B
Trotsky, L.   c.1

GLOTZER.
    TROTSKY: MEMOIR & CRITIQUE.

TROTSKY

TROTSKY

MEMOIR & CRITIQUE
ALBERT GLOTZER

PROMETHEUS BOOKS
Buffalo, New York

C.1

B

TROTSKY, L.

Library of Congress Cataloging-in-Publication Data

Glotzer, Albert, 1908–
    Trotsky : memoir and critique / Albert Glotzer.
        p.   3m.
    Includes bibliographical references.
    ISBN 0-87975-544-X
    1. Trotsky, Leon, 1879–1940. 2. Revolutionists—Soviet Union—
Biography. 3. Statesmen—Soviet Union—Biography. 4. Glotzer,
Albert, 1908–   . 5. Communists—United States—Biography.
6. Fourth International—History. 7. Communism—History—20th
century. I. Title.
DK254.T6055   1989
947.084′092—dc20
[B]   89-10926
                                                             CIP

Contents

Acknowledgments   7

Introduction   9

Kadikoy, Turkey, 1931   28

The Evolution of Trotsky's Political Life   87

"The Party is Always Right"   145

Paris—1934   176

"I am not a Jew but an Internationalist"   208

The Moscow Frame-Up Trials
and the Dewey Commision in Mexico   235

The Russian Question and the Split in American Trotskyism   282

Trotsky's Legacy   309

Bibliography   325

Index   331

In Memory
of
Sidney Hook and Max Shachtman

*

To Marguerite

Acknowledgments

I thank the following people who were kind enough to read the original manuscript, all of whom made important observations, criticisms, and suggestions, which are reflected in one way or another in the new version of these pages. First of all, I want to express my indebtedness to the late Sidney Hook. He made many important comments and criticisms and urged me on, believing it important to record the evolution of my political life: beginning as a young Communist and ending as a Social Democrat. His suggestions led me to recast my original draft. I also want to thank Emanuel Geltman, whose political association with me goes back to the earliest days of American Trotskyism. He made important criticisms and suggestions that recalled events grown dim with time. The late Sam Fishman, a political colleague and personal friend as well as an outstanding labor leader, read the manuscript in revised form, making important observations. Irving Panken, an old comrade and friend, whose historical and political judgments are outstanding, immensely improved the first part of the manuscript. The late Dr. Ephraim Friend, compatriot and political colleague, read the manuscript carefully and made helpful comments, especially on the history of Bolshevism. The same is true of Barry Miller, a friend of long standing and an acute observor. Dr. Werner Cohn, of Vancouver, British Columbia, a formidable critic of radical politics, gave me the benefit of his reading of the final draft. Last but not least, Don Slaiman, veteran of the labor movement, long-time political associate, and President of Social Democrats, U.S.A., discussed with me the place of Lenin in this re-examination of a particular past.

I would be remiss if I did not express my appreciation to Professor John P. Roche, who invited me to take over his seminars at Tufts University's Fletcher School of Law and Diplomacy, where I developed many of the ideas contained in the "critical" part of this book. I am also delighted to thank Gabriel Schoenfeld, who invited me to lecture in seminars he conducted at Harvard University's Russian Research Center.

Most of all, I am indebted to my wife, Marguerite, a severe critic of my elusive grammar and rhetoric, who is familiar with much of the history and politics of the last several decades. Her editorial work on the manuscript was essential. She also served as a prod for me to accomplish my original goal.

Although I am indebted to all the above, none of them is in any way responsible for what I have wrought, nor could they be. The responsibility is entirely mine.

Martha's Vineyard,
October, 1989

Introduction

Leon Trotsky's life was made up of brilliant struggles and tragic defeats. His leadership in the 1905 and 1917 revolutions—one democratic and the other authoritarian—was historic, but he faltered during his nation's most crucial period: Stalin's grab for total power. Trotsky was guided in this most important of all his battles by a newly acquired but no less unshakable devotion to Bolshevism and an adoration of Lenin and the Leninist Party. But in the end, that party betrayed and destroyed him. At what might have been a time of important rethinking of his political positions in 1940, he was assassinated by a specially trained agent of the Bolshevik secret police, the Spaniard Ramon Mercader. Thus the Party took its revenge on the man most responsible for its seizure of power in 1917.

My first association with Trotsky began on my fifteenth birthday, November 7, 1923, which coincided with the celebration of the sixth anniversary of the Russian Revolution, in Chicago's historic Carman's Hall. Trotsky's name was linked to Lenin's, and he was admired as the leader of the revolutionary battalions of Bolshevism that brought that movement to victory. On my birthday I joined the youth section of the American Communist Party, then called the "Workers' Party." I was influenced in part by the Socialist and anti-Tsarist traditions of my family, which had fled Russian oppression.

My joining the Communist youth organization was not entirely unexpected. My family had a history of urging political reform.

I came to this new country with my mother and older brother, Fred, to rejoin my father, assorted uncles, aunts, cousins, and close friends from our hamlet of Ivanik (named after Ivan the Terrible), a farming "suburb" of the historic old city of Pinsk in Belorussia, often (but wrongly) called White Russia.

We arrived in February 1913, at Castle Garden, New York, and continued on without a halt to Chicago, where a considerable number of my father's large family resided. Of my paternal grandfather Sholem's sixteen children, Chicago was the home of the families of Aunt Zlota, the oldest; Uncle Joe; Uncle Max, whose family was still living in Ivanik; my mother's younger brother, Nathan (Immigration's translation of "Noah"); and her very close cousin, Sam; together with cousins and landsmen, which included two peasants, Nicolai and Stepan, who worked in the Gary steel mills and felt themselves part of the old-country circle.

Grandpa Sholem's other children, born during his 108 years of life, were scattered in the northeast, mostly in New York; only a handful of daughters remained with him in Ivanik. His children produced many cousins in the States and in the old country; but, as is common in the United States, most of them seemed to scatter and "disappear" in our vast land.

To a boy who lived his first four years of life in a tiny Russian village, Chicago in 1914 was a joy. In the old country, my "hometown" consisted of one broad dirt street; we could easily count all the houses that lined it. Ivanik never had more than three or four hundred people. I remember that they would walk back and forth all day on this unpaved "Main Street" carrying out their tasks and visiting each other.

Farming was the main occupation in our village, whose first eight families (later joined by four more) received or purchased land from Tsar Alexander II, a "reform" ruler (by Russian standards, anyway), provided they agreed to farm it. This they did. And when winter came—it was always long and severe—many of the young people, married or not, took off to the city of Pinsk to work in one of the several factories there, mainly for a match manufacturer.

Given my origin, Chicago was like a magical circus. We lived on the northwest side of the city, where the bustle of Division Street dominated life. Indeed, our first residence was right on Division Street, a vibrant thoroughfare that sported an electric trolley, which traveled to the Loop, with a spur that went straight to the end, all the way to Lake Michigan. There were stores everywhere. Many of the earliest cinemas of the age—when Pearl White, Creighton Hale, Sheldon Lewis, Arthur Daley, and the phenomenal Charlie Chaplin worked their movie magic—were located around the corner from us. I remember the construction of three "movie palaces," one with a crystal chandelier that startled and amazed the neighborhood.

The population of our neighborhood was originally Scandinavian, predominantly Norwegian and Danish. But they gradually moved into the northwest section of the city, to be replaced by immigrant Jews and other first-generation Americans. Later on, large numbers of Poles moved into neighborhoods east of us, and Italians began to fill the neighborhoods near a huge closed quarry by Superior Street, south of Chicago Avenue.

A new world!—filled with paved streets, as well as with wide open areas we called "prairies," which contained wild rhubarb, sunflowers, and dandelions. And there seemed to be a countless number of attractive alleys, which could easily occupy the full attention and imagination of an immigrant boy growing up. My brother Fred and I were absorbed by sports, but most passionately and totally by baseball. Baseball was something not only to be played, but to be *studied*. It was through baseball that we came to read the newspapers—only the sports pages, to be sure, but that was a beginning. We learned the rosters of all the major league teams and the stats of the great stars, who were contemporary heroes: Ty Cobb, Honus Wagner, Grover Cleveland Alexander, Casey Stengel. We lived through the trauma of the Chicago Black Sox, having reveled in the talents of Joe Jackson, Eddie Collins, Buck Weaver, and Ray Schalk. (How heartbroken we were when the scandal broke! Fred and I even went to the courthouse, believing that it was our right—and our duty to the players— to express our solidarity with them. We couldn't know, since we didn't read the news section of the papers, that several hundred journalists were unable to get into the tiny courtroom. We were met by two burly, vintage Chicago cops on the floor of Judge Friend's trial rooms and disabused of our rights as only red-faced, beer-bellied, fat-rumped Loop policemen could put it. We disappeared from the trial area faster than we got there.)

We studied Spaulding's Baseball Guides and manuals, and pored over our growing collection of baseball cards, all of which shared our attention with school. But most of all we played the game, baseball and softball, on the improvised diamonds of corner lots, in the prairies of the city, the playgrounds, and the public parks, mainly Humboldt Park. We did this every day, unless there were heavy rains. Fred and I shared his baseball glove, an old piece of leather with little or no padding, wholly unlike the "baskets" used by ballplayers today. In those years, before we moved on to other games, like basketball and soccer, swimming was also a favorite sport. In the wintertime we used indoor pools; in the summer, Lake Michigan. We traveled the length of its coast from Chicago to Waukegan, searching for the perfect spot. Our favorite beaches were in Ravinia Park and Braeside. There were some towns in between that were "restricted." The beaches in those areas where the wealthy WASPs lived were ruled by lifeguards who made it abundantly clear: NO JEWS ALLOWED! Certainly no blacks were permitted near the water. Some beaches were even restricted for Catholics, especially the Irish.

*   *   *

Our household literally resounded with political talk. All of our family and relatives, and many of our closest friends, had fled oppression to become Americans. And we loved America. But this did not mean that we felt we had to be totally submissive to the new order. We tried to live like other free Americans. We were independent, vocal, and critical. We wanted to make our adopted land even freer and more just.

The nation in the early years of mass immigration was quite different from the United States of today, as it pushes its way to the end of a tortuous century. Particularly during the long years of the New Deal, its evolution was astonishing; the United States entered the modern age. Until the deep economic crisis of 1929–41, the country was socially conservative and backward. Federal and state governments supported the so-called captains of industry in all social conflicts, using the police powers of the land against American labor, initiating the violence that attended the many efforts of American workers to organize into free trade unions of their choosing. The country had newly emerged from the "Gilded Age," when the great trusts were formed and vast personal fortunes were accumulated, and great land grabs were aided by the federal government. The mass of Americans were hard-working but still poor, exploited, unorganized; their living standard was well below that of the politically more sophisticated and unionized workers in Europe.

Thus the beginning of the twentieth century was the scene of great strikes: the Colorado miners of 1912 and their slaughter by National Guardsmen in the Ludlow Massacre; the bitter Lawrence Textile Strike led by the International Workers of the World (IWW); the 1919 Gary Steel Strike; and the shooting of workmen at Homestead. The post-World War I strike wave involved tens of thousands of workers who put down tools: 35,000 needle-trade workers in New York City, together with 30,000 cigar workers; in Chicago 30,000 construction workers were locked out while 70,000 railroad shopmen struck. These were turbulent days, which saw the city and state governments, with their police and National Guards, rally behind industry against its working citizens.

Uncle Nate helped lead the famous 1910 Chicago strike against Hart, Schaffner & Marx, part of a long and bitter campaign to unionize its plants. Out of this struggle was finally born the Amalgamated Clothing Workers in the Second City. My Uncle Joe participated in forming this new union, too.

The "shop" and the "diabolical, scheming foremen" were nightly dinner discussion topics in our large household, since family members were always recounting their daily battles with the boss. Fred and I had an intimate knowledge of the heroic struggle of the workers and their abuse by the foreman, who always tried to cheat the men in a variety of little schemes to reduce their true daily earnings.

The second great dinner-table topic among the members of our family, and friends who came in afterward to socialize, was the slaughter in Europe, the astounding destruction of men, animals, land, and machines during the Great War. Except for one young cousin living with us who was militantly patriotic (as many immigrants were), most of us were antiwar and held no great sympathy for either side, especially before the United States became involved. The Germany of 1914 was an advanced industrial and cultured country; it simply craved its share of an already divided colonial world. How could we believe that the Allies were defending democracy and civilization against "the Huns" when Tsarist Russia, a land of violence and pogroms, was a leading member of the Allied team? (That it was not a war to save civilization or democracy was borne out by the peace treaty imposed on Germany.) Aside from the "politics" of the war, there was the more personal problem of the draft that concerned several family members. While my brother and I didn't feel the urgency of this problem, the concern of others communicated itself to us.

In a sense, it was inevitable, given our experience of life under Tsarism, that our family and close friends would be politically radical, if not always Socialist. Uncle Nate, whose intellectual and cultural influence on us was immeasurable in our formative years, was a member of Eugene V. Debs's Socialist Party, with prior membership in the Bund in Ivanik, where he had, along with some of his contemporaries, engaged in underground political activities in behalf of that organization and Social Democracy. (The Bund was the General Jewish Workers' Union, which helped found the Russian Social Democratic Party. The Bund left the Party in 1902, after it was denied an autonomous role in dealing with Jewish matters.) Without preaching, he provided the elementary ideas of socialism to us, just as he gave us a hint of the exciting world of art. (We were one of the first families to own an Edison permanent diamond-needle phonograph, which we listened to constantly as its quarter-inch thick records played. Chicago's Orchestra Hall and the Auditorium Opera House were well-known to us as boys because Nate was a regular patron, and Fred and I later studied music there.)

It is easy to imagine how elated all the families and friends from Ivanik and Pinsk were when the Tsar was overthrown in the February 1917 Revolution, which established the first democratic parliamentary republic in the history of Russia. (This was an achievement won without the participation of the Bolsheviks, who could not claim to have overthrown the Tsar, but only to have executed him and his family.) The great event was celebrated by all of us.

My brother and I had already been "involved" in the vigorous political campaigns of the Socialist Party in our radical Fifteenth Ward. In 1916, under Uncle Nate's direction, we distributed socialist campaign leaflets in buildings, mailboxes, and stores, calling on the electorate to vote for Allan L. Benson, the Socialist candidate, for president. (Debs was not a candidate that year.) Locally the party campaigned to elect the popular William Cunnea as State's Attorney for Cook County and William Rodriguez for alderman for the Fifteenth Ward. The old Chicago system of counting ballots was no doubt used to defeat Cunnea in what was a very close race. Rodriguez *was* elected as alderman, but he promptly turned his back on the party after taking office. All in all, the campaign was indeed a learning experience.

I cast my first "vote" in the 1916 presidential election. My lower-grade teacher in the noted LaFayette Public School in our neighborhood decided to poll her class of juveniles on their favorite candidate. She asked those who favored President Wilson to stand, and a large number of pupils rose; she followed by asking those who favored Charles Evan Hughes, the Republican, to rise, and most of the rest of the pupils stood up— except for two, who remained sitting, much to the indignation of this educator. "Why are you two sitting?" she asked. Julian Pevny (who attended the Socialist Sunday Schools) and I piped up: "We're voting for Benson." Her next comments made it clear that she approved of neither our independence nor our choice.

*   *   *

The "emigrés" rapidly became Americanized and learned to participate fully in the new country. This participation was fostered—and unified—to an important degree for tens of thousands by two important institutions: the Jewish *Daily Forward,* an extraordinary Yiddish newspaper with a strong Socialist outlook, and the Workmen's Circle, a fraternal organization, also Socialist in outlook, which had in its ranks thousands of immigrants. The two institutions educated the newcomers in their varied conceptions of socialism. The *Forward* in particular sought to make Americans of the immigrants. Its editor, Abraham Cahn, more than anyone else, encouraged such an attitude and goal. There were debates in our kitchen on this subject that often became sharp and divisive. Articles from the paper were often read aloud. In this period the *Forward* was deeply concerned with the developing schism between the Socialist Party and the rising left wing, which was heavily influenced by Bolshevism. This division of American Socialists and radicals was not a unique national phenomenon, for the schism was worldwide. The Americans only knew less about the ideas involved and the nature of the struggle; they were overwhelmed by the debate over a "real, living revolution."

In this turbulent political atmosphere, which shook the organized Socialists severely, Division Street was alive with debate. The Old Style Inn, opposite the entrance to Humboldt Park, was the scene of the many debates between the right and left wings. We were often taken to these meetings, at least the most important of them. The one that stands out for me was the one in which Seymour Steadman and Michigan's Dennis Batt confronted each other bitterly. I did not understand the issues; all I knew was that this stranger from another city seemed to make the well-known Chicago Socialist leader most uncomfortable. From discussions in our kitchen, I knew the debate had something to do with the Revolution in Russia and which of the groups contending for power there was more revolutionary.[1]

The dispute even reached the great corner of Division Street and Washtenaw, where large meetings were held. It was a tradition in the neighborhood to congregate at this corner, where the widest variety of topics were deliberated. I attended them often, if only briefly, never suspecting then that in less than a decade I would myself be holding forth at this open-air "hall," speaking on almost anything that came to mind, sometimes on organized topics, more often in an undisciplined free-wheeling way.

*   *   *

The great debate about Russia seemed as endless as it was stormy. Few understood the doctrinal differences, and that included those who spoke on them. The mass of people were interested above all in the destruction of Tsarism. We were impressed by the superior political organizational skills of the Bolsheviks, whose heroes, Lenin and the new Bolshevik, Leon Trotsky, also became heroes in the United States to those supporting the new regime. Left-wing Jews were particularly proud of Trotsky; even Jews of the "Right" did not conceal their admiration for the man's intellectual gifts.

When Uncle Nate, a thorough Social Democrat, joined the left wing of the now-unified Communist Party, he reflected the political confusion of the times. Like thousands of others, he believed the Bolshevik regime was the harbinger of a new freedom Socialists had long been fighting for. Nate wanted to go to the "new" land, but not as an "individual." He was the driving force behind the Commune Herald, whose goal was to go to Russia to aid the struggling society by setting up a commune near a large city to provide milk and dairy products to an undernourished population. (Among the Commune's members was Benny Goodman's sister.) Nate was selected to go to Russia to offer the services of the Commune Herald to the Socialist state, requesting only some decent farmland for cattle.

This was in 1923, long after Russia's Civil War, and a period of rising expectations. But already what dismayed Nate was the vast bureaucracy: rude, officious, and an impediment to any swift, intelligent action. He sat for hours in "buros" just waiting for some official to speak to him. The land offered the Commune was unusable, hundreds of miles from a city or even a large town, and this in a country without any arterial access to substantial population areas. Poverty was widespread. Housing was incredibly poor. The dictatorship of the one-party regime made itself felt everywhere. After six months of wandering about the country, buffeted by bureaucrats of various dimensions, Nate returned to the States. His negative report was rejected by a number of the Commune's members, who were enthusiastically ready to go to Russia to help the Revolution. But, in reality, the Commune, without land and without a welcome from the Soviets, was finished and disintegrated. Only one member actually went to Russia. Without Nate, the Commune could never have survived, and it didn't.

My uncle resigned from the Communist Party and its trade-union organization and returned to the Socialist Party, remaining a Social Democrat to the end of his life. I had joined the Communist youth movement while he was in Russia and in youthful arrogance disdainfully rejected his political course. I traveled the Communist road for years before I, too, returned to Social Democracy.

*   *   *

In this prosperous but politically reactionary decade of the Roaring Twenties, or the Jazz Age, I felt in my adolescence that I was part of the movement that would expand democracy and bring true freedom everywhere.

For the next five years, until my expulsion for the heresy of Trotskyism in November 1928, I was active in all phases of Communist Party life. At the time of my expulsion, I was a member of the National Committee of the Young Communist League.

Soon after I joined, I found the Party in an endless factional struggle between groups that sought to lead the organization and influence its sympathizing periphery. At that particular time, I saw the factions fighting with the intense passion of a guerrilla war. My "integration" into the life of the Party was initiated by my joining the majority Foster-Cannon faction, which held the national leadership (Chicago was the center of the organization). The faction's leadership was continuously challenged by the Ruthenberg-Lovestone faction. No matter what my activities were in the five years of my membership, whether organizing a Sacco-Vanzetti Defense Committee in Milwaukee, working for months in the Illinois coal fields as an organizer in the anti-John L. Lewis "Save-the-Union" movement, or directing a Communist youth school in New England, bitter factionalism imbued them all. Yet I found life in this new political world stimulating and exciting. I believed I was doing something important and serious. In any case, I was maturing fast in a milieu of older people.

When I was expelled from the Party and its allied organizations for the "heresy" of Trotskyism, it was on the basis of formal charges followed by the pretense of a "trial." The slightest suspicion that one held such heretical views brought into play investigative procedures that aped the Russian Party. Expulsion was as inevitable as it was automatic. One simply could not be a Trotskyist—or even express doubts about the Party's position on Trotskyism, above all other questions—and remain a member. For by 1928 the organization was far along in its total subordination to the Kremlin. Trotskyism was a state crime in the Soviet Union. If the American Party had had the same power as its Russian masters, those who held heretical views (Trotskyist or any otherwise) that challenged official doctrine would have suffered the same fate as Party dissidents in the Soviet Union: exile, imprisonment, and execution.

*   *   *

In 1925 the minority faction of the American Communist Party, led by Charles E. Ruthenberg[2] and Jay Lovestone,[3] came to the fourth National Convention determined to wrest the leadership from William Z. Foster and James P. Cannon.[4] (Lovestone became the sole leader of the faction upon Ruthenberg's sudden death in March 1927.) That they succeeded was not of their own doing but by the most drastic intervention into the internal affairs of the Party by the Kremlin, through the medium of the Executive Committee of the Communist International, which was totally dominated by the Russian leadership. I sat through this convention in Chicago on August 21, 1925, and observed this take place with great alarm and disgust.

The Foster-Cannon majority of the Party was deposed by a Kremlin far removed from the American scene and the political life of the organization. It was done by a cable addressed to the leadership and the convention that arrived in the midst of its proceedings. The cable was like a bombshell, exploding precisely at a time when the conflicts in the convention were resolving themselves on the basis of the true, relative strengths of the factions, but also under the baleful eyes of the Kremlin's watchman, P. Green (S. I. Gusev), a member of the new Stalinist leadership. Green was reporting every development to the Kremlin, and it was he who brought the cable to the attention of the leadership and the convention.

The cable said that the minority faction was more loyal and politically correct. No reasons were given or citations made in support of these contentions. And no discussions with the Executive Committee were, under the circumstances of the Kremlin's intervention, possible. The cable was fiat!

The majority of the convention was deposed in this way. How could it continue its leadership when it was stigmatized as being less loyal to the Russians and the Comintern leadership, especially since it was also politically wanting in its confusion on the question of advocating a labor party in the United States. Its knowledge of Communist theory was simplistic, and its analysis of American politics bewildering. The Lovestone group was more sophisticated in theoretical matters, but its internal politics were unsavory—reflecting the practices and personality of its leader. While the Ruthenberg-Lovestone faction was elated by the cable, the Majority was thrown into crisis. Foster's instant reaction was to reject the premises of the cable, to fight against its terms—and, failing in that course, to resign from the leadership on the logical grounds that he had been repudiated by the world organization. Cannon, the outstanding political figure in the faction, though unqualifiedly opposed to the cable and its political conclusions, nevertheless argued that his faction could only fight the Comintern at its peril. The dictates of Bolshevization required acceptance of their decision. He proposed a policy of "correcting" the Comintern in the course of time. While Cannon won a majority of the faction to his position, the caucus split. Cannon and his supporters constituted themselves as a smaller independent faction. The Fosterites, who felt themselves loyal to the Comintern and originally supported Cannon on this question, turned around and rejected his overall leadership in a pout for his trouncing Foster in the debate. (Three years later Cannon gave a different answer about loyalty to the Comintern when he embraced the political views of Leon Trotsky.)

The cable marked a turning point in the American Party, for its effect unquestionably established that the party was not at all independent; it functioned under the direction of a higher power. The higher foreign power was established by the "Twenty-one Points" of admission to the Communist International. Devised by Lenin, the Twenty-one Points governed organizational life of the new world body and subordinated every national party to the Executive Committee of the International politically and organizationally. The Executive Committee was, in turn, subordinated to the Political Committee of the Russian Communist Party.

The mystique of the Bolshevik Party rested on the successful insurrection leading to its state power. After all, it was the only party that achieved such successes. And so it intervened in all the national parties— but never so much as when Stalin came to power. From then on, many cables intervening in the affairs of the American Party came from the Comintern—so that one Party leader observed, with wit and accuracy, that the American Party was "suspended by cables from Moscow."

In the 1980s, revisionist historians of American communism, particularly Morris Isserman, have claimed a measure of independence for that party, especially in the Earl Browder period, that in fact never existed. They have forgotten, or perhaps never knew, that Browder was selected as the leader of the U.S. party by the Kremlin *by Stalin personally* (much to the extreme shock of Foster, who was waiting in the wings for a call), and that he was removed from the leadership by similar methods. Browder's reign came to an end in the form of an international attack on his leadership and policies by a leader of the French Communist Party, Jacques Duclos. There was hardly a person who did not immediately know that Duclos was acting for a higher power. From then on, everything was downhill for Browder, and with one or two exceptions, all of his closest coworkers joined in the chorus of denunciation that ended in his expulsion from the Party. Clearly, the American Party had little or nothing to do with the elevation of Browder as leader, and it did not initiate his removal.

Comintern "reps" were in constant attendance in the United States throughout Stalin's long reign. Financial aid from the Kremlin through the Comintern was steady and direct, interruptions occurring only during the war years.[5] One needs to add that an American political line was a "sometime thing," conforming in all important respects to the needs and demands of the Soviet Union. "Our Line Has Changed Again" was not merely a humorous song that Socialists sang at parties; it was a political statement regarding the American Communists' fidelity to the Kremlin and the Communist International.

*   *   *

The Sixth Congress of the Communist International, held in Moscow in the summer of 1928, was a bizarre event. I mention it for a couple of reasons: that out of this Congress came the beginnings of American Trotskyism; and that the Congress was typical of the chicanery of Stalin, his contempt for his followers, and their abject response to every whim of their international boss.

Nicolai Bukharin was a highly respected and beloved leader (all Russian Bolshevik leaders were, at one time or another, beloved, particularly just before Stalin destroyed them) and the head of a nonfaction in the Russian Politburo. (By "nonfaction," I mean a group of likeminded thinkers who did not function as an organized faction or struggle for Party leadership on behalf of its ideas.) Bukharin gave Stalin invaluable support in his grasp for total power by joining him in the destruction of Trotsky, Zinoviev, Kamenev, and their supporters in the Central Committee. Still nominally the president of the Comintern at the opening of the Congress, Bukharin presided over its sessions and delivered the main political report to the Congress. At the very moment he was standing on the podium surveying his fellow leaders of the International, shining in the glory of his leadership, enjoying the excessive plaudits of the sycophantic delegates, the "corridor congress" of Stalin's faction outside the official Congress precincts was preparing for Bukharin's removal, thus tightening the grip of the General Secretary on the International. Not only was Stalin preparing the political destruction of his erstwhile political ally and other political friends, he was also planning their physical annihilation.

Toward the end of the Congress, as it became certain that the rumors of Bukharin's impending removal were true, Jay Lovestone realized he, too, was in trouble. After all, he had made a public display of his political closeness to the Comintern's president, supporting Bukharin on international questions, he said, even as he endorsed Stalin's national policies, seemingly unaware that Stalin demanded *total,* not divided, support and would remember Lovestone's divided allegiance. Lovestone attempted a quick retreat by making a pathetic last-minute attack on Bukharin. He hoped by this ruse to retain the support of the Stalinist leadership, so he could continue in his American post. This political acrobatic act failed. The sessions of the Congress droned on ritualistically, while significant decisions took place elsewhere.

The International was now ten years old, and it still had not adopted a program defining its principles, world strategic aims, and political perspectives. Bukharin had been given the assignment of preparing such a program as early as 1920, but the International never fully reviewed his initial draft then or in later years. (It was published in pamphlet form and distributed in many countries to be used in Party classes in Communist principles.) One of the ironies of the Congress, given the deception that Bukharin was still its leader, was the creation of a Program Commission to consider again the adoption of a programmatic statement. The Stalin leadership regarded this Commission as a very minor affair. The Comintern had functioned for ten years without a program. By the time Stalin dissolved the International several years later, no program had been adopted yet. Hence Cannon's assignment to the Program Commission was considered strictly "minor league."

The Commission, for reasons unknown to this day (unless it was the "softness" of Bukharin asserting itself, or his secret respect and admiration for Trotsky—in the early years of the new revolutionary state, his esteem for Trotsky was quite public), received and distributed a voluminous document from Trotsky in his Siberian exile, highly critical of the political affairs of the International. This document was distributed to the Commission members in abbreviated form. The part given to them was titled "A Criticism of the Draft Program of the Communist International." It was given to the Commission members as informational material only, not to be discussed or considered by the body in any way.

What the members read in Trotsky's criticism was an indictment of the specific policies of the International in Great Britain, China, and several countries of Europe, areas in which the Comintern underwent severe defeats. Trotsky attributed these defeats to the policies of the leadership of the Russian Party and the International. Behind the political criticism was a scathing attack on the bureaucratic manner in which the leadership functioned and the way the Kremlin manipulated the Communist parties throughout the world. It was most anomalous that this document was distributed at all, because writings by Trotsky, or anyone connected with the Left Opposition, were officially illegal and forbidden in the Soviet Union and to the Comintern. Its appearance in the Program Commission was an additional reason for Stalin's determination, assuming he needed one, that Bukharin must go.

The document had a profound effect on Cannon. He felt cleansed and enlightened. He told his American associates that for the first time in five years he understood the meaning of "Bolshevization." And he had been the prime mover of the Bolshevization of the American Party!

During the sessions of the Commission, Cannon met his old acquaintance Maurice Spector, a founder of the Canadian Communist Party, who had for several years been privately sympathetic to Trotsky's views. Cannon and Spector revealed to each other their critical feelings about the Comintern and sympathies for the criticisms in Trotsky's document. The document explained to them many of the "mysteries" of the functioning of the world movement, its subordination to the Stalin bureaucracy, and the increasing personal dictatorship of Stalin over the International. They agreed that upon their return to their countries they would proclaim their support for Trotsky and do whatever they could to advance his views in the American and Canadian organizations and their peripheries.

There was a formidable obstacle to overcome first. Delegates to the Congresses, all of which were held in the Soviet Union, had to surrender their passports to the Russian secret police. These would be returned to permit departure from the country, provided the conduct of the delegate was "correct." All documents given out had to be returned, unless the delegates were told they could be kept. No one could keep Trotsky's document. In order to take the document out of Russia, Cannon and Spector stole a copy from an Australian delegate named Wilkinson, knowing that he would report the theft immediately and absolve himself of any guilt. Cannon and Spector had already turned in their copies and obtained their passports, so they were able to return to North America with a stolen copy.

Back in the States and in the Party national center, Cannon remained silent about his newly acquired views. He did show the document to his two closest political allies, Martin Abern[6] and Max Shachtman,[7] whom he was able to convince to join him. The maneuver of silence was not successful for long, and soon the whole Party was shocked to learn that this veteran Party leader, its one-time National Chairman, was a Trotskyist. No crime against the Party was greater! In October of that year, Cannon, Abern, and Shachtman were put on trial by the Political and Central Committees and expelled from the Party.

The Lovestone faction in the leadership and the opposition Fosterites vied with each other: Which side was the most intransigent in the struggle against Trotskyism? Neither group, however, could erase the stigma that was attached to them. They were, after all, leaders of a party that spawned Trotskyists. Stalin's paranoia would never absolve them of guilt, for if hated Trotskyism appeared in the party, the leaders were ipso facto guilty. But the presence of Trotskyism in the Cannon faction, made worse by the fact that its leader was responsible for it, caused unconcealed anguish to the part of the faction that remained loyal to the Party. The anti-Lovestone bloc of the Foster and Cannon factions, now tainted by Trotskyism, knew that they would be held equally responsible for its emergence.

An anti-Trotskyist campaign was launched in the American Party. Clarence Hathaway, a leading member of the Cannon faction and its representative student at the Lenin School in Moscow, was now reputed to be a "learned Leninist." He was assigned by the Political Committee to travel about the country in an effort to influence members of his own faction to reject Cannon's counsel as "political disaster." He accepted the assignment enthusiastically—armed, he thought, with the enhanced stature of the Lenin School and his sudden rise as an appointed national leader of a Stalinized party.

Early that November, Cannon sent me the galley proofs of the smuggled "Criticism." Arne Swabeck, an erstwhile leader of the Chicago District of the Party who was recently ousted in the Lovestone takeover, and to whom I was closely allied politically and personally, read the lengthy document with me in one sitting. We were profoundly influenced by it. As members of the Cannon faction from the time of its formation at the 1925 convention, our feelings regarding the internal situation in the Party were similar to Cannon's, as was our response to Trotsky's "Criticism."

Indeed, Trotsky convincingly explained for us what was wrong with the Party, the International, and beyond that, the Russian leadership. That year, 1928, was a turning point in my political life, as it was in the lives of many other American Communists. We went through a process of political reeducation, resisting the pressure put on us at the same time to condemn Cannon, Abern, and Shachtman—described by the Central Committee as "three generals without an army." We were under suspicion in our own faction and by the Fosterites, as well as by the official Lovestoneite leadership in Chicago. Hathaway made a special trip from the national office in New York to a joint meeting of the Foster-Cannon coalition in Chicago to persuade those who were moving in the "wrong" direction to shun Trotskyism and its new adherents in the American Party. His immediate goal was to influence the local Cannonites, particularly Swabeck and me as leaders of the group, not to join Cannon and his two associates, providing us with reasons for not doing so. He called me aside at this meeting and, in a secretive and confidential way, told me:

> I know why you are supporting Cannon. It is because you have given up all hope of ousting the Lovestoneites from the Party leadership. It is just despair. But let me tell you something: When I was at the Lenin School, I studied hard the first year, but I learned while there that you will never get anywhere in the American Party unless you have the right connections in the Russian party. I spent the next two years making "friends" in Moscow. [At this point he showed me a little black address book.] I have them right here, and I tell you this: In six months, Lovestone will be out of the leadership of the Party. Don't go with Cannon. The whole internal situation is going to change completely, I promise you.

I am certain now as then that I was not the only one favored with this confidence. Hathaway's secret and the advice that accompanied its telling did not sway me (or Swabeck, to whom I relayed Hathaway's admonition), and I told him so. Swabeck and I nonetheless continued our private discussions with Hathaway, and we discovered quickly that his knowledge of the theoretical and political questions in dispute between Trotsky and the Stalin leadership was feeble. Swabeck and I gave him a very rough time. He was just as ignorant as the rest of the American leadership. It was unfortunate that we were unable to confront Hathaway in a large meeting to show how really pitiable was the knowledge of our faction's Lenin School graduate. Hathaway simply couldn't debate the issues raised by Trotsky's criticisms. Trotsky's ideas were probably a forbidden subject in that bureaucratic educational institution. The student-leaders were, like the whole International, educated by the Kremlin's rewritten and falsified history of Bolshevism and the Revolution.

Lovestone and his faction, already discredited in the Kremlin for their support of Bukharin, and now additionally stigmatized as the leadership of a group that generated Trotskyism, were ousted from the leadership and expelled from the Party, as Hathaway foretold. The next thunderclap in the Party's turbulence was the surprise selection, personally made by Stalin, of the colorless, undistinguished Earl R. Browder as the new General Secretary of the Party over his faction's leader, William Z. Foster. This was not only a shock to Foster but the most unexpected choice to the whole Party. Foster, who was certain that the post and the leadership of the Party were his, never recovered from the blow, though he remained abjectly loyal to his Russian masters. It was clear in the selection of Browder that Foster would never achieve his cherished ambition to be number-one Party leader.

Six months after the expulsions of the first Trotskyists, the Chicagoans expelled with Swabeck and me formed a committee to arrange a national conference of other expelled Party members. The conference was convened in Chicago in May 1929. Out of this meeting came the Communist League of America and a National Committee to direct its affairs. The Committee consisted of Cannon, Maurice Spector,[8] Martin Abern, Max Shachtman, Swabeck, Karl Skogland,[9] and myself.

Thus out of Cannon's assignment to the unimportant Program Commission on a reluctant trip he made to the Sixth Congress arose something utterly unanticipated: the first appearance in the United States and Canada of a Trotskyist movement, destined to become the largest and most important of the many organizations supporting Trotsky outside the original faction in the Soviet Union. For Trotsky this was a most fortunate occurrence, because it gave new life to a small, isolated, struggling world movement.

Notes

1. In later years, Seymour Steadman, the bitter foe of communism, joined the Communist Party. He had also been imprisoned following a trial for malfeasance in office as a bank vice-president.

2. Charles E. Ruthenberg (1882–1927) was the executive secretary of the American Communist Party almost continuously from its founding in 1919 to the time of his death from peritonitis in 1927. Before and during World War I Ruthenberg was a leader of the Socialist Party in Cleveland, where he was born. As a Socialist, he showed considerable organizational and administrative skills; throughout his career in the Socialist Party he ran for offices of United States Senator, Congressman, and Mayor of Cleveland. After the Russian Revolution, Ruthenberg supported the Socialist Party's left wing and joined the American Party, where his leaderhip was supported by the Soviet Comintern. He advocated unity with the Communist Labor party and became its executive secretary. (See Johnpoll and Klehr, *Biographical Dictionary of the American Left.*)

3. Jay Lovestone (1889–   ) was born in Lithuania and came to the United States at the age of nine. A leader of the Socialist Club at the City College of New York in 1917, Lovestone joined the left wing of the party in supporting Lenin and the Bolsheviks. In 1919 he was elected to the Central Committees of both the Communist Party and the United Communist Party. In the bitter factional fight in the Party, he was Ruthenberg's ally, an expert in organizational matters. Lovestone became the Party's General Secretary upon Ruthenberg's death in 1927, and he remained so until 1929, when he was expelled from the Party for his sympathy for Bukharin. Together with Bertram D. Wolfe and Benjamin Gitlow, Lovestone organized an independent group called the Communist Party Opposition, which was active during the thirties and was dissolved in 1941. Together with Wolfe, Lovestone led the campaign against Trotskyism in the American party. After World War II Lovestone worked in the International Ladies Garment Workers Union and organized the "Free Trade Union Committee." He later worked in the AFL-CIO, editing their *Free Trade Union News* until his retirement. (See Robert Alexander's *The Right Opposition* and the *Biographical Dictionary of the American Left.*)

4. James P. Cannon (1890–1974) was a veteran leader of the Socialist Party as well as the Communist Party and was the principal founder of the American Trotskyist movement as the Communist League of America (1929). Cannon joined the Socialist Party in 1908 and the IWW in 1911, where he was active in free-speech campaigns, a leader of the party's left wing, and editor of *Workers' World* (1919). A founding member of the Communist Labor Party, he was elected to the Central Executive Committee at the underground Bridgeman convention. In 1920 Cannon was named to edit the party's newpaper, *The Toiler,* and was a delegate to the Fourth and Sixth Congresses of the Communist International. He was national secretary of the International Labor Defense from its founding until his expulsion by Lovestone's leadership in November 1928 for Trotskyism. (See

Draper's *American Communism and Soviet Russia*, Solon de Leon's *American Labor Who's Who*, and the *Biographical Dictionary of the American Left*.)

5. David Garrow, in his *The FBI and Martin Luther King*, tells the story of veteran Party leaders Morris and Jack Childs, who were informants for the FBI for three decades, until 1981. They were known as "Solo" and reported every aspect of Party life and activity. Morris reported on the political affairs as a member of the National Committee, and Jack, who was in charge of "international" finances and was caretaker of funds from Moscow and their distribution, reported on the monies received and the areas of expenditure. Independence, indeed!

6. Martin Abern (Abramowitz) (1898–1949) was a founder of both the American Communist movement and the Trotskyist CLA. At the age of fifteen Abern joined the IWW and Young People's Socialist League. At the age of twenty-three he was elected to the Central Committee of the Communist Party. Abern was national secretary of the Young Workers' League, the youth organization of the Workers' Party. On leaving youth work, he became assistant national secretary of the International Labor Defense during its first mass growth. He was a member of the National and Political Committees of the Communist League of America (CLA), and the Socialist Workers' Party (SWP), and the Workers' Party of 1940. (See Max Shachtman's obituary on Abern in *Labor Action*, 9 May 1949.)

7. Max Shachtman (1904–1972), born in Poland, came to the United States at the age of two. The *Biographical Dictionary of the American Left* records that "for fifty years he was the center of international social and political controversies and made significant contributions to the movements of the non-Communist Left as a tireless agitator, an informed and formidable debater, a pamphleteer, and a brilliant and witty polemicist." At seventeen, he joined the Workers' Council, led by J. B. Salutsky and Alexander Trachtenberg, which supported the Russian Revolution and the Communist International but was critical of the American Communist Party. In 1922 Shachtman met Martin Abern, who persuaded him to go to Chicago to edit the *Young Worker* and function in the leadership of the youth organization. At the age of nineteen, in 1923, Shachtman thus began his career as a "professional revolutionary." At the time of his expulsion from the party for Trotskyism with Cannon and Abern, he was an alternate member of the Central Committee and editor of *Labor Defender*, a photo journal of the International Labor Defense. Shachtman was the first editor of the *Militant* and founded, with Martin Abern, *The New International*. In 1930 he was the first American to visit Trotsky on the island of Prinkipo, Turkey. Shachtman later broke with Trotsky regarding the latter's view that Russia was a "workers' state." Shachtman then formed the Workers' Party–Independent Socialist League, which he led until it dissolved upon entry into the Socialist Party in 1958. Shachtman is the author of *The Bureaucratic Revolution, The Rise of the Stalinist State, The Moscow Frame-Up Trials*, and many pamphlets and theoretical and political articles. (See the *Biographical Dictionary of the American Left*; and Albert Glotzer, *Biographical Essay on Max Shachtman* [Taniment Library, 1983] and "Max Shachtman, An Obituary," *New America*, 15 November 1972.)

8. Maurice Spector (1898–1968) was a founder and leader of the Canadian Communist Party, editor of its paper, and a writer and orator of considerable ability. Spector joined the United Socialist Party of Canada in 1914 and was a member of the National Executive Committee of the Canadian Social Democratic Party in 1918. A delegate to the Fourth and Sixth Congresses of the Comintern and a member of its Executive Committee, he was the editor of the *Canadian Worker and Labor Monthly*. With James Cannon, Spector introduced Trotskyism to North America and founded the CLA; he was a member of its National Committee and, at times, its Political Committee. Spector left the organization at the time of the 1939–1940 split. After a brief involvement with the Socialist Party, he left organizational politics forever.

9. Karl Skoglund (1884–1960) was born in Sweden and emigrated to the United States. A railroad worker who became active in the Socialist Pary and the IWW, Skoglund was a founding member of the American Communist Party and was especially active in its Minnesotan chapters. He was expelled from the Party for Trotskyism in 1928, whereupon he joined the National Committee of the Trotskyist CLA and Socialist Workers' Party. A leader in the Minneapolis strike, he was convicted under the Smith Act and sent to prison in 1944.

Kadikoy, Turkey, 1931

Leon Trotsky was deported to Turkey from Alma Ata in Siberia in February 1929. Stalin did not permit him to select his country of exile. Whereas the Tsar had banished him and other political opponents to Siberia, the new "Socialist" state of his own creation went further, depriving him and his lifelong companion, Natalia, of citizenship. The act of deportation itself expressed the cruelty of Stalin's regime. Ten years after he led the insurrection and eight after his successful military leadership in defeating the counterrevolution, Trotsky was expelled from the Bolshevik Party, which regarded him as an interloper. Trotsky's deportation to Turkey, however, did have the effect of making him physically accessible to his followers in Europe and America, thereby strengthening the anti-Stalinist Communist movement.

In November 1929, not a year after the formation of the Communist League of America, Max Shachtman, editor of *The Militant,* our weekly newspaper, and Martin Abern, our organizational secretary, asked me to go to New York to work in the national office, help issue the paper, and serve on the Political Committee. Shachtman, an old friend and political colleague, was leaving soon for Turkey to meet with Leon Trotsky as a representative of our National Committee, and I was to replace him in New York during his journey to Prinkipo.

After working for two years as an active Trotskyist in the New York organization, I wanted to meet our movement's leader. Moreover, Trotsky wanted first-hand news of how we were doing. So immediately after the second convention of the Communist League late in the summer of 1931, I left for Paris on the way to Turkey. (A reflection of the time: My round-trip, third-class ticket on the *S.S. Albert Ballin,* the Hamburg-American ocean liner, was $136.50. A Depression price—but difficult to meet on the depressed income of a young revolutionary.)

Paris Interlude

I arrived in Paris in early October and went to the headquarters of the French Communist League on Boulevard de la Villette. It was closed, and no one was there to receive me, so I just sat down. Toward evening, Pierre Frank, one of the leaders of the organization, came by, saw me on a curb—I knew neither the language nor the city—and expressed great surprise at my presence. Why had I not informed the League I was to arrive on this day, he asked? I told him that I had written to Pierre Naville,[1] a founder of French Trotskyism, well-known Socialist intellectual, and a noted figure in the Surrealist movement. Frank made a derogatory comment about Naville. Right away, then, I got a hint of factionalism within the French League. I was to learn a lot more about it during my brief stay in Paris.

A few days after my arrival, the local section of the organization had a meeting at which the factional struggle revealed itself in a vigorous discussion. I was not familiar with French, but the bitterness of the debate was apparent from the volume and demeanor of the participants. Albert Trient,[2] a former leader of the Communist Party and member of the Executive Committee of the Communist International for France in the early twenties, had been expelled from these bodies at the peak of the struggle in Moscow in 1927, because he was a supporter of Zinoviev and the United Opposition Bloc. He was present at this meeting and seemed to have embarked on a fruitless campaign to foist his leadership on the League's unwilling membership.

Raymond Molinier[3] and Frank, as the leaders of the French organization, were also present. Molinier was known for his volatile personality; he was given to sudden outbursts, which were often punctuated by physical threats. (They said Molinier threw a table at Naville at one League debate.) Yet after the meeting, I went for coffee with Molinier, Naville, and Frank. Molinier dismissed my surprise at their amiability after the table incident, explaining it away as an example of French "temperament."

From the meeting of the Paris section, I was taken to a meeting of the so-called Jewish Group, a part of the general organization. Frank thought that since I was familiar with Yiddish, I would be able to talk to the members and follow the course of the meeting. I could participate in slow, personal conversations, which permitted me to ask some questions, but I could not follow the formal meeting, because their Yiddish contained so many French terms. I spoke to several members of the group privately and agreed to try to obtain financial help in the States for one or two of their more destitute leading members; but otherwise, this meeting ended my relations with the Jewish Group. (My visit to them was nonetheless to have repercussions involving Trotsky and me.)

The most important event of my stay in Paris, in a political-organizational sense, was my meeting with the International Secretariat of the world Trotskyist movement, which was made up of its secretary, M. Mill,[4] Myrtos,[5] who represented the Greek section, Souzo (Ercoll), an expelled leader of the Italian Communist Party, Pierre Frank, and Pierre Naville. The meeting was called to discuss the prospects of forming a British section of the International Left Opposition with a representative of the London Marxian League, Chandu Ram, also known as Aggrawala, who had come to Paris for that purpose.

Throughout the year, Trotsky and the International Secretariat had received letters from England expressing an interest in Trotsky and the movement he led. These inquiries came from members of the British Communist Party, trade unionists, political groups, veterans of the Socialist movement, and from other politically unaffiliated people. During the summer, the IS (as the Secretariat was commonly referred to) sent Pierre Naville to London to meet some of these people. As a result of his visit, the IS asked the Communist League of America to send someone to England who could remain there for a time in order to help in the formation of a Trotskyist organization. The League was unable to do so.

Speaking for the Marxian League and its leading personality, F. A. Ridley, Ram asked that his organization be recognized as the official Trotskyist group in Great Britain and given the status inherent in such recognition. I also attended a meeting that was called to determine whether the Marxian League did in fact represent the views of world Trotskyism. Indeed, some of its public statements seemed to *oppose* key elements of Trotsky's thinking.

Ram made a statement to the Secretariat citing several key programmatic positions of the Marxian League:

1. It was for the immediate creation of a new International and new parties wherever possible. This objective would require that the Trotskyist movement give up its position as a faction of the Communist International everywhere in favor of new parties.

2. It considered the trade unions in England to be moribund, without a future, and led by reactionaries.

3. Though it was willing to do some work in the Labor Party, it saw no important role or future for the party and no reason why the Trotskyists should be seriously concerned with it.

4. It regarded the establishment of a Fascist state in Great Britain to be an imminent possibility.

The International Secretariat unanimously rejected these views. At this Paris meeting, I reflected the views of the American League by also rejecting the positions of the Ridely-Ram organization. We were acquainted with these ideas in the States and had debated them with various groups there. I described our American experiences in the meeting and stated why we thought the positions outlined by Ram to be wrong for us. The International Secretariat was correct, I said, in refusing to recognize the Marxian League as the sole representative of the Trotskyist movement, with which it disagreed so sharply on programmatic questions. Indeed, I invoked the authority of Lenin himself in criticizing the sectarian views of the Marxian League by referring to his pamphlet *Leftism in Communism.* Reference to the godhead, Lenin, would have been enough, but I thought to make my references even stronger, buttressing my argument by citing Trotsky's articles on syndicalism and the positions adopted by the Communist International in its early congresses on working in the trade unions. Chandu Ram did not take kindly to my references to Communist scripture, nor to the remarks of other members of the Secretariat who concurred with me. He made it quite clear that, while an adjustment of views was possible on some issues, there could be no reconciliation of positions on the "principle" questions. Although we parted in a friendly way, it was clear to him, as well as to all of us, that the Marxian League was not going to be the basis for the Left Opposition in England, nor was there any certainty that it would even be a part of it. The question was to arise again in Turkey, where Trotsky himself was appealed to by the Marxian League.

The remaining days of my stay in Paris were spent in seeing the city and enjoying briefly some aspects of French life and manners, especially in sampling French cuisine, which suited my plebian American taste. I stayed at the home of Oscar Rosenzweig (also known as "Myrtos"), in the working class suburb of Clichy. He was a delightful companion on my strolls through Paris—until what he considered a dangerous visit to the renowned Père Lachaise Cemetery, burial ground of the Paris Communards and other noted Socialist and revolutionary figures.

I had wanted to go there to express my own sentimental solidarity with the martyrs of the Paris Commune, and off we went together. We sought the Wall of the Communards, and I scratched my initials on the wall. One could tell at a glance that they would never be seen again as they merged with the thousands of other graffiti of those who preceded me.

On our way out of the cemetery, we passed a new monument, erected to the memory of Jules Guesde, a founder and leader of the French Socialist Party and a man of high reputation in the world Socialist movement. The Guesde memorial was made a part of a single stonework structure in memory of Paul Lafargue and his wife, Laura, a daughter of Karl Marx, who had been long before interred in Père Lachaise. The combined monument was dedicated in the name of the Socialist Party of France. I lamented the fact that this enterprise was the work of the reformist French Socialist Party and not the Communists, that the French CP was derelict in its duty by permitting the Socialist Party to usurp the revolutionary traditions of Paul Lafargue and Laura Marx Lafargue, and, through them, of Marx and Engels.

On the rubbish heap near the monument, waiting to be carted away, lay two old, flat ceramic plaques with the names of Paul Lafargue and Laura Marx and the dates of their births and deaths engraved on them. I thought it was a shame for these headstones to be so treated, and, without hesitation, I picked them up from the rubbish heap, wrapped them in a newspaper, and prepared to remove them from Père Lachaise, feeling quite proud of my action. Myrtos became alarmed and cautioned me against such vandalism. I could not convince him that these stones had been discarded as junk by the cemetery workers; mine was a "revolutionary act," not one of thievery. But no assurances from me could prevent his quick disappearance from the area, certain as he was that I would leave the cemetery only in the company of les flics (the cops).

Left alone, I calmly walked out carrying my two treasures. Myrtos had, in the meantime, rushed to the headquarters of the French organization and informed whomever he met there of my "crime." By the time I arrived at Boulevard de la Villette, a large group of French comrades had gathered to await me and my loot! They were obviously prepared to express the wrath of the entire organization when I unwrapped my newspaper cover.

There was an instantaneous change of mood, however, when they saw what I had brought. Naville, clever and quick, laid claim to the plaques in the name of the French League and denied my right to remove these national treasures to the United States: "They belong to France!" For a moment I thought he sounded like Clemenceau, speaking with the full emotion of French chauvinism. Nevertheless, being a reasonable person and not an American "imperialist" unmindful of French "rights," I came to a compromise with them. We agreed that the French comrades could retain the plaque of Paul Lafargue and that I would take the one of Laura Marx back to the States as a memorial piece. I thought I made the better deal, even if Lafargue did come from the West Indies and was, in a sense, an American. But he lived most of his life in France and was a renowned leader of French socialism. Between leaving Paris and staying in Turkey and Germany, however, my plaque disappeared, and I returned home without it. The two plaques may still be somewhere in Paris.

Although I had written earlier to Trotsky from Paris that I would reach Turkey in two weeks, I had enough of the French organization for the moment and decided to leave at once for Marseilles, my point of embarkation for Turkey. The case of the cemetery "theft" came up on the very first day that I met and talked with Trotsky. Between my departure from France and arrival in Turkey, the "Old Man" (as he was affectionately called by almost every Trotskyist) had been alarmed by the story, which I was led to believe was sent to him by Molinier.

On to Kadikoy

I left Marseilles on October 16, 1931, in the small, run-down, and slow-moving *S.S. Caramanie,* a French Paquet Line vessel. I arrived in Istanbul on the twenty-second. The ship failed to make a scheduled stop at Naples, which would have given me the opportunity to see Pompeii, but sailed instead past the Lipari Islands and the smoking Stromboli. We continued through the Strait of Messina and by the colorful roofs of the city of Messina and Calabria on the mainland. The ship sailed through the deep-cut Corinth Canal to stop for a day at Athens and its beckoning Acropolis. We then headed for Istanbul through the Greek archipelago and the Dardanelles and Marmara Sea. Then: the city that was still often called Constantinople. We knew we had arrived when we saw the mosques and their minarets in the old Stamboul section, which faced the sea.

I had learned from friends in Paris how to get to Kadikoy from the boat area. Kadikoy was on the Asiatic side of Turkey, about forty-five minutes away by ferryboat, the name for which was *vapur*. Many ferryboats sailed from Istanbul to the towns and villages on the Asian mainland, and to the islands that dotted the Marmara coast. Prinkipo, Trotsky's main residence in Turkey, was one of these islands. The boats left from the Galata-Karakoy Bridge, which led into the Stamboul section of the city. The Bosphorus flowed from this point to the Black Sea and the Russian port of Odessa, and was the Kremlin's gateway to the Mediterranean and Middle East.

At the ferry ticket office, I was able to surmount language difficulties with hand gestures, and I bought a second-class ticket to Kadikoy. I was husbanding my meager funds, so instead of paying the equivalent of four cents for a first-class ticket, I paid about two cents for second-class. By this excess of thrift, I lost the opportunity of buying refreshments and enjoying the enclosed quarters of the boat. As we ferried past Scutari, the seat of the Selimuje military barracks, we heard the booming of cannon and small-arms fire, which I was to hear throughout my stay in Kadikoy. We were nearing my destination.

On disembarking, I went directly to the taxi area, expecting to find a driver who might know some German because of the German-Turkish alliance during the First World War. Luckily, I engaged one who had driven for the German military staff (so he said) and knew enough to get me to 22 Sifa Street, in the Moda section of Kadikoy, Trotsky's temporary residence. In those years, Kadikoy was known as an Anglo-American suburb of Istanbul, and Moda was a residential area adjacent to the town limits. The driver told me that he had often taken people to that address and also brought members of the household to the ferry station on their way to Istanbul.

We drove up the hilly, cobblestone street, passed several stores, and soon came to the very last house on Sifa Street. It was about ten o'clock in the morning. As I left the taxi, I could see the shoreline of the Marmara. Beginning at the water and running at right angles to it across the front of the house was a brick fence, surmounted by iron pickets, topped with barbed wire, and divided by a large, locked gate. I could see only the upper floor well and immediately recognized the shock of graying hair, horn rims, and goatee as Trotsky peered out of a second-story window and, I later learned, wondered who was arriving without warning at his new, isolated exile. (My letter from Paris had led him to expect me later.)

I was about to meet Trotsky! Only twenty-two, I saw for the first time in the flesh the heroic leader of our tiny, aspiring movement. Here was the legendary figure of the October Revolution, the president of the Revolutionary Military Committee, which led the Bolshevik insurrection, and the creator, with Lenin, of the new Soviet state. He was the man who built the Red Army out of raw peasant recruits; he was its first commander, leader of the victorious war against the counterrevolution, member of the Political Committee of the Bolshevik Party, and one of its five initial representatives on the Executive Committee of the Communist International in its formative years.

Jan Frankel, Trotsky's secretary and a member of the household, opened the gate for me. We instantly accepted each other as comrades in a common struggle—joined by ideas, organization, and allegiance to the historic figure in the rooms upstairs. More than that, Frankel was elated because I would relieve his solitude and automatically become a "relief battalion" to share his various burdens, which would soon be outlined to me. We put my things in the house and walked along the sandy paths of the garden.

I could see the house, probably once handsome, but now showing the decay of neglect. It had been rented, Frankel told me, after the fire in the Prinkipo dwelling. Forced to leave that favored spot—even in exile there is a choice of residence—this poor house in this small town was all that was available to Trotsky.

Jan was an excellent linguist, which was indispensable for one who would be Trotsky's aide. At that time, as I recall, Jan spoke French, German, Turkish, Czechoslovak (his native tongue), considerable Russian, and some English, with ever-increasing facility in the latter.

As a one-man staff, Jan had to deal with the Turkish government in all matters relating to the exile of Trotsky and Natalia Sedova, particularly with the defense of the household and its residents. Frankel had to receive political persons from many countries and answer correspondence in several languages. Thus, Frankel's qualification for his post was more than mere availability. He, like other dedicated comrades, decided on a self-imposed exile, a subordination of his life to the "greater good of the movement," which was identified with the greater good of society. There was no other way for any secretary to Trotsky. For a young man only a little older than I, life was often dreary during the grim years of the early thirties, especially since he was without assistance in political and defense duties.[6]

The Kadikoy house was taken because it was at the end of the town and street, overlooked the sea, and had enough ground surrounding it for maneuver in the event of an attack. The outer boards showed that it had been painted long ago. It was a square box with a front shanty and a rear door leading from the kitchen to a stoop; it was two stories high and had a slanted tile roof and windows with shutters on all four sides. Trotsky and Natalia occupied the rooms on the second floor, their bedroom windows opening to a small, plain balcony facing the sea. Frankel and I occupied the first floor's improvised bedrooms, where the dining room and kitchen were also located. Toward the northwest corner of the grounds stood a smaller, one-story structure, which housed a cook, a young fisherman, and the two policemen assigned by the government to guard Trotsky and oversee his movements.

The family household was made up of Trotsky, Natalia, and Vsievolod Volkow (Sieva), the five-year-old son of Trotsky's eldest daughter, Zinaida, born to him and his first wife, Alexandrovna, during his first Siberian exile. The boy's father was Platon Volkow, a devoted member of the Trotskyist group in Russia in the twenties, who perished during Stalin's early assault on Trotsky's followers. Zinaida left for Berlin on the morning of the twenty-second, just as I was arriving in Istanbul, to undergo treatment for a "nervous disorder" at a sanitarium in Germany. Little Sieva, as he was called, remained with his grandparents and attended a private school in the area.

Trotsky and Natalia[7] came downstairs to greet me with friendly smiles of welcome. Trotsky then shook hands with me. Jan made the introductions, which Natalia acknowledged first in Russian and then in French. Although I understood neither, the look in her eyes was enough for me. It was one of being pleased that another young comrade and friend had come a long distance to meet Trotsky, in a gesture of personal and political solidarity, and assist in whatever ways possible in this new, temporary residence. We spoke mainly in English; Trotsky's vocabulary was large, I would learn, but he would turn to German, where my vocabulary was weak, to rescue himself from occasional difficulty in English. Both he and his wife showed signs of fatigue, especially Natalia. They were plainly dressed and neatly goomed. Natalia was not five feet tall, small but sturdy. Trotsky was erect, taller than any of us. Prominent dimples punctuated his smile. I was beaming, inwardly and outwardly, as I looked into the faces of two people about whom I had read so much and who were so important to my young life.

Trotsky stood there smiling at a supporter from—of all places!—that quintessence of capitalism, the United States, where, since the days of Eugene V. Debs, no Socialist movement had made any significant progress. I thought he smiled, too, because he was meeting the youngest member of the leadership of a tiny group of struggling but determined Trotskyists.

He had been told about me and was not truly surprised at my youth. While I felt I had the political maturity of a veteran activist of the movement, I was young, and young as an American—that is, limited in intellectual and political experience, reflecting the rudimentary American socialism, which did not have the history that the mass parties in Europe did. However, the American Trotskyists—all of its leading committees and almost the whole organization—came out of the early Communist movement and so were not political neophytes. The experience of the Americans was important to Trotsky. He did not begin quite at square one with us.

Trotsky had been expelled from the Russian Communist Party in January 1927 and exiled to Kazakhstan, the capital city of Alma Ata, in Soviet Central Asia. He was joined there by Natalia and their eldest son,

Lyova. At the end of 1928, Stalin decided to deport Trotsky from the country and deprive him of his citizenship (at which time Bukharin wept in the meeting of the Political Committee), certain that the deportation would destroy his worldwide reputation as a revolutionary Socialist leader and discredit any activity in which he might engage.

On January 20, 1929, the deportation order was announced to Trotsky, and within two days the trek to the new exile began. He was taken by ship from Odessa to Istanbul, arriving in Turkey in February 1929, after a journey of six thousand kilometers in twenty-two days. After a short stay in the Russian Embassy, the new exiles went to the island of Prinkipo, where the first direct contact was made with them by their American supporters. A fire broke out in their rented house there about two years later and led to the move to Kadikoy for a stay of about a year.[8]

Merely to be in Kadikoy at Trotsky's exile residence forced the thought of the great change in his life. Once the leader of the most profound social revolution of this century, this man of extraordinary intellect, an exceptional literary stylist (George Bernard Shaw dubbed him the "prince of the pamphleteers" of socialism), Trotsky bore not the slightest air of defeatism, even though he had been almost crushed by the new bureaucracy organized and led by Stalin. Yet his self-imposed task, in his latest exile, was nothing less than to try to build a new movement from minuscule beginnings.

First Talk with Trotsky

In his accented English, he invited me to his *buro*. This being my first day, he said we would just chat. He wanted to know whether I was hungry or needed anything. I knew that Trotsky was physically distressed by smoke, yet I said, "I would like a cigarette." "But I don't smoke," he replied. "I know," I said. He laughed, went downstairs, looked for the fisherman, and dispossessed him of what I thought then to be his wonderful Turkish cigarettes. He brought them to me and I proceeded to smoke, acknowledging that I knew from his autobiography how smoking affected him.

"Today," Trotsky said, "you are a guest. You may smoke in my room. But after today, no more. You will have to smoke in your room or wherever else you are but not in my presence or in a room where I am." My excuse of an addict's craving compounded by the fatigue of the long journey was accepted, and that closed the matter.[9]

As I sat talking, I observed the famous head, with its shock of gray hair, the high forehead, the penetrating blue eyes behind the horn rims, the full lips framed by dimples that deepened with his smile or laughter. He spoke with deep feeling, assurance, and conviction, even in casual conversation, and with certitude about the future. The resonance of his high tenor reminded me of his legendary oratorical prowess.[10]

Trotsky said that he wished I had come to Kadikoy two weeks later, when he would have been finished with his *History of the Russian Revolution.* At the moment, he was being hounded by his publishers in the United States, Simon and Schuster, because, as he acknowledged, he was far behind his contractual deadline. The publishers were making it difficult for Max Eastman, who was Trotsky's literary agent and translator, as well as personal friend. In another two weeks he would be finished, and then we would be able to talk about the many things on my list, among which were the American economic crisis, the conditions of the American League, European Trotskyism, and the prospects for an organization in England. (As it turned out, he did not finish the second volume of the *History,* on which he was then working, until long after I left Turkey.)

I had the opportunity during my stay to "listen" to Trotsky write some of the *History.* He rose early and breakfasted quickly. Then he would return to the second floor workroom to continue the laborious task of dictating the *History* directly to the Russian typist; afterward he would edit what he had already done and prepare material for the following day. He dictated the three volumes of the *History,* chapter by chapter, pasting the typed sheets together in long rolls for easier reading, and meticulously correcting and revising pages, some as many as three times. He checked facts and events scrupulously. Sometimes he waited days or weeks for books and other corroborating materials to arrive from France and other places. He lamented his lack of a suitable, usable library in Turkey and found it very frustrating.

On a large table in his workroom, he spread out a large number of photographic street maps of Petrograd, maps that showed buildings, streets, corner crossings, the Nevsky River, and the bridges over it. As he wrote the story of the insurrection, he would check locations of the marches of masses of people and areas of the uprising against the detailed maps to make certain that not a street, building, or bridge would be described incorrectly.

He dictated consecutively for an hour or two, and sometimes longer. You could hear the clear and powerful inflections of his voice throughout the old worn house to the regular accompaniment of his pacing. From pages of notes held in his hand, he could compose a lengthy narration many times their length, in an unbroken outpouring of speech. (The theoretical and political faults of the *History* are systemic, since the work adheres to Bolshevism as a political system, justifying the dictatorship and claiming that the Soviet Union remained a true workers' state, though a "degenerated" one. The *History* nonetheless remains widely recognized as historical literature of a high order.)

He had an assignment for me while he was finishing the book. Having learned that I knew stenography, Trotsky gave me a file of correspondence in English and asked me to select a few letters I deemed, or he deemed, worth answering and to draft replies to them. I should also prepare a detailed list of topics I wished to discuss, and we would in the course of days get to them one by one. The rest of my time I could arrange with Natalia and Frankel.

I inquired in this first conversation about the state of his health, which was of concern to the American comrades, who had read all kinds of newspaper stories about a variety of ailments he was purported to have. He said, "My two main complaints are malaria and a stomach ulcer. I suffer these from time to time. Regarding my malaria, I can add very little to what I have already told the comrades before. There is very little that can be done for it in Turkey. The climate is extremely bad for malaria." (I later used my notes on his reply, which included this quote, in an article for the American paper *The Militant,* which I wrote immediately upon return from my journey.)

He dismissed the rumors that he had any problems with his heart or was subject to severe and continual headaches or any other organic problems. He was, he added, able to carry out what he had to do without interruption for health reasons. External, objective difficulties interfered with this work, but many of these would be overcome in time. I wasn't quite sure at the moment what he meant, aside from the general knowledge I had of the restrictive conditions of exile, but the "objective difficulties" would become clearer to me as the days passed.

After referring to my notes and outlining the general subjects I wanted to discuss with him, our initial conversation began to run down, and I became aware that Trotsky showed some discomfiture. I began to feel uncomfortable myself. He asked suddenly: "What have you done in Paris? I am informed that you have robbed a graveyard and have endangered our French comrades."

He appeared embarrassed when I burst out laughing at my recollection of the Père Lachaise incident. When I told him what happened, he seemed even more embarrassed and then dropped the subject abruptly. My other Paris "involvement," which came up briefly in a discussion after I returned to the States, concerned the factional situation in the French Trotskyist organization and its relations with the Jewish Group. I was charged by one or two of the leaders with lending political support to emigré comrades.

The factional situation in the French organization, which had abated slightly following agreements reached by the various contenders at their 1931 conference, flared up again. My attendance at the meeting of the Jewish Group made me automatically suspect by one of the factions. As in the case of the cemetery incident, Trotsky had been informed of my "dereliction." What to me was an amusing evening was presented to him with distortions typical of much political gossip. The Jewish Group differed with the Paris organization on the question of unity between the French trade unions and the Socialist- and Communist-led federations. It would have been presumptuous of me to take a position one way or the other on a question I did not fully understand.

Perplexed by the conduct of the French comrades who had written to Trotsky, I felt that I had to go through an elaborate explanation about how I came even to be at the meeting. After my explanation, there was no further discussion of the matter.

Kadikoy Life

Following my first meeting with the Old Man, I tackled the English correspondence file he gave me. It was an accumulation that could never have been fully acknowledged, let alone answered in detail, without a large staff. Nor should much of it ever have been. I waded through nuisance letters from souvenir-seekers and collectors of photographs and autographs.

As an ideological leader alone responsible for his movement's political program and activities, Trotsky received stacks of literature, newspapers, magazines, and materials from factions within the organizations—as well as documents from a myriad of intellectuals, political activists, and individuals of greater or lesser importance, for a multitude of purposes. Pleas, requests, and demands poured in on him from everywhere. He participated in each of the problems, large and small, involving his movement. Indeed, he involved himself far more than he should have, especially with the trivia of factional conflict. Moreover, he was deeply engaged in the *History,* as well as other literary works of a theoretical and political nature on the partisan crises in the Soviet Union, Spain, and Germany.

Of the half dozen letters that merited a reply, one was from H. L. Mencken, the editor of the old *American Mercury,* which had a great influence on American letters. Mencken had read about the fire in Trotsky's Prinkipo house that had destroyed his library and said he was sending Trotsky copies of all his (Mencken's) works; he also volunteered to send him any other books he might want. A gracious letter and a generous offer, which I thought to be a characteristic American expression of solidarity and kindliness on the part of one man of letters to another. But Trotsky seemed embarrassed by the gesture. He said he felt he could not accept Mencken's offer for two reasons: One, the kind of books he needed and used in his work were best supplied by European and American "comrades"; two, he did not feel he could obligate himself to one who, whatever his contributions to American letters, was politically conservative, even reactionary. My reply thanked Mencken for his kindness; Trotsky signed the letter.

Another letter I selected for Trotsky to answer offered him an honorary Vice Presidency of the Mark Twain Society. The letter was signed by Cyril Clemens, Mark Twain's son. Trotsky laughed aloud. The society's letterhead listed General John J. Pershing and, as one of the Vice Presidents, Benito Mussolini. Trotsky told me to write and thank them for their kind offer but to say that he could not under any circumstances serve on any committee, or in any capacity, with a General Pershing or a Benito Mussolini.

He asked me to answer a letter from an American in Waco, Texas, who lamented Trotsky's derogatory comments in a newspaper interview on the sport of casting, a method believed by thousands of fishermen to be the only way to pursue the art of fishing. Trotsky had compared casting unfavorably to his method of net fishing, which yields "massive" results. He obviously measured the quantity of the catch against the caster's pleasure in the skill of the sport. The Texan suggested in a friendly way that if Trotsky were to try casting, he would certainly enjoy its challenge, skill, and artistry. He invited Trotsky to Texas, where he would take him for an extended fishing trip. Trotsky was truly amused and pleased by the sentiments of the letter and told me to write that he would enjoy such a fishing experience but, unfortunately, was unable to travel to the United States because he had no visa. However, if this fisherman were able to obtain such a visa, he would be most happy to go to Texas and join him.

There was a letter from a young boy from the Bronx who asked Trotsky why he did not go to China and lead the Red Army in a war against Chiang Kai-shek to free the nation. Trotsky thanked him for his sentiments and explained how and why such a venture was not possible for him in his present exile.

A society asked Trotsky to donate one of his canes to its collection of world-famous personalities' canes. Trotsky said I should write and tell them that he could not meet their request because he did not use one. Yet there *were* photographs of Trotsky that showed him carrying a cane, perhaps because of recovery from an illness. He did not, however, frequently use a walking stick.

Then there were requests for his manuscripts, photographs, and specimens of his handwriting. Invitations came to participate in symposia, to contribute to books, to comment on a variety of matters, and to hold interviews. Trotsky could not and would not accede to these demands, for they would have occupied him fully in basically wasteful matters. Indeed, the slightest yielding to such curiosities would inevitably have opened floodgates of requests. Moreover, Trotsky could only rarely confirm the legitimacy of the letters. In at least one instance, a Jewish correspondent in Europe published an interview with Trotsky that never took place. One collector of trivia wanted Trotsky to name the one hundred most useful men in the world at that time. Another correspondent sent unsolicited advice on health.

I recall two other especially amusing letters from famous Americans. The first was from Upton Sinclair, asking: "Is it true that you are planning to translate my novels into Turkish?" We all laughed at the naivete, arrogance, egotism, and/or ignorance suggested by the question. I could not imagine Trotsky occupying himself in such an unrewarding way—assuming that he knew Turkish! Only Upton Sinclair could believe in such a possibility. The second came from the famous Will Durant, who, together with his wife Ariel, wrote popular versions of history and philosophy that sold millions of copies. Durant wrote: "I take it for granted that my name is unfamiliar to you; that you have been too actively engaged in doing things to read the writings of one who has done nothing." Here was astounding self-abnegation.

From the moment Trotsky was deported from Russia, friends and followers made strenuous efforts to obtain visas for him to countries where his life would be safer and somewhat easier, and his working conditions more convenient, than in Turkey. Efforts to obtain visas for France or Germany had repeatedly failed. Great Britain was another country that refused to admit him, though Trotsky would have preferred, I thought, Germany first and then France.

The material Trotsky gave me to review after our first discussion disclosed that George Bernard Shaw and H. G. Wells had each written appeals to their government to grant asylum to Trotsky. Great Britain was long noted for its democratic traditions and had often provided such asylum to various political exiles. It did so notably for Marx and Engels, for German revolutionaries of 1848, and for Paris Communards and Italian Garibaldians. Shaw and Wells thought they could obtain such a visa for Trotsky and sought support among England's noted men of letters, science, and other public figures. Shaw's letter was signed by Arnold Bennett, the Bishop of Birmingham, and Lord Olivier, a Fabian socialist and colonial expert.

Wells's letter was signed by John Maynard Keynes; C. A. Gregory, an editor; Lord Beauchamps, a Liberal peer; Graham Wallas, the noted Fabian socialist; Ramsay Muir, a liberal historian; A. Gardiner of the *Daily News;* Beatrice Webb; and Harold J. Laski. Wells received no replies from Gilbert Murray, A. P. Herbert, and Sir William Orjen. Among those who refused to sign either letter were England's four great scientists: Sir Arthur S. Eddington, Sir James J. Jeans, Sir J. J. Thomson, and Ernest Rutherford. Other nonsigners included Dean Inge, Lord Brentford, J. M. Barrie, John Galsworthy, E. L. Mond, Rudyard Kipling, the Bishop of Gordon, and the Archbishop of York.

Not a single name of an intellectual fellow traveler, let alone a member of the British Communist Party, appeared on any list. They were all unabashedly and totally subservient to the Soviet Union, notwithstanding its Stalinist degeneration. They all approved of the deportation of Trotsky.

Defense and Related Duties

Wanting to establish a routine, I sat down with Frankel. First there was the matter of guard duty. How Frankel managed it alone, I never understood; even for the two of us, the hours of duty were arduous. Shift changes kept one of us awake for almost a whole day. We had no way of establishing a more rational routine, because Jan also had to be available to Trotsky in his capacity of aide—and that meant almost any time during the daylight hours.

We had two pistols, a nickel-plated Browning, whose caliber I no longer remember, and a smaller one, a .22, which we changed in our patrols of the garden. We alternated night patrols. It was the damp and chilly season, and I would wear Trotsky's old military greatcoat to ward off the cold. During the days we kept a similar vigil while doing our work, making sure to take a turn or two around the garden. When Trotsky took his walks or went fishing, which he did frequently then, one or both of us inconspicuously watched from the garden or in the boat as a second fisherman.

We decided that I would accompany Trotsky on his fishing breaks, in order to leave Frankel to his other duties, which seemed to grow day by day. This division would enable Jan to make necessary trips to Istanbul to deal with government officials, make purchases of needed supplies, and discharge other household chores.

Trotsky's son, Lyova Sedov, had left for Germany to continue his engineering studies and political activities that could not be carried on in Turkey. He devoted his time mainly to the printing and distribution of the *Russian Bulletin,* edited by his father (in later years Sedov was the editor and wrote for it). When I arrived, Frankel had been with Trotsky in Turkey for more than a year and a half and was feeling the pressures of an unrelenting schedule and a circumscribed personal life.

The division of guard duty held throughout my stay, but my fishing trips ended temporarily one chilly and choppy day at sea when I became seasick. Fatigue brought on by my being unaccustomed to our erratic schedule and the steady diet of fish undoubtedly contributed. At one point in our fishing, Trotsky asked me if I felt all right. "You look green," he said. I denied it, and held out as long as possible because I knew fishing was the only consistent relaxation Trotsky had from his heavy daily writing schedule. He tried to avoid returning to the shore directly, hoping that I would overcome my nausea. Eventually we reached a point where I could no longer tolerate the rising and falling of the boat and we had to return. My deadly discomfort ended the moment my feet touched the solid shore.

After the incident, Trotsky did not want me to go fishing with him again. He insisted that I would get sick and he would have to turn back. The fact that I had been with him at least ten times before without incident meant nothing. Our protests—Natalia's, Frankel's, and mine—all made on grounds of safety, did not convince him. Trotsky insisted that if the GPU (the Soviet secret police) wanted to shoot him, especially when fishing, my presence would certainly be no deterrent. On the contrary, he added, it would help them. He argued, using pantomime, that while we were all busy pulling out pistols and trying to avoid shooting each other in a small boat, they would shoot us all. He did sneak off on several occasions with two policemen (one usually came along with us) and the not-too-competent fisherman. The policemen were often in a state of semireadiness, jackets unbuttoned or shoes unlaced. I resumed my right to accompany him on subsequent fishing trips not only to undertake my post as guard, but also because I genuinely enjoyed the sea in this small fishing boat. Across the water there were stupendous views of Istanbul and its mosques, and we could hear the guns from the barracks in Scutari. Fishermen in their high-sided boats with upcurved bows sang sad songs. Their singing surrounded us in the morning darkness and fog before the boat lamps began to shimmer.

We fished not merely for relaxation and sport, but for the table. I thought of Trotsky's "Russian style" as "mass fishing," though it was a common method in many other parts of the world. I had heard from Max Shachtman how they fished in Prinkipo, so I was not surprised the first time I went out with the Old Man to see, along with the folded net, two or three small piles of stones in the boat. We rowed out a mile or so and laid the net, which was about a hundred yards long, in an arc or semi-circle in the water. Then we rowed several hundred feet away from it, turned the boat around, and rowed toward the net, moving sharply from side to side, throwing rocks in all directions to drive the fish into this trap.

Our catch depended on how the fish ran. Sometimes we came up with a large number of fish, along with the debris of modern society that lay in the shore waters of this ancient land. On my first day, for example, we dragged in very few fish but a large number of tin cans, old shoes, and boxes, all intermingled with a number of inedible scorpions.

According to Shachtman, in these same waters at Prinkipo, about twenty miles distant and a year and a half earlier, they had caught many lobsters. At the time I fished, however, either Kadikoy had no lobsters or the new fisherman with us, whom Trotsky did not consider skillful, did not know the waters very well. Trotsky used to remark on how much he missed his very able Greek fisherman, Charalambos, who was away in military service.

Our main catch at this time of year was salt-water mackerel. They ran in huge schools, and when we fished for them with hooks and lines, each line having many hooks and no bait, we often pulled in five or more mackerels on a single line. I understood then why fish made up so large a part of our daily diet. It was available and cheap.

Most of the talk during our fishing trips was banter about the weather and fishing prospects for the day. In breaking up his daily grind with these fishing trips, Trotsky was far from indifferent to a good catch. When the fish didn't bite, he would be a little disappointed, but he enjoyed the physical activity, the pleasures of the sea and the boat.

Among other things during the fishing trips, Trotsky often spoke of his enjoyment of the English language, lamenting his lack of knowledge and experience in it. The first time he spoke to me about it, he insisted that if I remained in Turkey for six months, he would really be able to speak English fluently. Another time he said four months would be sufficient for him to learn to speak well. On a fishing trip toward the end of my stay, he said, "One more month and I will make great progress, Amerikaner Onkel." ("Onkel" was an affectionate title he bestowed on me because I had brought him a cashmere sweater from the comrades in New York, which we thought would ward off the chill of the Turkish fall and winter.) I might add here that whatever his deficiencies in English, a few years later during the Dewey Commission hearings in Mexico he was cross-examined in English. He answered most effectively and fluently in that language for eight successive days.

Trotsky had been tutored in English by Max Eastman during the early twenties when the famous editor of *The Masses* lived in Moscow. Trotsky now spoke with a strong accent, mixing in his native Russian, and French and German, which he knew well and used daily in his political life. In fact, he was a remarkably able linguist. One of the high points of the Fourth Congress of the Communist International in 1922 was Trotsky's report on the international situation, which he delivered first in Russian and then, at the insistence of the French and German delegates who refused a translation, twice more in each language before each respective body. His knowledge of English was considerable, and he read it fluently. But when I complimented him on his competence in English, he would protest. It was obvious that he wished to speak it as well as he did German and French and was frustrated by having no opportunity to speak it consistently.

At lunch one day, Frankel made some derogatory comments about the English language and its insufficiencies, extolling the French as far superior. He was not serious, merely joshing with me as I defended English against one who spoke many languages easily and fluently. Trotsky interjected in a serious way that he enjoyed the use of English because he found it the richest of all languages. He thought it especially useful to a writer because the language's choice of words and phrases was so broad. He argued that this was so because the language had borrowed so much from other tongues.

The talk around the lunch or tea table was often light. One day Trotsky looked at his gray cashmere sweater and, imagining the great amount of labor that went into making it, said, "Ah, made in Scotland," and laughed. A few days later he poked fun at me about the "great American economy," then in its severest crisis.

Another source of amusement was occasioned by a purchase I made one day upon returning from Istanbul. I decided to walk to the house from the ferry station, and on the way I passed a candy store. The Turks were noted for their confectionary skills; their products were exported to the Balkans and various parts of Eastern Europe, areas that had apparently acquired a taste for them during their Turkish occupation.

In the window of one particular store, I saw a tub-shaped mound of *halvah,* shaped like the old butter tubs used in the United States. Halvah was a confection from my childhood. It was introduced to the United

States, we thought, by the immigrant Jews from Eastern Europe. Those of us who pursued the subject learned that the candy, made of honey and sesame seeds, actually originated in Turkey. A taste for it is easily acquired. When I saw these enormous solid piles of halvah, I could not resist walking into the store to purchase the delicacy. Language and the metric system created problems, and the proprietor interpreted my gestures to mean one kilo—two and a half pounds—instead of one pound.

When I returned at tea time, everyone wanted to know what I was carrying; none was more curious than Trotsky. When I opened the package and revealed my purchase, he would have none of it. I cut off some pieces and laid them on the table. Trotsky's teasing humor went something like this: "Ah, the Americans! They have the greatest economy in the world, and mass production, and you would think they can produce everything. But when they want a good sweater they go to Scotland for it. Fine steel, to England and Germany. For wine and cheese, to France and other European countries. And for halvah, they come to Turkey. Still, it is a great country. Its products may not be as good as the European, but one has to admit it makes a lot of them."

The first few times that the halvah was served with tea, Trotsky refused it as the plate went around the table. One day he broke down and asked if he had my permission to take just a very small piece. Given the kind of table joshing that went on I made a big deal of granting such permission, as though it were a tremendous personal triumph. On the subsequent trips I made to Istanbul, he would always ask whether I had remembered to buy some halvah for the tea table.

*   *   *

After Natalia and Jan had taken my side in the dispute with Trotsky over my accompanying him on the fishing trips, I soon discovered that this kind of dispute was recurrent and was sometimes sharp. Because Prinkipo was an island, only the most elementary precautions had been taken there; but Trotsky's mainland residence posed a far greater security risk. Even so, Trotsky minimized the differences. Given the enormous resources of the GPU, and the power of the Russian state and its satellite Communist parties, Trotsky believed that it was impossible to defend himself against assassination.

In Kadikoy the house could be approached easily from the street. Our fence was no formidable obstacle. There were no high brick walls covered with barbed wire or broken glass. Our garden was only ten or fifteen feet away from the sea, so that an approach from that direction was easy.

The house was, in truth, indefensible. Still, despite the impossibility of establishing an adequate defense—especially with so few people—we could not let the subject be dismissed so easily. Natalia argued vehemently against Trotsky's fatalistic view and insisted that a defensive posture had to be assumed and maintained—if only to indicate to the outside world that our guards were in a constant state of alert.

The guards, indeed! They were two Turkish policemen assigned by the government, and they were always late for any appointment, let alone an emergency. I retain unfaded mental pictures of their running to the boat with shoes untied, pants unbuttoned, and shirttails flying. The police did carry regular holstered arms. Then there were Jan and I—and I only a visitor—with one Browning pistol and a small automatic between us. Trotsky always had his pistol by his side when he worked, and Natalia had a pistol. After getting to know her I did not doubt that this fragile-seeming but brave woman would have been able to use it.

We were three to one against Trotsky in the argument over guard duty, and Natalia's views prevailed. We decided to maintain a regular schedule, even if we were uncertain of its value. At night we sometimes carried a flashlight, but other times we walked in total darkness. Our object was to make it appear to any observer that the house was constantly guarded.

The two attacks on Trotsky in Mexico later, where he lived under far more protected conditions—a well-situated house, which had been turned into a semi-fortress with a guard force at least five times stronger than the one in Kadikoy—showed that Trotsky, in the last analysis, knew what he was talking about when he spoke of the power and resources of the GPU. A handful of faithful friends and supporters, essentially untrained and inexperienced, could not indefinitely fend off the enormous power of the Russian Stalinist state, which had at its disposal its dummy political parties, mercenaries, secret police, and paid agents.

There had been increasing difficulties between the Turkish government and Trotsky on the point of security, I learned during my first days in Kadikoy. The government was represented by the security police. Trotsky had objected to the weak measures taken by the government and asked for an immediate improvement of his security. The government response? To demand that Trotsky supply the names and addresses of all his visitors, information it supposedly regarded as essential to Trotsky's security. Trotsky felt that this demand was meant to harass his visitors and, further, that the GPU had begun to exert pressure on the Turkish government—an ominous sign.

One afternoon, two officers, lieutenants I believe, arrived at the house to confer with Trotsky. Frankel thought they had come to discuss the improvement of security measures and perhaps to replace the existing guards with some more capable ones. He joined Trotsky in the ground-floor dining room to meet the officers while I remained outside in the hallway. In no more than two or three minutes, Trotsky yanked the door open, stormed out, and sped up the stairs. Within a minute or two, out came the officers, visibly embarrassed, followed by Frankel, who bade them a curt goodbye.

I was about to ask what caused Trotsky's quick disappearance to the second floor when Frankel, who was laughing by this time, told me what happened. No sooner had Trotsky and Frankel sat down around the dining table, thinking they were to take up security matters, when the spokesman for the officers opened the discourse by saying that they had come to collect the names and addresses of Trotsky's visitors. Trotsky asked, "Is that all you came for?" Upon receiving an affirmative reply, he got up from the table, left the room at once, and ended the conference.

In his book *With Trotsky in Exile,* Jean Van Heijenoort, another of Trotsky's long-time secretary/guards, wrote, "In Prinkipo, aliens had to register with the local police. For persons living in Trotsky's house, this was always done quite simply."[11] As to why Kadikoy was different from Prinkipo, I do not know. Registration may have been an option of the local police, or it may have been the island character of Prinkipo that led to the measure. I know that *I* did not register with an official department of any kind while in Kadikoy, and I was not a day visitor. There were other visitors and I am not aware that any of them registered with the police. But people in the same position in Prinkipo apparently did so, according to Van Heijenoort, without objection from Trotsky, it would seem. Was it the routine nature of the one as against the governmental pressure of the other, indicating some specific but unknown purpose, that formed Trotsky's response in Kadikoy? Perhaps Trotsky's reaction to the visit of the Kadikoy officers was caused simply by his dashed hope that they had finally come to discuss his improved defense. Frankel told me Trotsky had advised the government he would not submit his visitors, often noted persons, public figures, friends, and associates, to the indignity of registering with the local police.

Grandson Sieva Volkow

One of my tasks in the house was to befriend the young boy, Sieva, Trotsky's grandson. The greatest difficulty in so doing was that he spoke only Russian. Nonetheless, the situation begged for some kind of effort on my part to relate to him. From what I was able to learn, his mother, Zinaida, was to stay in Germany indefinitely. Sieva was left with surrogate—and preoccupied—parents only, his aging grandparents. In Kadikoy the boy was sent to a private school where the children spoke French, which he could not speak or understand. There he suffered the usual little cruelties inflicted by children. He was living in a house with strangers and visitors, who came frequently and briefly, and was sustained only by the love of his devoted grandparents.

Trotsky and Natalia asked me one day whether Sieva could play in my room when he returned from school. They thought it would be good for him not to be alone too often. So from then on, I welcomed him daily and hoped I could, by friendly gestures if not conversation, make his time with me as pleasant as possible. Being a heavy smoker then, I used to buy strong Turkish cigarettes in boxes decorated in brilliant colors, some exhibiting enticing poses of nude or seminude women. I gave the boxes to him, and he played with them in a variety of inventive ways. I tried, I fear not too successfully, to play games with him.

Trotsky asked me if I could show Sieva how to box. He thought the skill might help him to fend off his peers.[12] But boxing was too much like fighting, and Sieva was too unhappy to enjoy facing this person who loomed physically large. The experiment failed as soon as it was tried.

Sieva's main communication at the time was with Trotsky and Natalia. He could exchange comments with Frankel, but Jan was always too involved with his responsibilities, and he was just another adult. Trotsky could give the boy only the most limited attention, so it fell to Natalia to give as much of her time and devotion as she could. Sieva slept in a room of his own on the second floor near his grandparents.[13] Naturally, he retired early, and we would hear him cry out occasionally in his sleep when mice, which were permanent residents, raced across his floor.

Much of the time at the dining table was devoted to Sieva. Trotsky and Natalia would coax the boy's reluctant appetite, although he looked physically robust. He had plumpish cheeks and a head of blond hair, closely cropped. I have never forgotten his high-pitched voice calling out "Lev Davidovich!"—though so many years have passed. After Kadikoy I would not see him for twenty years, in Mexico.[14]

Preparing for a Hunt

Trotsky's routine of literary work determined the schedule of activities in the confined environment of Kadikoy. He wrote all day, breaking only for lunch or to direct us in some way, particularly to communicate whatever matters Frankel had to take care of. We had tea late in the afternoon, and then he worked until dinner was served. After dinner, he returned upstairs to read and prepare for any writing he was to do the next day. While working on the second volume of the *History of the Russian Revolution,* he kept up a voluminous, worldwide correspondence. He wrote articles and drafted documents for a variety of purposes, using the pennames of "Gurov," "Lund," and "Alpha" as well as Trotsky. At that time he still had contact with Left Oppositionists in Russia. His own writings filled most of the pages of the *Russian Bulletin,* distributed by Trotskyist organizations in Europe and America. Disturbed by current political events, he wrote several pamphlets devoted to the most important problems created by the rise of Hitler and the Fascist movement in Germany.

Trotsky showed me a number of letters he had received from his supporters in Russia, some from Siberian exile, others from Moscow. They had been sent out clandestinely, some written with special inks, others in microscopic script, recalling the subterfuges of underground revolutionary life under Tsarism—except that life was far more onerous under Stalin! These letters told of the problems in the economy and in the Party. Some declared that Russia was no longer a workers' state. To these latter letters Trotsky would say, "Brilliantly written, but wrong." Despite his fervent clash with the Party and Stalin's leadership, Trotsky *never* revoked his belief that the Soviet Union was a "workers' state." This reluctance, of course, eventually drove away many of his supporters, including me. In any case, if Trotsky sometimes disagreed with his young Russian comrades, these letters were vital to him as his remaining living links to the Revolution and his country.

For all his great capacity for intellectual and literary work, the self-imposed tasks of writing and of building a new movement weighed heavily upon him. It was obvious that he needed to find something beside fishing and walking in the garden to break up his schedule of ceaseless writing and offset his restricted mobility. The walks around the garden were not idle strolls but swift marches; he bore himself as straight as a soldier and made an exercise of them. Frankel and I, stationed separately in the garden, stayed away from him because we knew he needed to be completely alone. They occurred at times, Frankel said, when Trotsky wished to think out some political problem or to work out some aspect of the writing of the *History.* His brisk walks always ended suddenly, and he would return to the house to resume work.

*   *   *

Trotsky began to speak of taking a full day off to go hunting. Frankel smiled, "It's an old Russian custom." Preparations for such an event were complicated in the Kadikoy environment. First of all, a trip inland required the approval of the Turkish government. Police guards, hunter guides, transportation to the hill country, and an automobile and chauffeur all had to be arranged. Trotsky needed the proper hunting clothes for the field, a gun, and even a pair of puttees. It took a bit of doing to organize this trip, and most of the burden fell on Frankel. Trotsky's dog Tosca would accompany him. Frankel and I were necessary as guards.

Secrecy had to be exercised because the shadow of the Kremlin was always present. Turkey bordered Stalin's Russia, and dozens of GPU agents moved about the country freely. In addition, many of the White Guard Russians residing in Istanbul believed Trotsky to be the man most responsible for their own exile; some were even employed by the Russian secret police! The possibility of an organized attack on the hunting party was not a fantasy.

Frankel carried the preparations through with his customary efficiency. On a dreary November morning, just before dawn, our party left Sifa Street and made for the inland hills, where the hunt for *schnepfen,* or woodcock, would take place. Frankel and I did not look very formidable, but we made the group larger. At the hunting fields, our party numbered ten: Trotsky, two policemen, one security guard, four hunter-guides, Frankel, and me.

Frankel was organizing the entire affair. Personally, I detested hunting, but how could I balk when Trotsky cheerfully called out, "You carry the birds!" Moreover, I understood the circumstances that brought about this excursion. Nevertheless, the prospect of my job was repugnant to me. I found the hunt itself extremely dull even as an exercise. We walked up and down hills for a long time. Trotsky was indefatigable and nearly wore us out. His dog, though she was a pointer, was not a thoroughbred and as often as not wandered into a flock of birds, of whose proximity Trotsky and the hunters were unaware until it was too late. While Trotsky was quite distressed by his dog's uncertainty, he managed to bag twelve birds—which were hung on me, one by one, dripping blood over my neck and shoulders. As we marched along, my antipathy to hunting only increased. (Perhaps it is out of this inherent feeling that I have developed a subsequent avid interest in birds, and shoot them on every possible occasion—photographically.)

When the hunt at last came to an end in the late afternoon, we walked back to the waiting car. As we reached it we heard a cry from the distance: "Trotsky! Trotsky!" Looking up in the direction of the voices, we saw two elderly bearded men run towards the car, waving greetings and arriving breathlessly. They spoke in Russian, but Frankel understood the general nature of the conversation. They were two Jewish farmers who lived in huts beyond the first hill, to which they pointed, and they were inviting us to have tea with them. Trotsky accepted the invitation. I thought at first that we joined the two men simply because of the fatigue of the hunt and the Russian penchant for drinking tea. Later I learned that these were farmers who had migrated from the Soviet Union to Palestine and were now residing in Turkey, and Trotsky was interested in their experiences as cooperative farmers in Russia and Palestine.

We walked to a group of small houses, which had white-washed exteriors and pressed dirt floors; sparsely furnished, they were also impeccably clean. As we drank our tea out of glasses, Trotsky became involved in an animated conversation with our hosts, asking many questions. I understood nothing of the conversation except its emotional overtone of seriousness. The farmers seemed most grateful for a visit that must have broken their isolation and the dull routine of their existence. In addition, they obviously felt honored by their renowned visitor. I know that they drank many glasses of tea. Frankel and I began to fidget because we needed to return at once if we wanted to avoid a trip home in total darkness. After an hour or so of conversation, Trotsky himself closed the discussion, and we started back as soon as the exchange of warm farewells was completed.

It was plain to see that the hunt had succeeded in completely relaxing Trotsky. There was the test of his marksmanship. When I told him that I thought he was a pretty good shot, he modestly denied it, saying that he was "only fair." He added that he did not have much opportunity to hunt anymore. We returned exhausted from the long day's activities and unaccustomed exercise. In the next few days, the birds were prepared for a celebration of the anniversary of the Russian Revolution and, incidentally, my twenty-third birthday on November 7. (I learned later that it was Trotsky's birthday as well, though nothing was said about it at the time.) Aside from an occasional pellet, the woodcock was a gamey, extraordinarily delicious bird. It provided the best meal of my entire stay in Kadikoy.

England Once Again

Although the dictation of the *History* remained Trotsky's main occupation during my stay, he was compelled by events to turn his attention first to England and then, far more seriously, to Germany, where the swift rise of fascism warned of a shattering social crisis there. So far as England was concerned, Trotsky knew that I planned on meeting Max Shachtman in London, where we would try to organize the British Trotskyist movement. He wrote to Shachtman, who was then in Spain:

> Comrade Glotzer, with whom we have formed a good friendship in the few weeks that he has been here, is being retained here for a few more weeks by our great administrator, Frankel. I regret that his visit coincides with a period in which I am very busy with my book. If I am not finished with it by the first of December, the agreement with the publisher is lost. This is the reason why we have only been able to discuss things a few times. But we discuss indirectly by the elaboration of the Theses and Countertheses on the English question, which are translated by Glotzer and Frankel into English.

The theses Trotsky referred to here were those received from the Marxian League to explain in more detail the positions Ram expressed in Paris. Meanwhile, I had written to the National Committee of the American League on October 24 on the problem of my extended stay in Turkey.

> I have been here for three days now and am working out a plan for discussion with LD. I may have to stay here longer than I planned for the following reason: Trotsky is now completing the second volume of the Russian Revolution and in two weeks he will be finishing the project. With that over, I am promised full time for the American question.

Although Trotsky spoke of a deadline of December 1, a month hence, he did not complete the second volume until the end of December. He had already read the minutes of the meeting of the International Secretariat, where I was present, and he was generally familiar with the views expressed by the representative of the Marxian League. He was not surprised, therefore, when he read the written views of the League now presented in theses form. He had also read the communications from England of the various people interested in the Left Opposition. These he gave me to review. I would discuss them with him later and we would figure out how to respond to them.

The English correspondence file contained letters and other material from a group of ex-members of the Communist Party who had only recently been expelled. They wanted to establish relations with Trotsky and the Left Opposition on the political premises of the time. Reg Groves spoke for these people, who were known formally as the Balham Group, named after the district in south London where they resided.

After studying various letters and documents in the England file, I felt that the people in the Balham Group were the most knowledgeable people there, and most consistently sympathetic to the views of our movement. It appeared to me that if a Trotskyist organization emerged in England, its core would be the Balham Group—an opinion that was confirmed several weeks later when I was in London. They had close relations with a group led by an old Socialist, Dick Beech, who was married to Margaret Connally, the daughter of James Connally, a noted Irish revolutionary Socialist leader of the Easter Rebellion. This faction also included Eadmonn "Ned" MacAlpin, a veteran Socialist who at one time lived in the United States, an associate of John Reed in the left-wing struggle in the Socialist Party following World War I. He was joined by Jack Tanner, a well-known trade union leader.

The Marxian League was a violently anti-Communist Party. F. A. Ridley and Chandu Ram, its leading persons, had never been members of the Communist Party, which appeared to be true for the rest of the membership, so there could be no objection to them on this ground. But they had no organizational experience, and they were isolated from any mass movement, which served to exaggerate their extreme sectarianism. Max and I had a preview of their theoretical and political views in Paris. Now the group had codified them in written form.

There was no change in the group's position. Among other things, the Marxian League still forecast the demise of parliamentary democracy in Great Britain and its replacement by fascism. They regarded the trade unions as reactionary, whose precincts the revolutionary movement should avoid. The League's leadership said that the movement required a new Party and new International—preceding Trotsky's call for such a new orientation by several years. They also attacked my intervention in the meeting of the International Secretariat I had attended in Paris, coming, as I did, from the States.

On November 7, the day of the birthdays in Kadikoy, Trotsky wrote a brief reply to Ridley and Chandu Ram (as Aggrawala signed himself in the thesis) under the title *Tasks of the Left Opposition in Britain and India: Some Critical Comments on an Unsuccessful Thesis.* Taking up the question of the imminence of fascism, Trotsky wrote:

> Democracy and fascism are here considered as two abstractions without any social determinants. Evidently the authors wish to say: British imperialism is preparing to free its dictatorship from the decaying parliamentary covering, and to enter upon the path of open and naked violence. In general this is true, but only in general. The present government is not an "antiparliamentary" government; on the contrary, it has received unprecedented parliamentary support from the "nation." Advancing the question of fascism to

first place today is not adequately motivated. Even from the standpoint of a distant perspective one can doubt in what measure it is correct to speak of "fascism" for England. If the "party" of Mosley and the "Guild of St. Michael" represent the beginnings of fascism, as the theses declare, then it is precisely the total futility of these two groups that shows how unwise it is to put the imminent coming of fascism on the order of the day.

Turning to the trade-union question, Trotsky wrote:

The American comrade Glotzer, in speaking of the necessity of working in the trade union organizations for their conquest, appeals in absolute correctness to Lenin's pamphlet *Left Wing Communism: An Infantile Disorder.* To this Comrades Ridley and Ram answer with four objections:

(A) They ask for arguments and not appeals to authority. . . .

(B) The authors deny Roman Catholic dogmas of infallibility. . . .

(C) Lenin was neither God nor an infallible pope. . . .

(D) Lenin wrote in the year 1920; the situation since then has changed considerably. . . . The reference to the year 1920 is in direct opposition to the fundamental thoughts of the thesis. If the trade unions from their origin were and remain to this day pure imperialist organizations incapable of revolutionary deeds, reference to the year 1920 loses all significance. We would have to say simply that the attitude of Marx, Engels, and Lenin was wrong to begin with.[15]

Thus ended Trotsky's relations with the Marxian League. We then turned our attention on those groups that promised better results. Meanwhile, I received a note from Shachtman, still in Spain, asking whether I was going to waste my life in Turkey or join him in England to accomplish great deeds!

Hitler and German Fascism

The world economic crisis deepened in 1931–32. Mass unemployment, hunger, and suffering were widespread. Many countries were in a state of severe political crisis resulting from their inability to solve the many social problems produced by the economic collapse. The second Labor Government in England fell. The newly created Spanish Republic, which had just replaced the monarchy and military dictatorship, was in grave danger. The political crisis in France deepened and was explosive. And the depression in the United States appeared permanent. But the greatest threat of all to democratic society, and the working class in particular, was Germany, which Hitler and the Nazi Party now dominated.

More than a half century later, it is easy to forget how blind, ignorant, stupid, and/or indifferent the world was in the face of Hitler's ascension to power. Many Western political leaders seriously believed that after he achieved the chancellorship of Germany, Hitler would conform to the mold of traditional ministers, presidents, and national leaders. None thought that Hitler would really try to carry out his program of transforming Germany into the dominant power in the world through the conquest of Europe. They were certain he would be too busy attacking Russia, communism, and the Jews, as well as trying to solve the economic problems of Germany, to concern himself with the program he professed in *Mein Kampf.* Trotsky was almost alone in sounding an early alarm.

Although Trotsky adhered to many Bolshevik notions of "revolutionary struggle" that were illusory and divisive, as Leszek Kolakowski has pointed out in his *Main Currents of Marxism,* he was the one world figure who understood the Fascist dilemma in Germany and proposed a way out. While otherwise a fair and acute observer of the period, Kolakowski seems singularly insensitive to what Trotsky attempted in those grim years of the early thirties when Hitler threatened everyone. In this he is at odds with others, such as Trotsky's critical biographers: Joel Carmichael, Robert Wistrich, and the late Joseph Nedava.

Despite Trotsky's blind rejection of the basic elements of democracy, his inability to accept its essential necessity for human progress, and despite his repeated derogations of Social Democracy, he persisted in warning that Hitler meant what he said and was not merely a lunatic, as he was viewed in the West. In the general complacency of the time, Trotsky tried to awaken "decadent bourgeois" movements, as he often described them, to what Hitler meant to them. But his greatest concentration was directed toward arousing and unifying the organized working class in Germany for a struggle against Hitler and the Nazis. No one lambasted Hitler with the initiative, tenacity, and scope of Trotsky. He was convinced that European and, indeed, world civilization were in danger if Hitler was not stopped.

Trotsky was also preoccupied with Spain and interrupted the writing of the *History* to produce two pamphlets: *The Spanish Revolution* and *The Spanish Revolution in Danger.* In these he hailed the establishment of the Republic and the end of Primo de Rivera's dictatorship. He also analyzed the instabilities of the new parliamentary democracy, which he believed could not survive unless the revolutionary process continued, following the Russian example, to a workers' state, or to the Bolshevik version of the "dictatorship of the proletariat."

My visit to Trotsky took place in this increasingly tense period in a Europe that seemed outwardly so placid. Most people were primarily concerned with the worldwide economic crisis. But in Trotsky's view, the *political* developments in Europe arising from the crisis were even more important. Trotsky was most concerned with Hitler's threat against the Soviet Union. Unavoidably, Russia concerned him deeply, and he wrote many essays on the "crisis" in the USSR, at least three of pamphlet length. His brief comments on Great Britain occurred after the fall of the Labor government in August, 1931, in connection with the statements of the Marxian League.

In the fall of 1930 he had written a pamphlet on Germany in which he first predicted a political crisis that would shatter the nation.[16] The Communist League of America was among the first to publish the essay. Now, almost a year later, the crisis in Germany deepened and Hitler's army had grown ominously. The Brown Shirts attacked working-class districts in the larger cities and assaulted meetings of the Social Democratic and Communist Parties. The Nazi propaganda machine raised the level of invective against Jews, Socialists, Communists, liberals, and democrats to a level of hysteria. All important urban centers had become strongholds of the young National Socialist Party, as the Nazis called themselves, and they acquired massive support in rural areas. Some of the largest monopolistic industries and conservative political groups were giving a measure of financial aid to Hitler's movement and supporting his demand to take over the government by presidential selection or concession by his political opponents on the right.

From comments made in passing to Frankel and me on more than one occasion, I knew that Trotsky was so disturbed by events in Germany that he thought of the situation constantly. Writing about the Marxian League provided Trotsky with an opportunity to focus on the acute problem of fascism. On November 15, 1931, he dictated a letter to me for Max Shachtman, who was still in Spain. In the letter, Trotsky asked:

What is fascism? The name originated in Italy. Were all the forms of counter-revolutionary dictatorships fascist or not? That is, prior to the advent of fascism in Italy?

The former dictatorship in Spain of Primo de Rivera is named by the CI [Comintern] as a Fascist dictatorship. Is it correct or not? We believe it is incorrect.

The fascist movement in Italy was a spontaneous movement of large masses, with new leaders from the rank and file. It is a plebeian movement in origin, directed and financed by great capitalist powers. It issued forth from the petty bourgeoisie, the lumpen proletariat and, even to a certain extent, proletarian masses. Mussolini, a former socialist, is a "self-made" man arising from this movement.

Primo de Rivera was an aristocrat. He occupied a high military and bureaucratic post, and was head governor of Catalonia. He accomplished his overthrow with the state and military forces. The dictatorships in Spain and Italy are two totally different forms of dictatorship. It is necessary to distinguish between them. Mussolini had great difficulty to reconcile many old military institutions with the Fascist militia. This problem did not exist for Primo de Rivera.

The movement in Germany is most analgous to the Italian movement. It is a mass movement with its leaders employing a great deal of Socialist demagogy. This is necessary for the creation of a mass movement.

The genuine basis [for fascism] is the petty bourgeoisie. In Italy it is a very large base—the petty bourgeoisie of the towns and cities, and the peasantry. In Germany likewise, there is a large base for fascism. In England there is less of that base because the proletariat is the overwhelming majority of the population; the peasants and farming strata [form] only an insignificant section. . . . In order to be capable of foreseeing anything in the direction of fascism, it is necessary to have a definition of that idea.[17]

Reading publications that reflected all political tendencies, as well as the daily press, distressed Trotsky, as we were made aware by his comments at the dinner table. At one time he called attention to the response of the German Communist Party leaders to his initial proposals for a broad united front among the Social Democracy and its unions and the Communists and the unions influenced or controlled by them. His call for such a united struggle against Hitler was met with a vitriolic political and personal attack by the leading figures in the capitulationist, wholly Stalinized German Communist Party.

One morning Trotsky came down to the breakfast table and briefly described the contents of a document he was dictating on the situation in Germany. The ideas were similar to what he had already discussed with us, he said, but more rigorously defined. He was making a desperate call for a broad united front, one which would include the political and trade-union sectors of the working class, the military arms of Social Democracy, and the Communist Party, a front that would attract allies from the democratic forces of Germany to stem the accelerating growth of the Hitler hordes. The discussion moved me to alert our members and sympathizers in the United States in an article I wrote for *The Militant,* "The

Struggle for Power in Germany," which appeared in January 1932.

Trotsky finished his document on November 26, two days after I left Kadikoy. It was sent to all the sections of the Trotskyist movement, reproduced and distributed widely in a number of countries, especially in Germany, France, and the United States. The pamphlet created a sensation in radical political circles, even among many Communists.[18] The pamphlet opened with a brief analysis of the social situations in Great Britain, France, the United States, China, and Japan. Despite brilliant passing observations, his main political forecasts of workers' power in England and France never materialized. As for the United States, he did not make the mistake of seeing a prerevolutionary situation, as he did later in the decade, but he did foresee the radicalization of the American working class once the country began to emerge from its economic crisis. Such radicalization would take the form of a break with the conservative craft unionism of the AFL and the emergence of a new militant unionism, characteristic of earlier explosions in American labor. This forecast was realized in the rise of the Congress of Industrial Organizations out of the AFL, under the leadership of the very able conservative leader of the coal miners, John L. Lewis.

As for China and Japan, Trotsky pictured a continuous defensive war by China against Japan's military invasion, leading to the disintegration of the Kuomintang; that party would never be able to contain the national and revolutionary impulses generated by the military occupation.

However grave these possibilities were, Trotsky deemed them all less grave than the social crisis in Germany. Germany was in a prerevolutionary condition, which

> must be transformed into a revolutionary or the counter-revolutionary [situation]. In the direction in which the solution of the German crisis will develop depends the fate not only of Germany herself but the fate of Europe, the fate of the entire world for very many years to come.

He spoke of "revolutionary weakness," by which he meant the lack of will among the working class movements to challenge the Fascist armed bands with their own militias. Trotsky was absolutely convinced that a united working-class struggle against the Brown Shirts could result in victory. Indeed, such a united resistance was exactly what the Nazis themselves feared, uncertain whether they could prevail in that kind of struggle. But Trotsky was concerned above all that the fight be made *in time,* or all would be lost. He recalled his experience in Russia as the creator of the Red Army and leader of the defensive war against the counterrevolution. And so he wrote:

No doubt the Fascists have serious fighting cadres, experienced shock brigades. We must not take a light attitude in this respect; the "officers" play a big part even in the civil war army. Still it is not the officers but the soldiers who decide. The soldiers of the proletarian army, however, are immeasurably higher types, more trustworthy, more steadfast than the soldiers of the Hitler army.

Trotsky was fearful that the failure to resist the Nazi surge would lead to disintegration of the ranks of the working class and an easy Fascist triumph. What the Nazis lacked before a victory in a military sense, they would certainly achieve in power when the Communists and Social Democrats surrendered. Trotsky wrote:

After the conquest of power Fascism will easily find its soldiers. With the aid of the state apparatus, an army of the pet sons of the bourgeoisie, of intellectuals, counter clerks, demoralized workers, lumpen-proletarians, etc., is easily created. Example: Italian Fascism.

Obviously, if there was no resistance to the Nazis, the composition of its armed auxiliaries would mean nothing. Trotsky knew that the Comintern's boast—that it had no fear of a Hitler takeover because the Communists would be in power within twenty-four hours—was a dangerous conceit, hollow in its essence. It merely indicated that the International and the German Party were preparing for a defeat. In a sequel to his pamphlet *Germany: The Key to the International Situation* (that appeared as "A Letter to a Worker-Communist Member of the German Communist Party"), he appealed for more direct action, over the heads of the Party leadership, which was slavishly carrying out policies imposed by Stalin, who personally laid down the line for the International and the Party.

The initial response of the Communist Party leadership to the idea of a united front was to abuse everyone who did not accept its program of capitulation to Hitler, especially Trotsky and the Social Democrats. Stalin had paved the way for Communist policy with one of his rare excursions in the field of theory. He wrote that the Social Democrats were a greater danger to Germany than Hitler and fascism. Such thinking led to the suicidal policies of the German Party under the leadership of his personally appointed spokesman, Ernst Thaelman, a ponderous, anti-intellectual, ignorant brawler.[19] Stalin announced his new theory of Social Democracy and fascism in the form of a dictum:

Fascism is the fighting organization of the bourgeoisie which rests upon the active support of the Social Democracy. Objectively, the Social Democracy is the moderate wing of fascism. There is no reason to admit that the fighting organization of the bourgeoisie could obtain decisive successes without the active support of the Social Democracy. . . . These organizations are not mutually exclusive but on the contrary are mutually complementary. They are not antipodes but twins.[20]

The whole Communist movement parroted these desperately false ideas. In April 1931, at the Eleventh Plenum of the Communist International Executive Committee, Dimitry Manusky, then one of Stalin's most abject followers, said: "The Social Democrats, in order to deceive the masses, deliberately proclaim that the chief enemy of the working class is fascism. . . . Is it not true that the whole theory of the 'lesser evil' rests on the presupposition that fascism of the Hitler type represents the chief enemy?"[21]

Thus the main struggle of the Communist Party was directed not against Hitler's National Socialists but against the Social Democratic Party and its trade unions. These attacks on Social Democracy coincided with each tactic of the Nazis: Intensifying the political situation and deepening the crisis were the aims of both the Fascists and the Communists. When the Nazis initiated a referendum in August 1931 to overthrow the Social Democratic government of Prussia, the campaign was joined by the Communist Party, whose activities in their united front with the Fascists became so intense that the campaign became known as the "Red Referendum." The Communist Party boasted that it had taken the play away from the National Socialists even as the Nazis gained immeasurably from it. Had the "Red Referendum" succeeded and the Social Democratic government been overthrown in the most important state in Germany—and it very nearly was—Hitler would have come to power much sooner than he did. The Communist Party boasted of a great victory as a matter of course. Its participation in the Fascist referendum was a product of Stalin's new vision that fascism and Social Democracy were twin phenomena.

When the Social Democratic Party (through one of its leaders, Rudolph Breitscheid) declared in the autumn of 1931 its readiness to conclude a united front with the Communist Party to fight the Fascist menace, Thaelman rejected the very idea of such an alliance in a vicious rejoinder that typified the betrayal built into Communist policy. Thaelman's article in *Die Internationale* (November–December 1931) is a striking illustration of Stalinist thinking regarding the struggle in Germany. The Social Democratic Party, he wrote, threatens to make a United Front with the Communist Party. The speech of Breitscheid at Darmstadt on the occasion of the Hesse elections and the comments of *Vorwaerts* [the Social Democratic newspaper] on this speech show that Social Democracy by his maneuver is drawing on the wall the devil of Hitler's fascism and is holding back the masses from the real struggle against the dictatorship of finance capital. And these lying mouthfuls . . . they hope to make them more palatable with the sauce of a so-called sudden friendship for the Communists and to make them more agreeable to the masses.

Ironic, indeed, was the simultaneous announcement of the murders of Breitscheid and Thaelman by the Nazis during their separate imprisonments after Hitler came to power. The Fascist sauce was good for both goose and gander when the Nazis united them in death. Stalin's theory of social fascism was torn to shreds. And what a grim joke was the Communist slogan: "After Hitler, Us."

Thaelman made a closing speech at the Thirteenth Plenum of the Comintern, in September of 1932, which appeared in the magazine *Communist International*. The rhetoric of the speech was suited both to the ideology he professed and his dull-wittedness in dismissing a political policy that offered some hope of defeating German fascism:

This is the theory of a completely ruined Fascist and counterrevolutionary. This theory is the worst theory, the most dangerous theory and the most criminal that Trotsky has constructed in the last years of his counter-revolutionary propaganda.[22]

This was Stalin speaking through the voice of his loyal servant. Why should anyone wonder, then, that Thaelman advanced the slogan: "Chase the social Fascists [Social Democrats] from their jobs in the plants and the trade unions." This was a sufficient tip to the CP youth organization, whose paper, *The Young Guard,* issued the infamous slogan: "Chase the social Fascists from the plants, the employment exchanges, and the apprentice schools." Given this lead by its older leaders, the Young Pioneers issued this slogan in their paper, *The Drum:* "Strike the little Zorgiebels [a Social Democratic chief of police] in the schools and the playgrounds."

Most of the German Communist Party's activities in this period were directed, with all the energies and power the Party could muster, against the Social Democracy and its political strongholds, the trade unions and auxiliary organizations. These activities of the Stalinists led Trotsky, with an eye on the Italian experience, to warn that if unity in a struggle against

Hitler was not achieved and the fight was lost, the consequences would be a devastating terror in the land. He wrote in *The Key:*

> The coming to power of the German National Socialists would mean above all the extermination of the flower of the German proletariat, the disruption of its organizations, the extirpation of its belief in itself and in the future. Considering the far greater maturity and acuteness of the social contradictions in Germany, the hellish works of Italian fascism would probably appear as a pale and almost human experiment in comparison with the work of German National Socialists. . . .
>
> Leaders and institutions can retreat. Individual persons can hide. But the working class will have no place to retreat to in the fire of fascism and no place to hide.[23]

As this prophecy was being realized, the German Communist Party could only reiterate the teachings of its political master, Stalin: "Without a victory over the social democracy, we cannot battle against fascism."

Trotsky followed the alarm of *Germany: The Key to the International Situation* with another brochure, as he watched the situation in Germany deteriorate and Stalinism drive hard toward certain disaster. He paid no attention to the abuse organized and directed by the Communist International against him. The new brochure, *What Next? Vital Questions for the German Proletariat,* was an extension of *The Key."*[24] Only this time he had an opportunity to reply to the objections raised by the Stalinist leaders in the Comintern and in Germany to a united front against fascism.

Following the political policy initiated by Stalin, German Communists responded like robots, stepping aside to let Hitler march to power as if in a holiday parade. Trotsky warned that a Hitler victory would ultimately lead to a war with Russia. Stalin's avoidance of involvement in any German upheaval was self-defeating. Trotsky thought such involvement might come through collusion with the West or in an alliance with Poland. Yet, almost simultaneously, he predicted the Hitler–Stalin Pact. The Pact led directly to the outbreak of the Second World War and eventually to the invasion of the Soviet Union. The war in the West, however, began as Trotsky prophesied as early as June 1933 in an article called "Hitler and Disarmament," in which he wrote that "an attack on the West in the more or less immediate future could be carried out only on condition of a military alliance between Fascist Germany and the Soviets."[25]

While some of Trotsky's observations regarding various social groups and the rise of fascism are open to debate, his call for a united front against fascism was on target. He did err in saying that Social Democracy would be the biggest obstacle to such unity. "We must force the Social Democracy into a bloc against the Fascists," he wrote. But, indeed, it is not at all certain whether or not this was a knee-jerk ritual or whether he really believed it, for his main fire in all his writings on Germany was directed at the Communist International and the German Communist Party, where it rightfully belonged.

The German Communists boasted their way to defeat. Herman Remmele, Party leader and Reichstag spokesman, bragged in a speech to the parliament in 1931: "Let Hitler take office—he will soon go bankrupt, and then it will be our day. . . . We are not afraid of Hitler assuming power."[26] "This means," wrote Trotsky, "that the victory of tomorrow will be Hitler's not Remmele's."[27] As the time for Hitler's taking office drew nearer, Willi Munzenberg, an outstanding leader of the Socialist Youth International before World War I but now a Comintern hack, wrote in the *Rote Aufbau* on February 15, 1932:

> Trotsky proposes . . . a bloc between the Communist and Social Democratic Parties. Nothing could be as detrimental to the German working class and communism and nothing would promote fascism so much as the realization of so criminal a proposal. . . . His role is indeed . . . plainly fascist.[28]

Isaac Deutscher, Trotsky's chief biographer, quotes even more from this supremely manipulating international bureaucrat, and adds: "Munzenberg ended his polemical campaign by committing suicide in exile."[29]

Molotov, Stalin's loyal aide and newly appointed leader of the Comintern, said there was nothing to fear in a victory by Hitler. In "twenty-four hours we will be in power." As Trotsky forecast, those Communist leaders who escaped the Fascist net had to flee the country. In the first meeting of the Executive Committee of the Communist International after Hitler took power, the Comintern pundits proclaimed that his victory was of no great consequence; their strategy and tactics for the German Communist Party were totally correct. To make certain that this view would prevail, the Executive Committee forbade any discussion or debate of the question. The only paramilitary battle against the tide of rising European fascism was the historic armed resistance of the Austrian Social Democracy in Vienna in 1934.

In sharp contrast to the views of Kolakowski, to which we referred earlier, that there was nothing special in Trotsky's opinion of the Hitler phenomenon in Germany, Joel Carmichael (in *Trotsky: An Appreciation of His Life,* a sympathetic but highly critical work) acknowledges without hesitation Trotsky's role in the pre-Hitler years. "He was practically the only observer who perceived the drive of the Nazi movement and its threat to the Soviet regime. Throughout the thirties this was his predominant theme. It produced some of his best writings." Again:

> Trotsky's warnings were timely and persuasive; they were filled with all the dramatic urgency his talent could infuse them with.
> They persuaded no one. . . .
> Trotsky was vilified right and left as a sort of malevolent nut—the Communist press, both in the Soviet Union and in Germany, called him a "panic-mongerer," an "adventurer," "an ally of counter-revolutionaries," and so on. His predictions, which in this case all came true, earned him nothing but abuse. His powerful appeal fell on deaf ears.

Carmichael recognized that in the case of Germany and Hitler, "Trotsky's intelligence and passion came into play; long before it became even remotely fashionable anywhere else, and especially not in the Soviet Union, he produced penetrating analyses of German politics."[30]

A similar view is held by Robert Wistrich in *Trotsky: Fate of a Revolutionary,* a penetrating critical examination of Trotsky's political career. In specific connection with the German situation Wistrich wrote:

> Leon Trotsky's analysis of National Socialism (and of fascism in general) stands out in the Marxist literature of the 1930s as one of the more lucid attempts to dissect "this stupendous phenomenon of social psychopathology." Trotsky was by no means the first Marxist writer to produce a coherent definition of fascism but he perceived more clearly than most of his contemporaries the inner dynamics of the movement and some of its potential consequences.

Still, Wistrich argues that Trotsky's failure to

> perceive the primacy of politics and technical efficiency of totalitarian methods of domination revealed the same limitations that were previously apparent in his analysis of Stalinism.

Indeed, this was the same point made by the minority of the Socialist Workers' Party in the 1940 split over the Russian Question. Nevertheless, Wistrich adds:

> Though he failed to provide a complete explanatory model for the rise of fascism, his appraisal of the cynical folly behind the Stalinist strategy in Germany remained second to none.[31]

Another pointed observation of Trotsky's contribution to the discussion of Germany and Hitler was made by Joseph Nedava, who in his *Trotsky and the Jews* noted:

> With regard to the German problem in the 1930s, Trotsky proved to be a far-sighted statesman, truly prophetic about what would occur in Europe and throughout the world once Hitler was allowed to rise to power. In retrospect, it is difficult to appreciate fully the depth of his foresight.[32]

And then we come to Edward Hallett Carr's distinctive tribute to Trotsky's vision of this period of European history. In *The Twilight of the Comintern,* he wrote:

> Trotsky maintained during the period of Hitler's rise to power so persistent, and, for the most part, so prescient a commentary on the course of events in Germany as to deserve record. . . .
> Both Trotsky's diagnosis and his foresight were astonishingly acute.[33]

Carr's book illuminates the period of Comintern history in the fateful years of 1930–35 as no other work has. He describes not only the main ideological error of the Comintern (i.e., of Stalin) in its estimate of Germany fascism but also the almost supercilious response in the programs and policies of the International's bureaus delegating those responsibilities. Its common springboard in all countries in Europe: *The main enemy is Social Democracy.* Even when it proffered "united fronts from below" in the critical period, it accompanied these with the simultaneous denunciations of the organizations with whom it sought common action.

The main Comintern strategy in the pretended fight against Hitler informed all its activities, whether they be the parties in Germany, France, the United States, or the Far East. The political situations in the various countries did not matter. Their size and influence, or lack thereof, did not matter. This policy continued in its most blatant form until war loomed as a real prospect. With a suddenness characteristic of Communist practice, it was dropped and replaced by the policy of the Popular or People's Front. This new line continued until the Hitler–Stalin Pact, when Stalin reversed himself again.

But it was not until 1936 in Spain that the new policy was carried out in an actual combat with fascism. The Communists joined the Socialist Party and other democratic forces, anarchists, and trade unions, in the war against the armies of General Franco. Even then, however, that struggle was deliberately subverted by Stalin's military units and agents of the GPU and the international brigades, including the American Lincoln Brigade, organized by the Communist Party and led by its loyal comrades, who operated in complete freedom. The main goal of the Soviet Union was the destruction of all working-class and leftist political movements that differed from or challenged the Stalinist drive for complete power in Loyalist Spain. The native Fascists won the Civil War more through the treachery of the counterrevolutionary activity of the Communist military forces and the Russian secret police than by the superior military might of the extreme right.

Hitler's victory precipitated the war that killed tens of millions and maimed millions more. It saw the Holocaust against the Jews, the spread of Stalinist communism in the new totalitarian states, and the emergence of a variety of dictatorial, antidemocratic regimes in the Third World. In this war to come, Germany was key indeed.

Other Questions

I had come to Turkey originally to stay two weeks. By the time I had been there for about six, Trotsky insisted that I fulfill my original plans to visit Germany and England and—most important—to carry out our decisions based on our correspondence with London. Natalia objected to my leaving when there was no one to replace me. I agreed, despite Trotsky's objections, to stay until we knew that someone was on his way to Turkey to join the household.

The French Trotskyists had been searching for a permanent replacement for some time, and before many days passed the news came from France that Myrtos had agreed to make the journey and was completing preparations to leave for Turkey. With the assurance that he would be arriving soon, I prepared to take my leave.

In the limited time left, and while pressures increased on Trotsky to complete the second volume of the *History*, we talked about the situation in the crisis-ridden United States and the prospects for the development of our movement in a nation where radicalism and socialism always had a difficult time. By 1931, at the time of my visit, two years after the beginning of economic collapse, the crisis in the United States showed no signs of ending. Official spokesmen of the Comintern and the American Communist Party disoriented their followers with their foolish notion of the "Third Period" of capitalist decline, by which they meant that immediate revolutionary prospects were opening up and the struggle for power was the reality of the day. The Communist League of America, in contrast, pursued activities along the lines of Trotsky, which, untrammeled by considerations of Moscow's interests, were in consonance with the League's own experience of American political life.

Understandably, Trotsky was keenly interested in the Communist League's progress in the United States. I informed him that the League had approximately two hundred members, with branches in New York, Chicago, Minneapolis, Boston, Philadelphia, St. Louis, Kansas City, and among the coal miners of Springfield and West Frankfort, Illinois. I reported that there were numerous supporters in Cleveland, Youngstown, New Haven, and Los Angeles, with prospects for activity elsewhere in the country. There were also organizations in Montreal and Toronto affiliated with the League. The official journal of the League, *The Militant,* though no longer a weekly paper, had a biweekly printing of two to three thousand copies, two thousand of which circulated in the cities where we had branches. All in all, scarcely a formidable influence among a population of almost 125 million! But our entire organization was suffused with confidence that a victory over the Stalinists in the Soviet Union and the International was a certainty. And if that were possible, given the miserable conditions in capitalist society—why, next the world!

While Trotsky appreciated the talents and activities of the League, he was disturbed by the factional division that had occurred early in 1930. To be sure, factional struggles plagued *all* the European Trotskyist organizations—and had destroyed some of them. Trotsky had hoped that because of the maturity, experience, and common origins of the leading members, an internal convulsion in the American League could be avoided. My report to him frankly reflected my own factional views that it could not. Even though the factional situation had subsided by the time of my visit, I did not feel or convey any optimism, but suggested that the differences remained and might break out again at any time.

Trotsky knew that the differences in the CLA were caused by a generational conflict over the nature and tempo of the League's progress. Cannon and the older members of the leading committee advocated a slower pace, while the younger members, led by Shachtman, Abern, Spector, and myself, pressed for greater speed.

I reported that before I left the States we had already initiated youth work with a special committee directing their activities, wherein I would function when I returned. I assured him that a full-fledged youth organization, with its own newspaper, would quickly materialize. A Jewish group had emerged from the Communist movement and was planning to issue a Yiddish paper. The Greek comrades, experienced activists who came out of Greece's Communist Party, spoke of issuing a Greek newspaper. None of these developments, I told Trotsky, would lessen tensions. (Upon my return, the first issues of the youth and Greek papers, *Young Spartacus* and *Communistes,* were published. Soon the Jewish paper, *Unser Kampf,* appeared.)

Trotsky cautioned the whole leadership against intensifying the factional situation. He emphasized that he was not interfering with the affairs of the League but hoped that the younger leaders would be more patient, warning that factional situations were easy to initiate but difficult to halt. The whole leadership of the League had a long experience with factional conflict in the Communist Party, and so knew of the hazards of internal strife and debilitating splits that Trotsky feared.

We could not prevent, however, the emergence of deep differences over the use of organizational methods to solve political differences, a method characteristic of Cannon, arising from his personal history and development. We could not conceal the division within the National Committee on the problems of bureaucratization or democratization of the inner life of the League, nor avoid disputes over the rate of progress of the movement. These differences persisted, sometimes muted, at other times in open conflict.

I told Trotsky that in the person of James P. Cannon, the founder of the League, we had a very talented leader, expert and astute in organization, trade unionism, and oratory, who had been the most competent leader of Communist Party in these areas. But I did not hesitate to say that he retained bureaucratic habits developed in the CP; he championed the "Bolshevization" of the Party, a policy introduced in the Comintern by its then-president, Gregory Zinoviev. The concept embraced a totally disciplined party, the inviolable nature of decisions of the leadership, the impermissibility of factions, and the transformation of the organization into a slavish imitation of its Russian master. In some circles of the American CP in 1925 and 1926, Cannon was jokingly referred to as the "Captain of Bolshevization." In my opinion, Cannon had absorbed some of the worst features of these bureaucratic organizational concepts and practices. The unfortunate fact is that the otherwise able Cannon believed in many of these principles that were employed so deftly by Stalin and improved on by this "Genghis Khan of communism," as Bukharin once called him. In addition, Cannon was intellectually lazy. For being the leader of American Trotskyism, his theoretical deficiencies and his shortcomings in conceptual strategic politics were clearly evident. Internal organizational politics and trade unionism were his forte, and in these areas he was often superb and effective, despite the sectarian political life of his organizations.

Trotsky was aware of these problems. Indeed, he had faced similar ones in other Trotskyist groups. He reminded me that he had written to our National Committee briefly about them, and he would repeat his suggestions again in the following year or two if our internal situations continued to be unsatisfactory. Trotsky was not unaware of what he called "remnants" of the Soviet Communist Party's bureaucratic practices, but did not believe them to be a real danger. Furthermore, he felt that the situation could be resolved with proper goodwill on the part of both factions.

He was very pleased with *The Militant* and hoped we could expand its circulation and improve the frequency of issue. It was obvious to me from all of our discussions that in those ragged years of economic poverty, the early thirties, he was gratified that a Trotskyist organization had managed to emerge in the United States.

*   *   *

From my brief experience, it seemed to me that Trotsky's humor was confined to political jokes. At the time of my visit, he had no patience for pure banter or small talk. On infrequent occasions, however, he would make sarcastic or ironic comments about events or persons. I recall that he made a comment at the tea table about Frankel's erstwhile "Tolstoyan vegetarianism," to the effect that someone totally devoted to such a diet could not be trusted politically. But since Frankel had dropped that strange dietary custom and began to eat meat, fowl, and fish, he had improved politically and could be relied on with more confidence. Trotsky would repeat this theme with variations.

With me, aside from references to the "Amerikaner Onkel," he would make sarcastic comments about the United States, as though I had a chauvinistic view of my country. Or he would tell jokes that came from Russia or were Russian in origin. I recorded two of them that indicated the direction of his interest. He related these to me with considerable relish, a humorous eye, and laughter.

One concerned a meeting in Odessa commemorating the Russian Revolution. The principal speaker at the meeting was Maxim Litvinov (it could have been any Party leader), an Old Bolshevik and People's Commissar of Foreign Affairs throughout the thirties. After his peroration, a peasant in the audience arose and asked:

Has the Revolution really changed everything, Comrade Litvinov?
Litvinov: Why, of course it did. It changed the whole society.
Peasant: It really changed everything and made a new life for us?
Litvinov: Oh, yes, we have created a new society.
Peasant: Has the Revolution changed the Black Sea?
Litvinov: Oh, no. The Revolution didn't change things of the natural world, or geography and the like. Why do you ask?

Peasant: Well, if it didn't change those things, or the Black Sea, why don't we get herrings any more?

The other was an "internal" joke having to do with one of the outstanding figures of the Russian Revolution, the economist and leading Left Oppositionist in the Party, Eugene A. Preobrazhensky, who was shot on Stalin's orders in 1937. Preobrazhensky, Trotsky related, was a great scholar and totally devoted to his economic studies and writings. In the Political Committee, so the story went, whenever an economic commission, committee on production, or coal board was set up, Preobrazhensky would be nominated for membership. At each nomination, and there were countless numbers of these, Preobrazhensky would respond with an affirmative blinking of his eyes, happy to be nominated and elected. As a result, at anniversary meetings and other celebrations, when the names of leaders and the posts they held were read out, Preobrazhensky's name led all the rest. But Preobrazhensky did not attend a single meeting of these many boards and committees, nor did he participate in their work; had he done so, he would have done nothing else. Yet his honors were greater than those of all the others. Trotsky chuckled over this story, told with an obvious fondness for the butt of the joke, and as if he had told it often, with the same bemusement. He displayed no broader examples of humor to me.

Trotsky gave me a few commissions in connection with his *History* before I left. I was to take up with Simon and Schuster, his publishers, the matter of advertising for the book, its sale price, and the timing— simultaneous or serial—of publication for the two volumes. Trotsky suggested that I visit Max Eastman before I saw the publishers, with the thought that he might assist in this discussion with them. In addition, I was to relay several other messages to Eastman which I no longer remember. I agreed to discharge his requests immediately upon my return to New York.

At my leave-taking, Natalia gave me a letter, some apparel, a large box of Turkish confections, and expressions of maternal love for her son, Lyova Sedov.

*   *   *

Meeting the revolutionary titan Leon Trotsky was a heady experience for a person of my young years. He had been so much admired in American Communist and radical circles, and by many Jewish groups whose views were sharply different from his. To have lived in the same house, discussing urgent world events *en passant* or in depth, was beyond my expectations when I had decided to make this journey. My initial purpose was to meet the founder of our movement and to discuss mainly American problems with him. But the talks became far more extensive and encompassed problems of the international movement and its sections, perspectives on Great Britain, and, above all, the grave dangers of fascism in Germany and on the Continent.

Trotsky expressed an affection for me that, while warm, was not intimate. I never forgot that I was one of many who visited him; my visit's significance was greater to me than to him. It could not be otherwise. He addressed me as "Comrade Glotzer," although his manner toward me warmed the longer I stayed. In general, he was formal and objective to most everybody. He maintained at all times a distance that I understood instinctively came with the vast responsibility he bore for the whole movement. He never slouched, standing or seated; his sweater was buttoned, his tie never loosened; his personal grooming was fastidious. He embraced one warmly at parting, as he did me, but was not given to expansiveness.

I recall talking to him one day about some aspect of the struggle of the Russian Left Opposition and asking him what Stalin's personality and character were really like. In those years, Stalin was still largely an unknown figure who had risen meteorically to the leadership of the world Communist movement. There was not much written about him, even by his most devout supporters. Such indecent panegyrics and godlike worship were unthinkable in the twenties, when the influence of Lenin was still strong. Like my comrades, I had read everything that was written about Stalin in the Comintern and by Trotsky, which had to do mainly with features of internal struggles. No true image of his person had emerged by then; the flood of biographies only arrived in the thirties, almost a decade after Lenin wrote his last "Testament," which described Trotsky and Stalin as the two most able men in the Party. I wanted more than the blurbs of Stalin's sycophants or the objective political statements of Trotsky. It seemed clear to me that there was much more to the man who now dominated the whole movement in a way Lenin never aspired to or had need of.

"Everything I have to say about him I have already written," Trotsky said. I knew that this answer just could not be true. Obviously it wasn't all he had to say about Stalin, as time and his biography of the General Secretary would later bear out. I could not then, nor years later, understand his reluctance to say anything more on a subject on which I was sure he could discourse at considerable length. Did he feel that he didn't want a young person to think of the great struggle through the distorted prism of mere "personalities"? Did he wish to maintain a rigid impersonal objectivity in order to reinforce the oft-repeated idea that the struggle of the Left Opposition was based on ideas and program and not on the personal relations among the leaders of the Bolshevik Party? Perhaps. But Trotsky's silence on this score disarmed his own followers in the early years, because it concealed the particular brutality Stalin's personality gave to the unfolding of internal struggles. We already knew, as early as the mid-twenties (though we suppressed our feelings even before we became Trotskyists), of the anti-Semitic aspects of Stalin's campaign against the Opposition leaders and the cruel measures he took against them: expulsion from the Party, imprisonments, beatings, and exile.

My own youthful idealism had already been dulled by some knowledge of how Stalin eliminated his rivals for power in the Russian Party and how the often ludicrous vascillations of Zinoviev and Kamenev inadvertently assisted the vengeful Stalin. Still, Trotsky could not bring himself to go beyond his published writings, which were totally insufficent in describing Stalin let alone the system, inherent in Bolshevism, that elevated him to the all-powerful post of General Secretary. Only much later did Trostky compare this political thug in the Kremlin to Cain and Torquemada.

Though I could not converse with Natalia except through Trotsky or (more often) through Frankel, I quickly learned during this first visit that she had a gift for friendship that transcended the barriers of language, age, experience, and evolving political ideas. She had been pleased by my concern over Trotsky's security and my willingness to stay on until a replacement was found. Though I did not see her in France, where I next saw Trotsky in 1934, we renewed our relations in 1937 at the Dewey Commission hearings in Mexico, in the fifties when I traveled to Coyoacan, and during her several brief visits to the United States. Our friendship endured to the end of her life.

A few days after I left Kadikoy, Trotsky wrote to Max Shachtman: "Glotzer has left very good and friendly memories here." So were those I carried away with me, even though the winds of historical change have put an entirely different perspective on events of that era and the lonely, eloquent exile who labored so mightily to change the drift of history and still did fail.

Throughout the thirties, I was a committed, active, and searching Trotskyist, and I continued to correspond with Trotsky from time to time, as did many other political colleagues throughout the world.

A Brief Visit to Germany

At the end of a three-day ride on a third-class wooden bench on the famous *Orient Express,* Eastern Division, I arrived in Berlin early on the morning of November 27, 1931. I was greeted by young Leon Sedov and Anton Grylewicz, a veteran leading member of the Left Opposition of Germany. Leon—or "Lyova," as he was more often affectionately called—was excited by my arrival because I had just come from his "home" with messages and gifts from his father and mother, to whom he was fiercely devoted. We went to the buro of a Comrade Joko (the pseudonym of Joseph Kohn), who directed a small advertising business related to radical papers. I was to stay at Joko's home in the Schoeneweide district during my visit in Berlin. I was pleased to be received with the kind of open friendliness that was reminiscent of Americans at home, friendliness that greatly contrasted with the cooler tone in Paris.

I sensed immediately the German political climate, even if superficially, in the short time I spent in Berlin. One incident sufficed to show me the charged political atmosphere. One day, walking along the streets of Berlin, I bumped into Herman, a young Jewish medical student from New York whom I had met earlier aboard ship and who was going to Germany to continue his medical studies. I asked him how things were going. He replied that he was near despair. Germany was dreadful. His medical school was full of Nazi students who intimidated the professors and made life intolerable for Jewish, liberal, or radical students. "They actually run the school," he said. After less than three months, his schooling was in an upheaval. The intolerance and brutality of the Hitler Youth went beyond anything he had expected in what he had regarded as a highly civilized and cultured nation. Especially dismaying was the fact that Nazi student activists had made "intellectual pursuits" impossible. Indeed, at the moment I saw him he was on his way to apply for a visa in order to study in another country.

Herman's experience exemplified the general tension in the country, and the battles between the Brown Shirts and the Social Democratic and Communist workers. The Brown Shirts invaded working-class districts of the city to provoke street battles, which were multiplying daily. The united front between the Nazi Party and the Communist Party in the "Red Referendum" of only a few months before caused bitter confusion in the anti-Fascist and non-Fascist circles. When I went to Liebknecht House, the headquarters of the Communist Party, to purchase books at their bookstore, there was a strange quiet surrounding the immense structure, which I knew was guarded by armed units of the Party. Few people were visible.

From reading the press and talking to various people, I was struck by the unabashed aggressiveness of the Fascist organizations and their leader's increasing boldness. They made no secret of what they would do once they came to power: They would destroy the Communist and Social Democratic Parties and their auxiliaries, the trade unions, and all democratic movements (from the most conservative to the most radical).

The tiny organization of the Trotskyists in Germany, severely hampered by inner schisms, concentrated its efforts on creating a united front with all the anti-Fascist forces in the country to challenge the Nazis. I was present at one meeting of the Berlin branch of the German League, which was at the moment considering ways to complete a large distribution of its written views and propaganda in behalf of its main political orientation. They knew nothing would change unless the big parties of the working class heeded Trotsky's alarm and united quickly for confrontation.

At this meeting, I met Oskar Seipold, who had been elected to the Prussian *Landtag* while a member of the Communist Party. Seipold had retained his seat after he broke with the Party to become the foremost spokesman for Trotsky's program for Germany. I also met the Sobolevicius (Sobolevich) brothers: One of them, Ruvin, called himself "Roman Well" and was the current leader of the German group; the other, Abraham, called himself "Senin," a ludicrous play on Lenin's name. They were personally exceedingly friendly, and in August of that same year Well, his wife, and Senin had visited Trotsky in Kadikoy, as my photographs show. They were later revealed to be agents of the GPU. Arrested in the United States, Senin, under the name Jack Soble, after testifying before a Senate Committee in November 1957, was sentenced to federal prison. Roman Well, now called "Dr. Soblen," was also named as a Russian agent and fled the United States. He sought admission to Israel, which was refused him. While being returned to the United States via London, he committed suicide. Before they were found out, however, they managed to disrupt the German Trotskyist organization by creating internal convulsions over political policy.

Two of the more interesting people I came to know in Berlin were Franz Pfemfert and his wife, Alexandra Ramm, Trotsky's German translator. I was familiar with Pfemfert's work before I arrived in Berlin, and knew that he edited the famous German magazine *Die Aktion,* a periodical of the German Expressionist movement (1911–1932). He was a veteran of the *Spartakusbund,* the revolutionary left-wing movement that emerged after World War I, which he tried to revive in the middle twenties. They were friends of Trotsky even though they had important differences with him. In addition to his work as editor and hers as a translator, Pfemfert was a dealer in books—Marxist, radical, out-of-print, and important historical works. People came to him for rare volumes of the early Socialist movement. He was also a superb portrait photographer. When friends like me visited, fresh from a stay at Trotsky's asylum, he would lead us into his studio for portraits.

Most of my time in Berlin was spent with Leon Sedov. Our closeness in age and my recent visit to Turkey led to an instant and open acceptance of each other. He asked all about life in Kadikoy. In what kind of house did his parents live? How was their health? And how was little Sieva getting on? I had no doubt he already knew how his family was doing, but he wanted reassurance from someone with recent personal knowledge.

Lyova was now editing the *Russian Bulletin*. Though officially named the *Bulletin of the Left Opposition (Bolshevik-Leninist)*, by then the publication no longer represented the views of such a large faction; the toll taken on Russians associated with Trotsky was severe. The *Bulletin* was now the voice of Trotsky alone. Still, the greatest problem faced by the magazine was not a dearth of material, or even, given the economic times, financial hardship, but circulation. Russian readership was limited to refugee circles, Russian institutions outside of the Soviet Union, functionaries of the Stalinist state who lived in all countries of the West, and Russians who had fled the country in post-Revolution years. Aside from the personal work of Lyova, the publication required the assistance of all the organizations of the world-Trotskyist movement in seeking out readers in the various emigré Russian circles.

In those years, there were still functionaries of the Party and State abroad who were covertly interested in what Trosky had to say about world and Russian affairs. That interest died with them. The breed of Stalinist functionary that followed had no such interest, secretly or in any other way. This situation forced us to deal with the problem of finding someone who would take responsibility for the *Russian Bulletin* in the United States. Knowing the importance of the magazine and how much Trotsky and his son desired its issuance and circulation, I promised to give it my personal attention when I reached New York and to see if something could be done for it in Great Britain on my visit, even though we had no organization there as yet.

At one point in our meetings, I spoke to Lyova about visiting Zinaida at the sanitarium, since I had missed her in Turkey. She had been receiving treatment for her deeply disturbing psychological problems. Lyova said this was not possible because her condition was not sufficently improved; and a visit from me, who had just spent a number of weeks with her parents and Sieva, would be too upsetting. I said no more about it. Neither I nor most others were privy to the details of her neurotic condition. We only knew that they were complicated. The family did not discuss the matter with others.

In 1932, isolated from her husband (Platon Volkow, of whose existence in Russia nothing was known), estranged from her father, and unable to cope with her condition, she took her life.[34] The fact that Sieva was living with her had no strengthening effect on her. The boy, now without his father and mother, came to live with Lyova, his closest next-of-kin in Berlin, and his wife, Jeanne Martin. They became his surrogate parents for the next half-dozen years.

I said goodbye to my new friends in our German movement and Lyova Sedov, and traveled to England to meet Max Shachtman to establish a Trotskyist organization in that country.

*   *   *

After his deportation to Turkey, some of Trotsky's supporters thought that Stalin and his GPU had lost their interest in him. To be sure, there seemed to be a kind of calm in the area of exile. Although Natalia was always concerned with the question and suspicious of Stalin's motives, Trotsky had the dual feeling about security I have already described. Still, in this period of extreme isolation, support to him, no matter how tiny, and expressions of solidarity, even the most tenuous, were welcomed, sometimes in a totally unguarded way. Trotsky was ready to employ even suspicious Russian stenographers and typists, certain that young ones could not do any real harm and positive that after a short time they would be won over by the "correct ideas" of the Left Opposition.

The seeming calm surrounding Trotsky was a period of preparation for deep penetration of the Trotskyist movement by Stalin. The GPU, as we now know with absolute certainty, sought out Eastern European Jews in and around the Communist movement and recruited them for this espionage.

Jakob Franck (or "Frank," as Van Heijenoort spells it), also known as "Graef," was perhaps the first of such recruits. He came to Prinkipo on the recommendation of Raisa Adler, wife of Alfred, old friends of Trotsky and Natalia, and spent five months as secretary. He may already have been Stalin's agent. If not, he certainly became one shortly afterward, when he became acquainted with the Sobolevicius brothers. Of Franck, Natalia wrote:

> We later learned that he was a GPU informer, as was a certain Sobolevich or Sobolevicius, another Latvian, who paid us a much shorter visit. Sobole-

vich's brother, Roman Well, was an *agent provocateur* among Opposition circles in Paris and in Central Europe, a fact that was not discovered until later.[35]

Were these people agents to begin with or "turncoats" (Trotsky's word for them)? Trotsky's own appraisal of them often confuses the issue, as does Isaac Deutscher's, who made many important mistakes in the third volume of his biography of Trotsky. With respect to Senin and Well, he wrote:

> The trouble was that not all those who were exposed as *agents provocateurs* necessarily acted that part, whereas the most dangerous spies were never detected. Sobolevicius, for instance, thirty years later imprisoned in the United States as a Soviet agent, confessed that he indeed spied on Trotsky during the Prinkipo period. Yet his whole correspondence with Trotsky and the circumstances of their break throw doubt on the veracity of this part of his confession. Sobolevicius himself broke with Trotsky after he had openly and repeatedly expressed important political disagreements, which was not the manner in which an *agent provocateur* would behave. Trotsky denounced him in the end as a Stalinist, but did not believe he was an *agent provocateur*. Whatever the truth, both Sobolevicius (Senin) and his brother enjoyed Trotsky's almost unqualified confidence the first three Prinkipo years. They were no novices to Trotskyist circles. Sobolevicius had been in Russsia as a correspondent of the Left Marxist *Saechsische Arbeiterzeitung* and there he joined the Trotsky Opposition in 1927.[36]

Deutscher adds that correspondence with the Sobolevicius brothers makes up two files in the Trotsky archives (at the Houghton Library at Harvard University), describing a close political relationship between them and Trotsky, which would indicate that they were not spies but turncoats. The fact that the brothers had political differences and debated these with Trotsky does not prove they were not *agents provocateurs* for Stalin. Nor would their active participation in Trotskyist events prove anything Deutscher contends. This evidence could just as easily prove that they pursued their aims very cleverly, in order to create disruption in Trotskyist ranks and produce internal convulsions, as happened in the German organization.

The foremost Tsarist spy in the Bolshevik Party was Roman Malinovsky, close associate and friend of Lenin, who defended him against all charges of subversion, especially those that came from the Mensheviks. Malinovsky, a long-time *Okhrana* (Tsarist secret police) agent who penetrated the leadership of Lenin's party, rose to the leadership of the Bolshevik faction in the parliament (or Duma), and carried on an enormous amount of activity on behalf of Boshevism. This did not preclude his being a spy; such effectiveness is one way in which spies function successfully. He became a "pet" of Lenin's, who stuck by him even as the charges became more pointed and persistent.

When Malinovsky suddenly resigned from the Duma, he left Russia still enjoying Lenin's support, the Bolshevik leader asserting that Malinovsky had a breakdown because of the attacks of the Mensheviks.[37]

Van Heijenoort in his *With Trotsky in Exile* writes about Senin and Well: "As is now known, they were agents of the GPU recruited and trained in 1927 and functioned as such agents in Spain, after they could no longer function in the French and German organizations." He points out that "Deutscher mistakenly accepts the thesis that the Sobolevicius brothers were not trained GPU agents but political defectors."[38]

Trotsky contributed initially to that mistake, one repeated in the case of the most harmful and deadly of Stalin's agents, Mark Zborowski, known in France as "Etienne," who became a constant companion of Leon Sedov. Even after his implication in the murder of Sedov, he continued to serve Trotsky. Zborowski's knowledge of Russian facilitated his penetration, as he used his membership in the French Trotskyist League to become an aide to Sedov in Russian matters and in publishing the *Russian Bulletin*. As Stalin's leading agent, he successfully concealed his true role even though suspicions about him were raised in the French League, especially by Pierre Naville.

When Zbrowoski complained about these suspicions in a letter to Trotsky, Trotsky defended him, saying that some French comrades wanted to deprive him of his collaborators. During these years, Zborowski was responsible for fingering Ignace Reiss, a former GPU agent who broke with Stalin, and Rudolph Klement, International Secretary of the Trotskyist movement. Both were brutally murdered. Klement's head was severed.

Still, Zborowski continued to function as a "replacement" for Sedov in what passed for the Russian Opposition. He was a "refugee" brought to the United States by American Trotskists and became an anthropologist and protegé of Margaret Mead, who continued to defend him even after he was exposed as an agent of the GPU. (Professional solidarity meant more to her than the truth about this Stalinist killer.) In December 1955 he was sentenced to five years in a federal penitentiary for perjury, having been arrested in a sweep of Stalinist agents.

Beginnings of British Trotskyism

I arrived in England on December 5, 1931, and made my way to the home of Reg Groves in the Tooting section of London. Once I settled there, we went to search for Max Shachtman, who had arrived the day before. He had been through one of the severe storms of the English Channel and was now recovering at the home of Dick Beech in Clapham, sleeping on a tiny love seat, green-faced from what he said was a twelve-hour trip from Calais to Dover.

We began a round of discussions with the English people with whom we had been corresponding. This did not include the Marxian League, on whom we had given up after our discussion in Paris, compounded by its exchange with Trotsky. (We learned that in fact the League was now experiencing internal difficulties. One of its leading members, an individual who was later to become prominent in the Trotskyist movement, one Hugo Dewar, resigned in a dispute over the ideas, program, and the bureaucratic nature of the League's political life. The two leaders, Ridley and Ram, had kept from the membership Trotsky's reply to what he called their "unsuccessful thesis," contending that there had been misunderstandings that they were in the process of clarifying.) Shachtman and I felt that a meeting with the Marxian League would be useless; it would only waste the precious little time we had left in London.

We spent a good deal of our time getting acquainted with well-known figures from the older radical-Socialist period, including Dick Beech, Jack Tanner, and Ned MacAlpin. Their friendliness made our work more pleasant, even if they did not help much in realizing our goal.

Shachtman and I presented the views of the Left Opposition at a joint meeting of several groups as well as individuals. My remarks included a commentary on my conversations with Trotsky on the English movement. This was the first organized presentation of Trotskyism for the English. Many had come from the labor movement and the Communist Party. The discussion was animated because they were politically experienced and highly articulate people. During my stay in London and in the brief period that remained to Shachtman, no organization emerged, but the spadework had been done. My earlier feelings, developed in Turkey, that the formation of a Trotskyist organization depended on Reg Groves appeared justified during the course of our discussions.

Some months later, Groves and his associates—Harry Wicks, Hugo Dewar, Henry Sara, Stewart Purkis, and others—were responsible for the first Trotskyist organization in Great Britain. This development is described briefly in a booklet by Groves, published in 1974 under the title *The Balham Group: How British Trotskyism Began*. It is far from the whole story, being essentially a sentimental and nostalgic memoir of a cohesive and enduringly friendly group of comrades residing in the Balham area of London.

In a letter of November 5, 1931, dictated to me, Trotsky informed

Shachtman that he had written to Ivor Montague in London about the possibility of reissuing *Where is England Going?*, which had been published in the United States under the title *Whither England?* Trotsky suggested that Montague might "facilitate your stay in London in every respect." I assumed Montague was a good friend of our movement. But our visit with Montague was surprisingly brief, especially in view of Trotsky's letter to Shachtman. Montague was formally cordial, but we could not help feeling that he was unenthusiastic about our visit and our suggestions that he do something for the Opposition or for Trotsky personally. Trotsky had warned against compromising Montague, whose business organization and interests were related to the Soviet Union. It was clear to us that Montague would never allow himself to be "compromised" by the Russians, let alone by Trotsky.

After I returned to New York, my visit to Montague continued to rankle. He exhibited an unmistakably frigid attitude toward us. Shachtman and I later talked about our puzzlement. Why had Trotsky asked us to see him? Was he reaching out to just *any* straw for help?

In later years it became known that Ivor Montague was a member of the Communist Party's Executive Committee. Neal Wood, in his *Communism and British Intellectuals,* wrote in 1959 that many radicals of the thirties "seem to have been the first intellectuals of new bourgeois families," among whom he lists Montague. And he adds, "Wogan Philipps and Ivor Goldsmid Samuel Montague are the only intellectuals who are sons of peers." Wood continues: "There is, then, a high probability that the House of Lords will have its first Communist members within the course of a few years. The father of Ivor Montague was the second Baron Swathyling."[39] Having the best of two worlds, why should Ivor Montague have done anything for Trotsky except to deceive him? When I returned to New York, I wrote to Trotsky regarding our failed visit, making special note of the uneasiness I felt about Montague.

Shortly after my return to the States, I began a tour of cities where Trotskyist branches or groups were located. The tour took me as far west as Kansas City, and north to Montreal and Toronto. My meetings were successful, given the smallness of the Communist League, because many came to hear my account of the life and work of Trotsky in exile. The alarm sounded by Trotsky was the foremost message I carried; the dreadful consequences of a Hitler-run Germany made my voice stronger. The Communist League penetrated larger circles of concerned people who realized, little by little, that we alone raised the cry of danger.

Notes

1. Pierre Naville (b. 1904) and Pierre Frank (1905–198?) were founders and leaders of the French Trotskyist Communist League. Naville, a well-known intellectual and one-time editor of the *Revolution Surrealiste,* was actively involved in the affairs of French Trotskyism. Frank was secretary to Trotsky during the early thirties in Turkey, but his main work was with the French League. He wrote a history of the Fourth International.

2. Albert Trient (1889–1972) was a well-known member of the Central Committee of the French Communist Party, and a familiar name in the Communist International. His speeches in Moscow and his articles were always published in the widely circulated *International Press Correspondence,* known as *Inprecorr.* After a brief membership in the Communist League of France, he became active in the syndicalist movement.

3. Raymond Molinier (b. 1904) cofounded the French Trotskyist movement, but was expelled, with his faction, in 1935 for "violation of discipline." Attempts at reunification were unsuccessful. He participates in the Fourth International to this day.

4. M. Mill (Pavel Okun, sometimes referred to as Obin) (b. 1905) helped found the French Trotskyist organization and its paper, *La Verite,* in 1929. He was secretary of the International Secretariat at the time of my meeting with him. Questions about his competence, coupled with "differences" he developed, led to his removal from the post. Originally from the Ukraine, he came to France following a stay in Palestine. A former member of the Communist Party of France, he eventually returned to the Stalinist movement. My latest knowledge of his whereabouts is that he had returned to the Ukraine, reputedly to city of Kharkov. Some in the French movement thought that Mill may have been a GPU agent all along; others felt that he left the Trotskyist movement because he was humiliated by his removal from his post with the IS.

5. Myrtos, whose real name was Oscar Rosenzweig, was born in England but for the most part lived with his family on the Continent. In his early twenties he was an accomplished linguist and a professional violinist, performing in trios and small orchestras in Czechoslovakia, Turkey, and Greece, often in the British embassies. In Paris, he played with a trio of his own in a cafe that I had the pleasure of visiting on several successive evenings.

6. Jan Frankel (John Glenner) (1906–deceased, date unknown) was born in Czechoslovakia. In 1929 he became a member of Trotsky's secretariat and guard in Turkey. I used to call him Trotsky's "foreign minister and janitor." Frankel was unusually devoted to Trotsky and his special needs as the leader of a movement of international supporters. He took care of certain movement correspondence, dealt with the unending organizational problems among the different groups, handled financial problems of the little *buro* in Kadikoy, supervised household matters together with Natalia, and represented Trotsky to officials of the Turkish government and police. Frankel was not a scholar or wide-ranging intellectual,

but he was quite intelligent and well-read. He left the "Secretariat" in 1933 to work in the International Secretariat of the Trotskyist movement in France; then he went to Norway to be Trotsky's secretary, until both were deported. He rejoined Trotsky in Mexico, where he was the only other witness in the Dewey Commission hearings.

Frankel came to the United States in 1937. There, he supported the Minority in the great debate over the "Russian Question" and functioned on the national and political committees of the Workers' Party. In the 1950s Frankel abandoned leftist politics and moved to Los Angeles, where he entered private business and broke off all relations with his political past. It was said that he died there. Neither I nor other one-time personal friends know exactly when or how. It has proved impossible to learn anything more about the later years of this key figure in the Trotskyist movement.

7. Trotsky was never spoken to or called by his first name—Leon, Lev, or Lev—but everyone called his wife Natalia. It seemed both natural and proper to do so. There was always a barrier at one point or another to greater intimacy with Trotsky. Whether he could not brook or was embarassed by it, I could not say. I found no such barrier with Natalia, nor did others.

8. The Turkish government under Kemal Pasha accepted Trotsky's residence as an exile under stipulated conditions. He was not free to move about the country or do as he pleased, and he was not to participate in Turkish politics. What agreement Kemal made with Stalin to accept Trotsky is not known, but for several years Turkey was the only country to offer residence to him.

9. In later years, this piece of trivia assumed some minuscule political proportions arising from a visit James P. Cannon made to Trotsky in the fall of 1934. About ten years afterward, in a once-over-lightly history of American Trotskyism, Cannon referred to his own smoking incident. Cannon wrote that he smoked cigars daily in the presence of Trotsky and Natalia, admitting, however, that "Glotzer and others came back with fierce tales" about this matter. Cannon claimed that Trotsky said: "No, go ahead and smoke. For boys like Glotzer I don't allow it, but for a solid comrade it is all right." By this tale Cannon thought to establish Trotsky's preference for his political leadership and faction against the minority to which I belonged. In doing this, however, he was making an uncomplimentary observation of Trotsky, who, in Cannon's mind, was making such incidents a matter of hierarchical significance. At the same time, Cannon exhibited a certain guilt for his own boorishness. In any case, I doubt his reportage is entirely accurrate.

10. In his *Revolutionary Silhouettes,* A. V. Lunacharsky wrote: "The chief external endowments of Trotsky are his oratorical gift and his talent as a writer. I consider Trotsky probably the greatest orator of our times. . . . Effective presence, beautiful broad gesture, mighty rhythm of speech, loud, absolutely tireless voice, wonderful compactness, literariness of phrase, wealth of imagery, scorching irony, flowing pathos, and an absolutely extraordinary logic, really steel-like in its clarity— these are the qualities of Trotsky's speech. . . . I have seen Trotsky talk for two and a half to three hours to an absolutely silent audience, standing on their feet,

and listening as though bewitched to an enormous political treatise. . . . " (See also Max Eastman's *Since Lenin Died,* Appendix I.)

11. Van Heijenoort, *With Trotsky in Exile,* pp. 11, 16, 18.

12. In my early adolescence I had boxed a little, and periodically visited the famous Kid Howard's Gym in Chicago, where the boxers of the twenties trained. It was there that I saw Jack Johnson, the great heavyweight champion, spar long after he ceased to be champion. I also saw Sammy Mandell, the lightweight champion, and Joe Lynch, bantamweight champion—as well as noted fighters Joey Sanger of Milwaukee and Joe Burman. The great wrestlers of the day also trained there: Strangler Lewis, Joe Stecher, and the Zybysko brothers. Trotsky did not know this but either assumed that my Chicago origins qualified me, or heard about it from Frankel, with whom I talked about the sport.

13. Although Natalia was not his blood grandmother, she devoted herself to him as though she was, and he spent more time with her than with anyone else.

14. Sieva eventually left Turkey for France with Van Heijenoort, rejoining his mother in Berlin, in December 1932. Zinaida committed suicide in a mood of hopelessness one month later. Sieva then lived with his uncle, Lyova Sedov, in Berlin. Since Hitler came to power soon after, Sieva then went to Vienna and subsequently to Paris to rejoin Sedov and his wife, Jeanne Martin, formerly the wife of Raymond Molinier.

When the Stalinist assassins took Lyova's life in a Paris hospital in 1937, Sieva remained with Martin until he made his way at last to Coyoacan, Mexico, to be reunited with Trotsky and Natalia in their final exile together. Martin was reluctant to surrender Sieva, but legal efforts finally resolved the matter. He was now a teenager who had lived through a difficult childhood and boyhood. His later years were a period of more normal growth, and he became the father of his own family.

In the May 1940 abortive assassination attempt on Trotsky's life by the GPU gang headed by the artist-turned-gunman David Siqueiros, Sieva was the only one wounded; he lived through the murder of Trotsky several months later—all of this in the short period he lived in Mexico.

15. *The Writings of Leon Trotsky,* p. 335.

16. "The Turn in the Communist International and the German Situation," by Leon Trotsky, in *The Militant,* October 1930.

17. *The Writings of Leon Trotsky,* "What is Fascism?", p. 99.

18. *Germany: The Key to the International Situation,* Pioneer Publications, New York, 1932.

19. Ernest Thaelman (1886–194?) was Stalin's favorite leader of the German Communist Party. He began his career as a seaman and transport worker active in Hamburg's trade unions, eventually joining the Social Democratic Party. Beginning with the *Spartakusbund,* he joined the Communist movement. Through the intervention of Zinoviev, and then Stalin, Thaelman was elevated to the Party's leadership. Thaelman was a coarse and brutal debater, whose intellectual level was low. Loyally carrying out Stalin's fatal policy in Germany, he was imprisoned by

the Nazis and murdered there.

20. Stalin's comments appeared in *Die Internationale*, February 1932.

21. Quoted in *The Communist Parties and the Crisis of Capitalism*, p. 112. This reference is in the Introduction by Ted Grant to the English edition of *Germany: The Key to the International Situation.*

22. Thaelman, *Communist International*, nos. 17/18, p. 1329.

23. Trotsky, *The Key*, p. 23 (English edition).

24. Leon Trotsky, *What Next? Vital Questions for the German Proletariat.*

25. *The Writings of Leon Trotsky*, p. 246.

26. *Communist International*, no. 36, 1933, p. 17, cited in the *Russian Bulletin*, nos. 36–37. Remmele fled to the Soviet Union after Hitler came to power and was executed by the GPU in 1937.

27. *What Next?*

28. From *Rote Afbau*, February 1932, one of the numerous publications of the German Communist Party, very likely issued by one of Munzerberg's many enterprises.

29. Deutscher, *The Prophet Outcast*, p. 142f.

30. Carmichael, pp. 384–385, 389, and 388.

31. Wistrich, pp. 176 and 177.

32. Nedava, p. 22.

33. Carr, pp. 433 and 436.

34. Everyone in the Prinkipo house knew that Zinaida suffered deep personality problems, which exacerbated the conditions of her life in exile with Trotsky and Natalia. While living there, two minor fires and one major fire broke out. (Joel Carmichael, in his *Trotsky*, records that members of the household believed her to be responsible for the fires.) She was at odds with her father because he would not accept her as an aide in a role similar to her half-brother Lyova. She was simply not capable of such a role, but refusal only disturbed her the more.

35. Victor Serge and Natalia Sedova, *The Life and Death of Leon Trotsky*, p. 164.

36. Deutscher, *The Prophet Outcast*, p. 25.

37. Conquest, *V. I. Lenin*, p. 146.

38. Van Heijenoort, pp. 96 and 154.

39. Neal Wood, *Communism and British Intellectuals*, pp. 82-83.

The Evolution of
Trotsky's Political Life

1903-1917: Trotsky's Polemic with Lenin

Between the time the Russian Social Democratic Labor Party was illegally convened in Minsk on March 1, 1898 (on the initiative of the Jewish Labor Bund[1]), and the momentous Second Congress in London in July 1903, the Party had no official program, no elected leadership, and no formal constitution.

Russian Social Democracy, like all other independent political movements in the country, functioned illegally—within the national borders of a backward peasant country ruled by a tyrannical Tsarist monarchy. Its units in the cities and towns had to work "underground." Indeed, many of its leading figures were in prison or in Siberian exile. Even there, the work went on, as they met in small groups, studied Marxism, debated political questions, wrote for the Party press, published tracts, and—above all—planned ways to escape.

Other outstanding leaders of the Party lived in European exile, where, though relatively free, they felt the frustrations of emigré life, physically separated from their country and movement. The one thing that nourished these exiles and the illegal Party in Russia was the influential paper they published, *Iskra* (*The Spark*). The paper's editorial board was comprised of G. V. Plekhanov, founder of the Russian Marxist movement, Lenin, Julius Martov, Paul B. Axelrod, Vera Zasulich, and A. N. Potresov. Because of their individual and collective authority, the board functioned as an unofficial leadership of the new organization. They gave the Party a whole body of theoretical and political ideas. *Iskra*'s Russia-wide readership looked to it eagerly for political, programmatic, and practical guidance in their illegal activities.

The Party was groping slowly toward a truly representative congress that would, under free conditions, permit an open discussion of the program and organization for the first time. Although the editors were not without their differences concerning the Party's ideas, they agreed on the need to create an organization capable of challenging the Tsar and his intolerably oppressive government. A strong, resolute, unified party was the key. On the eve of the Second Congress the Party leaders appeared to agree on this point.

Before the congress convened, the Party was presented with a pamphlet by Lenin, *What Is To Be Done*. Despite the initially warm reception it received, the pamphlet was destined to split the organization—forever. At the time of its publication, however, Lenin's political and editoral associate Potresov expressed enthusiasm for the pamphlet. As he wrote Lenin, "I have read your little book twice running and straight through and I can only congratulate its author. The general impression . . . is superlative."[2]

Trotsky read the pamphlet in Siberian exile and was likewise impressed. In the illegal, dispersed, and amorphous Social Democracy of the time, Lenin had commenced a welcome discussion of the most immediate organizational problems of the Party. How could they build a centralized, disciplined, revolutionary party under Tsarist absolutism? Most of the leading figures of the Party were, like Potresov, sympathetic to Lenin's aims in the pamphlet. But the real meaning of Lenin's ideas on organization, as they evolved, was not revealed until the Second Congress.

*   *   *

Trotsky's descriptions of Siberian exile are extraordinarily vivid. He was sent by boat to the village of Ust-Kut for his first exile.

Ust-Kut had known lusher times, days of wild debauches, robberies, and murders. When we were there the village was very quiet, but there was still plenty of drunkenness. The couple who owned the hut that we took were inveterate tipplers. Life was dark and repressed, utterly remote from the rest of the world. At night, the cockroaches filled the house with their rustlings as they crawled over table and bed, and even over our faces. From time to time we had to move out of the hut for a day or so and keep the door wide open, at a temperature of 35 degrees (Fahrenheit) below zero.

In the summer our lives were made wretched by midges. They even bit to death a cow which had lost its way in the woods. The peasants wore nets of tarred horsehair over their heads. In the spring and autumn the village was buried in mud. To be sure, the country was beautiful, but during those years it left me cold. I hated to waste interest and time on it. I lived between the woods and the river, and I almost never noticed them—I was so busy with my books and personal relations. I was studying Marx, brushing the cockroaches off the page.

The Lena was the great water route of the exiled. Those who had completed their terms returned to the South by way of the river. But communication was continuous between these various nests of the banished which kept growing with the rise of the revolutionary tide. The exiles exchanged letters with each other, some of them so long that they were really theoretical treatises.[3]

Siberia was in many ways Russia's intellectual, subversive center:

The aristocracy among the exiles was made up of the old Populists who had more or less succeeded in establishing themselves during the long years they had been away. The young Marxists formed a distinct section by themselves. It was not until my time that the striking workers, often illiterates who by some freak of fate had been separated from the great mass, began to drift to the north. For them, exile proved an invaluable school for politics and general culture. Intellectual disagreements were made the more bitter by squabbles over personal matters, as is natural where a great many people are forcibly confined. Private, and especially romantic, conflicts frequently took on the proportions of drama. There were even suicides on this account. At Verholensk, we took turns at guarding a student from Kiev. I noticed a pile of metal shavings on his table. We found out later that he had made lead bullets for his shotgun. Our guarding him was in vain. With the barrel of the gun against his breast, he pulled the trigger with his foot. We buried him in silence on the hill. At that time, we were still shy about making speeches, as if there were something artificial about them. In all the big exile colonies, there were graves of suicides. Some of the exiles became absorbed into the local populations, especially in the towns; others took to drink. In exile, as in prison, only hard intellectual work could save one. The Marxists, I must admit, were the only ones who did any of it under these conditions.

It was on the great Lena route, at that time, that I met [Felix] Dzerzhinsky, Uritzky, and other young revolutionaries who were destined to play such important roles in the future. We awaited each arriving party eagerly. On a dark spring night, as we sat around a bonfire on the banks of the Lena, Dzerzhinsky read one of his poems, in Polish. His face and voice were beautiful, but the poem was a slight thing. The life of the man was to prove to be one of the sternest of poems.

Soon after our arrival at Ust-Kut, I began to contribute articles to an Irkutsk newspaper, the *Vostochnoye Obozreniye (The Eastern Review)*. It was a provincial organ within the law, started by the old Populist exiles, but occasionally it fell into the hands of Marxists. I began as a village correspondent, and I waited anxiously for my first article to appear. The editor encouraged my contributions, and I soon began to write about literature, as well as about public questions. One day when I was trying to think of a pen-name, I opened the Italian dictionary and *antidoto* was the first word that met my eye. So for several years I signed myself "Antid Oto," and jestingly explained to my friends that I wanted to inject the Marxist antidote into the legitimate newspapers. After a while, my pay jumped suddenly from two kopecks a line to four. It was the best proof of success. I wrote about the peasantry; about the Russian classic authors; about Ibsen, Hauptmann, and Nietzsche; de Maupassant, Andreyev, and Gorky. I sat up night after night scratching up my manuscripts, as I tried to find the exact idea or the right word to express it. I was becoming a writer.[4]

The young Trotsky's intellectual ability made itself felt in these circles. Because of his talent in this area of Party work, he was given the pseudonym of *Pero*, the Pen, by Anton Krizhanovsky, a member of the *Iskra* group in Samara. Krizhanovsky, known as *Ker*, and his wife were friends of Lenin, and it was he who wrote to Lenin about Pero. When Trotsky later made his way to London, Lenin enthusiastically awaited him.

In 1902, Trotsky succeeded in his celebrated escape from Siberia, making his way across the whole of the Russian Empire to Vienna and then to Zurich. In Zurich he was directed to go on to London and seek out Lenin's residence. "Knock on the door three times," he was told. This he did, waking Lenin and Nadezhda Krupskaya, Lenin's wife, in the early dawn. The Revolution's two most forceful minds thus met. Trotsky was then an idealistic young man of twenty-three, full of zeal and totally absorbed in the hopes of Social Democracy. He was also an acute observer of the social and political scene in Tsarist Russia. All of this Lenin immediately caught, and he was pleased with what he saw and heard. Trotsky was as impressive in person as he was in the letters from Ker. Lenin would be able to put this man to effective use.

Trotsky talked to Lenin for many hours that night, and the next day he was taken to the *Iskra* editorial office to work on the paper. The young exile was euphoric to be at the *Iskra* quarters, among all the editors whom he had long admired. Robert Wistrich has written that Trotsky "had fallen in love with *Iskra*, displaying a reverence for the Party veterans which most of them reciprocated. His ties of friendship to Vera Zasulich and Paul Axelrod were particularly close."[5]

In these first days, young Trotsky was unaware that a conflict was looming on the editorial board between Lenin and Plekhanov. Lenin had proposed that Trotsky, despite his youth, be formally added to the board. He was a person "of rare abilities," argued Lenin, and Martov, Axelrod, and Zasulich agreed. But Plekhanov was strongly opposed and unyielding, suspecting, not without justification, that Lenin was seeking to control the board and build a majority against him. From this point on, Plekhanov's hostility to Trotsky was quite open and was often accompanied in an unsavory way by an anti-Semitic bias.[6]

In the years before the Second Congress, Lenin, like all Party leaders, talked of the fight for "political liberty" in Russia. He wrote that Social Democracy must "carry on propaganda not only in support of the ideas of scientific socialism, but also in support of the ideas of democracy." Lenin repeatedly emphasized this theme:

> Having made the overthrow of absolutism its immediate task, Social Democracy must come out as the vanguard in the fight for democracy, and this fact alone compels it to give every support to all the democratic elements of the population of Russia and to win them as allies.[7]

There is a unity of thought and logic here that Lenin later lost, when power and the exclusive rule of his party became his paramount objective. Before 1903, however, Lenin's remarks on liberty and democracy led other leaders of the Party and the editors of *Iskra* to believe that they and Lenin shared the same vision.

From the time of the founding First Congress in Minsk to the Second in London, no one in the leadership believed Russia was anything but a very backward peasant nation, economically and culturally, or that socialism was the next stage of social development. All seemed to acknowledge, with Marx and Engels, that socialism was not possible unless and until Russia became a developed industrial country. And that meant that a modern proletariat had to emerge from the peasant population. Notions of skipping the stage of capitalist industrial development came only after the Second Congress or, more accurately, after the 1905 Revolution. And this notion primarily came, surprisingly, from Trotsky. He had begun, under the influence of the well-known Parvus (A. L. Helphand), a noted Marxist of the turn of the century, to develop his theory of the "permanent revolution."

The theory of "permanent revolution" argued that backward nations could *skip* the capitalist phase of economic development and directly set up the political dictatorship of the proletariat. According to Trotsky, the

Russian bourgeoisie was simply incapable of carrying through a democratic revolution.

Prior to and during the Second Congress, of course, more standard visions of revolution prevailed. The thinking was that the "intermediate" stage of economic development was expected to bring on advanced capitalism. And both Mensheviks and Bolsheviks believed that this "advanced" stage would last for an undetermined period of time, until the inexorable contradictions of the system forced itself to collapse and pave the way for the Workers' Revolution. Until 1917 the Bolsheviks employed the slogan: "democratic dictatorship of the proletariat and peasantry." But the question of timing was not really in dispute at the Second Congress. The main questions to be decided were: What kind of party should be built? What will its relationship to the working class be? And who will be regarded as party members? The matter of the relations with the Jewish Labor Bund was a separate question, but it was logically related to the main questions of party organization.

What Happened in London

The mood of the Party was generally a happy one because the leadership, in exile and in Russia, had looked to the Second Congress as the assembly to finally organize a national, unified Party for the long struggle ahead. All the leaders of the Party and its most important and influential units believed in the necessity of the revolutionary overthrow of the monarchy, which denied even the most elementary of freedoms to the Russian people. The leaders agreed that Russia needed a centralized and disciplined party to achieve and guarantee these freedoms. So far as it was revealed during these formative years, the Party accepted the teachings of Marx and Engels. There seemed to be no great dissension among the leadership. The membership hoped that the Congress would put the Party onto the high road to eventual triumph. But the Congress was to produce an altogether different and unexpected result: a permanent split that would last until and beyond 1917, one that can still be felt today.

On the eve of the Congress, Lenin already knew where his ideas of class and party would take him, and for a brief time he seemed, despite his intransigent style, to foresee reconciliation on what would turn out to be irreconcilable relations with other Party leaders. The personalities of the leaders, as we shall see, were factors in setting the *tone* of the debates, not the outcomes.

The first sharp dispute, and the split in the Congress, came in the twenty-second session. The Congress was drafting the rules of the Party, and this question arose: Who exactly *were* the Party members? This seemingly innocent question brought out two proposals, one by Lenin and another by his close friend and political colleague, Julius Martov. Trotsky played an important role in supporting Martov, but he did not presume to be the main political opponent of Lenin on the organization question until after the Congress. This fateful opposition was to last for fourteen years.

Lenin defined a Party member as one "who accepts the program and supports the Party, both materially and by personal participation in one of the Party organizations." Martov's formula defined a member as one "who accepts the program and gives material support to the Party, but additionally gives the Party his regular personal cooperation under the direction of one of the Party organizations."

Tension in the Congress rose as the discussion over the two proposals became very sharp. At first glance, the difference did not appear to warrant a fiery debate, but the arguments of Lenin, Martov, and their respective supporters went far beyond the formal motions to reveal conflicting conceptions of Russian Social Democracy, its organization, and its relationship to the working class.

The Congress debate ended with Martov's proposal winning by a vote of twenty-eight to twenty-three. The tension of the discussion seemed to subside. The loss of the vote did not deter Lenin. Indeed, the defeat strengthened his vow to continue the struggle, because he could never concede that he was wrong on what he believed to be a high principle. Moreover, as Bertram D. Wolfe wrote, what set "Lenin apart from his associates was his absorption with the mechanics and dynamics of organization. . . . Lenin was an *organization* man, indeed *the* organization, of whatever movements he planned or took part in."[6] This trait led to the split in the Congress on the question of membership and produced two factions in the Party, factions that became known (inaccurately) as the Mensheviks (the Russian word for *the minority*) and the Bolsheviks (*the majority*), though their relationship was in a constant state of change. These appellations were coined, ingeniously, by Lenin himself, and did much over the years to boost Lenin's propaganda at the expense of his erstwhile colleagues.

The Menshevik/Bolshevik split continued through 1917, the strength of the factions changing often, with one or the other having the majority. Whether or not Lenin's wing actually held a majority, he called his faction the Bolsheviks, and indifference of the Mensheviks to the propagandistic value of the designations not only exhibited an obtuseness in the organizational-political area, but had unfortunate results. "It was a measure of the factional ineptitude of Martov and his followers," wrote Leonard Schapiro, "that they accepted the damaging nickname even at times when their supporters were in a majority on the Party committees."[9]

A sharp change in the relative strength of the Congress's factions occurred when the Bund moved that it be given a special right in the Party to guarantee its independence so that all matters concerning Jewish workers and Jewish questions would become its independent and exclusive province, not the Party as a whole. The *Iskra* editors united against the Bund, and they received the support of the overwhelming majority of Congress delegates—whereupon the Bund delegation withdrew from the Congress. Since the Bund had been the largest section of the Party, and for the most part allied with the Mensheviks, the majority now shifted to Lenin.

Lenin took advantage of his sudden majority and, not knowing how long it would last, proposed to elect an *Iskra* editorial board of only three members: Plekhanov, Martov, and Lenin. Potresov, Axelrod, and Zasulich would be dropped. He was reaching out to dominate the Party by controlling *Iskra* as well as the Central Committee and the Party Council, the two executive bodies of the Russian Social Democratic Labor Party.

If many of the delegates were taken aback by Lenin's thrust for power, it was because they misread or misunderstood *What Is To Be Done*. The fact that Lenin advocated a highly centralized, disciplined, and dictatorial party seemed lost on many Party members, who seemed to focus instead on the importance of *merely having* a functioning Social Democratic party, which did not then exist in fact. The *form* of Lenin's party, the true nature of Lenin's organizational vision, was concealed—but not for long. The democratic centralism advocated by Lenin came to be seen as all centralism and little or no democracy. The illegality of the Party supported Lenin's drive for the priority of centralism over any and all democracy.

Martov, too, as an authoritative leader of the Mensheviks and a highly respected member of the Party, believed in a *democratic* Social Democracy, but neither was he then ready, at a time of Tsarist absolutism and oppression, for a party functioning with full openness and democracy. All the Mensheviks, as well as Bolsheviks, understood the necessity for an illegal organization that could not be a totally democratic one. But what was a temporary condition and tactic for Martov was a permanent high principle for Lenin.[10] Since both wings of the Party accepted the necessity for an illegal organization, their fundamental differences were momentarily concealed.

When Lenin first presented his views of the Party, many leaders believed he thought as they did, in creating an active Party to help a newly formed working class to become imbued with Socialist or social democratic consciousness, so that this class would become the mass base for the developing party. The relationship between the Party and the working class would become an intimate one, the expected result of the interchange of economic and political struggles of the time and the active physical participation in these battles by an organized, cohesive Social Democracy.

The leaders in conflict with Lenin believed they represented the traditions of Marxism and the great working class parties of the Continent. But Lenin cared little about those traditions. His traditions were rooted in native Russian, nineteenth-century, pre-industrial, peasant revolutionaries, and these traditions intruded on the struggle of Menshevism and Bolshevism. Although Marx and Engels did not write extensively on theories of Socialist organization, their own activities and their participation in the First International were enough to indicate the direction of their ideas, and it was to these that Mensheviks attuned themselves. In the middle of 1879, Engels had written in behalf of Marx and himself a letter addressed to the German Social Democratic leaders:

> When the International was formed we expressly formulated the battle-cry: The emancipation of the working class must be achieved by the working class itself. We cannot therefore cooperate with people who say that the workers are too individualistic to emancipate themselves and must first be freed from above by philanthropic bourgeois or petty bourgeois.[11]

As if in anticipation of Lenin's views, Engels wrote in *Principles of Communism,* "None know better than [the Communists] the futility and, indeed, the harmfulness of conspiratorial methods."[12]

It is important to note that Engels did *not* say that such methods could not succeed; he just emphasized their harmfulness. And he was not talking about "special moments" when Socialist parties would be forced into an underground existence and to adopt subversive tactics; he was referring to the general life and character of the Party. These two points made by Engels went to the heart of the struggle between Menshevism and Bolshevism as it evolved in the post-Second Congress years. There is no doubt that Menshevism reflected the democratic tradition of Marxism; Lenin's Bolshevism, in this question as in others, was the "revisionist" position.

In *The Communist Manifesto* Marx and Engels dealt with the experiences of working class engagement in the social struggle as a process of evolutionary growth. Although the *Manifesto* was propaganda, they foresaw in it the general development of the workers' movement: "This organization of the proletarians to form a class, and therewith to form a political party, is continually being upset again by the competition among the workers themselves. But it ever rises up again, stronger, firmer, mightier."[13]

After the Second Congress

From the time of the Second Congress to 1917, Lenin had many differences with Marxists in Russia, usually not on important theoretical questions but on organizational or Party practices. He was fanatical in his determination to create his kind of party. Although he won the majority in the Congress after the Bund withdrew from it, he lost that majority not too long afterward. Plekhanov withdrew his support, rejecting Lenin's desire to crush his former colleagues. Lenin then lost control of *Iskra* and the majority of the Central Committee when he proposed to seize the paper.[14]

While exhibiting his determination to control and mold the Party, Lenin tried to allay the fears and suspicions Party leaders had about his goals and the fierceness with which he pursued them. Whether it was Lenin's guile or uncertainty in these early years is difficult to assess with absolute sureness. In his article "One Step Forward, Two Steps Back," Lenin wrote, "At present the dissensions that divide the two wings are for the most part only questions of organization, and not of program or of tactics," though he charged his opponents with "opportunism on the question of organization." Nonetheless, in behalf of Russian Social Democracy and in reply to those who pointed to its internal dilemmas, Lenin defended the Party: "The Russian Social Democrats," he wrote, "have already been sufficiently steeled in battle not to let themselves be perturbed by these pinpricks and to continue in spite of them, with their work of self-criticism. . . ."[15]

In one exchange with Paul Axelrod, Lenin wrote in 1904, "I absolutely do not consider our disagreement so fundamental that the life and death of our party depends on it."[16] Lenin was not forthright in saying this, because he was trying at the same time, immediately after the Congress, to convene a Third Congress to change the decision of the Second on the nature of Party membership.

To the dismay of the majority, which had refused to schedule another congress immediately after the Second, Lenin went ahead to prepare a Third Congress. Lenin was defiant and indefatigable in pursuing his proposal. And from April 23 to May 10, 1905, in London, he succeeded in convening a rump Congress. Lenin had created a party within the Party, as it was only his supporters who attended this London meeting. Despite his public utterances in defense of the organization of Russian Social Democracy, and his assurances to Axelrod and others, Lenin went ahead with his own movement. Referring to those who rallied around Lenin in 1905, Schapiro has written:

Lenin's forcible methods counted for more with [the underground professionals] than theoretical niceties. His success in calling this Congress emphasized the lines in which the Bolshevik Party was developing—a disciplined order of professional committee men grouped around a band of conspirators, who were linked by personal allegiance to their chieftain, Lenin, and ready to follow him in any adventure, so long as his leadership appeared sufficiently radical and extreme.[17]

The Bolsheviks following Lenin were still several paces behind him at this point. His proposal at this rump Congress to condemn Plekhanov failed to pass, as did his proposal requiring the Mensheviks to submit to the discipline of the Party or be expelled. The Congress adopted a resolution (in secret, like everything else that took place at the meeting) that the newly elected Central Committee seek the reunification of the Party, subject to the approval of another congress. But most important to Lenin was the adoption by this "Third Congress" of *his* proposal on the requirements for Party membership.

*   *   *

The relations between the Mensheviks and Bolsheviks after 1905 went through alternate periods of rapprochements and hostilities. Local organizations would unite, then separate. As often as not, the Mensheviks were in a majority. Yet Lenin always acted as if he were in the majority, striving to dominate the whole movement, while the Mensheviks would characteristically fail to take advantage of their majority to act as the leadership. Lenin's strategic aim in these years was always to avoid a reunification with the Mensheviks. He maintained this posture through 1917.

In his own political evolution before 1905, Lenin revealed the considerable influence of N. G. Cherneshevsky and P. N. Tkachev, two outstanding nineteenth-century antimonarchist revolutionaries. The title of Lenin's pamphlet *What Is To Be Done* was taken from Cherneshevsky's popular revolutionary novel and paid respect to the old writer. (In his youthful days, when he first began his serious reading, and before his acceptance of Marxism, Trotsky wrote that he was "carried away by the realistic aesthetics of Cherneshevsky," but made no other references to the politics, revolutionary perspectives, and influence of this nineteenth-century Russian figure.[18])

Tkachev's visions of a revolution by a small, conspiratorial group of professional revolutionaries also influenced Lenin's thinking about the revolutionary process in his time. Tkachev did not think in terms of democracy or a free society. Lenin suggested that his followers study this nine-teenth-century figure, even though Engels was very critical of him.

Adam Ulam regarded Cherneshevsky's novel as "inept, dull, and peurile work," which nevertheless fascinated the young generation of the time, who compared him to Tolstoy, Turgenev, and Dostoevsky. Plekhanov, for ex-ample, defended Cherneshevsky's *What Is To Be Done*.

So far as Tkachev is concerned, his description of what direction the professional revolutionary organization should take was exceptionally clear for that period in Russian history. He believed only an organized minority could achieve revolutionary power: "This minority, in view of its higher mental and moral development, always has and ought to have intellectual and moral power over the majority."[19] The revolutionary organization, he insisted, needs "centralization, strict disciplines, speed, decisiveness, and coordination of activities."

Vladimir D. Bonch-Bruyevich, a Bolshevik from the time of the origi-nal split in the Party, wrote in his memoirs that in the old days among the most sought-after writings were those of Peter Tkachev; whatever they found they "handed . . . over to Vladimir Ilyich (Lenin). Not only did V. I. himself read these works of Tkachev, he also recommended that all of us familiarize ourselves with the valuable writings of this original thinker. More than once, he asked newly arrived comrades [in Switzerland] if they wished to study the illegal literature. 'Begin,' V. I. would advise, 'by read-ing and familiarizing yourself with Tkachev's *Nabat*. This is basic and will give you tremendous knowledge.' "[20]

When Tkachev wrote that power could be achieved "by about a thou-sand well-organized revolutionaries," he was providing the intellectual nour-ishment for the development of Bolshevism. One can see this relationship in the statement that "The very difference between a violent revolution and a so-called 'gradual evolution' lies precisely in the fact that in the case of the former, a revolutionary minority is no longer willing to wait but takes it upon itself to force consciousness on the people."[21] Bolshevism clearly evolved from just such a theoretical premise, as is reflected in Lenin's view of the working class's inability to develop a Socialist consciousness. There is no question but that Tkachev even more than Cherneshevsky was the spiritual ancestor of Lenin's party. Trotsky wrote in his *Portraits* that even "the father of Russian Marxism," Plekhanov, "in spite of the strong influ-ence of the French literary masters . . . remained entirely a representative of the old Russian school of publicists."[22]

By 1905, Lenin had pretty well marked out his main course. He dis-carded his early ideas about political liberty and democracy. Though he still adhered to his slogan, "democratic dictatorship of the proletariat and

peasantry," as the fullfillment of the bourgeois revolution, he moved rapidly away from this position in mid-1917. His own particular type of one-
party dictatorship, as he elaborated his conceptions of it, was in contrast
to the view of Marx and Engels, who believed that "the first task in the
workers' revolution is to make the proletariat the ruling class, to establish
democracy."[23] The two old leaders were thinking of the Paris Commune
with its ruling council made up of many parties and groups. Lenin thought
in terms of the exclusion of all other parties and groups and the monopoly
of government by his own party. After 1905 he no longer spoke seriously
of political liberty or democracy.

The differences in the Party over the nature of Social Democratic
organization concerned the conceptual differences over the nature of and
relationship to the working class, the problem of spontaneity in the class
struggle, and the development of Socialist consciousness. They also included
questions concerning the political activity of Social Democracy and Lenin's
drive to create a party limited in the main to professional revolutionaries.
Lenin's party would be a cadre organization. When Lenin wrote in *What
Is To Be Done,* "give us an organization of revolutionaries—and we will
overturn the whole of Russia," it meant one thing to him and another
to his *Iskra* comrades. Plekhanov, too, was worried then about "the entrance into the Party of all sorts of opportunists," and like Lenin he desired
to keep the Party pure by exclusiveness. In time, however, he would learn
that his views and Lenin's were really far apart. As Martov said, "For
me a conspiratorial organization only has sense in so far as it is enveloped
by a broad Social Democratic working class Party."[24]

After 1903 the Party was in the early stages of understanding the
differences overwhelming it. Lenin had begun to state his differences clearly, which he punctuated with internal maneuvers backed by his formidable
separate and permanent faction. In *The Origins of Russian Bolshevism,*
Theodore Dan writes that Lenin believed "the antirevolutionary and anti-
proletarian character of Menshevik 'opportunism on questions of organization' in fact is contained in its 'hostility to the bureaucratic idea of
constructing the Party from the top down,' in its revulsion against proletarian discipline, and its indulgence, on the other hand, toward the anarchist
individualism of intellectuals with weak nerves."[25] On the same point, Lenin
himself wrote:

> Bureaucracy versus democracy is the same thing as centralism versus autono-
> mism. It is the organizational principle of revolutionary political democracy
> as opposed to the organizational principle of the opportunists of Social
> Democracy. The latter want to proceed from the bottom upward and,

consequently, wherever possible and to the extent that it is possible, it supports autonomism and "democracy," which may [by the overzealous] be carried as far as anarchism. The former proceed from the top, and advocate the extension of the rights and powers of the center in respect of the parts.[26]

The harshness of Lenin's attack, not to mention its groundless nature, was characteristic of his attitude toward his Party comrades, whom he tried to assure, as we have seen in his letter to Axelrod, that he did "not consider our disagreement so fundamental that the life and death of our Party depends on it." But that is exactly what he went on to make it! Why? We can see a partial explanation in this statement concerning "consciousness and the working class," which revises Marxism considerably:

We said that there could not yet be Social Democratic consciousness among the workers. This consciousness could only be brought to them from without. The history of all countries shows that the working class, exclusively by its own efforts, is able to develop trade-union consciousness, i.e., it may itself realize the necessity of combining as unions, to fight against the employers, and to strive to compel the government to pass necessary legislation.

The theory of Socialism grew out of the philosophical, historical, and economic theories that were elaborated by educated representatives of the propertied classes, the intellectuals. The founders of modern scientific Socialism, Marx and Engels, themselves belonged to the bourgeois intelligentsia.[27]

Thereupon Lenin sought to create a party of professional revolutionaries and armed contigents trained to take power in the name of the Party as the self-appointed spokesmen and representatives of the whole working class, *whether or not the working class understood what was taking place or supported it.* The Marxist idea of building a mass working-class party, educated in Socialist ideas and programs, learning its lessons in the process of its economic and political struggles, was vigorously challenged by Lenin, who disputed the notion that such a development was possible, necessary, or even desirable. He built his party as a tightly knit, highly disciplined, armed, cadre organization, Blanquist in its psychology and ready for a *putsch,* if necessary, to achieve state power.[28]

Trotsky's Break with Lenin

The Second Congress saw Trotsky's separation from Lenin. Lenin's activities after the Congress only widened the breach. Ideas of organization and class relations were not what gave Lenin his distinction in the struggle with Menshevism. It was his driving personality, the great force, anger, and determination to win any conflict he was in that set him apart from other leaders. His opponents were not without their intellectual abilities and practical achievements. But they lacked those qualites that Lenin had in the extreme, in areas of organization and the sheer art of leadership. Trotsky, according to Robert Conquest, called Lenin "the most highly charged utilitarian who ever came out of history."[29] He described Lenin as "irreconcilable" and "relentless" in the manner in which he sought to control the Party.

Trotsky was a delegate to the Second Congress, representing Siberian exile circles in the area to which he had been confined. After the Congress, he wrote his report, *Vtoroi Syezd (The Second Congress)*, in which he described the proceedings, especially its internal conflicts. Trotsky described Lenin as advocating "bureaucratic centralism" and made this sharp observation: "With the talent and energy characteristic of Lenin, [he] assumed the role of the Party's disorganizer." He had stated in the course of the discussion that Lenin was engaged in a struggle for power and that bureaucratic centralism would "dissolve opposition . . . slam shut the doors of the Party."[30]

Isaac Deutscher, the indefatigable biographer (and sometimes hagiographer) of Trotsky, attempts to make a life-long Bolshevik or Leninist of Trotsky. Describing Trotsky's report, Deutscher writes,

> Bronstein [Trotsky] set down his views in an essay which was widely circulated and hotly debated in the Siberian colonies. The biographical interest in this now little-known essay lies in the fact that in it he expounded broadly a view of the organization and the discipline of the Party identical with that which was later to become the hall-mark of Bolshevism, and which he himself then met with acute and venomous criticism.[31]

There is absolutely no historical truth to this. Enough has been written on this point to show that, try as he might, Deutscher cannot change the early history of the Russian movement. Indeed, he contradicts himself by reporting that Trotsky met Lenin's view "with acute and venomous criticism." We, too, think his views were "acute" and his criticism sometimes "venomous," but on the whole they were penetrating statements of the organizational principles of a *democratic* Socialist. Trotsky's concept of a disciplined and centralized Party was shared by the Menshevik leaders, and at no time had he "expounded broadly a view of the organization and the discipline of the Party identical with that which was later to become the hall-mark of Bolshevism." Moreover, Trotsky's speeches and activities at the Congress, as well as his writings afterward, deny Deutscher's implications. Deutscher's ludicrous statement takes its place alongside the biographer's belief that Trotsky *won* his struggle with Stalin because Stalin and his successors were carrying out Trotsky's program! With that belief, he titled the last chapter of his three-volume biography of Trotsky "Victory in Defeat." That Deutscher could sincerely believe this is evidence that he either did not understand the essence of Trotsky's struggle against Stalinism or that he misunderstood Stalin's murderous response to it.

Following the 1903 Congress and after a period of reflection, Trotsky wrote his booklet *Our Political Tasks,* a very thoughtful but unmistakably anti-Leninist statement of democratic Socialist organization. The work has never been fully translated into other languages or been reissued, so this classic statement remains largely unknown. Trotsky did not push for its republication in the years between 1904 and 1917. The Trotskyist organizations from 1929 to the present, while professing to be the bearers of Trotsky's literary legacy, have never, in all their many publication ventures to reprint everything he ever wrote, brought out a new edition of *Our Political Tasks.* The reason for this failure seems simply that it is an anti-Leninist work. Trotsky's long-held views remain largely unknown both to the movement that bears his name and to the world at large.

We are therefore fortunate that Baruch Knei-Paz, in his *Social and Political Thought of Trotsky,* reviewed the ideas in Trotsky's hundred-page essay with copious references. Our own references to it are taken from Knei-Paz's penetrating work.

Trotsky's ineptitude in his fight against Stalin and Stalinism has sometimes been attributed to his weakness in organizational matters. The organizational difficulties in Trotsky's last great struggle were rooted, however, in the contradictions created by his late and sudden adherence to Bolshevism and his unrealistic conception of Russia as a workers' state, not in any intrinsic, personal weakness. Despite his claim to have been the "best" Bolshevik after he joined Lenin in 1917, he was never truly able to adjust to that kind of party. He exhibited a revolutionary toughness and severity in the mass activities he was involved in as the Chairman of the Petersburg Soviet and the creator and top commander of the Red Army, but he could not adjust to the kind of inner life in the party Lenin created, where he was never accepted by a top leadership made up of Lenin's closest coworkers. Knei-Paz observes:

> Far from lacking an understanding of organizational questions, of the relationship between the Party and power—a charge often made against him— Trotsky here revealed an acute grasp of the power which such a party may accumulate, and of the manner in which it may degenerate, precisely because

it presumed to speak in the name of a democratic mass ideology. His criticism of Bolshevism raised the specific issue of organizational techniques as well as the wider issues of the autonomy of political action and the roles of intellectuals in political action.

The whole work was in fact an argument with Lenin—sometimes crude, often extreme, and always passionate. But beneath the polemics, beneath the almost violent language and personal denigration of Lenin, there lay a critique which even today, and perhaps especially today, when the subsequent evolution of Bolshevism is a matter of common historical knowledge, constitutes the most cogent analysis—dissection would perhaps be a more appropriate word—of the Bolshevik phenomenon.[32]

Trotsky thought in terms of educating and winning large numbers of the working class to the Party; of gaining the basic Party membership from the class whose political and organizational education was in its hands. He spoke of a politically developed proletariat arising from the activity of the Social Democratic Party. He wrote:

I remember the times [when] the propagandist set himself the goal of making clear to the worker . . . [the worker's] place in the universe. The propagandist began with a cosmology. Then he separated, happily, man from ape. Proceeding through the history of culture he reached (with difficulty) capitalism, then socialism. The basic idea of all this was to turn the simple proletarian into a Social Democrat imbued with a complete materialistic world outlook. Today, this respectable doctrinarism is already out of fashion, and much forgotten—reemerging, as it would appear, only in its most miserable caricatured form.[33]

This was written in 1904, and the language reflects the infancy of the movement as it does the romantic nature of the twenty-four-year-old Trotsky. But he was reaching to the heart of things when he said that "the self-activity [samodistelnost] of the proletariat has become a living slogan and, let us hope, that in the future it will be rejuvenating."[34] He talked about the "barracks regime" of a Leninist party, and in a very penetrating observation said, "The task of Social Democracy should be to set the proletariat against a system of discipline which replaces the working of human thought by the rhythm of physical movements."[35]

In this polemic Trotsky emphasized the democratic nature of Social Democracy and of Party life. He did not believe that centralism was necessary in order to establish the power and authority of leadership but only to create an institutional framework for the Party's activities; that it was a technical method by which the Party sought to educate the worker-member through participation in its political life. In one of his most prescient observations about a party existing in a most backward nation, he added: "Of course, I am talking about a 'European' centralism and not about an autocratic 'Asiatic' centralism. The latter does not *presuppose* but rather *excludes* such participation."[36]

Earlier, in his report on the Second Congress to his Siberian groups, Trotsky referred to the bureaucratization of the Party under Lenin's principles, and made an analogy with Robespierre and the Robespierriade:

> The process of self devourment has begun. . . . Comrade Lenin has transformed the modest [Party] Council into an all-mighty Committee of Public Safety so that he may play the role of an "incorrupt" Robespierre. All that has stood in the way has had to be swept away so that Comrade Lenin . . . could become, through the medium of the Council, the man who unhampered plants a "republic of virtue and terror." Robespierre's dictatorship through the Committee of Public Safety was able to keep itself alive, firstly, only by a fixed selection of "reliable" persons from the Committee itself and, secondly, by replacing the holders of all distinguished state posts with the protegés of the "Incorruptible." Otherwise, the omnipotent dictator would have hung in the air. In our caricature Robespierre, the first condition was attained through the dismissal of the old [*Iskra*] editorial board; the second was secured immediately through the fixed selections of persons to the first triumvirate of the Central Committee and, afterwards, by passing all candidates through the filter of "unanimity" and "mutual cooperation." Appointments to all other official posts will depend on the discretion of the Central Committee, whose own work is under the vigilant control of the Council. Such, Comrades, is the administrative apparatus which must rule over the republic of orthodox "virtue" and centralist "terror."

Lenin was outraged at being so described and compared. Trotsky's reply: "It is a pity [Lenin] has taken the Robespierre [comparison] in earnest; [our] report . . . spoke only of a caricature Robespierre. The latter differs from its great historical model approximately as a vulgar farce differs from historic tragedy."

For those who were in the modern Trotskyist movement during its long existence, these early and unknown views of Trotsky may come as a minor shock. (Indeed, for those who remain loyal to the memory of the old leader's ideas from the era of the Revolution and the post-Revolution decades, they may produce convulsive reactions.) But they will not be able to say that Trotsky's uncompromising and vigorous debate with Lenin was due to "a misunderstanding," for his writings in this field, exaggerations and vehemence aside, were written with order, clarity, and certainty. If there was a youthful shrillness in the writing, it was to be found in the harsh adjectives "demogogical," "malicious," and "repulsive."

Trotsky dedicated *Our Political Tasks* to Paul B. Axelrod, whom Lenin sought to drop as an editor of *Iskra*. The dedication made sure that no one would misunderstand where Trotsky stood in the great debate. Like the other Mensheviks, Trotsky was a centralist who wanted the Party governed by democratic methods. He favored leadership and direction of activities, but not by a self-perpetuating hierarchy, and he felt that Lenin's party was hierarchical, antidemocratic, and bureaucratic .

Martov charged Lenin and his acolytes with being Jacobins, to which Lenin replied, "A Jacobin indissolubly linked to the organization of the proletariat, aware of its own class interests—that is just what a Social Democrat is."[37]

In his own reply, Trotsky said it was not possible to be a Jacobin and a Social Democrat; a Social Democrat could no more be a Jacobin than a French Jacobin or any other kind could be a Social Democrat. "Their method was to guillotine the slightest deviators, ours is to overcome differences ideologically and politically. They cut off heads, we enlighten them with class consciousness."[38]

History has shown that if a Jacobin could not be a Social Democrat, he could easily be a Bolshevik. And Lenin, an endless polemicist, tough and combative in his differences, did not take kindly to the criticisms made of him, particularly by Trotsky, who only a short time before the Congress had come to him as a young, eager, and promising Party leader. In his article "The Historical Meaning of the Internal Party Struggle in Russia," Lenin rejected the criticisms of Martov and Trotsky, especially because he was worried in those years about what the German Social Democratic leadership might think about the Russian factional struggle.

> Martov sums up the "Russian" experience saying: "Blanquist and anarchist lack of culture was victorious over Marxian culture." (Read: "Bolshevism over Menshevism.")
> Trotsky follows in the wake of the Mensheviks and camouflages himself with particular sonorous phrases.
> Martov and Trotsky are presenting [in articles in the German Party's *Neue Zeit,* edited by Karl Kautsky] to the German comrades liberal views, painted up to look like Marxian views.[39]

In the same volume, Lenin writes of "Trotsky's anti-Party policy" and his "utter lack of theoretical understanding." Later on in the same volume he speaks of "the lengths to which Trotsky will go in degrading the Party and exalting himself before the Germans. . . ." Trotsky, wrote Lenin, "makes a jesuitical reservation. . . ." On the following page, Lenin went on:

> We now regard Martov as one of the leaders of liquidationism, who is the more dangerous, the more "cleverly" he defends the liquidators by quasi-Marxian phrases. But Martov often expounds views which have put their impress upon whole tendencies in the mass labor movement of 1903–1910. Trotsky, on the other hand, represents only his own personal vacillations and nothing more. In 1903 he was a Menshevik; he abandoned Menshevism in 1904, returned to Menshevism in 1905 and merely flaunted ultra-revolutionary phrases; in 1906 he left them again. . . . Trotsky one day plagiarises the ideological stock-in-trade of one faction; the next day he plagiarises that of another, and therefore declares himself to be standing above both factions."[40]

To enforce his position before the membership, Lenin called upon the authority of Karl Kautsky in those early years. Kautsky was involved in a debate inside the German Party over the meaning of "Socialist consciousness." In the *Neue Zeit* of 1901–1902 he wrote an article that seemed to support Lenin's views. In fact, he did quite the opposite. He wrote:

> Socialist consciousness is represented as a necessary and direct result (it is said) of the proletarian class struggle. But this is absolutely untrue. . . . Socialism and the class struggle arose side by side and not one out of the other; each arises out of different premises. Modern Socialist consciousness can arise only on the basis of profound scientific knowledge.[41]

Although this quotation from Kautsky seemed at first glance to be almost identical to Lenin's on the same point, the reality was that the translation of the idea into practice produced two entirely different parties. Lenin created a tightly knit cadre organization of bureaucratic centralism; Kautsky and the Germans developed a mass working-class, democratic organization of social democracy, centralized and disciplined, approaching the descriptions of Martov and Trotsky. To be sure, this German party became the model for Social Democratic parties throughout Western Europe and in other countries, while Bolshevism remained only a Russian phenomenon until 1917, when Lenin's seizure of power led to the establishment of Russian-type parties in other parts of the world. Then the split in the Russian movement became a split on a world scale.

In those early years, Trotsky believed in a democratic Socialist party. This reflected his conception of a Socialist revolution based on democracy, equality, freedom of choice, self-determination, and liberation from hierarchy and bureaucratism. Trotsky regarded Lenin's cadre party as a form of "substitutionism"—i.e., Lenin was substituting the Party for the working class and speaking exclusively, in the name of Marxism, for the working class. *Our Political Tasks* presents this quite clearly:

> In one case, we have a system of *thinking for* the proletariat, of political *substitution* of the proletariat, a system of *educating* politically the proletariate, *mobilizing* it, so that it may exercise pressure on the will of all groups and parties. These two systems produce political results which are, objectively, totally different.[42]

Prior to 1917, Trotsky still believed that the Socialist struggle under Tsarism would take a long time; the working class of Romanoff Russia was too backward in economic, political, and cultural terms to achieve revolutionary success quickly. When Trotsky thought about the process of the Socialist revolution and its evolution from the initial overthrow of the monarchy, he thought in Marxian terms. He was, of course, quite familiar with the writings of Marx and Engels on the subject. In a letter from Cologne to Arnold Ruge in May, 1845, for example, Marx had written:

> Men—means intellectual beings; free men—means republicans. The common philistines do not want to be called either. . . .
>   One will have to reawaken in the breast of the people the sense of the self-worth of men—freedom. Only such a sense, which vanished from the world with the Greeks and evaporated into the blue with Christianity, can transform society again into a community of people working for their highest ends—a democratic state.[43]

Engels put it most succinctly when, in a criticism of the Erfurt Progam of the German Social Democracy adopted in 1891, he said:

> If one thing is certain it is that our party and the working class can only come to power under the form of the democratic republic. This is even the specific form of the dictatorship of the proletariat, as the Great French Revolution has already shown.[44]

This sense of Marxism was absorbed by Social Democracy and became integral to its tradition. In the Second Congress and the years thereafter this was Trotsky's firm conviction and the basis for his long quarrel with Lenin. He foresaw the degeneration of Bolshevism and was quite specific about the form it would take. In the oft-quoted description of the unavoidable evolution of Lenin's party, he had written:

The dictatorship over the proletariat [means] not the self-activity of the working class which has taken into its hands the destiny of society, but a "powerful commanding organization," ruling over the proletariat, and, through it,
over society, thus securing presumably the transition to socialism.[45]

Rather than the transition to socialism, he prophetically saw the inevitable degeneration of the Party.

Lenin's methods lead to this: The Party organization at first substitutes itself
for the Party as a whole; then the Central Committee substitutes itself for
the organization; and finally, the single "dictator" substitutes himself for the
Central Committee.[46]

I have found it important to present these references from Trotsky's
virtually unknown work of 1904 not only because they are necessary for
an accurate historical record of the early struggle in Russian Social
Democracy, but also because Trotsky, after his conversion to Bolshevism,
ignored or treated his past as though it did not exist. His followers are
still largely ignorant of that past; those who do know something about
it are forced to avoid reference to the long years before 1917. In reviewing
the disputes of 1903–1904, Robert Wistrich concluded that:

Trotsky was at this stage completely committed to the principle of rank-
and-file consent, to the "self-activity" (*samodistelnost*) of the proletariat, its
mass participation in the collective struggle. The democratization of Party
life entailed the rejection of all mechanical forms of discipline associated
with the capitalist production system and the "barracks regime." Leninism
had merely perpetuated these evils.[47]

Rosa Luxemburg, the revolutionary Socialist leader active in the Polish and German Social Democratic Parties, also opposed Lenin's "ultra-
centralism" as the "negative spirit" of the "night watchman." Lenin, she
said, was the "taskmaster," not the "gatherer and unifier." Leonard Schapiro put forth the now more frequently accepted view that Lenin reflected
the "Russian conspiratorial heritage and its populist traditions of revolutionary centralism."[48] Trotsky's polemic emphasized the rejection of that
tradition in the post-Second Congress dispute.

1905 and Afterward

Trotsky predicted the Revolution of 1905 in his early writings, and it came
in the midst of the internal crisis of Social Democracy.[49] Russia's humiliating

defeat by Japan in the Russo-Japanese War of 1904–1905 revealed the profound ineptitude of the monarchy and brought masses of protesting people into the streets of the leading cities. The deep political crisis emerging from the war and the restlessness of the people drew Trotsky to the very center of the struggle in Petrograd, where the first spontaneous People's Soviet arose. Trotsky became the chairman of this Soviet, where a great revolutionary drama was played in which all the political parties in opposition to Tsarism were represented.

Trotsky became the spokesman for this new revolutionary political body, where his outstanding oratorical ability catapulted him to the leadership of the movement.

The 1905 Revolution was a rehearsal for 1917 in the sense that it gave birth to the Soviet as an instrument of political power of a new kind. Trotsky grasped its significance and possibilities and described the Soviet as the "first appearance of democratic power in modern Russian history." Only twenty-six when he became the tribune of the Soviet, he provided unusual leadership to it and helped to bring about joint work between the Mensheviks and Bolsheviks, though the former dominated the temporary union. What contributed to this uneven relationship was the sectarian attitude of the Bolshevik Party to the events of 1905. The Party was often isolated from the important happenings in the Soviet—or it isolated itself. Bolshevism was not a factor in the revolution. The leader of the Party was not involved in the work of the Soviet and did not speak there. Given the political reality of the bitter split between the two wings of Social Democracy, any joint action of the two took place only through the person of Trotsky, who was by then not affiliated with either faction, though he remained politically closer to the Mensheviks.

The Revolution of 1905 did not and could not succeed; a spontaneous eruption, it was essentially premature. While there was broad opposition to the monarchy, there was no unity between the working class and peasantry; and the army, made up mainly of peasants, remained loyal to the regime. The Socialist parties, surprised by the turbulence, had neither the necessary influence nor the political programs to meet the demands of this initial and primitive revolution. Once the monarchy recovered from the shocks of the rebellion, it proceeded to arrest its leaders and imprison them while they awaited trial. The entire Soviet of workers' delegates was brought to trial in 1906. As Trotsky described the event in his autobiography, "The trial itself was carried out with a certain amount of freedom. . . ."[50] Four hundred witnesses were on call; two hundred testified!

The contrast with the "legal" system of the future Bolshevik state, in which there were no rights for defendants, is striking. The Bolshevik form of justice was a prosecutorial system that contrasted unfavorably to the "looseness" of the Tsarists' uncivilized system. Alas, Trotsky recognized this only during the Moscow show trials of the 1930s. As we will see in our discussion of the Dewey Commission hearings in Mexico, Trotsky was concerned mainly with the democratic rights of Party leaders and members—particularly the Left Opposition—not of the society. He expressed in his own political and legal tribulations the essential antagonism between Bolshevism and democracy. Trotsky used his trial in 1905 as another revolutionary tribunal. He defended the right of the defendants to overthrow the Tsarist monarchy as the only available means of redress the people had in this closed society. Since there was no democratic right to meet, organize, speak, write, or publish—in fact, no liberty of any kind—only revolutionary means were left to the people.

These arguments did not persuade the courts, of course. Trotsky and his Soviet comrades were found guilty and received various sentences of imprisonment and Siberian exile. The chairman of the Soviet was sent away once more to Russian Asia. According to A. V. Lunacharsky, the one-time Minister of Education and leader of Soviet Cultural Affairs, an Old Bolshevik and associate of Lenin after the Revolution of 1905,

> Trotsky undoubtedly showed himself, in spite of his youth, the best prepared, and he was least stamped by the narrow emigré outlook which, as I said before, handicapped even Lenin. He realized better than all the others what a state struggle is. He came out of the Revolution, too, with the greatest gain in popularity; neither Lenin nor Martov gained as much. Plekhanov lost a great deal because of the semiliberal tendencies which he revealed. But Trotsky from then on was first rank.[51]

In 1905 Trotsky and Parvus (Alexander Helphand) began to publish *Nachalo,* a journal "in alliance with" the Menshevik faction. Because of its faithful reflection of the revolutionary events and its more powerful interpretation of them, the paper far outstripped the Bolshevik journal *Novaya Zhizn.* This was no mean achievement, since neither Trotsky nor Parvus was organizationally affiliated. Despite his remarkable role in 1905, Trotsky wrote in his autobiography twenty-five years later that "Lenin spoke approvingly of my work in prison (awaiting trial), but he taunted me for not drawing the necessary conclusion, in other words, for not going over to the Bolsheviks. He was right in this."[52]

Why? There was no reason for Trotsky to agree with Lenin, particularly in 1905. The gulf between the two wings of the Party remained wide even though Lenin did say at one time during the revolutionary events that the division was untenable; and 1905 pushed the question of unity once more to the forefront. Why did Lenin push, when he was in fact deepening the split and strengthening the organizational separation of his faction from the Party and its Menshevik majority?

The rekindling of desires for unity in 1905 led to a Fourth Congress in April and May, 1906, in Stockholm. This was the last time the Mensheviks and Bolsheviks would meet together in a congress. The Fourth Congress came on the heels of an election for a new Duma. The Bolsheviks, on Lenin's insistence, had boycotted the elections, while the Mensheviks participated actively and elected eighteen of its candidates. Years later, Lenin admitted publicly he had been mistaken. The Mensheviks strengthened themselves considerably.

Trotsky was closely attuned to the Party situation during 1903–1906, and to the Second, the illegal Third, and the unification Fourth Congresses. He was fully aware of the continuing internal struggle, yet he remained close to the Mensheviks. So, if Lenin was "right" in asking him to join the Bolsheviks, it was a statement Trotsky could make only after he actually joined Lenin eleven years later.

The Fourth Congress was a triumph for the Mensheviks. Superior policy in the Duma election gave the Mensheviks great strength, and they were able to elect a majority of the Central Committee. With Lenin professing publicly the need for unity, it appeared that the factional in-fighting might actually recede. Schapiro describes the new circumstances in the following terms:

> Thus, the Fourth Congress ended with the two factions nominally reunited, in very changed conditions from 1903. Revolution was at the ebb, the constitutional era had dawned, and a strong middle-class party had emerged upon the scene, determined to create conditions of political and civil liberty. New opportunities seemed to be opening up for Social Democrats, of a kind which in some of the countries of Western Europe were already leading to the emergence of the working class as a conscious political force. The Russian party was not destined to profit from these opportunities.[53]

An important, if not decisive, reason for the failure of the Party to profit from the apparent unity was that the Bolsheviks had set up their own illegal Central Committee, to which its members were disciplined adherents. The Bolshevik center was made up of Lenin, A. A. Bogdanov, and Leonid B. Krassin; and the faction's secret funds, obtained largely through deceit and bank expropriations, were administered, as before, by Krassin. All of this was kept secret from the Party as a whole. The unofficial activity of the Bolsheviks was directed by Lenin, and despite the public show of unity, Russian Social Democracy remained sharply split. The reality was that two Social Democratic parties functioned in opposition to each other. The responsibility for this situation was Lenin's, and he accepted it gladly.

*   *   *

After the unification Congress, Trotsky was a Social Democrat without organizational affiliation. He had not altered any of his views of Lenin's concept of a party and the nature of the development of the Russian working class. What contributed to his separation from the Mensheviks was his theory of the permanent revolution, which kept him apart from the Bolsheviks, too, because it sharply contrasted with Lenin's slogan of the "democratic dictatorship of the proletariat and peasantry." Trotsky considered the slogan unreal and too similar to the position of the Mensheviks.

Trotsky remained an independent and isolated leader of Russian Social Democracy, a man of considerable standing outside of the Party after 1905. Convicted in his 1905 trial and exiled to Siberia, he escaped again from his Asian isolation and made his way to Vienna, where his wife, Natalia, joined him. They lived there for several years before beginning a new journey westward.

During his residence in Vienna, Trotsky became close friends with Rudolph Hilferding, a Marxist theoretician and, for a time, a left-wing Socialist. Karl Kautsky, whom he had met in earlier years and whom he admired and respected, also became a frequent visitor. Through Hilferding, he met the leaders of Austrian Social Democracy: Otto Bauser, Max Adler, and Karl Renner. He renewed his friendship with Victor Adler, which had begun in 1902. He met for the first time Franz Mehring, a biographer of Marx and a literary critic. In his Vienna period he also attended the Congresses of the Party.

*   *   *

During the Fourth "unification" Congress in Stockholm, the mood of reconciliation and unification was strong in both factions, as noted above. Tsarist reaction after 1905 contributed to this mood, but it was considerably strong among Mensheviks who felt that the political condition of the country demanded unification, believing that the existence of two organizations to be unnecessary and undesirable. But Lenin saw the division to be both necessary *and* desirable, and he made sure that the split in reality remained permanent. However, Menshevik pressure in the pre-Congress period compelled the Bolsheviks to participate and accept momentarily the Menshevik majority.

Immediately after the Fourth Congress, Lenin and his followers began to agitate for a Fifth Congress, on the ground that the Menshevik majority Central Committee was not carrying out the will of the Fourth Congress. Although the Mensheviks opposed another congress so soon after one had been held, they finally conceded. The Fifth Congress met in London in 1907. Lenin's superior organizational ability and persistent drive gave him a bare majority at this Congress of about ninety votes against the Mensheviks' eighty-five. Schapiro, citing an "important source," said that voting on different propositions in the Congress varied, with the Bolsheviks winning one vote ninety to eighty-one, and another, eighty-five to eighty. Variations in numbers occurred because of the presence of Polish, Lettish, Trotskyist, and Bundist delegations, whose votes changed back and forth on specific issues. The Bund had returned to the Party with mixed support, including Lenin's.

No important programmatic questions came up at the Congress, but the meeting in the end strengthened Lenin's new majority, even though he lost two votes on important questions. For example, the Bolshevik resolution condemning the Menshevik Central Committee elected at the Fourth Congress for not carrying out "the will of the Party" was defeated by the Mensheviks with the support of the Poles and Letts.

The most controversial and debated question at this Congress was the decision of the gathering, by a vote of 170 to 35 (with 52 abstentions), to denounce the Bolshevik policy of expropriations and robberies, and to demand their immediate cessation. The question arose because Lenin's faction maintained a special apparatus to direct and carry out this demoralizing and degenerating activity as a means of keeping the Bolshevik treasury well-supplied with funds.

Stalin's Georgian friend and comrade, Kamo, an unusual character totally devoted to the Bolshevik Party, was the organizer of a group of expropriators, which drew into its circle many unsavory elements. Kamo was the personal leader and active participant in its many robberies. The most notorious was the Tiflis bank robbery in June, 1907, which netted Lenin's organization 250,000 rubles, a considerable sum in those years.[54] The affair gave the Bolsheviks an enormous advantage over the Mensheviks, who suffered from a lack of funds. Such monies were used in the Party to assist various groups, gestures that did not hurt the Bolsheviks in votes on various questions. Some of the monies taken in the bank affair were marked 500-ruble notes, and the attempt to pass them in several

European capitals led to the arrest of a number of Party figures. Unfortunately for the Bolsheviks, a police spy was well situated in the Party—and kept the police apprised of the Party's plans to obtain cash for the notes.

Russian Social Democracy was severely compromised when the expropriation became publicized and the news of the arrests in Europe spread. There was turmoil in the Party because this action in Tiflis came only two to three weeks after the Fifth Congress had condemned such activities and called for their end. Since everyone knew that the Bolshevik leadership was responsible for the robbery, large numbers in the Party felt this was a deviance of the Congress decision and a mockery of the organization. The Tiflis affair became a scandal in the Second International, to which the Bolsheviks adhered. Lenin, who in those years sought approval of the world-renowned leaders of Social Democracy, was embarrassed by the arrests, as were other leaders of the Bolshevik faction. It was the pertinent reason why Lenin agreed to end the practice of "expropriations." Still, the Bolshevik policy in this field did not cease for several more years.

Despite public appearances of greater unity in the Party, the actual relations between Menshevism and Bolshevism were caustic. Although the reaction seemed dominant and the Tsar triumphant following the 1905 Revolution, the Mensheviks, at least, felt that an opening to constitutionality was achieved and the time was appropriate to begin activity creating a legal party to carry out public work among the working masses, supplementing the illegal organization. Lenin unfairly denounced the idea as an aberration of Menshevik liquidators who sought the dissolution of the illegal underground Party. There were some who did, but the leadership did not.

The Bolsheviks were able to exercise their majority in the Congress to elect a new Central Committee of fifteen with twenty-two candidates.[55] As an indication of how even the factions were, the Bolsheviks had five members, the Mensheviks four, and two each went to the Bund, the Poles, and the Letts. This was obviously a compromise political leadership. The military organization of the Party, however, remained in the hands of the Bolsheviks.

An important reason for the continued Bolshevik activity as a separate aggregate was that the "unified" Party had no authority or control over the faction, which simply ignored Congress decisions. The Menshevik journal, *Golas Sotsial Democratii,* denounced the Bolsheviks, stressing that either the Party would destroy the clique or be destroyed by it. Even Plekhanov, whom Schapiro described as "an enigma" in the Party, "ruffled by vanity," and ambiguous in his relations to the factions, moving from one to the other and back again, urged a complete break with Bolshevism. Many Bolsheviks were equally shocked by the Tiflis affair. When Lenin agreed to stop the expropriation activity in 1907, he was yielding to unanswerable criticism, but also with an eye to what the respected Western parties, particularly German Social Democracy, might think of it. Within a few years he, too, rejected this means of financing his party; he may even have felt that such an activity was evidence of the social and cultural backwardness of the country, and outside the tradition of Marxism.

At the end of the Fifth Congress, anticipating that the unity achieved was akin to a "shot-gun marriage," as Zinoviev described it, and despite their own internal differences on the question, the Bolsheviks, on Lenin's insistence, set up their own "new" center as an editorial board of its paper, *Proletarii*. The editorial board was the operating leadership of the Bolshevik faction, which functioned as an independent organization apart from the official Party. The Bolsheviks, as Rosa Luxemburg said, fought to win the Party majority with "Tartar–Mongolian savagery."[56]

In these years, Trotsky's *Pravda* avoided factional polemics, not because its editor was squeamish about such debates, but because of his political position of conciliator and possible role as unifier. He and his paper were popular with those who desired unity in the Party. *Pravda* was also the most popular paper among Russian emigrés and in the illegal circles in Russia, although it was under constant attack by Lenin, the butt of his hard attitude and polemical nature. For Lenin, "conciliator" was not only a political description, it was a useful epithet.

The Central Committee Meeting in Paris

The condition of the Party for the next several years after the Fifth Congress and the new Duma elections declined severely. The post-1905 depression was now widespread. Whole units of the Party disappeared; others lost many of their members. This was true for both Bolsheviks and Mensheviks. In 1910 Trotsky estimated the Party had a mere ten thousand members.

The varying strength of the two factions depended on developments inside of Russia, and since the 1907 Congress these brought new support to the Mensheviks. Its strong positions enabled it to force a plenum meeting of the Central Committee in Paris in 1910. Menshevik leaders felt confident that with strong differences inside the Bolshevik wing over unity, a plenum might advance that possibility, despite the fact that they were warned by a leading Bolshevik, V. P. Nogin, who favored reconciliation and unity, that Lenin would never permit a joint Central Committee of Mensheviks and Bolsheviks. His adamant position was not softened, although at this particular time he was in a minority in the Party and in his own faction on the question. But the plenum went ahead, and on the basis of a compromise was able to achieve the following agreement:

1. The possibility of creating a mass party now existed.
2. To issue a call for a unity conference as soon as possible.
3. Local conferences of legal and illegal workers should meet first. [Lenin opposed numbers 2 and 3.]
4. A Party organization to be reconstructed on the basis of the Central Committee elected at the Fifth Congress of 1907.
5. The paper *Sotsial Democratii*, now controlled by the Bolsheviks, would become a Party journal.
6. Both factions agree to stop publication of the Menshevik *Golas Sotsial Democratii* and the Bolshevik *Proletarii*.
7. The journal *Vpered* would be the paper of a "literary group."
8. A subsidy would be provided to *Pravda*, Trotsky's paper.

There was also a complicated agreement regarding the disposition of monies controlled by the Bolsheviks for funding the "united organization," which was carried out mainly in the breach. The Bolshevik treasury of tens of thousands of rubles financed the faction, paid its functionaries and the expenses of delegates attending official gatherings, and supported Bolshevik papers. The official Party had no funds (for reasons already cited). To have expected Lenin to carry out an agreement to provide funds for the Party now under the direction of the Mensheviks was to misunderstand his goals and how he fought for them. He would not and did not carry out the agreement of the plenum.

Trotsky's *Pravda* received the agreed-to subsidy, but only for a very brief time. The Bolshevik representative to the paper, Leon (Lev) Kamenev, quarreled with Trotsky, and Lenin thereupon withdrew the subsidy. At this time, Lenin reestablished relations with Plekhanov, which had been broken off in 1903, using Plekhanov's hatred of Trotsky to win his collaboration on the Bolshevik paper in Russia, which was in competition with the Vienna *Pravda*.

Despite the new unity of the 1910 Central Committee plenum in Paris, Lenin decided to call his own plenum on June 5, 1911, a plenum of hand-picked delegates. The Jewish Bund and Mensheviks walked out of the meeting because there was no legal authority for it. But the illegitimate meeting went about its affairs anyway—and in greater comfort, once the Bund and Mensheviks departed. Lenin was slowly consolidating his group despite the decisions taken at the 1910 plenum of the official Central Committee, bearing out Nogin's warning to the Menshevik leaders. Lenin's illegal plenum made preparations for an "all-Party" conference of his own to be held in Prague on January 12, 1912.

Lenin's Prague conference met as planned and recorded one new turn by the Bolshevik faction: After denouncing the Mensheviks for their efforts to carry out legal activities, describing them as "liquidators," Lenin reversed Bolshevik policy and decided to compete with the Mensheviks for the right to legal struggle. The Prague conference also decided to issue its own paper. Its name: *Pravda,* brazenly stolen from Trotsky's Vienna journal. Having no organization of his own and, therefore, no means or power to resist this usurpation, Trotsky had no recourse but to accept, with complaints, this example of Bolshevik ethics. In *My Life,* Trotsky refers to the expropriation of his paper's name but attributes it to the Bolshevik paper in Petrograd rather than to the Prague conference; he ignores Lenin's initiative in the matter. In any case, the new paper helped Lenin rebuild his Bolshevik Party. The Mensheviks then issued their own paper, *Luch (The Ray)*.

Despite Lenin's pretense at Prague that Bolshevism represented all of Russian Social Democracy, excluding the Mensheviks, it was obvious that the Party was still in utter disarray. Trotsky tried once more to make a stab at bringing the Party factions together under one fold. So, he summoned the various currents to a conference in Vienna.

The conference met on April 25, 1912. It became known as the meeting of the "August Bloc." It was most fiercely denounced by Lenin, but it was endorsed by a number of leading figures, including Rosa Luxemburg. Among those present in Vienna were the Bund representatives, Trotsky's *Pravda, Golas Sotsial Democratii,* and two Bolshevik conciliators who broke with Lenin and called themselves "Party Bolsheviks." The Prague Central Committee ignored the invitation from the "conciliators." When the meeting agreed to call an all-Party conference of all groups and factions, the Polish Social Democrats and Plekhanov opposed it. In his perverse way, Plekhanov blamed the Mensheviks for the split in the Party.

There was present at the conference a Bolshevik delegate from Moscow (a police agent) with instructions to break up the conference in Vienna, if possible. He was aided by Alexinskii of *Vpered.* Little agreement existed among those present, except their common anti-Leninist viewpoint. While Trotsky was anxious to create a mood of harmony, Martov's reference to Lenin and the Bolsheviks as "charlatans" offended many. Instead of setting up a Central Committee to continue the purposes of the conference, an organizing committee of seven members was elected to direct work inside of Russia.

As a political policy, the Vienna conference agreed on the objective of creating a mass party and the maintenance of the illegal organization subordinate to it; they also adopted a conciliatory resolution on the state of the party. There was now added to the picture the Prague Bolsehvik Central Committee and the Vienna Organizing Committee, as far apart as it was possible for these old political contestants to be.

With Lenin's acceptance of legal activity alongside his underground organization, a policy not unlike the Menshevik's, the two factions seemed less at odds politically. Nevertheless, there were still two Party papers, both representing Social Democracy. Trotsky contributed writings to the Menshevik *Luch,* and, oddly, Plekhanov wrote for the Bolshevik paper, *Pravda.* Despite Lenin's denunciation of the Mensheviks as liquidators, by 1913 the Mensheviks had an extensive illegal organization persecuted even more than the Bolsheviks. The situation remained this way until the outbreak of the Great War.

Meanwhile, the International Socialist Bureau had offered to mediate the Duma split directed by Lenin and executed by the spy Malinovsky. The Bureau was especially motivated to mediate because of the division in Russian Social Democrats. It thereupon arranged for a "unification" meeting in July 1914. Present were the Menshevik Party, the Caucasian Social Democracy, the *Vpered* Group, the Jewish Bund, the Lettish Social Democrats, the Polish Socialist Party, the Plekhanov-Edintsov Group, and the Bolsheviks, who were represented by a committee of three, headed by Lenin's personal friend and colleague Inessa Armand. Though he did not appear in person, Lenin wrote Armand's statement to the Bureau, in which he reasserted the Bolshevik policy, emphasizing that "we will not retreat from it."

Lenin had few supporters at the Bureau meeting, and Plekhanov tersely explained that Lenin wanted no agreement because he didn't want to share the large sums of money the Bolsheviks had accumulated. He showed a singular lack of political insight at this particular moment in confining the differences to a financial matter. Lenin paid little attention to all of this and kept churning up the conflict. For its part, the Bureau adopted a resolution, summarized below, directed toward the unification of the Party, which everyone favored except the Lettish Social Democracy.

Beginning with the observation that no factional disagreement existed which justified the split in the Russian Party, the Bureau called for unity of the party on the basis of:

1. Acceptance of the Party program.
2. Recognition of the principle of minority acceptance of majority decisions.
3. Organization of the Party must be secret at present.

4. All groups reject blocs with bourgeois parties.
5. All groups agree to participate in a unification conference.

This decision was to have been reported to a Congress of the Socialist International in August 1914. By then, however, Europe had exploded in a devastating war. To guess what might have happened had there been no war is idle speculation, for history took a new turn. The catastrophic event hastened the breakdown of Tsarist society, and the world came to the era of Bolshevism.

*   *   *

Many of Trotsky's most important predictions about the inevitable evolution of Lenin's organizational principles and practices, following the great division of Social Democracy at the Second Congress, came to pass. One can see in the evolution of the Party, its many turnings and churnings, the essential conflict between the desire of one half of the Party to build a democratic Socialist organization based on a mass development of working class struggle, and the other half of the Party's attachment to Lenin's conception of a party based on rigid discipline; the one looking toward the replacement of Tsarist absolutism with a democratic stage of social development on the road to socialism in the vortex of Russian political, economic, and cultural backwardness; and the other determined to create a one-party state destined to evolve into a brutal, bureaucratic society under totalitarian conditions.

The Bolshevik Revolution and Trotsky's Conversion

The Tsar and the decaying monarchy were overthrown in February 1917. The story is now generally familiar in many versions, most of them true in part. Elements of the liberal bourgeoisie, the middle and the working classes, the intellectuals, and the peasantry with its soldier-sons coalesced into an irrepressible rebellion that the regime was too feeble to resist. For the first time in Russian history, the nation became a democratic political state, governed by a provisional government in which all anti-Tsarist political forces participated except the Bolshevik Party. The main forces of the provisional government were the Constitutional Democrats (also called the Cadets) and the Social Revolutionary and Menshevik parties.

The February Revolution was largely confined to the cities, especially the capitals of Petrograd and Moscow. The vast country, backward in the extreme, was in great measure untouched by the turmoil of the revolutionary outburst. But it did not have to be significantly involved because the ruling centers of the nation remained in the two capital cities (Petrograd was the winter capital), as all important and decisive events flowed to and from them.

Emigrés, men and women of wide political allegiances, who had been away from Russia for many years, now returned in vast numbers. Constitutional Democrats, Social Revolutionaries, Mensheviks, Bolsheviks, Anarchists, Bundists, unaffiliated intellectuals—every political current found its way back, certain it was going to find a new democratic haven where its members could live, work, and participate in the political life of the country under a new freedom.

Lenin and a Bolshevik emigré cadre returned in a sealed train that was permitted to pass through a war-engaged Germany by its government and military leaders; they hoped that Lenin and his staff would create enough disturbance in Russia to take it out of the war and end Germany's strife on the Eastern Front. Trotsky, Bukharin, and others came from the United States in the late spring, after they were interned by the British in a Nova Scotian prison camp. Emigré circles all over Western Europe trekked back to their home country.

Factional struggles of great intensity between the political parties were now transferred from Western Europe to Moscow and Petrograd. The new and weak provisional government was besieged by endless pressures to deal with the land question (i.e., giving land to the vast numbers of landless peasants) and, most of all, to end Russia's participation in the First World War. Tsarist Russia's role in the war had already devastated the nation and taken an extraordinary toll on the poorly organized, trained, and equipped army. The provisional government, goaded on by France and Great Britain to continue fighting a war thoroughly hated by the whole country, found its very stability and capacity to govern in danger.

Trotsky returned to Petrograd certain that he was seeing his theory of the Permanent Revolution unfolding. Under Lenin's unceasing persistence the Bolsheviks had changed its long-held view that a "democratic dictatorship of the proletariat and peasantry" (as reflected in the provisional government) was a necessary stage. Now Lenin called for the immediate establishment of a "dictatorship of the proletariat." Many believed, Trotsky most certainly included, that the Bolsheviks had adopted the essential perspective of the Permanent Revolution. The Social Revolutionaries pressed for an immediate land revolution, while the Mensheviks sought to strengthen the new democracy by bolstering the provisional government. The Social Democrats had never been farther apart.

The most important factor in this tense revolutionary situation was the Bolshevik Party, with its armed battalions held in readiness, awaiting the most favorable moment to seize power as a minority party and to rule the country on behalf of the small Russian working class. In the midst of this revolutionary situation, there occurred the sudden and bewildering transformation of the political ideology and practice by Trotsky.

Trotsky was known throughout the Russian movement and Europe as a Menshevik, if an unorthodox one. There was no doubt, however, based on the long internal history of the Russian Social Democracy, that he was anti-Bolshevik. But suddenly, in the midst of the revolutionary months of 1917, he joined the Bolshevik Party.

The Bolshevik Party gained a figure of immeasurable strength. As in 1905, Trotsky again rose to the leadership of the Petrograd Soviet and became the tribune of the opposition to the provisional government. Lenin, to whom political agreement cancelled out all previous differences and disputes, courted Trotsky, whose enormous talents as a leader and organizer of masses he most appreciated. He wanted Trotsky's aid in fighting against those in his own party who opposed dropping the traditional position of Bolshevism toward the "permanent revolution." Driven by his own theory of the revolution, convinced that Lenin was now closer to his own views, Trotsky moved to Bolshevism in an amazing and abrupt switch. Such a switch involved surrendering every fundamental idea he had of Party organization and the role of the working class that he had held for almost fifteen years.

There was a not quite visible evolution in Trotsky's shift to Bolshevism. It occurred during the war, when he participated in the Zimmerwald–Kienthal conference of antiwar socialists.[57] He wrote the main document for the conference, a statement of views that invited Lenin's critical comments. Still, one could not assume from this event that Trotsky would soon join Lenin's organization; he seemed too strongly committed to his views on the nature of a Social Democratic party. The shift, when it did come, was abrupt. He became, next to Lenin, the outstanding voice of Bolshevism—to the bewilderment of all political currents in the revolution, including the leading cadre of the Bolshevik Party. However, the intensification of the revolutionary situation, and the Bolshevik decision to seize power in the political chaos of the moment, pushed Trotsky's transformation into the background. He now became a determined advocate of Bolshevism. He fully endorsed Lenin's theory of the centralized and disciplined party, and of the one-party state. All the long battles, the severe polemics, Trotsky's theory of organization, his anti-Bolshevism, his anti-Leninism, all disappeared as though they never existed. "In one stroke," Knei-Paz has written, "the bitter controversies of fourteen years were buried; he abandoned his role of 'conciliator,' denounced the Mensheviks, and became as if a long-standing ally of Lenin."[58]

My Life: An Attempt at an Autobiography is one of Trotsky's most unsatisfying writings, and one of which he was himself highly critical. In it he distorts his own ideological history. He wrote:

> I had resisted for several years Lenin and his methods.
> Whatever I may say about it, the Second Congress was a landmark in my life, if only because it separated me from Lenin for several years.[59]

How could he explain his "several years" of separation from Lenin, a separation that stretched into fourteen years? He continued:

> My break with Lenin occurred in what might be considered "moral" or even personal grounds. But this was merely on the surface. At bottom, the separation was of a political nature and merely expressed itself in the realm of organization methods. I thought of myself as a centralist.
> But there is no doubt that at that time I did not fully realize what an intense and imperious centralism the revolutionary party would need to lead millions of people in a war against the old order.[60]

In another rationalization, he wrote, "Lenin's scheme of organization aroused certain doubts in me."[61]

Merely to recall the many things Trotsky wrote in *Our Political Tasks* and elsewhere confirms that he was evasive and inaccurate in explaining these long years of struggle with Lenin. His differences may have contained moral and personal elements—there is no doubt, for example, that he was outraged by Lenin's proposal to drop most of the original editors from *Iskra*—but the split with Lenin was essentially political and objective. Is it credible to believe that this veteran of the revolutionary process in 1905 did not realize what an "intense and imperious" centralism a Leninist-type of party needed? Lenin had made that more than clear in 1903 and in all the years afterward; and it was because he understood its bureaucratic and antidemocratic nature that Trotsky fought vigorously against what he called "bureaucratic centralism."

The Bolshevik view of the revolutionary process was not to "lead millions of people" to freedom and democracy. Trotsky understood from the beginning that Bolshevism meant the seizure of power by the Party through its own armed forces, a *putschist* or Blanquist strategy utterly contrary to the Marxism he championed. His polemic with Lenin revealed an acute perception of the Social Democratic Party and Bolshevism as Marxism's negation, an ideology that rejected and usurped the historical role of the modern proletariat envisaged by Marx and Engels. Trotsky explained away these deep differences in *My Life* with a literary flourish and an odd loss of memory.

The sudden surrender of his ideas and the acceptance of everything he had fought against for so long left him vulnerable in the Bolshevik Party once the heroic period of the Revolution had passed, the Civil War ended, and Lenin died. He could not truly adapt to a bureaucratic party in power in a period when there was less revolutionary turmoil, when the biggest concerns were with the reconstruction of the country's economy. This was so not because he could not face the "quietude" of the new stage. He was deeply involved in the problems of peace and reconstruction, and he was often in advance of the leadership with ideas and proposals to improve the state of the nation. But the Old Guard of the Party, with Lenin gone, would not tolerate this dangerous newcomer to the leadership, particularly one who fought them for so many years and was capable of assuming the place of Lenin as the leader of the new society.

Trotsky came into the Bolshevik Party in 1917 without an organization, long separated from the Mensheviks and Bolsheviks. He was alone in a party sense, and though his public acceptance and his reputation were next to Lenin's, the envious Party leadership rejected the very idea that the old enemy could or would be an equal in the stewardship of the dominant cadre. They treated him as dangerous, and they were eager to destroy him. An anti-Trotsky vendetta was hatched in 1922 when the initial conspirators against him—Stalin, Zinoviev, and Kamenev (Trotsky's brother-in-law)—made their move. Lenin was still alive but ailing. Trotsky's base in the cadre was weak; he had been a member of the Party for only five years. After Stalin broke with Zinoviev and Kamenev—and made a bloc with Bukharin, Rykov, and Tomsky in 1926—the fight against Trotsky continued more purposefully, and more publicly.

As the struggle unfolded, Trotsky was hampered psychologically. He was unable to adjust to the kind of party Lenin created, a party at once uncompromising, brutal, and destructive of people. Trotsky was to learn in a bitter way that the individual counted for nothing in the Party—as if to mock his debate with Kautsky—and that the appartus was everything.

One can say with a certain justification that Lenin reversed his long-held perspectives of the Russian Revolution and accepted in one form or another Trotsky's view of an overturn of the absolutist regime. There are those who dispute this, but their close agreement in 1917 led to their reconciliation. Trotsky suggested more than once that the abandonment of the classic Bolshevik position, expressed in the slogan of the "democratic dictatorship," made his separation from Lenin no longer of any moment. But he was not required to drastically change his conception of the revolution. That was only one side of the coin. How could Trotsky accept, without explanation or public rejection of his old position, the organizational principles of Bolshevism and Lenin's concept of the Bolshevik state power as an antidemocratic dictatorship? What we have quoted from *My Life* is no explanation at all. What he wrote over the years after 1917 was simple hero-worship of Lenin. When Lenin once said of Trotsky, during the revolutionary days of 1917, that from a certain point in time he was "the best Bolshevik," Trotsky gained some stature in the ranks of the Party. He quoted this comment of Lenin repeatedly (and with increasing pathos) to the deaf ears of Lenin's cadre, which continued to regard him as an interloper.

From the time he became united with Lenin in the insurrectionary thrust of Bolshevism (a revolt he could not have organized or led, being virtually alone and without an organization), he became a totally uncritical admirer of the man he had fought so bitterly for so long. There is no doubt that in 1917 he became infatuated with Lenin, and it would seem, too, with Bolshevism. This is one of the reasons he could never resolve the theoretical problems that rose to haunt him. "Nothing so failed him," wrote Knei-Paz, "as the Bolshevik success itself, and the *History of the Russian Revolution,* when it deals with that self-consciously, becomes an exercise in impassioned but transparent apologetics."[62]

In 1924, in memory of the great leader, he issued his book *Lenin,* made up of articles he had written in praise of the man. The book was the expression of a cultist. Years later, he made known his great dissatisfaction with the book, which read like so many other panegyrics written by lesser Party leaders for mass consumption. These writings puffed up Lenin to godlike proportions; they were followed by the placement of a mausoleum containing his body in Red Square next to the Kremlin. Near the end of his life Trotsky began a new biography of Lenin, but was only able to finish one volume on his youth, which was highly prized by several critics who read it. The eminent Edmund Wilson wrote in 1946 that "this book, had it been finished, would have been one of his most remarkable works. . . ."[63] One can venture a guess that it would have been a eulogy of Lenin.

For example, in *My Life* Trotsky recalls that at the 1903 Congress Plekhanov said to Axelrod of Lenin's role in the meeting: "Of such stuff Robespierres are made." At one time, Trotsky would not have regarded this as high praise, but in his autobiography he quotes Plekhanov *approvingly.* Part of Trotsky's transformation, more serious than the charge on the Robespierre matter, is his rude public reply to the Menshevik leader

Theodore Dan, who had lamented the Bolshevik seizure of power and destruction of the newly established but weak democracy. With the zest of a high-flying victor, Trotsky wrote:

> I replied to Dan and, in him, to the yesterday of the revolution: What has taken place is an uprising, not a conspiracy. An uprising of the masses of the people needs no justification. We have been strengthening the revolutionary energy of the workers and soldiers. We have been forging, openly, the will of the masses for an uprising. Our uprising has won. And now we are being asked to give up our victory, to come to an agreement. With whom? You are wretched, disunited individuals. You are bankrupts; your part is over. Go to the place where you belong from now on—the dust-bin of history.[64]

Had Trotsky been able to foresee his treatment by the Bolshevik leadership after Lenin's death, he would have been less arrogant in his reply to Dan. He was filled with the euphoria of victory and well aware that as an individual he contributed more than anyone else in the transfer of power to the Bolsheviks. His mean treatment of Dan contrasted sharply with Lenin's approach toward Martov, then the leader of Russian Menshevism. Lenin had not been a personal or political friend of Martov's since 1903, at which time and prior thereto they were extremely close. In the deeper recesses of his memory, he never forgot their warm association and common work in creating the Russian Social Democracy and founding *Iskra*. Martov remained in Russia after the Bolshevik victory and tried hard to cooperate with the new regime, supporting it, together with his comrades, in the Civil War. In 1920, when he no longer found it possible to function, he asked to leave Russia and was granted permission to emigrate on Lenin's order. When Lenin was dying, he remarked to his wife Krupskaya rather sadly that he heard that Martov, too, was dying.

Trotsky felt compelled to be especially harsh on his old comrades; he had the problem of proving himself (without much hope, as it came to pass) to his new comrades. At the same time, in writing of the revolutionary action of 1917, he described how Lenin's cadre failed him while he, Trotsky, was the "best Bolshevik." Even through it was true that he was most responsible for the seizure of power, and next to Lenin the most capable Party leader, he was precisely for these reasons hated by Lenin's coworkers. For when Trotsky wrote in *My Life* that "I come [to the Bolshevik party] . . . more surely and seriously than those 'disciples' who, during the Master's life, repeated his words and gestures—not always at the right moment—but, after his death, proved to be nothing but helpless epigones and unconscious tools in the hands of hostile forces," he was not only dismissing Lenin's cadre as incompetents, he was indicting Lenin's party, which failed him and the Revolution despite Lenin's fourteen years of creating, training, and educating its leaders. In *My Life,* only Lenin and Trotsky remained theoretically and politically true to their revolutionary postures.

What Lenin Wrought

Tsarism was a highly centralized power structure, monopolistic and totally despotic. Four centuries of its rule in a swamp of ecomonic, political, and social backwardness left its mark on Bolshevism, because Lenin absorbed much of his thinking from this society. His years of exile in Western Europe and England left him untouched, absorbed as he was in Russian affairs. Adam Ulan observed about Lenin that

> His deeply felt nationalism became evident during his long years of exile. He moved through Paris, London, Cracow, and other cities almost oblivious of his surroundings (except for libraries and parks) as long as they had nothing to do with politics. In his two years in Austrian Poland he failed to learn Polish, even to the point of getting the gist of a newspaper article. Yet the proximity of the two Slavic languages is so great that it is almost incredible for a Russian to spend two years in a Polish-speaking environment and not learn it. . . . [H]is very parochialism made him leave an imprint of nationalism on Bolshevism, and this set the stage for Stalin.[65]

Lenin's revision of Marxism expressed itself, as we have noted, in his view of the working class, the theory and practice of a Bolshevik cadre party, and the nature of political power. In 1920 he had written that "dictatorship is a harsh, heavy, and bloody word." But, he explained:

> The scientific concept *dictatorship* means nothing more nor less than unrestricted power, not limited by anything, not restrained by any laws, nor by any absolute rules and resting directly on force, *that and nothing else but that* is the meaning of the concept dictatorship.[66]

He went ahead in 1917 to create this kind of state. His revision of Marxism is nowhere so clearly stated than in this description of its form and character. It differed sharply from the agitational phrase "dictatorship of the proletariat," employed by Marx and Engels several times, contrasted to a "dictatorship of the bourgeoisie." Their "dictatorship" was filled with a democratic content. Charles Rappaport, a leader of French communism after the Revolution, called Lenin's ideology "Marxism with tartar sauce." In his little volume *V. I. Lenin,* Robert Conquest said of Lenin's Marxism that it was "of the early Marx," but "it was the Marxism of a backward Europe." This is borne out by a knowledge of the basic writings of Marx and Engels.

The almost accidental phrase of Marx and Engles, which did not reappear in most of their writings, saw the "dictatorship of the proletariat" as a temporary social period filled with democracy, which would be extended with time. Lenin educated his generation of Bolsheviks in an antidemocratic mold, with a hatred of freedom and individual rights. Trotsky, in his conversion, denounced democracy repeatedly and sneered at individual rights and liberties, as blatantly stated in his debate with Kautsky. No wonder t˙ at G. L. Piatakov, a young talented Party leader, a Trotskyist during the early days of the factional struggle (later executed by Stalin in the second of the Moscow Frame-Up Trials), spoke of the unobtainable goals achieved by the Party through "boundless power."

Neither Marx nor Engels wrote much, if anything, about how a Socialist state would look to an outside observor. They did not write about its organizational forms or the manner in which the economy would be conducted except in the most general way, such as when Engels described it as a democratic state, in contrast to the "dictatorship of the bourgeoisie." Lenin developed his own blueprints in creating a despotic state, and he was supported by Trotsky in his main objectives. Similar to the Tsarist monopoly of political power, Lenin's "Socialist" state reflects a monopoly of political power—but by a political party rather than a royal family. It contains the following main features:

1. A one-party dictatorship, which is the exclusive ruler of the country, makes all the important social, political, and economic decisions, and rests upon a nationwide internal police network, akin to an army, whose size is a "state secret."

2. A totalitarianism, tighter and more complete than fascism and Nazism.

3. A new class society of exploitation and oppression in which the bureaucracy rules in a Bureaucratic Collectivist system.

4. As a one-party dictatorship, it allows no other power centers. The regime is free from "outside" criticism or intervention and correction by organized groups of professionals or specialists, let alone political opponents.

5. There is no right of free speech, press, assembly, or free association. (These were later guaranteed by the Stalin Constitution, which
legalized the one-party dictatorship). None of these rights can be
tolerated by a Leninist state.

6. Only the Party press and publications are permitted to exist; those
issued outside the state or Party are by definition illegal. The possession of a mimeograph machine is a criminal act, a threat to
the security of the state.

7. The atomization of society follows from the legal and practical
organization of this society. It is further maintained by the world's
largest system of gulags, prisons, exiles, and the most perfidious
interference in the daily life of the people by the secret police;
even psychiatric hospitals become a political weapon of coercion
and punishment.

8. Purge and terror, together or separately, are an adjunct of the
system of political rule, used whenever the regime deems it necessary. (They were merely "overperfected" by Stalin.)

9. Inner-party democracy in this state is limited to the leading cadre
of the Party and its hierarchy. It has remained so under every
leadership from the day of the revolution.

10. The Leninist state is expansionist and seeks the universalization
of its forms and aims in a world divided by advanced, middle-
developed, and underdeveloped nations. (In fact, its success is almost wholly confined to underdeveloped and peasant nations, in
contradiction to the original vision of Marxism.)

11. The Leninist state is rigid and infallible. It intervenes in every phase
of life, from science and industry to education and the arts.

Changes do occur in this society, as they must in all societies, but
they occur here "within a single-centered, closed, highly centralized society
run by a power both undivided and all-embracing."[67] The people, unin-
volved in the governing process, have no role in the selection of government leaders and have nothing to say about their bunglings, misdirections,
and malfeasance in office. Nor are there any means for them to intervene
in the managerial corruption that is built into the industrial landscape.

Back in 1903–1905 Lenin, not having fully developed his views, was still able to write that "anyone who attempts to achieve socialism by any other route than that of political democracy will inevitably arrive at the most absurd and reactionary deductions, both politically and economically." In case anyone had any doubts about what he meant, he added, "Everyone is free to say and to write what he pleases without the slightest restrictions. Liberty of speech and of the press shall be complete."[68]

Boris Souvarine, one-time leader of French Communism and a biographer of Stalin, noted an example of Lenin's determination during the days of upheaval in 1917 that "the bourgeoisie had postponed the Constituent (Assembly) when the Bolsheviks demanded it, and began to demand it when the Bolsheviks suppressed it—a reversal of roles which emphasized the anachronism of an institution inherited from bourgeois revolutionary traditions in other lands and defenseless against the accomplished fact of a new 'specifically Russian system at home.' "[69] One notes that after the October seizure of power, the Bolshevik regime did finally call for elections to the Constituent Assembly but dissolved the body immediately when it turned out that the Bolsheviks, even after they became the new rulers, ran badly behind the Social Revolutionaries and Mensheviks. The victorious opposition did not have arms to enforce their electoral victory. Lenin never again experimented with a democratic form or institution.

Suppression of the two parties increased despite Lenin's public statement that "now that the insurrection is over *we have no intention whatever of suppressing the journals of other Socialist parties* except in the case of incitement to armed rebellion or sedition." Was he mocking the Mensheviks and Social Revolutionaries, or was he in an ambivalent stage of feeling his way to total power? A press decree drawn up by him assured that "immediately after the new order is consolidated, all administrative pressure on the press will be at an end. Complete liberty of the press will be established on the principle of legal responsibility on the widest and most advanced principles."[70] But even as the regime was "consolidated," becoming more powerful with the defeat of the counterrevolution, the "widest and most advanced principles" of a free press, or even a limited one, were unknown in the Soviet Union.

The unwillingness of Lenin's dictatorship to grant the right of a press to the Social Revolutionaries and Mensheviks held, even though in these years both opposition parties worked loyally with the government and fought side by side with the Bolsheviks against the White armies. When Trotsky wrote that "every group of citizens should possess its own printing press and materials," he was deceiving the people as well as himself—for it was utopian to think that the Bolsheviks would permit an opposition to exist legally.[71] Lenin set the standard of suppression from the very beginning. When Justice Kursky was at work codifying internal laws, Lenin wrote him:

> The court should not eliminate terror. To promise that would be either to deceive oneself or to deceive others, but should give it a foundation and a legalization in principle, clearly, without falsification, and without embellishment.[72]

The exclusive political power of the Party was inviolate. In this new type of state, the Party's power was permanent and made legal, thus emphasizing the myth of "Soviet Democracy." The Party ruled on the principle of unshared power; it could not tolerate the existence of any other political organization, for the very existence of such contained the possibility of organized opposition. Trotsky, in his hard-hitting critique of the Soviet Union in 1936, *The Revolution Betrayed,* was dealing in fantasy and self-deception when he wrote:

> The opposition parties were forbidden one after the other. This measure, obviously in conflict with the spirit of Soviet democracy, the leaders of Bolshevism regarded not as a principle, but as an episodic act of self-defense.[73]

An "episodic act" against whom—an annihilated, dispersed, and totally disorganized bourgeoisie? Or against the Social Revolutionaries and Mensheviks, who joined in the defense of the new state and were no threat, having been completely disarmed? Trotsky could not but know that the "episodic act" was a permanent feature at the time he wrote his book almost twenty years later. On the seventieth anniversary of the Soviet Union, the "episodic" act still continued, though Russia was the second strongest military power in the world.

Self-deception pervaded Trotsky's attitude not only toward the Leninist state, but also toward the Leninist party, for he wrote in the same discussion in his book that "the forbidding of factions was again regarded as an exceptional measure to be abandoned at the first serious improvement in the situation."[74]

There is no doubt there has been a steady improvement from a peasant nation to a noteworthy industrialization, but there was never consideration given to removing both prohibitions, for that was contradictory to the essence of Bolshevism. Stalin dealt with the problem in the mid-thirties when he announced the completion of socialism by the vast purges and the show trials—carnivals of murder.

None of this should have surprised Trotsky. He had forecast all of it in his debates with Lenin. The wonder is that he could forget it all, even as he wrote:

> The prohibition of oppositional parties brought after it the prohibition of factions. The prohibition of factions ended in a prohibition to think otherwise than the infallible leaders. The police-manufactured monolithism of the party resulted in a bureaucratic impunity which has become the source of all kinds of wantonness and corruption.[75]

These prohibitions did not end that way; *they began that way,* for that was the purpose of the prohibitions. The prohibition of oppositional parties came at the very beginning of the Bolshevik power and the abolition of factions in the Party at the Tenth Congress in 1920. It is in the nature of this one-party state to prohibit any form of independent expression as a preventive measure. This is done with enormous power and brutality whether dealing with a strong rebellion like that of the Kronstadt sailors, the weak, dispersed, and incarcerated Refuseniks, or the divided and physically beaten dissidents.

*   *   *

After the Bolsheviks seized power, Karl Kautsky wrote his *Terrorism and Communism* as a critique of Bolshevism. He argued that socialism could not be realized anywhere except as a democratic change; it could never be activated by a party *putsch*. If the movement did not have the support of the majority of the people, argued Kautsky, then Socialists would have to wait, since they had no right to impose their rule on an opposing people. The Bolsheviks made a *putsch* just as Trotsky said they would many years before. The *putsch* violated the traditions of Social Democracy, he wrote.

Lenin tried to meet such arguments:

> Marxism teaches us that only the political party of the working class, i.e., the Communist Party, is capable of uniting, educating, and organizing such a vanguard of the proletariat and of the working masses as is capable of resisting inevitable petty-bourgeois waverings of these masses [and] their trade union prejudices.[76]

But Marxism doesn't teach anything of the kind. This is a Marxism totally revised by Lenin to fit the Russia he now ruled.

In *Terrorism and Communism* Trotsky wrote a mocking reply to

Kautsky: "The rights of the individual were irrelevant nonsense. Moreover, we were never concerned with the Kantian priestly and vegetarian-Quaker prattle about the 'sacredness' of human life." Like Lenin, Trotsky asserted that "the dictatorship of the Soviets became possible only by means of the dictatorship of the Party."[77] By 1936, in his *The Revolution Betrayed,* Trotsky acknowledged that it was a myth that the nation was ruled by the "dictatorhip of the Soviets." By then, too, he found it necessary to write, "The regime had become 'totalitarian' in character several years before the word arrived from Germany."[78]

In the revolutionary days of 1917, he was still revelling in his assault on Kautsky, and in reply to the question, "How do you know your party is right and represents the historical interests of the working class?", he replied in one of his most wretched observations: "We have suppressed the Mensheviks and SR's [Social Revolutionaries] and they have disappeared. This criterion is sufficient for us."[79]

Hardly an "episodic act" of self-defense, but a sufficient criterion for the period from 1917 to 1920 became for Stalin a justified premise for wiping out all opposition groups. Their disappearance proved that he was right!

Schapiro has said that by 1921 Lenin could have buried past differences "and attempt to build up Russia on the basis of cooperation and legal order and not the dictatorship of an unpopular minority. He chose total suppression of the Mensheviks and Social Revolutionaries."[80] And Trotsky, who had warned of this kind of Bolshevik dictatorship and its inevitablity, now became a leading part of it. Conditions had become so severe that Maxim Gorky, a one-time "Left Bolshevik" and personal friend of Lenin, wrote with alarm in the journal *Novaya Zhizn:*

> Lenin, Trotsky, and their disciples are already intoxicated with the poison of power, as is proved by their shameful attitude toward liberty of speech, personal freedom, and all the rights for which Democracy has fought. . . . How does Lenin's conduct with regard to the freedom of speech differ from that of Stolypin, Plehve, and other caricatures of humanity? Does not Lenin send to jail all those who do not think as he does, just as the Romanovs did?[80]

This one-time defender of Lenin described the Bolsheviks as "blind fanatics," "conscienceless adventurers," and spoke of Lenin's "anarchism on the Nechayev and Bakunin level." The Bolsheviks, wrote Gorky, "think they have license to commit every crime."[81]

There is a striking parallel between the early views of Trotsky and

Rosa Luxemburg relating to the October Revolution. From her prison cell in Germany she admonished Lenin in this way:

> Freedom for the supporters of the government alone, freedom only for the members of one party—that is no freedom at all. . . . All that is instructive, wholesome, and purifying in political freedom depends on this essential characteristic. . . . With the repression of political life in the land as a whole, life in the Soviets must also become more and more crippled. Without general elections, without unrestricted freedom of the press and assembly, without a free struggle of opinion, life will die out in every public institution. . . . Public life gradually falls asleep. A few dozen leaders . . . direct and rule. . . . An elite of the working class is invited from time to time to meetings where they are to applaud the speeches of the leaders and approve resolutions unanimously . . . not the dictatorship of the proletariat but a handful of politicians, a clique. . . . Such conditions must inevitably cause a brutalization of public life: attempted assassinations, shooting of hostages, etc.[82]

The only error in this observation is that the assassinations and shooting of hostages were carried out by the regime itself, as it brutalized life in the Soviet Union. Luxemburg herself did not live to see her prophecies realized. But Trotsky did.

The Stalin Era

The rise of Stalin to power in the Party and the state did not come as an abrupt break from the Leninist period but as a continuity. Stalin's rule was not a revision of Leninism in the same sense that Lenin's was from Marxism. As a paranoid seeking to create his personal dictatorship over the country, he believed he was a leader in the image of Lenin—nay, greater than Lenin, for he was the total leader beholden to no one, not to the governing state, not to the Bolshevik Party and its leading Political Committee. The center of power in this dictatorship was embodied, unshared, in him.

To achieve this goal, he determined to physically destroy all rivals, or those he believed to be such, not only to ensure his power, but to place him in the forefront of the historical revolutionary pantheon. He thereupon unleashed history's longest and greatest purge and terror, taking a toll of almost twenty million people, including the entire remaining generation that made the October Revolution. Yet in all the years of his reign, he never changed a single principle of state and Party organization as enunciated by Lenin, nor brought back capitalism to Russia as predicted by Trotsky; he *did* drive the nation with unprecedented brutality to become the military equal of the West over the bodies of his fellow Russians.

The Stalin epoch was the most vulgar period of Soviet political leadership. He was himself a vulgar person, of low development culturally, filled with intense hatreds, envious of those of greater intellectual talents and accomplishments, those who could write and speak with competence and authority. His own authority lay in his power over the Party cadre he created during his secretaryship of the Party and in the immense bureaucracy to which he catered.

Roy Medvedev, Russia's revisionist historian, who has done valuable research in the Stalin period and written important works on the nature of the Leninist and Stalinist periods of the country's history, speaks of Stalin's excesses. Excesses are not a system, writes Medvedev, but an extension of or degeneration of a system. The system itself, Medvedev admits, was created by Lenin. Because of his own infatuation with Lenin, embalmed and laid out so that all may come and look upon the deified founder of the Bolshevik society, Medvedev believes the country could have evolved in a different direction. No doubt under Lenin the details of the national development would have been altered in many ways. So would they if Trotsky had taken over the leadership of the Party and state. But the basic forms of the society, the one-party state, the dominance of the Bolshevik Party, the suppression of any and all other political parties and organizations would not have been altered, and there would not have been universal freedom of speech, press, or assembly. Medvedev turned to Stephen S. Cohen's essay "Bolshevism and Stalinism" for support, but the same difficulties exist for Cohen as they do for Medvedev, as we will soon observe.

In discussing the distinctions between Bolshevism and Stalinism, Medvedev writes:

> These historians [who see no distinctions] fail to see that there was a critical difference between the two authoritarian regimes that existed in Soviet Russia before 1929. Although there were many signs of Authoritarianism before 1929, it was only in this year and afterwards that authoritarian rule was characterized by the highest degree of extremism. . . . Khrushchev's years were frequently referred to . . . as "Stalinism without the terror and excesses." But these excesses were precisely what constituted the essence of Stalinism, and this is what has to be explained.[83]

Undoubtedly, the personalities of different rulers or leaders in a given society, government, and political party exert their leaderships in different ways under the same set of principles. Therefore one has to look in the direction of the basic principles to see if the differences go to the heart of the system or systems, or if they are merely secondary or cosmetic. If Stalin is measured by the facts of history, the differences seen by Medvedev tend to fade. Less than a page after he emphasizes how different the new society would have been under Lenin, he writes:

> Of course, many features of authoritarian rule developed by Stalin first appeared under Lenin and in some cases he played a direct role in introducing them. The one-party system, restrictions on democracy and democratic practices and discussion within the Party are all obvious examples. But these are by no means inherent features of Leninism.[84]

Medvedev's unresolved difficulty is that he is simply wrong to write that these "restrictions" were not "inherent features" of Leninism. We have cited enough from Lenin's writings to show that his antidemocratic acts were not confined to the insurrectionary period, or from 1918–1920, but extended over the years of his leadership. The question is not whether Stalin made Lenin appear soft-hearted and weak, but whether the Georgian killer changed a single attribute of the Leninist state or the Leninist party. Did he carry out his "excesses" and entire program within and through the basic Leninist structure? On that question there can be no doubt: He changed nothing in principle.

"The one-party system was not," writes Medvedev, "established without the participation of Lenin, and the same may be said of his limitations of freedom of speech and the press. . . ."[85] Isn't this the heart of the matter? These characteristics were deeply rooted in the long history of Bolshevism. In its primitive disciple, Stalin, it took forms more extreme, brutal, and inhumane, because he was as a personality more determined in his quest for personal dictatorship. He lacked Lenin's intelligence, theoretical and political achievements, or respect for fellow leaders. He was the ultimate and supreme destroyer in Bolshevism. This, too, reflected the centuries-old Russian traditions of harsh autocracy.

*   *   *

In 1922 Lenin ordered the closing of the journal *Ekonomist* and the deportation of its leading contributors. In the same year, the editor of *Golos Minuvskego (Voice of the Past)*, Sergei Mulgunov, was expelled from the country, along with a group of contributors, and the paper closed down. The Petrograd *Mysl (Thought)* was shut down in 1922 and its contributors exiled, among whom were the philosophers Nicola Berdayev, Lev Shestov, N. O. Lossky, and Semon Frank.

Medvedev acknowledged that Stalin continued the policy Lenin initiated with a long list of his own. We note his suppressions: *Novaya Rossia,* closed in 1926; *Byloe (The Past)* in 1927, after having been issued for twenty-seven years. Also suppressed: *Russki Sovremennick, Movaya Epoka, Volnaya Zhihn, Slova O Istiny, Vestruk Literaturii;* and the almanacs *Krug, Kovsk,* and *Zhizn Iskusstva.* "By 1929," says Medvedev, "there was not a single nonparty publication left nor any private publishing house that could have served as vehicles for opposition views."[86] Or on any other subject, he could have added.

Tsarist authoritarianism was a milder form of dictatorship than the Leninist type, if indeed one can make such a comparison between two evils. The Tsarist type was less complete, not nearly as tightly closed as the Bolshevik state. Between the years 1866 and 1917, for example, Tsarism officially arrested 183,949 people and executed 14,000. Siberian exile, severely condemned in the Western world, saw the victims living under unquestionable difficulties, but many were able to read, write, hold classes, and maintain a measure of relationships with other exiles. Others married in exile. It was easier to escape, too, as many (including Trotsky) did.

Official Soviet figures show that in the twenty years of the Stalin regime there were 8,877,430 arrests. Executions ran into the tens of thousands; deaths in the purges, deportations of whole populations, and famines took the lives of many millions. Exile in Soviet society was for the most part a brutal experience; it consisted of intense exploitation, incessant beatings (especially of Party members), and near starvation. Camp directors in the *gulag* were trained to make life intolerable for all inmates, and most of all for political prisoners, former Party leaders, and cadre people. Often common criminals ruled the camps, incited by KGB officials to be especially cruel to the politicals.

Robert Conquest's *The Great Terror* is a compendium of the brutal society of Soviet communism, and it is shocking in its detailing of the many forms that the terror took. Latter-day spokesmen for the rulers of Russia, many with full knowledge of the facts of Conquest's study, may acknowledge all or part of it, but they explain it away as "mistakes" of individual Party leaders who "erred." There is nothing wrong with the system itself, they argue, only with certain leaders who wrongly "interpreted" the principles. All the General Secretaries from Brezhnev to Gorbachev speak in praise of Stalin, criticize his "mistakes," and cover themselves with excessive praise of Lenin, the father of them all. And Stalin is great: He saved the country because he defeated Trotsky. (Indeed, this was a major theme in Gorbachev's speech on the seventieth anniversary of the founding of the Soviet Union.) There is nothing wrong with the system, even though it has a built-in mechanism for repeating the experiences of the twenties and thirties, even employing something new: the use of psychiatry and psychiatric hospitals as political weapons against critics and dissidents.

Lenin called for the removal of Stalin as General Secretary because he feared that personal relationships between the members of the Politburo might split the ruling party and endanger the new regime. He had become worried about Stalin's cruelty and tremendous power in the Party created through a system of appointment of officials who were loyal only to their sponsor. Of overriding significance in this recommendation to the leadership is that Lenin's party refused to honor their leader's "will" or "testament." Stalin remained, but all his contemporary leaders whom he feared as rivals disappeared, destroyed physically at his direction.

The General Secretaries since Stalin, men of disparate personalities and abilities, trained in the Stalinist school of falsification, did not tamper with the one-party state which nurtured them. Khrushchev may have startled the main cadre of the Party with his revelations at the Twentieth Congress, but the leading staff already knew all or part of the story of Stalin's reign, and together they all agreed to keep the report hidden from the Russian people.

The latest General Secretary, Mikhail Gorbachev, faced with a stagnant, unproductive economy, and trying to loosen the grip of a stultified conservative bureaucracy, now demands accountability from the managers of industry and agriculture. But his Glasnost and Perestroika meet iron resistance from managers who are defending their special privileges, revenues, and status in the society. However their conflict may develop or be resolved, in no way do Glasnost and Perestroika threaten the basic one-party structure of this totalitarian society.

Gorbachev says that "democratization and nothing but democratization" will help to realize his program and help the nation emerge from the economic doldrums it has suffered for so long. His call for democratization has gone further than Trotsky's well-known demands for reestablishment of Party democracy during the long struggles of 1924–1927. John Dewey, months after he chaired the Commission of Inquiry to take Trotsky's depositions in Mexico, noted in an interview with Agnes E. Meyer in the *Washington Post* of December 19, 1937:

If Trotsky had remained in power, he might have attempted to retain more democracy within the Party itself. But he had never faced the question whether democracy within the Party can be maintained when there is complete suppression of democracy outside of the Party. The idea of democracy is an exacting matter. The limitation of it to a small group invokes such a contradiction that in the end democracy even within the Party is bound to be destroyed.[87]

After Gorbachev's pronouncements about a new democratization, Boris Yeltsin, once a vigorous Gorbachev supporter and the leader of the Moscow Party, sharply criticized the slow pace of the General Secretary's reform program; he was removed from his important political and organizational post and reassigned to a minor activity. The struggle within the leadership over how far to allow criticism of Party history and current Party programs, especially criticism of the staff, the cadre, and the managerial system, is severe. The winds of change in the leadership varies; how it will end is difficult to say. (Yeltsin made a comeback in the elections to the new parliament running as an independent, hinting at varying democratic possibilities if the openness Gorbachev advocates continues.)

David R. Shipler, an acute observer of the Russian scene who wrote an excellent book on the country, *Russia: Broken Idols, Solemn Dreams,* as recently as May 1988 said, "Democracy is a truly alien culture here." The "secret ballot [is] unsavory." He added, "M. Gorbachev presented a sketchy set of ideas, which bear a scant resemblance to Western concepts."[88] Democracy is the heart of the problem for this society, the more so that the culture is antidemocratic. Weighed down by centuries of authoritarian traditions, ruled from above under both Tsarism and Bolshevism, accustomed to taking orders, to be told what they could or could not do, unaccustomed to free and independent action in all aspects of social life, the Russian people seem paralyzed by the conflict between Gorbachev and his Party supporters and the old-line leaders and cadre. The people are fearful of the democratic critics, advocates of human rights, those who demand the freedoms of emigration, speech, assembly, and organization.

Whatever openings were made by Gorbachev to win support for his program, they brought into existence the widespread opposition of ordinary citizens who consider people who make demands "trouble-makers." There has even come into the open organized groups of anti-Semites, who are now distributing the forgery known as the *Protocols of Zion*—in the self-proclaimed Union of Socialist Soviet Republics! This anti-Semitism is nurtured in the leadership, in its stubborn resistance to the right of emigration, which is thus far the demand mainly of Jews, as well as in the elimination of Jews from leadership of the Party.

The symbolism of victory over Nazi Germany, impossible without the material aid of the Allies combined with Hitler's two-front war, covers a multitude of dissatisfactions: Ceremonies and statues take the place of meat; the ballet is a substitute for shoes, clothing, and even potatoes. After seventy years, the Soviet Union remains technologically backward. Aside from the modern and extensive military production and organization, Russia is economically a second-class country. It lacks the new high technology of the West and Japan.

The paucity of consumer goods depresses the living standard of the Russian people. Housing is lacking, and what is available is of poor quality. There is grinding poverty in the villages, and rural housing is deplorable. These ramshackle huts lack hot water, as do the village hospitals. Hospitals in general lack surgical tools, operating and examining gloves, and disinfectants. The quality of their manufactured goods, according to Russian specialists, is only 8 to 18 percent that of world standards. There is still no widespread network of roads to connect cities to towns and villages. The mass production of automobiles is hence a fruitless objective.

Tourists who visit the two main cities of Moscow and Leningrad never see the real Russia. They see the Kremlin, St. Basil's Cathedral, and Lenin's tomb, but they rarely see behind this facade. Charles T. Powers, writing for the *Los Angeles Times* in the Spring of 1989, makes the point that the tourist "never sees the city where it seems impossible to find an unwarped window glass, or concrete that doesn't crumble, or a locally made elevator that doesn't seem as though it were fashioned from old packing crates slapped over with cheap formica. . . . One of the greatest surprises for a first-time visitor to Moscow is the general shabbiness of a city that is a superpower capital, for the very term superpower suggests at least some minimum standard of efficiency and maintenance. . . ."

Powers says the buildings where Muscovites live are in unbelievable disrepair. And long queues are everywhere. "The people are docile. They will stand in lines, sometimes for hours, for the most mundane of consumer products—shoes, ice cream cones, canned fruit, wallpaper. . . . Customers wait in line just to buy two kinds of processed meat, something like the product Americans call baloney. People wait in line for hours for the most simple needs and are forced to deal with rude, indifferent, and discourteous clerks." Is it any wonder that under these conditions the black market flourishes?

The question pushed forward by the situation of the Soviet Union (and China) is the nature of the Revolution based on backwardness, poor economic and cultural development, and the Leninist doctrine of a plebian dictatorship transformed into a totalitarian society. In such a country there is less socialism than in the welfare states of the West. Neither a utopian socialism nor the "scientific socialism" of Marx and Engels exists in the Soviet Union. The Soviet Union represents a new type of society of exploitation, and the bureaucracy is a new ruling class in a land of collectivized or nationalized productive property. Hardly anyone today truly believes that the Soviet Union and China are classless societies pointing to the future of mankind.

The Leninist system has been extended only to backward, peasant countries where the regimes created, one-party dictatorships, are in the image of their Russian model, with "local" variations. It does not matter whether we look at Albania, Vietnam, Cuba, or Ethiopia—the regimes are brutal, the prisons are full, and the economies are close to collapse. In Ethiopia starvation is used, as under Stalin, as a political weapon of an extraordinarily brutal ruling party. If the evolving one-party regime has not yet been completed by the Sandinistas' boss, Ortega, the economy has already been put into crisis by the sheer incompetence of the new rulers. Will they be influenced by the Gorbachev reforms? They have shown no signs of it; they are closer to the Stalin period of rule than to the regime of the seventieth anniversary.

The next stage of Soviet society obviously depends on the direction the Gorbachev phenomenon takes. If the democratization he calls for is confined to the Party leadership and cadre, it will have little meaning. If there is not a complete revision of Russian political history, which is currently based on a complete falsification of every event in Party and government history since 1924, there cannot be an honest turn in the direction of the country. The rehabilitation of Bukharin and the defendants in his trial, campaigned for by Stephen F. Cohen, his biographer, is of secondary importance, so long as the most important Party leader in the fight against Stalin, Leon Trotsky, continues to stand officially condemned by the Soviet state and Communist party. In praising Stalin for defeating Trotsky, and defending Bukharin for helping Stalin achieve that same objective, Gorbachev has followed a long tradition of all the General Secretaries since the Georgian dictator. And while Professor Cohen denied that history is the issue, Gorbachev *made* it so by stating in his anniversary speech that a commission had been set up by the leadership to reexamine the history of Stalin's reign and the post-Stalin era, to seek the truth of that long history, because what history consisted of in all those years were lies or distortions of the truth.

There is no doubt that Gorbachev has shaken up the bureaucracy in his effort to turn the economic course of the country around. Gorbachev has responded to the clear failures of the economy and realizes that the country has reached a point of danger that could lead to the nation's decline. Can he make the necessary changes? That is far from decided. The situation in the Soviet Union is extremely fluid. Gorbachev has marked out new directions in order to save a nation in deep crisis. These new directions have only just begun to develop, but the bureaucracy is strongly resistant to them. While this openness has resulted in a number of democratic reforms—reforms by Leninist standards, anyway—economic progress has been very limited.

Gorbachev has created a situation that, if successful, will be irreversible. But an alliance of the bureaucracy, the secret police, and the military could destroy it all. The pressure the present Soviet leader is now exerting on his country's system of government could result, ironically, in a more militant, Fascist, and anti-Semitic regime. Meanwhile, taking advantage of the "new freedom," historians, writers, and intellectuals are engaged in a vigorous reexamination of the nation's past. The lies of official history are revealed more and more each day. Stalin is pilloried for his role as the director of the most malevolent period in Russian history. Not even Lenin is left untouched in this enlightening revision of history. Trotsky is spoken of more softly, and his role as a founder of the Soviet state is being accorded recognition at last.

Notes

1. The Jewish Labor Bund was the leading force in the creation of the Party at the founding conference. With the technical assistance of the Bund group in Kiev, this unrepresentative congress, with delegates from only three cities (Kiev, Moscow, and St. Petersburg) and some from the Union for the Liberation of Labor, constituted the first formal organization of Russian Social Democracy. The Bund was not only responsible for this first gathering, it made up the bulk of the membership.

2. Quoted by Theodore Dan in his *Origins of Bolshevism,* p. 238.

3. *My Life,* pp. 124–125.

4. *My Life,* pp. 126–127.

5. Robert Wistrich, *Trotsky: Fate of a Revolutionary,* p. 25.

6. *My Life,* pp. 152–157, and Joel Carmichael, *Trotsky: An Appreciation of His Life,* pp. 73–75.

7. V. I. Lenin, *Selected Works.* Vol. 1, *A Protest by Russian Social Democrats,* pp. 520 and 526.

8. Bertram D. Wolfe, *Revolution and Reality,* pp. 137–138.

9. Leonard Schapiro, *The Communist Party of the Soviet Union,* p. 53.

10. A detailed discussion of disputes at the Second Congress appears in Schapiro's *The Communist Party;* Dan, *Origins;* Knei-Paz, *Social and Political Thought; My Life;* and Lenin, *Selected Works,* Vols. I through IV.

11. *Letters of Marx and Engels,* edited by Saul Padover, p. 376.

12. Friedrich Engels, "Principles of Communism," in *The Communist Manifesto,* p. 330.

13. Karl Marx and Friedrich Engels, *Communist Manifesto,* pp. 218–219.

14. See Schapiro, especially Chapter 2.

15. Lenin, *Selected Works,* Vol. 2 (1904), p. 408.

16. Dan, p. 251.

17. Schapiro, p. 61.

18. *My Life,* p. 99.

19. Tkachev's *Collected Works,* quoted in Ulam, *The Bolsheviks,* p. 83.

20. Albert L. Weeks, *The First Bolshevik: A Political Biography of Peter Tkachev,* p. 5.

21. Tkachev quoted in Weeks, p. 51.

22. Trotsky, *Portraits, Political and Personal,* p. 37.

23. Marx and Engels, *Communist Manifesto,* p. 52.

24. J. Martov, quoted by Dan, p. 245.

25. Quoted in Dan, p. 245.

26. Lenin, *Selected Works,* Vol. 2, pp. 447–448.

27. Lenin, *Selected Works,* "The Iskra Period," pp. 114–115.

28. Volumes I and II of Lenin's *Selected Works* contain many of his polemics in the still unified Party and also reveal his total devotion to the problems of organization.

By *Blanquism* we mean the theory of revolution through an insurrection carried out by a small conspiratorial group. Marx and Engels were vigorous opponents of Blanqui. Trotsky never shared Lenin's sympathies for Blanquism and its theorist. Knei-Paz notes: "It should be emphasized that when Trotsky spoke of this nucleus or 'revolutionary army' he did not mean a party of professional revolutionaries but workers themselves, albeit the 'cream,' so to speak, of the proletariat" (p. 126).

Rosa Luxemburg said that Lenin's view of revolution effected "a mechanical transfer of the organizational principles of the Blanquist movement of conspirators into the Social Democratic movement of masses of the workers." (As quoted by F. L. Carsten in "Freedom and Revolution," in *Revisionism,* edited by Leo Labedz, p. 61.)

In short, Blanquism is another form of the *putsch.* It is the opposite of the open mass movement and mass action advocated by Social Democracy, and observed in the Philippines and China, one leading to the overthrow of the corrupt Marcos regime, the other drowned in blood by a heavily armed Communist government.

29. Robert Conquest, *V. I. Lenin,* p. 20.

30. Quoted in Knei-Paz's *Social and Political Thought,* pp. 180–183.

31. Deutscher, *The Prophet Armed,* p. 45.

32. Knei-Paz, p. 193.

33. Knei-Paz, p. 189.

34. Knei-Paz, p. 190.

35. Knei-Paz, p. 192.

36. Knei-Paz, pp. 184–185.

37. Lenin, *Selected Works*, Vol. II, p. 433.

38. Lenin, *Selected Works*, Vol. III, p. 499.

39. Lenin, *Collected Works*, "The Iskra Period," p. 122.

40. Lenin, *Collected Works*, "The Iskra Period," p. 123.

41. Karl Kautsky, *Neue Zeit*, 1901–1902.

42. *Our Political Tasks*, p. 50.

43. *The Letters of Marx and Engels*, p. 25.

44. Engels, *Letters*, p. 486.

45. *Our Political Tasks*, p. 102.

46. *Our Political Tasks*, p. 90.

47. Wistrich, p. 29.

48. Schapiro, p. 36.

49. *My Life*, Chapter 14.

50. *My Life*, p. 190.

51. A. V. Lunacharsky, *Silhouettes*, quoted in *My Life*, p. 185.

52. *My Life*, p. 200.

53. Schapiro, p. 85.

54. Lenin put the figure at 360,000 rubles. *Collected Works*, Vol. XII, p. 566.

55. Although the Bolsheviks later themselves participated in Duma elections, it was not until 1920 that Lenin admitted they were wrong to do so.

56. Luxemburg, *Russian Revolution and Marxism and Leninism?*

57. *The Zimmerward-Kienthal conference was made up of antiwar, left-wing European groups that met in Switzerland in September 1915 and April 1916. Trotsky wrote the conference's manifesto, ending it with the words, "Workers of All Countries Unite!"—a direct appeal for a revolutionary end to the war.*

58. *Knei-Paz*, p. 225.

59. *My Life*, p. 164.

60. *My Life*, p. 162.

61. *My Life*, p. 157.

62. Knei-Paz, p. 510.

63. Knei-Paz echoed Wilson's view by saying that "*The Young Lenin*, the first installment of what was to be a full-scale biography but which never materialized beyond this single volume . . . is a work on a grand scale, [with] all those elements characteristic of the Trotsky style and of Trotsky's dramatic sweep—so conspicuously absent from the 1924 biographical sketches. . . ," p. 524.

64. *My Life*, p. 328. There were several versions of this statement. Robert Wistrich quotes Trotsky differently, perhaps due to a translation from a European edition of *My Life*. He has Trotsky making the statement to Julius Martov, who spoke for the Left Mensheviks. (Wistrich, p. 88.) Isaac Deutscher also wrote in *The Prophet Armed*, p. 313–314, that it was made to Martov. His authorities are the important historian of the Russian Revolution, N. Sukharov, and possibly John Reed. Knei-Paz, too, writes that the statement was made to Martov (p. 509).

We know that Trotsky wrote *My Life* immediately after his deportation to Turkey on the basis of memory and the limited archives he had at the time. It is difficult to say what is true without a further search into archives, but Trotsky's writings reveal a sharp memory of events. I think it's safe to accept his statement for the time being.

65. Adam Ulam, *The Bolsheviks,* p. 210.

66. B. D. Wolfe, *Revolution and Reality,* p. 312.

67. Robert Conquest, *V. I. Lenin,* p. 33.

68. Quoted in Schapiro, p. 78

69. Boris Souvarine, *Stalin,* p. 211.

70. Quoted in Schapiro, p. 33.

71. *The Revolution Betrayed,* p. 96.

72. *Revolution and Reality,* p. 293.

73. *The Revolution Betrayed,* p. 96.

74. *The Revolution Betrayed,* p. 96.

75. *The Revolution Betrayed,* p. 100.

76. Lenin's Trade Union Resolution of the Tenth Party Congress, directed against the Workers' Opposition.

77. Trotsky, *Terrorism and Communism: A Reply to Karl Kautsky,* p. 60.

78. *The Revolution Betrayed,* p. 100.

79. *Terroism and Communism,* p. 106.

80. Schapiro, pp. 193–94.

81. Quoted in Boris Souvarine, *Stalin,* pp. 195–196.

82. Rosa Luxemburg, *The Future of the Soviet System,* pp. 312–313.

83. Roy Medvedev, *On Stalin and Stalinism,* p. 196.

84. Medvedev, p. 187.

85. Medvedev, p. 186.

86. Medvedev, p. 187.

87. Quoted in "Interview with John Dewey," *Washington Post,* December 19, 1937.

88. Shipler, *New York Times Magazine,* May 8, 1988.

"The Party Is Always Right"

The leadership of the Petrograd Soviet in 1917 fell to Trotsky just as it had in 1905—the consequence of his sheer energy, skill, and eloquence. By 1917, however, the Bolshevik Party was no longer isolated—it was the most active and politically organized force in Petrograd and Moscow. What it lacked in elected representatives to the Soviets it made up for with its own armed battalions.

Lenin arrived in Russia in April in the midst of the Seventh Party conference, which had adopted a policy of support for the provisional government because the "bourgeois democratic revolution" was not yet completed. This was the policy of the interim Party leadership under Stalin and Kamenev. Lenin was enraged and proceeded to use his immense authority to revise the just-adopted policy. He forced the leadership to accept his "April Theses," which advocated that the Party seize political power by force. There were some in the leadership who accused Lenin of "Trotskyism," and they fought hard to prevent the adoption of the new policy.

A month later Trotsky arrived in Petrograd, quickly rose to the leadership of that Soviet and, with the adoption of the April Theses, drew close to the Party, so close that he wrote many of the Bolshevik documents. He knew from the April Theses that the Party had revised its main perspective under Lenin's pressure. Two eminent Party leaders led the organization to support the provisional government in the belief they were carrying out Party policy. Trotsky's opposing perspective now seemed to him almost identical to Lenin's Theses, and he felt himself, in the heat of the revolutionary conflict in the two capitals, now to be an advocate of Lenin's policy. The Bolsheviks were disoriented and unable to mold themselves to what Lenin and Trotsky believed to be new conditions and requirements of the Party.

As was always true in this kind of party, the membership was not involved in this fundamental policy change. Under Bolshevik principles, there was no need even to consult the membership. Nor did the membership expect to be consulted in those unsettling revolutionary days. Lenin's view became the Party's.

Trotsky responded to Lenin's invitation to join the Bolshevik Party in a sudden, climactic change, as I have said, which left all revolutionary sectors in Moscow and Petrograd stunned. In joining the Party he fought for so long, he finally had the organizational means of testing his theory of revolution. He joined the Party at the top, as a member of the Central Committee and, almost immediately, its Political Committee. The combination of his powerful intellectual gifts and his new alliance with Lenin made him a formidable figure in the Party. Edward Hallett Carr comments on this very subject:

> Lenin had planned and directed the main strategy [of the October Revolution,] but it was Trotsky who actually organized the revolutionary coup. It was Trotsky who created and led the Red Army, which was victorious in the Civil War and which beat off the Allied internvention.[1]

Lenin, Trotsky, and the Bolsheviks were incalculably aided by the blunders of the Kerensky government, chief of which was keeping the country in the destructive and fruitless war with Germany that the whole nation hated. Now, in the heat of the revolutionary upsurge, the idea of joining the Bolshevik Party was no longer an absurdity to Trotsky, as it was when Lenin first made the proposal after 1905. He was now highly pleased to be asked to join the Party and serve on its Central Committee precisely at a time when events pointed to a coming political upheaval. His role in the Party kept growing, as did his popularity with the masses, and he was never more pleased when in the course of the many-sided strifes of 1917, Lenin said that he—Leon Trotsky—was "the best Bolshevik."

As long as Lenin lived, Trotsky's role in the Party and the new state was secure. He was a leading member of the Party's Political Committee, head of the military affairs of the country, and commander of the Red Army; he also became one of the Party's five delegates to the Executive Committee of the newly formed Communist International, a position he held through the first five congresses of the new world body. Yet, when Lenin became fatally ill and incapacitated, unable to exercise his leadership, two of his subordinates, Gregory Zinoviev and Joseph Stalin, began scheming to replace him. Zinoviev was president of the Communist International, head of the Leningrad Party, and a long-time associate of Lenin. Stalin had become the General Secretary of the Party, head of the Secretariat and Organizational Department, which was staffed by secondary leaders chosen by him. Together with Kamenev they plotted to prevent Trotsky from assuming Lenin's leadership role. Such a goal was far from Trotsky's consciousness. After all, how could he not but have a feeling that the Central and Political Committees would never tolerate such a role for him?

*   *   *

The leadership cadres never forgave or forgot Trotsky's long differences with Lenin. Especially galling to them was Trotsky's famous description of the inevitable "degeneration" of a party organized on the principle of "bureaucratic centralism." Many regarded Trotsky as an enemy in their midst, notwithstanding his colossal achievements in behalf of the October Revolution, achievements that made his opponents' power possible.

In 1922, at the time of Lenin's first illness, Party affairs were pretty much in the hands of Zinoviev, Kamanev, and Stalin. The trio controlled the Party and the cities that had the largest Party membership. It was then that the first seeds were planted in the struggle against Trotsky. There were danger signs for conflict ahead and a possible split, which Lenin foresaw. Trotsky would have had to have been totally insensitive to the political scheming going on among his "comrades" in the Politburo, and he was anything but that.

The Party had come through the Civil War and the internal crises of 1920 aligned with the Workers' Opposition faction in the trade unions and the Democratic Centralist faction in the Party, both of whom led an attack on the bureaucratization of the organization and the government. Though there was not the slightest possibility that these groups could triumph, the fact that they emerged at all in this tightly knit Party was troubling. In leading the fight against these factions and defeating them, Lenin was not only conscious of the danger but he was concerned that much of it was due to the emergence of Trotsky as the leading state and Party figure next to himself. He knew this presaged Party turmoil, particularly if he were no longer there to control it. The Tenth Party Congress was the beginning of his efforts to prevent a smash-up of the leadership. He chose badly, as it turned out, by adopting measures that gave Stalin the weapons he needed to seize the Party.

Lenin sought to end the factional situation at the Tenth Party Congress by prodding it to adopt a resolution barring factions in the Party, limiting political discussions, and generally inhibiting the expression of differences. The difficulties arising during the Revolution were enough to threaten the existence of the new government as well as the Party, he argued. The measures he proposed to prevent a civil war inside the Party increased the bureaucratic potential in an organization that had already moved swiftly and inexorably in this direction. By 1922, the build-up of the bureaucracy was so rapid and dominating that Lenin was unsuccessful in trying to halt it.

The banning of factions in the Party following the destruction of the Mensheviks and Social Revolutionaries closed off the last possibility for open and tolerant debate in the one-party state. Lenin's polemical style became the model for the state and Party: He was often cantankerous, intellectually brutal, and intolerant. His opponents were always rhetorically crushed. Still, if Lenin could see little good in an opponent's views, he never physically destroyed a Party leader with whom he disagreed. Once differences were resolved, he might collaborate with an erstwhile opponent, though that opponent might no longer be a respected leader.

Lenin was very conscious of the danger of "cannibalism" in the Party leadership. He warned against such a possibility and proposed measures that he thought guaranteed that no physical violence would be used against members of the political elite. Such an agreement may have worked had Lenin remained alive, but Stalin made a shambles of Lenin's effort to save the leadership. More than any other Party, the Bolsheviks were isolated from European or Western societies and reflected the backward culture of the Tsarist centuries.

From 1922 to Lenin's death in January 1924, the turmoil in the Party and state increased. Lenin was deeply concerned with Stalin's brutal activities, specifically his intervention in the "Georgian affair" against the leadership of the Party in Georgia under the ideology of "Great Russian nationalism."[2] Outraged by events there, which threatened the stability of national relations with a minority people, Lenin asked Trotsky on March 5, 1923, to "urgently undertake the defense of Georgia in the Central Committee." Lenin's secretary, Fotieva, told Trotsky that Lenin "was preparing a bomb for Stalin at the forthcoming Congress." Trotsky readily agreed, eager to make this political bloc with Lenin and represent him before the entire leadership as his surrogate. Lenin thereupon sent all his notes on the national question to Trotsky for use in the debate. This was a great opportunity for Trotsky to appear as an opponent of Stalin in a show of unity with Lenin, the unquestioned Party leader.

But Trotsky failed to carry out his agreement with Lenin at the Twelfth Party Congress in April 1923, and this failure was to play an important part in Stalin's strategy to eventually seize the Party. He knew that Trotsky's long struggle against Lenin would inhibit Trotsky's acquisition of power. In addition, Trotsky's failure to intervene in the Georgian affair as Lenin explicably requested was the beginning of a series of inexplicably half-hearted efforts against Stalin in the factional struggle. When he revealed to the Congress that he had Lenin's notes on the Georgian question, he did so only because Fotieva, for some unknown reasons, had already forwarded a copy of them to the Politburo. Both Trotsky's and Fotieva's actions were unaccountable, because Lenin specifically did not want his notes known to Stalin before the question came before the Congress. Schapiro believed Stalin "was rescued by Trotsky, who with all this ammunition in his hands remained inactive. Stalin passed that crisis in triumph."[3]

In the Congress, Trotsky did not speak as he had promised Lenin he would, thus inadvertently assisting in the exoneration of Stalin. He told the Central Committee that he had Lenin's notes but he didn't display them, and even this partial revelation was expunged from the record of the meeting by Stalin. Up to April 25, 1923, the end of the Congress, Trotsky had yet to say one word on the national question. He lost utterly the opportunity given him by Lenin. When the Politburo adopted a motion to publish the notes, only Bukharin opposed it. The Politburo took the opportunity to explain that Trotsky withheld the notes from the Party, thus creating doubts concerning Trotsky's intentions in this secrecy. Though Stalin had packed the Congress and his power already seemed limitless, it is difficult to know how the delegates would have responded had they known that it was Lenin who was fighting against Stalin and Ordzhonikidze through Trotsky.

In *My Life*, Trotsky said he could have won the fight for Lenin at the Twelfth Congress. He failed to act, he said, because he feared that if he had done so the Party would have considered it an effort to take Lenin's place, "of which the very idea made me shudder." At the moment of the debate, Trotsky was concerned with endangering the stability of the Party apparatus by the removal of Stalin! Trotsky had discussed the question with Kamanev and told him: "I am against removing Stalin."[4]

There is a fuller explanation in *My Life* of the Georgian incident, but it does not improve Trotsky's position in the matter. Lenin's secretary, according to Trotsky, told him the leader was reconciled to informing Kamenev of his plans, even though he did not trust his old associate, knowing he would inform Stalin. On a visit from Kamenev, Trotsky told him of Lenin's plan, including his breaking off of relations with Stalin. Here is Trotsky's explanation:

I gave him [Kamenev] my opinion. . . . "Remember and tell others that the last thing I want is to start a fight at the Congress for any changes in the organization. I am for preserving the status quo. If Lenin gets on his feet before the Congress, of which there is unfortunately little chance, he and I will discuss the matter together anew. I am against removing Stalin and expelling Ordzhanikidze and displacing Dzerzhinsky. . . . But I agree with Lenin in substance. I want a radical change in policy on the national question, a discontinuance of persecutions of the Georgian opponents of Stalin. . . . On the national question, Stalin's resolution is good for nothing. . . . And . . . when you are in Tiflis, [you] must arrange a complete reversal of the policy toward Lenin's Georgian supporters on the national question."

Kamenev gave a sigh of relief. He accepted all my proposals. His only fear was that Stalin would be obstinate. "He's rude and capricious."

"I don't think," I answered, "that Stalin has any alternative now." Late that night Kamenev informed me . . . Stalin had accepted all the terms.

I gained the impression, however, that Kamenev's tone was different from that of our parting a few hours earlier. It was not until later that I realized the change was the result of Lenin's more serious condition. On his way to Tiflis . . . Kamenev received from Stalin a telegram in code telling him that Lenin was paralyzed again and unable to speak or write. At the Georgian conference Kamenev carried out Stalin's policy against Lenin's. Cemented by personal treachery, the trio had become a fact.[5]

There is revealed in this recital an important ingredient in Trotsky's failed struggle. In contrast to Lenin's threatened "bomb" against Stalin and the breaking off of personal relations with the Party Secretary was Trotsky's opposition to the removal of Stalin. He wanted to preserve "the status quo"! He ended up, however, failing his idol, Lenin. Trotsky made a fetish of unity in the Bolshevik Party, precisely because he was an "outsider" to the cadre, and he felt like one. But he faced opponents who had no such reverence for a "totem pole," or even for Lenin. As a matter of historical fact, though he carried on an historically heroic ideological war against the Stalinized Party and International, his organizational faltering led to the destruction of the Party leadership, the Party itself, and lay waste to the entire country.

It's impossible to understand Trotsky, I believe, without knowing of his polemic with Lenin, for that long debate reveals Trotsky's intense distaste for inner-party conflict and intrigue. This great revolutionary leader simply could not bring himself to give the factional struggle of the next three years the organizational passion needed to fight a Stalin in a party whose traditions and methods he so long rejected. Trotsky was the personification of a Party leader beset by the severe contradictions of his sweeping theoretical and political ideas in relation to the mean requirements of organization. This dichotomy accounted for the basic failure of his weird factional thrust against Stalin. His failure was tragic for himself as well as for the nation.

The Lenin "Testament"

Lenin's illness continued through 1923. By the end of year he was incapable of functioning or asserting his authority. Unofficially, and in bits and pieces only, the leadership learned that Lenin had written a "Testament." In the same period, Stalin, in an unusual display of rudeness where Lenin was concerned, had insulted Krupskaya personally. (Lenin was so infuriated by Stalin's crude manners that he demanded that Stalin apologize to his wife under the threat of breaking off all personal relations with the General Secretary.) The "Testament" was a commentary on the top leadership. Lenin observed that the two most able men in the Politburo were Trotsky and Stalin, and that there was a danger of a split in the relationship between these two.

At the very end of 1923, Lenin wrote a postscript to the document, which called for the removal of Stalin as General Secretary as a way of reducing the danger of lethal warfare in the leadership. Stalin was described as rude and disloyal, a cook who would serve up a "peppery dish."

The next event of importance in the developing conflict came on October 9, 1923, when Trotsky attacked the Central Committee and the Central Control Commission for endorsing a proposal made by the chief of the GPU, Felix Dzerzinski, that all Party members act as informers for the secret police. Trotsky was outraged at this intimidating proposal, and to confront it he began a public campaign for the democratization of the Party. The call for democratization received a significant response from the Party ranks and former leading opponents of the bureaucratization of the entire society. The issue was so popular that at the end of October the joint plenum of the two leading Party committees adopted Trotsky's criticism about the lack of democracy in a resolution and articles in the press. The leadership at the very top had been caught unprepared by the criticism and for the moment went along with the tide. Although Trotsky was absent due to illness, the committees had discussed a resolution on Party democracy with him beforehand to obtain his approval. Trotsky thus seemed to have won this skirmish.

But the victory was in truth an illusory one, and Trotsky's difficulties were increasing. He saw all the elements of the developing conspiracy inside the Kremlin. The principal conspirator at this stage was Zinoviev. In an interview conducted by George Urban in *Survey,* Boris Bazhanov, a secretary to Stalin from 1923 to 1926, said Zinoviev opposed the insurrection of 1917 and was put in "a state of panic" by General Yudenich's offensive against Leningrad during the counter-revolution. "It was Trotsky who came to his rescue, plucking victory out of impending defeat. From then on, no love or trust was lost between Zinoviev and Trotsky."⁶ Perhaps this is history of a kind, but if it is, it is certainly not the whole history and not even the important phases of what occurred. Bazhanov was merely telling Urban his impressions of the internal crisis from his post in the Kremlin.

Events surrounding the Twelfth Party Congress had already demonstrated where Trotsky's strategy would take him in the post-Lenin period. The question of who should make the political report to the Congress arose because Lenin, who always made the statement for the leadership, was too ill to do it. Stalin proposed that Trotsky do it "as the Party's favorite son"! Stalin was being very wily. On the one hand, he showed a deference he never before expressed, or believed; at the same time, he was forcing the issue of Lenin's successor, an issue that he knew disturbed Trotsky. He was also putting down Zinoviev, his fellow conspirator, who no doubt believed himself to be, next to Lenin, the "Party's favorite son."

Trotsky refused the suggestion, as Bazhanov recalls, "not wanting to create the impression that he was exploiting Lenin's illness in order to build up his own position." This was a common thread in Trotsky's political strategy throughout the struggle of the Left Opposition. Bazhanov thought Trotsky had a number of advantages in the fight against the Triumvirate, "but he did not know how to make use of them."

Roy Medvedev believed Trotsky simply "opted out." In searching through available archives in Moscow, Medvedev formed the following view of Trotsky's initial response to the conspiracy, a forerunner to the strangest tactical execution of a struggle to survive in the history of Socialist factional politics.

At the time Trotsky considered it beneath his dignity to engage actively in the struggle for power, even in a manner that was perfectly decent and appropriate for that objective. And yet in the spring of 1923, before the Twelfth Congress, no one was in a stronger position for such a struggle than Trotsky. Although Zinoviev, Kamenev, and Stalin had already formed a triumvirate aimed against Trotsky, they had not yet resolved to come out into the open, either at the Congress or before the Central Committee. Moreover, when the Politburo came to discuss the question of the Central

Committee's report to the Party Congress, it was Stalin who insisted that Trotsky should be the one to deliver it. Kamenev, who presided over the Politburo, supported Stalin's suggestion. When Trotsky appeared to be unwilling, Kalinin, the chairman of the Central Executive Committee, and other Party leaders appealed to him to accept. But at the beginning of the discussion, Trotsky had come up with an odd proposal: There should be no report at this Congress, he said, in order to avoid the impression in the Party that Lenin, so very ill, could be replaced. His proposal was rejected, but Trotsky refused to deliver the political report in the name of the Central Committee, and this task was entrusted to Zinoviev. Trotsky also refused to take on the defense of the "Georgian Affair," despite the fact that Lenin had insistently asked him to do it. He had come to a general decision to avoid raising acrimonious questions of any kind at the Congress, although he was well aware that if he were to read out any one of a number of Lenin's letters, whether on the national question or on the foreign trade monopoly, there would have been no question of re-electing Stalin to the post of general secretary.[7]

Trotsky verifies much—but not all—of what Medvedev wrote on the internal Party struggle in his autobiography. Unless one can show that Medvedev's account is fiction, one has to believe that Trotsky's version of the event in *My Life* omits essential facts and thereby distorts the picture. Referring to the Twelfth Congress, he wrote:

> Zinoviev demanded that he be allowed to make the political report. Kamenev was asking the "Old Bolsheviks," the majority of whom had at some time left the Party for ten or fifteen years: "Are we to allow Trotsky to become the one person empowered to direct the Party and state?" They began more frequently to rake up my past and my old disagreements with Lenin; it became Zinoviev's specialty. In the meantime, Lenin's condition took a sharper turn for the worse, so that danger no longer threatened them there. The trio decided that the political report should be made by Zinoviev.[8]

The two versions of the event are clearly contradictory. Trotsky's account may have been hampered by the fact that he was writing from memory alone. Or perhaps Medvedev misread the facts he cites. I find this latter possibility difficult to accept in view of Trotsky's failure to carry out his commitment to Lenin in the Georgian affair at the same meetings of the Central Committee and the Twelfth Congress. His action in connection with the political report to the Congress fits in with his feelings that any step in taking the place of the incapacitated Lenin "made me shudder." If he was "the most able man" in the leadership, as Lenin believed, why should he have shuddered to take over the leadership from one who was no longer able to carry out his role as the Party leader? If Lenin were thereafter able to return to his post, Trotsky could easily have relinquished his temporary post. Obviously, the problem of his becoming the Party leader was deeper than it appeared. To this day, it is an endless puzzle to biographers and historians.

*   *   *

On December 8, 1923, Trotsky wrote an article for *Pravda* called "The New Course." After giving a warm endorsement to the resolution promoting Party democracy, Trotsky stated that the impetus for carrying out the resolution was "from below," through Party control of the apparatus and the powerful secretaries (Stalin's area of Party function). Only Party democracy can make for proper guidance of the economic enterprises, he wrote. The rule of the secretaries was an inefficient system. In the course of his commentary he made a special appeal to the new generation of youth to keep the old guard on the revolutionary path.[9]

I recall that in the American Communist Party there was outrage at Trotsky's "New Course"—which no one saw, let alone read—a response initiated by the Kremlin throughout the Communist International. Trotsky was denounced for seeking to mobilize the youth against the Party. Those of us who were in the youth movement thought well enough of ourselves, but we had gone through long discussions of "vanguardism" and were persuaded that the youth were not the leaders of society or the Party. ("Vanguardism" was the idea that the youth movement was endowed with such remarkable qualities that it stood at the head of the revolutionary movement, noble and free from the deviations and opportunism that afflicted the "adult" movement.) We were wary of anyone who attributed to us the leadership of the proletariat! Since Trotsky was presented to us as seeking to create a division between the mature leadership of the Party and the inexperienced youth, we joined in the fierce rejection of his views.

One thing Trotsky did not say, although he was continuously accused of it, was that permission should be given for the existence of groups and factions inside the Party. He was *not* in favor of such a step in those years, for the decisions of the Tenth Congress were still fresh in his memory, as was the fact that it was Lenin who initiated the antidemocratic resolutions of the Congress.

There is no doubt that "The New Course" drew a favorable response among many sections of the Party, sections that felt a new period was opening up in the ranks as well as in the leadership because of the resolution on democracy and the fact that Trotsky's writing appeared publicly. But these hopes were in vain. Whatever decisions were made would never be carried out by the bureaucratic apparatus. Since Trotsky believed in a monopoly of power by the Party, he did not appeal to the "revolutionary working class." Discussions in the Party and its press followed the publication of the "letter" in *Pravda,* which then came out in book form. But the dice were loaded. Trotsky, still ill, did not participate in the public discussion.

The Thirteenth Party Conference convened in January 1924. The meeting was a gathering of hand-picked participants. Trotsky was unable to attend. His few supporters present had no vote, and they knew in advance they were beaten. The Conference adopted a resolution, with only three dissenting votes, condemning Trotsky, the one who dared initiate a discussion on democracy. It was Stalin who led the attack on him, supported militantly by Zinoviev and Kamenev. Trotsky and his supporters were warned that "decisive measures" would be taken against those passing out "forbidden documents." The exact moment of this warning came after Stalin's disclosure of the "secret clause" of the Tenth Congress. At the Tenth Party Conference, faced with the Workers' Opposition and the criticisms of the intellectual Democratic Centralists, Lenin had produced two secret resolutions, on "Party Unity" and "The Syndicalist and Anarchist Desecration in Our Party." The first resolution declared that separate platforms and oppositions in the Party gave encouragement to the Kronstadt uprising. "Everyone who criticizes . . . must keep in mind the situation of the Party in the midst of enemies by which it is surrounded," Lenin wrote.

The resolution then called for the immediate dissolution of all groups that had their own platforms; groups that didn't comply would face immediate expulsion from the Party. The secret clause gave the Central Committee full power of expulsion, with the proviso only that a two-thirds vote of the Central Committee's members, candidate members, and the members of the Control Commission was required. The second resolution condemned the Workers' Opposition and contained Lenin's view of the Party, the triumph of his central doctrine of *What is to Be Done.* Lenin wrote:

Marxism teaches that only the political party of the working classes, i.e. the Communist Party, is capable of unity, educating and organizing such a vanguard of the proletariat and the working masses as is capable of resisting the inevitable petit-bourgeois waverings of the masses . . . [and] their trade union prejudices.[10]

Trotsky voted for both these resolutions, thus marking the end to two decades of struggle for Party democracy. In becoming a Leninist, he adopted Lenin's bitter attitude toward Social Democracy in particular and democracy in general.

A purge of the Trotskyists began. General M. V. Frunze was made Deputy Commissar of War, which meant that he actually displaced Trotsky. The measures taken against Trotsky were symbolic, a warning to his supporters. The Thirteenth Congress of May 1924 confirmed the decisions of the Conference, and its actions were unanimously approved. Trotsky, E. A. Preobrazhensky, and six signers of the "Declaration of Forty-six," the Opposition statement to the Congress, were present but had no vote. There was not a single voting Opposition delegate in attendance. The Congress then adopted a resolution that officially declared the Dictatorship of the Party to be identical with the "dictatorship of the proletariat."

The leadership of the Party was momentarily in the hands of Stalin, Zinoviev, and Kamenev, supported by the "Right" group of Bukharin, Rykov, and Tomsky. The cult of Leninism was fostered by a collection of speeches in pamphlet form, Leninism or Trotskyism, the title being the brainchild of Zinoviev, who mistakenly believed that he headed the "new collective leadership." The pamphlet marked the first action taken by Stalin as an important leader, and the Congress showed how overwhelming his strength was in a delegation largely selected by him. Stalin was in fact now dominating the Party.

Krupskaya delivered Lenin's Testament, or "will," to the Congress, together with other notes by Lenin. The Testament was read to the delegates, almost all of whom owed their various Party and state posts to the General Secretary. Stalin made the gesture of offering to resign, knowing full well that it would be rejected by the adoring delegates. They insisted that their benefactor remain at his post to lead the nation and the Party, which he as a good soldier agreed to do! Stalin claimed that Trotsky, too, voted for the motion to keep him in office. (In another period, sometime before the Congress, Trotsky did oppose the removal Stalin from his post, but it could not have been at the Thirteenth Congress, where neither he nor his supporters had a vote.)

Bazhanov's version of what occurred at the Congress on this question differs from the official one. Trotsky, he wrote, "looked upon himself as a man on par with Lenin—which he was—and refused to be drawn into this unseemly wrangle for succession." Kamenev moved, after the reading of the Testament, that Stalin should remain in office, and though he kept no written record of the vote, Bazhanov states that Trotsky, Piatakov, and Radek voted against the motion.[11]

At the Congress Trotsky, undoubtedly deeply shocked by Lenin's death, was confronted with a political offensive against him by the Triumvirate, outraged as it was by the criticisms of them contained in "The New Course." The booklet questioned the political acumen and Party loyalty of Zinoviev and Kamenev. Trotsky was surprised at the reaction of the Congress leadership, which attacked him violently and demanded disciplinary action be taken. Trotsky thereupon acknowledged to the assembly that he was wrong, saying weakly:

> In the last instance, the Party is always right, because it is the only historic instrument which the working class possesses for the solution of its fundamental tasks. . . . One can only be right with the Party and through the Party because history has not created any other way for the realization of one's rightness. The English have the saying: "My country, right or wrong." With much greater justification we can say: "My Party, right or wrong. . . ." It would be ridiculous perhaps, almost indecent, to express personal statements here, but I hope that should the need arise I shall not prove to be the lowest soldier on the lowest Bolshevik barricades.[12]

What else is there to say about a "Socialist" political party that compels the first authentic hero of the Revolution to respond in such an abject way, where the Commander of the Red Army is ready to serve his nation and Party as the lowest soldier on the lowest Bolshevik barricades? And what of the hero himself, who could utter the dreadful historical distortion again and again, as the Party continued to err? Schapiro writes:

> Though it is easy to criticize Trotsky for throwing away his opportunities to rally wide support for the overthrow of Stalin while this was still possible, it is also necessary to remember that this was a course he could not lightly pursue. For a small minority, ruling by force in the teeth of proletarian and peasant opposition, can ill afford to saw away the only firm branch which supports it—a well-disciplined organization. All Communists had recognized the necessity of such a party machine in 1921. It was too late for them to draw back, even when that organization threatened to engulf them.[13]

For these very reasons the country and the Party paid dearly in accepting the rule of the Communist hierarchy and its vast bureaucracy. The toll of the dead and suffering cannot be redressed by a dozen Glasnosts or Perestroikas.

Lessons of October

In the autumn of 1924, as the seventh anniversary of the Russian Revolution approached, Trotsky published his book *1917*. He entitled his introduction "Lessons of October," in which he discussed the Party's ideological and political unpreparedness for the October insurrection until Lenin arrived and "rearmed" the leadership. The introduction was not only a criticism of Zinoviev and Kamenev, who initially opposed the insurrection, it was also a criticism of Stalin and Molotov, caretakers of the Party at that time who supported the provisional government. Why did Trotsky choose this moment to challenge the whole leadership and question its authority, when he was now weaker than at any time since the Revolution? With Lenin he might have won that battle; without him, there was no possibility of victory. This act of criticism emphasized to the Central Committee that Trotsky was indeed an "alien" to Bolshevism.

Consciously or unconsciously, what Trotsky was saying to the Party, and particularly to the Triumvirate, was that in the most crucial period of the revolutionary events the Party without Lenin proved incompetent and unprepared, until he, Trotsky, assumed leadership of these events and, as in 1905, became the voice of the Soviet. Equally important, his book denied that "the Party was always right" or that "one can only be right with the Party and through the Party." He was also saying that the Party was not always "the historic instrument of the working class"—that, indeed, it was often an impediment to the working class's progress. This book tended to elevate the role of the individual in history, an idea not usually interpreted by Bolshevism to be a pillar of Marxism. Most incredible of all, Trotsky "smeared" the Party and its leadership soon after he had acknowledged his errors, accepted the discipline of the leadership, and was prepared to be "the lowest soldier on the lowest Bolshevik barricades."[14]

*   *   *

Long after he had been deported from Russia, Trotsky elaborated on his view of Lenin's role in 1917, and his own. He wrote in his *Diary in Exile, 1935:*

> Had I not been present in 1917 in Petrograd the October Revolution would still have taken place—on the condition that Lenin was present and in command. If neither Lenin nor I had been present in Petrograd, there would have been no October Revolution: The leadership of the Bolshevik Party would have prevented it from occurring—of this I have not the slightest doubt.[15]

Trotsky had not the slightest doubt of this when he wrote "Lessons of October." Neither was there any doubt that the leadership of the "bureaucratic centralist" Party, without Lenin, could tolerate the "Menshevik" Trotsky in their midst. Because it could not tolerate him, the leadership continued its pressures on the Left Opposition and its main leader. He endangered the unity of the Party, it said in 1925, and so the Central Committee resolved

> to give Trotsky a most serious warning that membership in the Bolshevik Party requires not merely verbal but genuine submission to Party discipline as well as complete and unconditional repudiation of any struggle against Leninism.

The Party required "genuine submission," not merely acceptance; it required "complete and unconditional repudiation" of a struggle against . . . Leninism! The leadership implied that whatever Trotsky did in reviving or developing any new differences with the Party would be a struggle against Leninism itself.[16] Why was this warning necessary when Trotsky had already acknowledged his errors, accepted the primacy of the Party decisions and its leadership, and denied at the same time that he sought a "special position" in the Party? ("I am ready to do any work assigned to me by the C.C. in any position or without a position and, it goes without saying, under any kind of Party control," he said.[17]) For two reasons: One, the leadership could never be sure that Trotsky would not turn around and begin his criticism again. Two, the leadership of the "historic instrument of the working class," which demanded surrender from the Party's "favorite son," did not and could not accept his surrender as genuine. What it wanted was to destroy him, not merely to defeat him politically and organizationally.

After the "Lessons of October," Zinoviev published his book *Leninism or Trotskyism* as an anti-Trotskyist exercise and to establish that *he* was the true pupil of Lenin and his natural successor. But it was to no avail, for at that very same time Stalin was preparing to destroy the chief of the Leningrad Party and establish his own base there. Meanwhile, the January 1925 plenum of the Central Committee condemned Trotsky once more. The Fourteenth Congress, which convened in December of the same year, endorsed everything the Central Committee decided. The Fourteenth Congress was the "hoodlum congress," where the Stalinist majority delegation hooted, whistled, and jeered all oppositionists. The Left Opposition was in disarray. Trotsky did not take part in the Congress. His failure to assume leadership there demoralized his followers.

Out of this Congress came the wide dissemination of the pamphlet *Leninism or Trotskyism*. The worldwide distribution of the Bloc of Three's speeches—Zinoviev, Kamenev, and Stalin—marked the opening of the campaign in the Communist International against Trotsky and the Left Opposition, catapulting Stalin to the top leadership of the world movement (a person heretofore unknown for the most part outside the Soviet Union).

Stalin was particularly unknown to the American movement. I recall that when his picture first appeared in the Party's theoretical magazine, members, especially in the youth organization, were asking about Stalin. The Party leaders were not very enlightening; they themselves knew little about the Russian leadership or Party events. But it soon became evident that he was the single most powerful force in the Russian Party, and that is what mattered to the Americans.

There is no doubt whatever, as history records, given the nature of a Leninist party and International, that the campaign undermined any tendency toward Trotskyism in the world movement and destroyed Trotsky's high place in the leadership in the International, though he *was* a Russian Party representative to the Executive Committee from the First up to the Fifth Congresses. The "Old Guard" closed ranks against the alien Old Menshevik. His past would haunt him until his assassination—Stalin's final victory.

*　　*　　*

Between the Plenary meeting of the Central Committee in January 1925 and the Congress in December, Max Eastman published *Since Lenin Died* in the United States. Eastman told the story of the factional struggle in the Russian Party, largely unknown to the outside world at the time. He named its principals, referred to the main issues, and added an appendix that reproduced the Testament of Lenin, which was as unknown to the Russian Party at large as it was to the International. It was in Eastman's book that the document was first published in an unrestricted, public way. *Since Lenin Died* had a considerable circulation in the United States and abroad. The Soviet leadership responded by saying that rumors of such a Testament were untrue, that Eastman was trying to create difficulties for the Soviet state, split the Party, and help the enemies of the Revolution. Moreover, everyone knew that he was a Trotskyist, the leadership said.

Eastman had been a long-time supporter of the American Communist Party, a prominent intellectual defender of the Russian Revolution, a well-known admirer of Lenin, the Bolshevik Party, and its leadership. He was also a friend of Leon Trotsky, his tutor in English; he had first-hand knowledge of the internal situation in the Russian Party in part because he had resided in Moscow for an extended period of time. We now know that he received the Testament either from Trotsky himself or from some other leader of the Left Opposition. What he wrote in the book was gone over by a responsible Oppositionist leader, said to be Christian Rakovsky, next to Trotsky the most outstanding leader of the faction.

Under the severe pressure from the Politburo, Trotsky repudiated Eastman, saying that no Testament existed. There was no factional struggle inside the leadership of the Russian Party, Trotsky lied. Eastman was completely stunned by Trotsky's public statement; it told the world that he had invented the whole story.

As we have already indicated, the existence of the Testament in the version published by Eastman, as well as the one with the clause breaking off all personal relations with Stalin, became known to leading circles of the Party and state almost from the time it was written. The Left Opposition and the Opposition Bloc, a later formation, made it known to their followers, after which it filtered through the Party in all directions. I find it strange to read the following observation in Bertram D. Wolfe's autobiography:

> It took me many years of examination of all available evidence to reconstruct the full story of the Testament, for all the close witnesses were under intense strain! It justifies my feeling in 1926 that Max Eastman's release to the *New York Times* was genuine. To be sure, the last words of Lenin to Stalin were not included in Eastman's release because it was Krupskaya, as I learned, who had sent Eastman the Testament, and she was too modest to tell him the final story because it dealt with her personally.[18]

Either Wolfe did not read Eastman's *Heroes I have Known*—that is hard to believe—or he forgot the story of Eastman's involvement in the American publication of the Testament. The year 1926 was when Wolfe was very active in the inner leadership of the American Party as a top leader of the Lovestone faction. He was undoubtedly the leading anti-Trotskyist spokesman, at work on his pamphlet excoriating the Trotskyists and the United Opposition. He was also a leading spokesman of the Party in its organized denunciation of Eastman. The probability is very strong that he made no strong examination of this incident, because a strong one would have led him to Eastman and his friends as a source of the truth. His curiosity, if indeed it existed, did not take him that far. I would find it hard to believe otherwise, as I witnessed the immense amount of anti-Trotskyist material that came from the National Educational Department under his direction.

In his essay on Trotsky in *Heroes,* Eastman told of his role in the news release and the origins of his book *Since Lenin Died.* Eastman wrote that Trotsky

> disavowed my book. He disavowed it, although he himself had given me the key facts and done so with the express understanding that I would publish them. He denied over his signature that there was any such thing as this document, called "Lenin's Testament," which I had quoted directly from his lips.

We know now that Eastman presented the draft of the book to Rakovsky, Trotsky's closest personal friend, who approved the manuscript. Krupskaya never entered the picture of this particular event in the varied history of Stalin's thrust for power, and Wolfe's reference to her role is incomprehensible. Wolfe's Party activity continued from 1926 to 1929, when he was expelled from the Party together with the Lovestone faction for "American exceptionalism" in his support of Bukharin.[19]

Many years later, Trotsky tried to make amends for this indecent repudiation of Eastman's book, written primarily to aid the cause of the Left Opposition, and motivated by savage pressure from the leadership and his own desire to preserve Party unity. Here, too, it is certain the Party was *not* always right. Someone other than Eastman might have broken with Trotsky over such a repudiation, but Eastman had larger issues in mind, and he took Trotsky's act with sadness and disappointment. Eastman continued to support the Left Opposition and its leader. He was, in later years, to render inestimable aid to the American Trotskyist movement in its formative period. Moreover, he continued to be Trotsky's friend, American translator, and literary representative.

*   *   *

After the Fourteenth Congress, a bloc was formed between Zinoviev and Kamenev, who had broken with Stalin. The two took the name of "United Opposition." These two members of the Triumvirate had become aware of Stalin's plan to take over the Party and state, an aim that did not include their participation. Feeling his new power, Stalin took on the mantle of "theoretician" and developed a new orientation for the nation and Party, which he termed "Socialism in One Country." Bukharin was his accomplice in repudiating the traditional position of Lenin and the Bolshevik Party; he supplied the theoretical justification for the concept, enabling Stalin to argue for it. In practice, Stalin's theory meant that there would be less emphasis on the "internationalism" of Bolshevism and a greater concentration on national tasks. The change was justified, Stalin wrote, on the grounds that the Soviet Union could build a Socialist society on its own; it was not dependent upon a European revolution. This idea repudiated traditional Bolshevik thinking. Indeed, Lenin often explained that the Revolution was made in the hope of serving as the catalyst for a European revolution, without which the Soviet Union could not survive indefinitely or build a Socialist society.

The newly formed United Opposition Bloc was a precarious unity, and in the following year or more it was battered from crisis to crisis before it finally disintegrated. During its brief existence it prepared a platform for the Fifteenth Party Congress, where the Bloc demanded discussions before the membership in the Party cells on the issues of Party democracy and the growth of the Party and state bureaucracies. The attack on the Bloc for its audacity was vicious, particularly in the abuse of Trotsky, Zinoviev, Kamenev, Preobrazhensky, Sokolnikov, and Evdokimov, who were all charged with "violating Party discipline"! Once more they had to agree that their ideas were wrong. Why not, since Trotsky publicly admitted that "one cannot be right against the Party"?

At a plenary meeting of the Central Committee held in January 1926, Trotsky made a speech on Lenin's Testament. His repudiation of Max Eastman, however, came back to haunt him, for Stalin, replying for the majority, called attention to the fact that even Trotsky denied that such a document existed when the matter of Eastman's book came before the Politburo.

On the eve of the Fifteenth Congress of December 1927, the Party leadership arranged a mass demonstration for the tenth anniversary of the Revolution in Red Square. The Bloc decided to hold its own demonstration within the larger and official one, in which it carried placards bearing the following slogans: "Let Us Turn Our Fire to the Right—Against the Kulak, the Nepman, and the Bureaucrat," "Let Us Carry Out Lenin's Will," "Against Opportunism, Against a Split, and for the Unity of Lenin's Party." The Bloc's demonstration was broken up violently. Trotsky noted that those engaged in this physical violence against the Opposition were "volunteers in the fight against 'Trotskyism,' notoriously nonrevolutionary and sometimes sheer Fascist elements in the streets of Moscow. . . ."[20]

As early as 1927, then, Trotsky referred to Party-organized hooligans as "sheer Fascist elements," an appraisal he was to broaden nine years later in *The Revolution Betrayed,* when he described the Party regime and state to be Fascist and totalitarian, respectively. In Gorbachev's time, under Glasnost and Perestroika, at least one Fascist organization has emerged, the Pamyat, a nationwide group of intellectual hooligans, violently anti-Semitic, which spreads the spurious *Protocols of Zion* as a propaganda weapon. The group flourishes in the anti-Semitic atmosphere of the Party leadership. Gorbachev has disassociated himself from this gang, but in a low-key way—evidently in the hopes of not giving it publicity. At any rate, if Perestroika limps or collapses, Pamyat and other Fascist organizations will no doubt grow in the attendant discontent, as similar ones did in 1927, when the proletariat in Red Square looked on passively as the Opposition leaders and supporters, veterans of the Revolution, were mauled by the secret police.

Stalin's first official measure against the United Opposition came at the Fifteenth Party Congress. He proposed to expel Trotsky, Zinoviev, Kamenev, and their respective followers from the Party, and to deport Trotsky to Siberia. Only Bukharin opposed the proposal. Zinoviev and Kamenev, to the surprise of no one in the United Opposition leadership, soon repented and asked to be readmitted to the Party, acknowledging that they were wrong not merely in their factional activity but in even thinking the ideas they had defended up to the day before their capitulation. Since Trotsky and a number of his followers would not do this, they found themselves in Siberia. (It was his third Siberian exile.) Zinoviev and Kamenev, Stalin's partners in the initial campaign to destroy Trotsky, began a new period of surrender and suffering under the most punishing *Vohzd* in the history of the Party. Stalin dangled the two like helpless puppets.

Trotsky, despite his stated acceptance of Party discipline, his agreements to end his factional activities, and his preparedness to carry out any assignment given him, could *not* carry out his promise not to fight the outrageous political methods of the leadership. As a "new" Bolshevik, unfamiliar with and untrained in Bolshevik internal organizational practices, he reflected a contradiction produced by his revolutionary temperment, informed by his theory of the "permanent revolution" and his long-held democratic concepts of Socialist organization. He demanded a tolerance from Stalin's party it would never give him. Nor would it accommodate him with an inner-party pluralism incompatible with Bolshevism.

Trotsky tried—vainly, continually, and desperately—to prove he was a good Bolshevik, a loyal and disciplined Party member, totally devoted to the interests of the organization and the state. And Stalin, who owed everything to him, abused him mercilessly, returning to Trotsky's pre-1917 polemics with Lenin in order to defeat him politically and organizationally in the mid-twenties. Since the Bolshevik Party was never a democratic body, Trotsky's appeals for it to return to a nonexistent past-Party democracy were ludicrous—and in view of his struggle, pathetic. It is often said that because the Bolshevik Party had to function illegally under the Tsarist monarchy, it had no experience with democratic methods or knowledge of the essential nature of democracy. There is only some truth to this. After all, the Menshevik Party functioned under the same conditions as an illegal organization, yet it tried consciously to exercise as much internal democracy as was possible or permissible. Certainly, as emigrés, the Mensheviks operated democratically; in contrast, the Bolsheviks flouted democracy even in the democratic West. Simply put, the difference between the two wings of Russian Social Democracy was in the democratic outlook of the one and the conscious rejection of that outlook by the other.

*   *   *

If the thought of taking Lenin's place—not *being* Lenin, merely taking his unfilled place—made Trotsky shudder, why didn't he just let it go at that and allow Stalin to become the leader of the Party? He already had the support of the majority of the leadership. Again, if the fight for the leadership would have demoralized the Party—"we would have had to pay too painful a price for it even in victory," wrote Trotsky[21]—then why did he struggle at all? Why not let Stalin have it peacefully and avoid demoralization?

Stalin won the struggle and the nation paid a price no one would have believed possible. Lenin recognized Stalin's threat, but he did not believe his evil would encompass the whole nation. Trotsky's explanation of his feelings about seeking power and taking Lenin's place was a prescription for defeat. And therein may be the explanation for the failure to fight in a timely, consistent, and unending way until victory, if such were possible. The way he fought was a waste of his enormous courage.

If the thought of taking Lenin's place made him "shudder," was he simply carrying on a struggle for the sake of *ideas?* Did he hope to *convince* Stalin, the totally unintellectual bureaucrat-killer? Trotsky once said that he "avoided the struggle until the last possible moment," always seeking instead "to preserve a basis for collective work." As we observe the evolution of the conflict, it seems impossible that Trotsky could write that he rejected a total offensive against the regime because of "the lack of sufficient political basis. The fact remains that I chose the first course and in spite of everything do not regret it. There are victories which lead to a deadlock and defeats which open up new paths. . . ."[22]

His strategy led to neither. In the very beginning of the struggle, in October 1923, during Lenin's fatal illness, he did not sign the platform of the "Forty-Six," though it was based on his ideas. Only his followers signed. Yet he was held rightfully responsible for it anyway. The publication of "The New Course" and "Lessons of October" continued to establish that there was more than "sufficient political basis" for the struggle.

Writes Knei-Paz: "Why Trotsky did not strike out with more than words against the new post-Lenin leadership of the 'triumvirate,' why he did not attempt to make a real thrust for power, remains the great enigma both of his personality and of his political judgment."[23] Knei-Paz rejects as unconvincing Joel Carmichael's belief that Trotsky's hesitations were caused by "shyness."[24] Angela Balabanova, on the other hand, thought him "too self-conscious."[25] Knei-Paz writes that Trotsky's "overriding sense of loyalty to the Party in general, and to Party unity in particular, was not an insubstantial factor in his reticence."[26] The sense of loyalty was particularly severe in Trotsky precisely because he was a newcomer to Bolshevism and had in fact been allied with the Menshevik cause before 1917. He was, in fact, not eligible for membership in "the Society of Old Bolsheviks."

Medvedev is certain that Stalin could not have succeeded in winning power if the "big three" (Trotsky, Zinoviev, Bukharin) had been united in their respective struggles against him.[27] But the three could never be joined. The struggle was initiated by Zinoviev's burning passion to take Lenin's place, which led him into the original plot with the organizational strongman, Stalin. Bukharin formed his alliance with Stalin with open eyes, because his political perspectives were antagonistic to Trotsky and the Left Opposition. These two laid the groundwork for Stalin's triumph. Anton Antonov-Ovsyenko, in his book *The Time of Stalin,* observes, "One of the keys to Stalin's success was the consistent failure of his opponents to unite. . . . Zinoviev and Trotsky could not unite and did not want to."[28] Their first try, he could have added, was a troubled and brief one. A reading of their works show that Medvedev and Ovysenko, historians of that period, looked to Trotsky as the only one capable of leading the struggle. There was a crucial question here: What was most important, programmatic purity or the prevention of monstrous Party leadership? We think history has already answered that question.

Much has been written about Bukharin's role in those years as a possible opposition center that could have been joined to the other oppositions to achieve a majority against Stalin. We have already indicated why this did not happen. Bukharin and his allies in the Politburo, Rykov and Tomsky, supported Stalin in all his machinations against Trotsky and the Trotskyists, and later against the United Opposition. The fact that Bukharin was an unhappy ally of Stalin is not too important. While Bukharin, Zinoviev, and Trotsky misunderstood Stalin's goals, they also misunderstood each other. And this latter point is the key one: Such a misunderstanding prevented a unified opposition.

Bukharin's Responsibility for Stalin

When the first manifestations of Stalin's anti-Semitism appeared, Trotsky talked to Bukharin about the problem. Stalin made the false charge that the leaders of Trotsky's Opposition were all Jews, when in fact, except for Trotsky, they were all "indigenous Russians." Jew-baiting in Moscow factories was introduced by Stalinist agitators, saying of the Opposition that "the Zhids are rioting." In a nation with a long tradition of anti-Semitism, still widespread after the Revolution, Stalin's motives were obvious. Trotsky sought Bukharin's help. Joseph Nedava in *Trotsky and the Jews* records Trotsky's reference to this incident:

> At one of the sessions of the Politburo I wrote Bukharin a note: "You cannot help knowing that even in Moscow in the struggle against the Opposition, methods of the Black Hundred demagogues [anti-Semitism, etc.] are utilized." Bukharin answered me evasively on that same piece of paper. "Individual instances, of course, are possible." I again wrote: "I have in mind not individual instances but a systematic agitation among the Party secretaries at large Moscow enterprises. Will you agree to come with me to investigate an example of this at the factory 'Skorohad' (I know of a number of other such examples)?" Bukharin answered: "All right, we can go." In vain I tried to make him carry out the promise. Stalin most categorically forbade him to do so.[29]

Trotsky and Bukharin were wrong about each other. Bukharin was not the friend of the Kulak, in the sense described by Trotsky. His own modest proposals for a more rapid industrialization did not threaten the Revolution. Yet Trotsky rigidly rejected an alliance with Bukharin. As he wrote in a letter to the Oppositionists: "With Stalin against Bukharin? Yes. With Bukharin against Stalin? Never."[30] This was a fatal error on Trotsky's part, but Bukharin's conduct was no better. He had opposed Trotsky's proposals for a planned, reasonably paced industrialization; but when Stalin embarked on his mad-paced program of super-industrialization, Bukharin (in private correspondence) called the General Secretary a Trotskyist. Later, when he found himself in a political situation similar to Trotsky's, he referred to Stalin as a Ghengis Khan. Bukharin simply had no perspective for a struggle against Stalin, and after he participated in the defeat of Trotsky, Zinoviev, and Kamenev, *et al.,* he was quite alone. Medvedev, in reviewing the relationship of forces in the party, said of Bukharin and the Right,

Their main leaders, and above all, Bukharin himself, proved to be inadequate politicians. Bukharin was quite good at theory and a man of great charm, but he was far too gentle and complacent to lead a factional struggle against Stalin. There was, in fact, no such thing as an organized Right Opposition in the Party in 1928–29, nor had Bukharin ever created any kind of Party faction, although it would still have been entirely possible to do so. Bukharin's supporters were not even able to press for a general Party debate. . . . Bukharin never managed to devise any kind of broad platform, analagous to those produced by the Left in 1925–27.[31]

Trotsky, in turn, always maintained the mistaken belief that Bukharin was a greater danger to the Revolution than Stalin. His voice was "the voice of the Kulak," wrote Trotsky—an absurd position and historically inaccurate. Bukharin desired to *reduce* Stalin's pace of industrialization in favor of a more open peasant economy. Even if Bukharin was mistaken, he was no more a so called "capitalist restorationist" than Stalin was.

Medvedev asserts that at the end of the twenties many of the senior military men and officers of the GPU were supporters of Bukharin and sympathetic to his policies. His is the first mention of such support in strong terms, though evidence for it is difficult to establish. Even so, Medvedev is compelled to reiterate that "the Right was unable to take advantage of this favorable situation."[32]

In a preliminary working paper prepared for a conference at the Hoover Institute at Stanford University in October 1964, Max Shachtman, whose knowledge of the history of the Comintern was acute and extensive, made the following observations:

It wasn't the Stalinist faction that fell under the hooves of the counter-revolution, as Trotsky believed. It was the Right Wing.

All previous oppositions had been defeated only after an open struggle in which they presented their views, their platforms, for consideration by the Party public. . . . Not so in the case of the Right Wing.

Bukharin's supporters in the Party machine were systematically removed without his open protest, often with his reluctant agreement. . . .

In early 1929, finally, Bukharin spoke of the need for Party democracy and sealed his fate when he spoke against control by a collective being replaced by control by a person.[33]

Questions of inadequate political-organizational abilities are undoubtedly involved in assessing Bukharin's role, but Stephen F. Cohen indicates that

Of the several circumstances favoring the General Secretary, the most important was the struggle's narrow arena and covert nature. This situation, abetted by Bukharin, Rykov, and Tomskii [sic], confined the conflict to the Party hierarchy, where Stalin's strength was the greatest, and nullified the Bukharin Group's strength, which lay outside the high Party leadership and indeed outside the Party itself.

This factor was as true for Trotsky, too, as it was for Zinoviev and Kamenev. "It derived," added Cohen, "from the Bolshevik dogma that politics outside the Party was illegitimate, potentially, if not actually, counter-revolutionary." Bukharin "shunned overt . . . factionalism" and was reduced to ineffectual "backstairs intrigue." "He conformed to 'Party unity and Party discipline' to the narrow intolerant politics he helped to create." But above all, Cohen writes,

> His position was politically incongruous—driven by outraged contempt for Stalin and his policies, he remained throughout a restrained, reluctant oppositionist.[34]

Though Medvedev believed that the defeat of Stalin was possible on the basis of a united struggle by Trotsky, Zinoviev, Kamenev, Rykov, and Bukharin, the idea was without real foundation; he shows as well as anyone why they could never have united.

Perhaps the saddest expression of Bukharin's disorientation, as a person as well as a politician, came in his return to the Soviet Union from Western Europe in 1936. He had been out of the country with his wife on some mission having to do with the purchase of archives in Europe; their child was in Russia. Social Democrats suggested that he defect, remain in Europe; they would see to his physical protection and financial support. The Moscow Frame-Up Trials had already begun, and Bukharin knew what fate awaited him. Yet he could not bring himself to leave the Party. Knowing that he was going to his death, the "Old Bolshevik" in him guaranteed his destruction. Stalin had counted on that! Shortly after he returned to Russia, he was indicted, tried in a judicial farce acted out by the vile Andre Vyshinsky, and murdered on orders of the Party boss.

*   *   *

The demoralization of the Party that Trotsky thought he could prevent by declining to "fight for Lenin's place" went on at a swift pace without his fight. The "painful price" he refused to pay was paid anyway, as the entire old Bolshevik Party and the Old Guard leadership was wiped out, to be replaced by new chiefs of the contemporary bureaucracy.

Stalin was now the supreme boss of everything: the Party, the state, the military, industry, agriculture, and all forms of cultural activity, from literature to music, theater, and painting. A paranoid personality, he demanded and received accolades no other national leader, Hitler and Mussolini included, ever received. His pictures were stuck on walls all over the country, in every state and Party institution; they were produced in the millions. Faked photographs were published showing Stalin with Lenin on occasions that never existed. Antonov-Ovysenko lists some of the more important "qualities" of the master leader in *The Time of Stalin.* They are the measure of the man who, rather than halt the fawning, asked for more:

Great Leader of the Soviet People
Great Friend of the Children
Great Friend of the Women
Great Master of Daring Revolutionary Decisions and Abrupt Turns
Transformer of Nature
Supreme Military Leader
Father of the People
Father, Leader, Friend, and Teacher
Distinguished Academician
Genius of Mankind
Leading Light of Science
Greatest Genius of All Times and Peoples[35]

How could a Workers' State, even a degenerated one, have tolerated such official humbug? One saw this characteristic of Stalinist leaders to an equal or lesser degree throughout world communism, from Mao in China to Tito in Yugoslavia, Castro in Cuba, Hoxha in Albania, the royal Communist family in North Korea, and his royal Communist highness in Romania. Whatever their names or titles, they are the absolute rulers for life of their self-styled Socialist or "Peoples' Democracies."

Stalin did not create the Soviet police state. He merely perfected it. The mass purge was the outstanding contribution of his political rule; the slaughter it produced was unprecedented in twenty centuries of mankind's civilization. Spy scares were constant. Police measures were employed indiscriminately against Party leaders and members, state functionaries, Party and non-Party national minorities, the peasantry, and peoples at large. So vast were the purges that Robert Conquest, in his account of them, *The Great Terror,* estimates that twenty million died in them.[36]

Solzhenitzyn claims that Stalin's terror took 66 million lives and World War II 44 million more, for a total of 110 million.[37] The Russian demographer Maksudov rejects these figures and sets down an estimate of his own. He states that 7.5 million in the military were killed at the warring fronts and another 7.5 million civilians were killed in the German-occupied territories. Adding starvation, mass repressions, and other means of destroying populations, he brings the figure to 20 million. To this he adds two or three million more as a result of artificially induced famine and repression, arriving at a total of 22 to 23 million. Maksudov also states that if Solzhenitzyn's figures were accepted, it would mean that not one person died a natural death between 1918 and 1953.[38]

Solzhenitzyn obviously exaggerates, but a dispute over the number of Stalin's victims is merely a macabre game. The Stalinist holocaust was overwhelming. Medvedev, however, in pointing out the greater accuracy of Maksudov's figures, writes:

His figures show that during the years of Stalin's rule almost half the male and one-quarter of the female population did not fulfill their natural lifespan. Given such extraordinary figures, there is hardly a need for exaggeration, doubling or tripling them as certain emigrés have tended to do. Our losses during the Stalin years thus exceeded the losses of all countries taken together in the course of both world wars.[39]

Maksudov concluded his study with the following comment: "No tyrant, past or present, was able to erect such a mountain of skulls, those of his own subjects as well as those of his bitterest enemies."[40]

The regime of the so-called Workers' State discovered spies everywhere: in the Party, the government, in all the bureaus of all the institutions of the country, and not least of all, in the economic and military arenas. One never knew when he or she would be called up to answer the charge of being a spy or "wrecker," or an agent of a foreign power, and be forced to confess to the most pernicious, depraved, and murderous counter-revolutionary acts. Confessions came easily; the secret police had refined its methods of torture so that almost any person would confess to the most heinous crimes. Antonov-Ovsyenko refers to Leonid Zakovsky, former Commissar of Internal Affairs for Byelorussa, whom Stalin appointed to replace the demoted Filipp Medved after the Kirov assassination, as head of the Leningrad secret police (now known as the NKVD). Zakovsky once boasted: "If Karl Marx himself fell into my hands he'd soon confess to spying for Bismarck."[41]

*   *   *

As I mentioned before, in 1931 I put a question to Trotsky about the character of Stalin, certain that he was very familiar with him, at least from the time of the Revolution to his expulsion from the Party in 1927.

His reply was odd: Everything he had to say about Stalin he had already written.

Now, up to 1931 Trotsky had not written very much about Stalin, except in the form of political debate. I had difficulty accepting Trotsky's response. He must have known Stalin in certain intimate ways as a co-member of the Politburo and during the Civil War, when he had to deal with Stalin as an undisciplined, interfering, and scheming subordinate. It was hard to believe that, from the whole period since the October Revolution, Trotsky, always a penetrating observer of people in the large sense, had nothing more to say about the man.

Trotsky's broader writings on Stalin—the political man, Party leader, and revolutionary personality—came in later years, but I was certain at the end of 1931 that his political and organizational relationship and struggles with Stalin from 1923 until his deportation could not but encompass an evaluation of the personality of his opponent and bitter enemy. I felt that it was an evasion for him to say he had nothing more to add. Why this most peculiar silence? Perhaps, again, to maintain an exclusively *objective* political attitude toward the conflict, to show that the struggle in the Russian Party was not a *personal* quarrel. It was this rigid, and in a sense honorable, posture that left Stalin unimpressed. Stalin was ready to destroy anyone who stood in the way of his drive for total power.

I talked to Jan Frankel about Trotsky's insufficient reply, explaining that Stalin hit the "American scene" as a great surprise. I told him that there was considerable disturbance over the vicious attacks on Trotsky, Zinoviev, and Kamenev, who were familiar figures to the Americans as leaders of the Revolution and companions of Lenin. Frankel had no explanation. Robert Wistrich, concerned about the manner in which Trotsky developed his struggle with Stalin, was struck that his "fight around ideas" was a form of passivity and wrote: "Trotsky's behavior during this period was that of a man who did everything *except* to concern himself with the succession."[42]

In the factional struggle, Stalin displayed craftiness, slyness, and total devotion to the goal of replacing Lenin in the Party and state. Carmichael saw this as dominating Stalin's determination to destroy the Opposition. He thought Trotsky's inadequate assessment of Stalin "incomprehensible," but he was impressed that

In overestimating ideas, in rationalizing his refusal to "stoop," "deign," and "demean himself," he was evading the unmistakable fact that he was simply incapable of navigating in the protean relationships of a large organization. While capable of expressing with mystical conviction the generalizations of Marxism, he was blind to the real-life interests of his opponents, who exploited such generalizations in order to make them dovetail with their private ambitions.[43]

Wistrich noted, too, what many in the struggle felt for some time: that Trotsky "was remarkably blind to Stalin's capacities, and incapable of uniting the Bolshevik Old Guard against him."[44]

Max Shachtman and I had many conversations concerning the significance of Lenin's Testament in singling out Trotsky and Stalin as the two most able men in the leadership. We had no doubt that Trotsky was the *most* able man in the Politburo next to Lenin, but we had difficulty, given our ignorance in those early years, in understanding why Lenin considered Stalin outstanding as well, especially when he regarded Stalin as a future danger to the Party. Lenin knew well the evil qualities of his "Old Bolshevik" colleague. But Stalin was already the master of the apparatus by the time Lenin wrote his Testament. Wistrich suggests that Stalin's true character was "lost on his adversaries, on all except the dying Lenin, who saw the danger and desperately sought to avert its potential consequences."

Trotsky "dug his own grave" with his hesitations, ambiguities, strategic and tactical blunders. Antonov-Ovsyenko believed that "Stalin had a satanic hatred of Trotsky and at the same time feared him. He feared Trotsky's indisputable authority as a leader of the Revolution and the Red Army and his great popularity within the Party and among the people."[45] But as Trotsky's strange struggle unfolded, Stalin's grip on the Party tightened, and he became bolder in his ruthless drive against all those might stand in his way.

Stalin more than once lectured Trotsky for failing to acknowledge or understand the monolithic nature of Bolshevism. By 1925, eight years after the Revolution, Trotsky resigned the last of his posts, President of the Revolutionary Military Council. Despite his acceptance of Bolshevism, Trotsky never quite grasped the inner rhythm of this most unique political cadre; he could not really adjust to it after the heroic days of the Revolution ended and Lenin, whom he came to idolize, died, leaving him without the one person whose leadership he gladly acknowledged.

Notes

1. Carr, *The Russian Revolution,* pp. 140–41.

2. The "Georgian Affair" was Stalin's effort, aided by Ordzhanikidze and Dzerzhinsky, to seize the Party in the republic of Georgia in a coup against the native leadership. Lenin, outraged by what happened but very ill and unable to intervene, asked Trotsky to do so. In a letter to Trotsky in March of 1923 Lenin wrote: "I wish very much to ask you to take upon yourself the defense of the Georgian case in the Central Committee of the Party. . . . I cannot trust [the] impartiality [of Stalin and Dzerzhinsky]. Quite the contrary, if you would agree to undertake the defense, my mind would be at rest."

3. Schapiro, p. 269.

4. *My Life,* p. 486.

5. *My Life,* p. 486.

6. Quoted in "Interview with Boris Bazhanov," *Survey,* Summer 1980 issue, p. 66.

7. Medvedev, *Stalin and Stalinism,* p. 47–48.

8. *My Life,* p. 489.

9. Trotsky, quoted in Eastman's *Since Lenin Died,* pp. 145–153.

10. Schapiro, pp. 211–212.

11. Quoted in "Interview with Boris Bazhanov," p. 98.

12. Report of the Thirteenth Party Congress, Moscow, 1924.

13. Schapiro, p. 307.

14. Trotsky's letter to the Central Committee, quoted in *Since Lenin Died,* pp. 155–158.

15. *Trotsky's Diary in Exile,* pp. 53–54.

16. Report of the Central Committee, 1925.

17. Trotsky's letter to the Central Committee, quoted in *Since Lenin Died,* pp. 155–158.

18. Wolfe, *A Life in Two Centuries,* pp. 65–66.

19. Eastman, *Heroes,* the chapter devoted to Trotsky. The term *exceptionalism* arose in the American Communist Party and became a sharply debated issue in the factional struggle between the Lovestone leadership of the Party and the Foster and Cannon faction—mainly, however, with the Foster faction. The term itself had a pejorative intent in the Party debates, for it embodied a view expressed most strongly by the Lovestoneites, that American capitalism had a development unlike the capitalist countries of Europe, at once rapid and extensive, and reflected by mass-production technology, making it the most advanced industrial nation in the world. This view was vigorously fought in the Party, if not most militantly by Foster, certainly by Browder, who held that there was nothing "exceptional" about American progress and unique growth for a nation just 150 years old.

Although the Lovestone faction was able to win the debate and could point to the unusual characteristics of the "prosperity period" of the twenties, the essential capitalist character of the country revealed itself in 1929 with the stock market crash, which presaged the worst economic crisis in American history; it also established that the United States confronted the same fundamental problems as other capitalist nations in what became a worldwide economic crisis unrelieved until the Second World War. Actually, both sides were right: There were exceptional and unusual features in America's vast growth, and in its transformation from an agricultural to an industrial country, but it was finally beset by the common problems of capitalism in crisis.

20. *My Life*, p. 534.
21. *My Life*, p. 482.
22. Quoted by Medvedev in his *Stalin and Stalinism*, p. 49.
23. Knei-Paz, p. 379.
24. Carmichael, p. 301.
25. Balabanoff, *My Life as a Rebel*, p. 250.
26. Knei-Paz, p. 379.
27. *Stalin and Stalinism*, pp. 62 and 63.
28. Antonov-Ovsyenko, *Time of Stalin*, p. 30.
29. Nedava, *Trotsky and the Jews*, p. 176.
30. Trotsky letter quoted in *Stalin and Stalinism*, p. 62.
31. *Stalin and Stalinism*, p. 62.
32. *Stalin and Stalinism*, p. 62.
33. Shachtman "Hoover Institute Paper," pp. 15 and 46.
34. Cohen, *Bukharin and the Russian Revolution*, p. 325.
35. Antonov-Ovysenko, p. 229.
36. Conquest, *The Great Terror*, Appendix A, p. 525.
37. Quoted by Medvedev, p. 140.
38. Quoted by Medvedev, p. 140.
39. *Stalin and Stalinism*, pp. 140–141.
40. Maksudov, quoted in *Stalin and Stalinism*, p. 141.
41. Zakovsky, quoted in Antonov-Ovsyenko, p. 96.
42. *Fate of a Revolutionary*, p. 128.
43. Carmichael, p. 301.
44. *Fate of a Revolutionary*, p. 126.
45. Antonov-Ovsyenko, p. 108.

Paris—1934

Trotsky's vision that "the hellish works of Italian facism would probably appear as a pale and almost humane experiment in comparison with the work of German National Socialists" became reality all too quickly. On January 30, 1933, the Junker president of the German republic, General Paul Von Hindenburg, appointed Adolph Hitler as Chancellor. As Trotsky predicted, Hitler proceeded at once to rearm the country, to create a "Greater Germany" that would be the most powerful nation in the world. He first consolidated his domestic power, then carried out his long-declared policies exactly as he said he would.

After the appointment of the new chancellor, the February 4, 1933, issue of *The Militant* ran this headline: *Hitler in Power; Civil War Starts*—an assertion based on hopes rather than reality, because there was no internal resistance of any kind, let alone a civil war, against the new Hitler regime. A week later, *The Militant* was compelled to note that "Hitler is consolidating the power of fascism in Germany." But the editorial board still had not faced reality. "Whoever blocks the Workers' United Front," they cried, "is a traitor." But no "united front" of workers ever emerged. Nor could it. The time for struggle had passed.

As Trotsky had warned, it was too late to do anything. Nazi hordes swarmed over the country to carry out the destruction of the labor movement, the political parties of the working class, and all democratic organizations and institutions—from trade unions to fraternal organizations. Within a brief time there were no longer any independent organizations of the working class or other social groupings that did not fit into the mold of the German Fascist state. Social Democracy, politically disoriented and psychologically unprepared for the new reality, was an easy victim of the Nazi assault. The trade unions were taken over by the new regime and transformed into state institutions completely subservient to the new power.

The regime was particularly vicious in its destruction of the Communist Party and its various front organizations, if only because it believed these to be agents of the intensely hated Soviet Union. The Nazis were merciless toward their recent partners in the Red Referendum in Prussia, where they had linked arms to assault the Social Democratic government, seeking its overthrow. Little time remained to the leader of the Communist Party, Ernst Thaelman, now in prison, to explain to Breitscheid, the noted Social Democrat, why "Social Democracy was the main enemy in Germany."

The Communist International, completely subservient to Stalin's direction and policies, with the duplicity characteristic of Stalinism, proclaimed in its boastful appraisal of the new situation in Europe that its policy on Germany was absolutely correct "up to and including the time of the Hitler coup d'état." When Stalin concluded his pact with Hitler in 1939, which in effect opened the way for World War II, it was altogether fitting that the Soviet Foreign Minister, Molotov, Stalin's close associate, should proclaim that "fascism is a matter of taste." (It was no accident that in Lenin's time Molotov was known as "lead-ass" for the sluggishness of his mind.)

The future of Europe looked bleak indeed as one observed reaction sweep across the Continent. Fascists, quasi-Fascist, and a variety of other reactionary movements arose in all European countries. An endless stream of refugees escaped to havens in the West. Among the first were leaders and activists of the democratic left. And then there were refugees of the *totalitarian* left. Many more of those who fled were Jews who sensed their dark fate.

For the Trotskyist movement, the easy victory of German fascism ended its basic political and organizational orientation, which was joined to the Stalinist International and its parties. In all countries where the Trotskyists had been expelled from their respective Communist Parties, they had tried to function as expelled factions of the parties, in the manner of the Russian Left Opposition. Reform of the International and the parties summarized the Trotskyist perspective, and its organizations confined themselves to the propagation of the views of Trotsky and the Russian Left Opposition, certain that eventually they would return triumphant, welcomed back by a movement that must finally acknowledge that Trotsky and his followers were right. History has since shown that this was *never* a tenable perspective. The European Trotskyist groups were no more successful than their Russian comrades.

Trotsky and the movement he created were ambivalent regarding Stalinism from the very beginning.[1] Indeed, it was Trotsky who gave us the name "Stalinism." But even as Trotsky wrote about the Russian "Thermidor," the Stalinist counterrevolution had already begun. The new Bolshevik Party was the party of the Stalinist bureaucrat, free of revolutionary Socialist zeal. Its old membership was now for the most part politically isolated; it would be decimated during Stalin's purges. Yet none of these degenerative developments convinced Trotsky to change his position. Only the German debacle could do that.

Trotsky called for the creation of new parties everywhere and an immediate end to the prospect of reform of the Communist International. He now urged the immediate formation of a *new* International. The response in the Trotskyist organizations was instantaneous. For a long time, many of them felt stifled by the traditional view, and the events in Germany reinforced those feelings. Even before the proposed change, speakers and writers ceased to stress the old view of reforming the Third International, because it had no appeal for members or followers.

It would have been politically absurd to continue the old line after Hitler. The call for a new movement only emphasized the defeat of Stalin's policy. Stalin responded to Trotsky's call with anger and violence. Like Nazi storm troopers, whom they resembled in political disputes, Party Stalinists literally attacked the Trotskyists' public functions, thinking they could in that way stop the agitation for a new International.

Despite Hitler's triumph, however, Trotsky still wrote with unwarranted optimism. In *The Tragedy of the German Proletariat,* for example, we read: "The German workers will rise again. Stalinism never."[2] Alas, only one half of this prophecy came true: The German workers did rise again, in West Germany, by reestablishing their trade unions and the Social Democratic Party. But Stalinist totalitarianism rose as well, by creating the Russian satellite states of East Germany, Poland, Hungary, and Czechoslovakia. Aided by the Russian armies and the political stupidity of the Allies, principally the United States (whose political pundits and leaders seemed never to have understood Stalin or Russian society), Stalinism revived and triumphed in Eastern Europe.

The Trotskyist organizations were not the only ones to respond sharply to the new political events. Independent Socialist organizations moved in the same direction, at least for the moment. Most prominent of these was the Socialist Workers' Party of Germany (SAP), and the Independent Socialist and Revolutionary Socialist Parties of Holland (OSP and RSP, respectively). There were other organizations in Norway, Sweden, and France that made feints in the direction of a new world body. Even the Independent Labor Party of Great Britain (ILP) made some weak gestures in that direction, but the ILP was anchored to a conservative past by strong Stalinist sentiments, dominated by the ideological and political confusions of its spokesman, Fenner Brockway.

As a result of their sharp criticisms of the Socialist International and the Comintern, the "Declaration of Four" was signed on August 22, 1933, by the three Socialist parties and the Trotskyist International Communist League. These organizations became known as the "Bloc of Four." They formed a shaky "united front," brought together in an attempt to create a "new international of revolutionary socialism."

The Bloc of Four endured through a year of internal crisis. There were at least two reasons for this instability: the grave doubts of the Dutch and SAP cosigners about a new International, and Trotsky's pressure that the Committee advocate the formation of a "Fourth International" based on the first four Comintern congresses rather than a new one. A "new" one, he felt, would permit a variety of programmatic views, essentially "centrist" rather than revolutionary. Although he initially used the term "new International" rather than "Fourth International," he now felt it was possible to move a step forward. The other organizations, however, resisted Trotsky's pressures and would never have accepted a "new" International based on the early congresses of the Comintern, for that meant accepting the political premises of Leninism, or Bolshevism.

The Stalinists' response to the new turn in the Trotskyist world movement and other independent Socialist parties was a campaign of physical violence. The United States was the main arena, because the American Communist Party was the most ignorant and abject in the Comintern, responding with Pavlovian reflexes to every whim of the Kremlin. It organized hooligan gangs to attack public meetings whenever the Stalinist movement was severely criticized, especially when these gatherings discussed the need for a new Party or a new International. These attacks, brutal as they could be, were merely relatively weak foreshadowings of the Moscow Frame-up Trials of the thirties, which cannibalized the Russian Communist Party, the GPU apparatus, the army, and the nation at large.[3] The violence of world Stalinism against its political opponents was in inverse ratio to its cowardice and passivity in the rise of Hitler and German fascism.

*   *   *

In the summer of 1933 the youth organization of the Independent Socialist Party of Holland proposed a conference of youth organizations to review the new political stage brought about by the debacle in Germany. Among the questions they wished to consider was the formation of a new youth organization as part of the movement for a new International. Trotsky was greatly interested in this youth conference, he hoped it would do what the Bloc of Four had been unable to do. The situation was not very clear to us in the States, because we did not know too much about the negotiations and problems within the Bloc during the second half of 1933.

Neither I nor the American Party leadership knew much about the Bloc of Four or what led to its collapse. But I was enthusiastic about the change in the international Trotskyists' policy, which freed us from the onerous task of claiming we were the expelled left-wing of the Communist International and its affiliated parties. From 1929 on, we decreased our "factional" activity around the Communist Party and its periphery. We tried to make a broader appeal to various radical circles as well as to the labor movement. We met with tiny successes, nothing that gave us any confidence that we were at last on the road to building mass parties. It was a liberating period, however, because we no longer felt as though we were an appendage of the Communist world. We felt that our movement could not be tainted by the CP's betrayal in Germany. We thought it might now be possible to enjoy a time of broader support and significant growth. The youth conference in Holland could be a stepping stone to such progress, I hoped.

The summer of 1933 was also the time when Trotsky left his Turkish exile. By some quirk in the strange and intense political atmosphere in France, he obtained a visa to reside in that country, and on July 17 Trotsky, Natalia, his staff, and two Americans, Max Shachtman and Sara Weber (Trotsky's Russian-language secretary in Turkey, France, and Mexico), boarded the Italian vessel *Bulgaria* and sailed for Marseilles. (The bizarre events attending the ship's arrival is described in some detail by the late Jean Van Heijenoort, for seven years Trotsky's secretary, in his book *With Trotsky in Exile*.) The trail of his movements ended for a time in St. Palais, near Royan, and then in Barbizon, near Paris.[4]

After Trotsky arrived in France, he wrote to the National Committee of the American Communist League about the proposed youth conference. The conference was to concern itself specifically with the danger of an impending war, the victory of fascism in Germany, and the necessity of a new International. Trotsky believed the conference to be of great value to the international Left Opposition and asked if it was possible for me to attend the conference as a representative of the International Trotskyists and the American youth organization. He considered me knowledgeable in youth matters and a competent representative for our world movement.

In face of this request, the National Committee could do nothing but accept.

I wrote to Trotsky, saying I would be unable to attend the conference if it was convened before the end of the year; if it was postponed to January or the early part of the following year, though, I would be able to attend. On November 21, Trotsky answered:

> Just received your letter on the Youth Conference. Hasten reply to it in view of the extreme importance of the matter. . . . The conference is postponed; . . . I am giving you below the address of Com. Held in Amsterdam and through whom you may get in touch directly with the initiators of the conference.[5] . . . You are quite right that the conference could produce serious results only on condition that our delegation comes united and well-prepared. . . . The direction of the preparatory work was assigned by the International Secretariat to Com. Souzo.[6] . . . Your presence at the conference, as well as sometime before the conference, would, of course, be most useful.

At the same time he wrote in German to Walter Held:

> The Youth Conference is postponed. To what date? This is of the greatest importance for America. We have a comrade there, namely Glotzer, who in questions of the youth movement is very well informed and also has a very clear head. Glotzer's work at the conference and also before the conference is of great importance.[7]

I then made preparations to leave for Europe, the most difficult part of which was to raise the money to make the trip during this period of extreme poverty for our League and its members. The League, except for a few members, did not help at all; it was the Spartacus Youth League that did the main work of raising funds. So, after some delay, I left the States for France, arriving in Paris on the morning of February 6, 1934.

The political situation in France was desperate; a general strike had begun that very morning. The labor unions, the Socialist and Communist Parties, and other independent democratic organizations took to the streets to demonstrate their readiness to fight the country's rising tide of reaction, which was headed by the *Croix de Feu* under the leadership of Colonel (Count) Casimir de la Rocque, a French army officer and the leading Fascist spokesman in France. Paris had the air of a great national holiday in that the ordinarily bustling city was strangely quiet; nobody moved except on foot. The great square in front of Gare du Nord was filled with taxicabs so mixed up that only the skilled drivers who created the maze could have unwound it. Without conveyance, I walked, bag in hand, to

15 Vaugirard, the headquarters of the French League.

After I exchanged greetings with old and new comrades, I was taken to quarters I shared with a pleasant Indo-Chinese (so they were called in those days of the French Empire) comrade, Nguen Van Nam, known in the organization as Anthony. Anthony spoke no English and I spoke no French. We started communicating with gestures, but I soon learned that he had studied English in school and that, although he had never had an opportunity to use it, he could read and write it. Anthony was a warm person and gracious host. We managed remarkably well by writing notes to each other. Years later he became a victim of the brutal Stalinist regime in Hanoi, when all independent political groups, especially the Trotskyists, were slaughtered.

Soon after my arrival, I renewed my acquaintance with Lyova Sedov, who had fled Germany and now lived in Paris with Jeanne. He told me that Sieva had been living with him after Zinaida's suicide, but that in the critical days of Hitler's assumption of power, he had been sent to Vienna. This was before Hitler forced his *anschluss* of Austria. Sieva was to rejoin them very soon in Paris. I met Raymond Molinier and Pierre Frank again after a lapse of three years. I also was able to talk to some of the young members I had known at the end of 1931, outstanding of whom was Ivan Craipeau, a popular and leading Trotskyist who was to participate actively in the Amsterdam Youth Conference.[9]

The International Secretariat met with me upon my arrival to discuss the youth conference, the role of the ICL, and the documents we would present to express our particular views on the matters considered by it. Several short documents were mentioned, the content of which was inspired by Trotsky's comments on the world political situation in the light of the Fascist takeover of Germany. The meeting was held in a cafe—not a very clever arrangement, given the political-emigré status of most of the participants. The half dozen people who participated spoke in a babble of English, French, and German. Given the jittery mood of the country since Hitler's German victory and the attendant prospect of war with the French, it was not surprising that a detective interrupted our meeting without warning and demanded to see the documents of everyone present.

Along with my French comrades and me, our meeting included exiles from German and Italian fascism, the International Secretary, Erwin Bauer,[10] the Italian Souzo, and Sedov from Stalinist Russia. None of them had valid passports, though they all traveled with papers signifying that their residence in France was legal, if circumscribed. The detective did not reveal the purpose of his search, and that made us nervous: We could not trust the government to be devoted to one's right of asylum. Sedov was the most vulnerable, because he lacked what they termed "strong papers"; he was truly a man without a country, as was his father. It had been made clear to him in many direct and indirect ways that he was a resident of France only by the grace of the French government. After the officer completed his inspection, we speeded up our discussion and dispersed.

The general strike that had greeted me on my arrival climaxed in a call for a mass demonstration against French fascism and the increasing conservatism of Premier Edouard Daladier's government. A united front made of all the anti-Fascist political organizations, plus the two national trade union movements of France, was initiated as a statement to the indigenous Fascist forces that they faced a battle if they made a move to take power. The French Trotskyists anticipated a conflict with the government forces that might take the form of a street brawl, so we instructed all emigrés to play it safe and absent themselves from the march; an arrest in the area could mean instant deportation. Sedov in particular was ordered to stay away.

Sedov and I thereupon made an appointment for the day of the demonstration to discuss a number of matters, most particularly the ever-present problem of circulating the *Russian Bulletin* in the United States and Canada. We set a meeting place on the Boulevard Saint Michel for late morning. I waited for him for two hours before I decided that some kind of emergency must have prevented him from keeping the appointment.

Something *had* happened. Sedov violated the instructions of the Secretariat and the French League and had gone to the demonstration. Fighting broke out in several sections of the march, and the police began mass arrests. Sedov was grabbed by a policeman in one of the skirmishes, but he managed to free himself, a fact he related to me with great excitement later in the day. I silently noted to myself that his bravado could have ended tragically.

*   *   *

During my first week in Paris I met a number of German emigrés who had escaped the Nazi roundup of known or potential "enemies of the new Reich." Awaiting my meeting with Trotsky, I spent a great deal of time with these Germans, from whom I learned a great deal about the situation in the country under Hitler prior to their flight.

On February 12 Sedov gave me a letter from Trotsky, who was now living in Barbizon. The letter, preparatory to our meeting, dealt with several matters:

Dear Comrade Glotzer:

I am very glad that you have come to Europe at this particular time, a time which is for you, as for us, of great interest. You will be able to report in New York that in the most conservative country in Europe, France, things, including the League, are on the move. In a little while, of course, as soon as things have quieted down a bit, you will give the [French] League a report on the work and successes of the American League.

It goes without saying that the most important thing is your participation in the youth conference. I am sure that your presence will be of great value. If you meet the youth representative of the Weisbord organization in Holland, treat this comrade—if I may take the liberty to give you a piece of advice— in a friendly and objective fashion and make clear to him the senselessness of [Albert] Weisbord's positions.[11]

Don't you think by applying pressure from all sides Weisbord could be compelled:

1. to publish a theoretical organ together with the League;
2. to stop all public attacks against the League;
3. to agree to a division of labor with the League?

I have not received any answer from the American comrades on this proposal or, better put, this suggestion.

Of course, we will see each other and have an extensive discussion about all pending questions. For the moment, a couple of practical matters:

1. Have you seen Comrade Maria Reese? It is absolutely necessary that you visit her and discuss practical details of her trip to America.
2. You probably have heard that [Arkadi] Maslov and Ruth Fischer are about to join us (this is not to be made public!).[12] Since they are both concerned with Anglo-Saxon affairs, I consider it very desirable for you to visit them to bring them information about America. You can arrange this through Comrade Schwarz [Sedov]. I will write these comrades about you.

Until we see each other,
Your Old Man

Before I met with Trotsky, I did make the acquaintance of Maria Reese, a Communist Party member of the German Reichstag who fled Germany, broke with the Party, and declared her adherence to the Trotsky- ist movement. She had been Ernst Torgler's companion, the leader of the Reichstag parliamentary delegation of the Communist Party. He was a defendant in the Reichstag-fire frame-up trial who was acquitted and sub- sequently arrested and confined to a concentration camp for the duration

"The Best Bolshevik" in exile, circa 1934.

The author in Kadikoy, Turkey, in 1931.

Trotsky "mass fishing" with his favorite fisherman, Kharalambos, in Prinkipo, Turkey, in 1930; the Trotsky residence in Kadikoy, 22 Sifa Street.

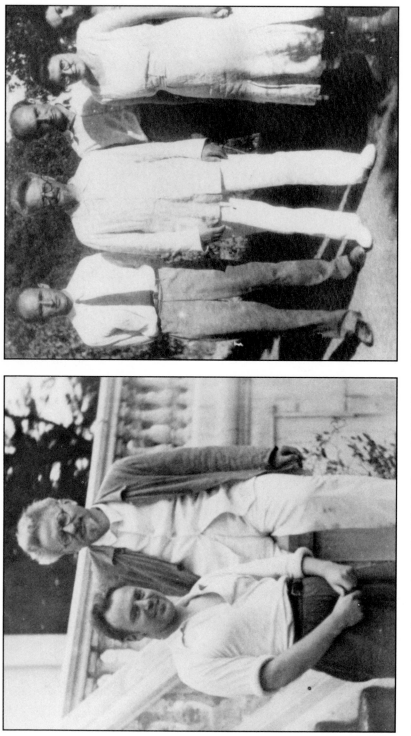

Trotsky and his son, Leon Sedov, in Saint Palais, France, in 1933; Roman Well (Sobelvicius), Trotsky, Adolph Senin (Sobelvicius), and Zinaida Trotsky Vokow (Trotsky's daughter), in Kadikoy, Turkey, August 1931. The Sobelvicius brothers turned out to be GPU agents.

Maria Reese, a German Communist who returned to Germany to support the Third Reich; Walter Held, brilliant Trotskyist Youth organizer murdered by the GPU in the Soviet Union; Max Shachtman and James P. Cannon, two of the United States' most prominent voices of the non-Communist left, in Paris gathering support in 1938.

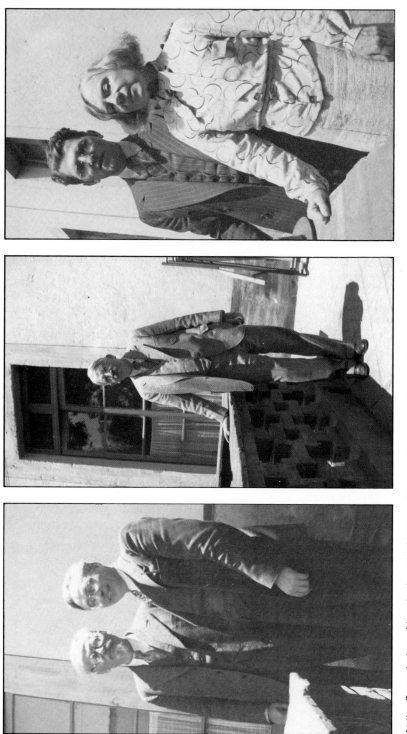

At the Commission of Inquiry into the Moscow Trials, in Coyoacan, Mexico: Trotsky with his lawyer, Albert Goldman; Commission chairman John Dewey; Trotsky's wife, Natalia, with author.

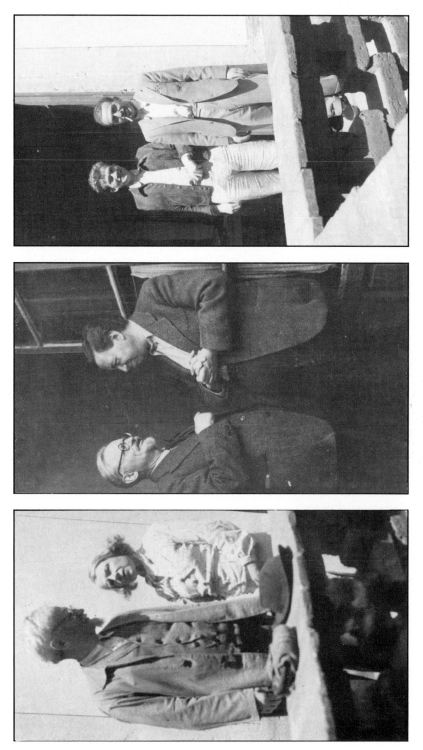

Trotsky with his wife, Natalia Sedov, and with Diego Rivera, at whose house the Trotskys first stayed upon their exile to Mexico; Jean Van Heijenoort and Jan Frankel, two of Trotsky's most loyal assistants.

of the war, at the end of which he joined the SAP. Reese had become well-known in Western European emigré circles. Her popular pamphlet, *I Accuse Stalinism,* was given increased stature by a November 1933 article of Trotsky's entitled "Maria Reese and the Comintern," which later became an introduction to the pamphlet. Maria was a buxom German woman in her mid-forties. Even before I left for Europe we had discussed her desire to come to the United States. She had failed to be admitted to Holland and wanted to establish new roots in America. Arne Swabeck, then National Secretary of the Communist League of America, without knowing very much about Reese, suggested that I marry her and bring her back with me when I returned to the States. Having read something of her history, I knew she was older than I, so I had some doubts about the proposal. I was then just past my mid-twenties, and I looked even younger.

When we met, Maria convulsed with laughter at the disparity in our ages. "You know," she said, "if we tried to enter through Customs as husband and wife, we would be arrested immediately for breaking the immigration laws. I look like your mother. We would both end up in jail." Our projected "marriage" was—agreeably on both sides—unconsummated.

Well, that settled a matter that greatly troubled me before our meeting. There was no doubt at all that American authorities were closely following the political events in Europe in those years and would have given special attention to this political marriage had we tried to enter the States with that status.

Still, I saw Maria Reese frequently in Paris, since she was now a part of the German Trotskyist emigré group. We "took in" Paris, as they say, visiting several museums and churches and walking about the city. Along the "Boul Mich" there were at that time stores called "Chamberlands," which were centers of the mechanical production of music. They were equipped with devices which, when fed a coin, played rather good music. We tried all of these centers for musical entertainment. I liked to listen to small chamber music groups and she preferred the famous German tenor Richard Tauber.

Underneath it all, however, she seemed to me unhappy; she felt dislocated in France, apparently unwilling or unable to withstand the rigors of her exile. She talked often about her loneliness for Torgler and for her many old friends.

Later in 1934, she broke with the Trotskyist movement and socialism, returned to Germany, and gave her services to the New Reich!

*   *   *

Even before Trotsky's letter and his suggestion that I visit Ruth Fisher and Arkadi Maslov, I learned from Bauer and several other Germans that these two former German Communist Party leaders, long-time supporters of Gregory Zinoviev in the Comintern, were residing in Paris. They had declared themselves supporters of Trotskyism and wanted to join the German section. The majority of the German League in Paris, however, was opposed to their membership, or even to any relations with them. Fisher and Maslov were considered "intriguants" rather than true Trotskyists.

I went to see Maslov and Fischer, on Trotsky's suggestion, in a meeting arranged by Sedov. Communication with these two was easy because Ruth spoke sufficient English for the occasion. Our exchange of greetings was friendly and open. Whatever their past political relations, I accepted their comradeship without question, keeping Trotsky's letter in mind. We discussed many topics, but mainly the economic crisis in the United States and about life generally in my country. They knew a great deal about the United States, especially Maslov, who was obviously the intellectually dominant of the two.

Ruth was a leader of the Germany Communist Party in her own right, an accomplished agitator whose entire life was wrapped up in the movement. She was the sister of Gerhardt Eisler, who was prominent in the affairs of the German Communists and a notorious agent of the GPU; and Hans Eisler, the Stalinist musician who helped organize the German pro-Soviet literary circle of exiles in Hollywood, including Berthold Brecht, Heinrich Mann, and Lion Feuchtwanger.

An important part of our discussion was related to their attitude toward the Trotskyist movement. German Trotskyists had questioned the reality of their new solidarity and raised a number of old questions, the strongest of which was their long-time active opposition to Trotsky and his movement in the Soviet Union and abroad. The Germans warned that in organizational matters they were Zinovievists, i.e., intriguants who could bring nothing but misfortune to the German League, whose movement was indeed a very tender shoot.

Even without Fischer and Maslov's participation, the German Trotskyist organization had more than its share of internal crises and not a little of its own political intrigue from the very beginning of its existence. It had suffered, for example, from the disruptive presence of the Soviet agents Roman Well and Adolph Senin. What the German group in France failed to grasp was that these two internationally known former leaders of the German Communist Party declared their adherence to the Trotskyist movement. It was sheer sectarianism to refuse their collaboration.

In 1934 Maslov and Fischer's adherence to Trotskyism was not yet a public matter. Trotsky's reference to the point in his letter was sufficient warning to me that there was good reason for caution. Obviously, he did not request that I visit them simply to make a friendly gesture: My visit would be an act of political recognition demonstrating a willingness to accept them irrespective of past divergences. Trotsky reinforced his acceptance of them in a letter to them about my impending visit.

During our meeting, I raised the question of their former association with Zinoviev and the opening of the campaign against Trotsky under the rubric "Leninism or Trotskyism," the very phrase an invention of the then-president of the Comintern. They denied that they had participated in that vicious struggle, which led eventually to Stalin's triumph. When I mentioned this denial to Trotsky in my later discussion with him, he related that in the beginning Maslov was undecided concerning what position to take in this political conflict, but confirmed that they *had* supported Zinoviev. At an important meeting in Moscow, Maslov decided to take sides and actually made a speech against Trotsky. They were in that factional position and continued for a number of years to be members of Zinoviev's corp of international supporters. However, Trotsky felt that the past should not be held against these veterans nor prevent collaboration with them in a new political setting. He tried hard to get the German section to agree.

I was to meet with Trotsky three weeks after my arrival. The youth conference was drawing nearer, and it was necessary to settle matters relating to it with him. When Sedov brought Trotsky's letter to me, he also gave me instructions on how to get to our meeting place. I was to go to an apartment located near the Arsenal Metro station. The owner of the apartment was unknown to me, though someone suggested that it could have been that of Simone Weil, who at one time had some deep interest in Trotsky and his ideas, to the point where she had some discussions with him. I was admitted to this apartment by "Comrade Steen" (Rudolph Klement).[13]

The meeting with Trotsky to take up the matters outlined in his letter was also a renewal of personal relations. I was startled when I first saw him. The goatee was gone, and his hair was trimmed, but his carriage was as erect as ever, and he showed no signs of aging. He greeted me with a warm embrace and immediately inquired how I fared in Paris during the intervening weeks, laughingly saying that I still looked young. I told him briefly about the people I had seen and the meetings I had attended. I then inquired after Natalia, regretting that I was unable to see her. He replied that if it were possible, we would make up for her absence after the youth conference. Then he added that their life in France, while generally better than in Turkey, was more confining for security and political reasons.

The first question Trotsky raised in our discussion was the problem of Albert Weisbord and his small group in New York, the Communist League of Struggle. Trotsky had written to the American CLA several months before about establishing some kind of relationship with Weisbord. The "Weisbord question" had a little history in the American movement, and we were all, irrespective of faction, disgusted with both him and his group.

Several attempts to work with Weisbord and his group were made. Joint discussions were held. He addressed the New York branch of the CLA several times, and during these we found our views sharply divergent on the assessment of the political situation in the country, and the trade-union question; he had not quite given up his dual unionist views. He was a strong advocate of "making a revolutionary situation" where none existed, on the theory that this depended on the "subjective factor" of leadership; if leaders had "the will," they could transform almost any critical or "crisis" situation into a revolutionary one. And, of course, *he* was that type of leader, in contrast to the leadership of the CLA with whom he wanted to collaborate!

The individual characteristics of Weisbord, whom all the leading committee members knew from Communist Party days, made even working with him, let along unifying with him, most difficult. He was egotistical to the extreme and intolerant of any differences. He conducted the affairs of his group in a totally dictatorial and bureaucratic way. He was, after all, the only leader in his group. Both the leadership and membership of the CLA felt that he was unassimilable; collaboration with him would have a negative effect on the organization. When Trotsky made his proposal originally, the Committee decided to reject it for the reasons I cited, but apparently no reply was sent to him. Trotsky therefore wrote Max Shachtman on January 20, 1934:

> I want to ask you about Weisbord. If he should firmly obligate himself not to attack the League, etc., would you consider it possible to fuse both theoretical organs, including Weisbord in the editorial board as a minority and guaranteeing him a certain freedom of "discussion"? I do not make this proposal. I merely try to get preliminary information from you. If such a plan were realizable its advantages would be obvious not only with regard to Weisbord but with regard to other groups and individuals who would convince themselves that the League knows how to gather people and grant them freedom of discussion without, however, giving up its principles.[14]

We had decided to reject Trotsky's original proposal, and the Committee agreed unanimously that I relay this decision to Trotsky. Some of us felt his letter to Shachtman was merely another attempt to seek acceptance of his proposal. This participation by Trotsky in the internal life of an individual organization was in the tradition of the Communist International, where it was exercised in at least two ways: fraternally and bureaucratically. The fraternal way was the manner used in the very early years of the International, which was breached often by Zinoviev and was nonexistent under Stalin. In the Trotskyist movement, participation by Trotsky in the internal problems of the League or other groups was in large part the result of the pressures put on him by national sections, factions, and individuals. What Weisbord was unable to obtain from his direct relationship with the CLA he sought by involving Trotsky and securing his intervention. We knew his pressure on Trotsky was unceasing. Trotsky did not order any policy or action; people called upon him as the political leader of the movement to aid them in any particular design.

I was not surprised, therefore, that Trotsky, thinking that unity with Weisbord would increase the strength of the Trotskyist movement in the United States (a grievously wrong idea), reiterated our personal discussion with the Weisbord question. First, he informed me that the "Weisbord youth" of his letter was a person called Fred (Raphael) Browner. I assured him that I would treat Browner with the necessary respect and friendliness. If Browner responded well to my fraternal treatment of him, we would have no problem working together in the youth conference. (So it turned out, and eventually Browner joined our organization. My decent relations with him and the events in Holland, Belgium, and France undoubtedly contributed to his political change.) At the moment, Trotsky seemed satisfied that I would carry out my promise.

Putting the Browner matter aside, we turned to the thorny question of Weisbord and his group. My immediate reply was direct and brief: "No. In this matter, I speak for the whole Committee, every single member of it," I said.

The unanimity of the rejection puzzled Trotsky for the moment. I pointed out that we had been dealing with the Weisbord question for over four years. It had taken much time and effort in pursuit of some conciliatory road that could lead to the unification of Weisbord's Communist League of Struggle with our organization. It had all been in vain. I then added: "It is not only the leadership that feels this way, but even more so, and in a sense more importantly, the New York organization, which was the scene of the many efforts made. The New York League bore the brunt of it and absolutely refuses to go through another debilitating experience with Weisbord, who now thinks he can achieve his purpose, break his isolation, through you, Comrade Trotsky, as the most important authority and influence in our movement."

Trotsky hastened to say that he was only making a proposal he hoped would eliminate once and for all the annoyance of Weisbord from the outside. He believed one more effort might lead to some kind of unification and a calming of Weisbord's attitude toward the CLA. Although he had publicly criticized Weisbord's views, he thought now, on the basis of Weisbord's latest representations, that the time was most auspicious for another try. However, Trotsky added, he was in no way insisting on his proposal because, in the last analysis, "I am aware that only the League can decide this question. And if you are all against it, there is nothing more for me to say." The matter was thus closed.[15]

As I mentioned earlier, we spent a good deal of time discussing my visit with Maslov and Fischer. He was pleased that I had had a friendly meeting and a far-ranging discussion of American affairs with them. Their past attacks on him were unsavory, but, he added, it made no difference what the past was; they now declared themselves in agreement with us and wanted to collaborate with the organization. We should not raise barriers to that collaboration. (Nowhere perhaps was Trotsky more unlike Stalin than in his friendliness toward one-time opponents.) We agreed that on my return from Amsterdam, I would visit them again. Trotsky stressed that Maslov and Fischer had many talents that could be very useful to our movement. As it turned out, sometime later, despite the opposition of the German group in Paris, Ruth Fischer, using the name "Dubois," became a member of the International Secretariat and functioned in that body from 1934–1936.[16]

I told Trotsky about my visits with Maria Reese, informing him, too, of Swabeck's proposal that I marry her. He laughed at the idea that I could pass as her legitimate husband and was quite amused when I told him that she called me "das kind" ("the child"). No matter; he was pleased that I spent time with her, because her emigré existence was extremely difficult.

We then turned to the impending youth conference, which was, after all, the reason I was in Europe. He was deeply concerned about the event, and most of our discussion was on the problems related to it. Trotsky reviewed the events of the previous months: the creation of the Bloc of Four and its first efforts in behalf of a new International, difficult though that road was. He thought it significant that the call for the youth conference came from Holland through the initiative of the youth section of the OSP. Trotsky advised that while relations with the OSP were difficult—because it hesitated to carry out its own program—we had to push the Party to follow the logic of its political declarations. It was very possible that the youth section was a step ahead of the Party, but he was really not certain of that, or how much the Party was involved in the call for the conference.

At this point Trotsky spoke generally of the importance of the youth movement in the struggle against Stalinism and for an uncompromising break with the old organizations. He was absolutely convinced that Hitler's victory would be the death-blow to the Comintern, which he considered up to then a more important factor in the revolutionary struggle than the Socialist International. He repeated what he had written to me shortly before I came to Europe, that while he considered the initiative of the OSP symptomatic of the times, he was nevertheless "worried that they would not follow the logic of the struggle for a Fourth International because they are really centrists who are afraid of a complete break with the Second and Third Internationals." I did not conclude from our discussion that the "new versus Fourth" controversy was a breaking point with these people, although that was the impasse at which we were to leave the conference with a ringing and defiant declaration.

We discussed the main purposes of our participation. Trotsky thought we should press for the adoption of a resolution on a new or Fourth International and one on the danger of war. My interpretation of the main point made by Trotsky was that we were to strive for the most, i.e., push the conference as far as we could along the road to a Fourth International, knowing that we were dealing with political forces that seemed to be moving in our direction but which lacked our "political clarity." It was this view that governed my approach to the conference.

Trotsky then discussed my departure for Amsterdam, named people I would meet en route, and said that Lyova would take care of other matters for me before I actually took leave. I learned from the discussion that the main ideas for resolutions had been already discussed with the International Secretariat and that Erwin Bauer would draft a resolution on the need to create a new youth International. Souzo prepared a draft resolution on the danger of fascism, and I prepared two resolutions, one on the danger of war and the other on what I thought the main declaration of the conference should be: The creation of a new International.

Before I left, Trotsky asked me if there was anything I needed or wanted. I said yes: an autographed photo from him. He laughed and said he would see that I get one. (Lyova later gave it to me when I returned from Holland and Belgium.) We embraced when I left our meeting place, and from then on the matters we discussed were dealt with through correspondence.

Following my discussion with Trotsky, I met with Lyova for a last-minute talk about the conference, at which time I received some financial assistance for myself and others to make the trip to Amsterdam. My departure was already arranged, and following the end of this meeting I left for Brussels. One Belgian youth met me at the station and brought me to the tiny apartment of the newly wed Camille and Nora Saxe, daughter of a prominent Socialist Party leader. George Fux, the leader of our youth organization in Belgium and in charge of the ICL correspondence in connection with the conference, came to the apartment, where we talked at length about the impending meeting.[17] Georges Vereecken, the leader of the Belgian Trotskyists, arrived just as I began to tell our young friends about my discussions with Trotsky and the importance he attached to the youth conference.

After a brief visit to the old city (passing the funeral of King Albert, who had died about the time I arrived in the country), I went on to Amsterdam to the home of Henricus Sneevliet, the veteran revolutionary Socialist, opponent of Dutch colonial policies, Trotskyist, and member of the Dutch Parliament.[18] Walter Held, an emigré from Germany and representative of the International Secretariat in charge of youth matters in Holland, was Sneevliet's secretary residing in his home. After a very stiff and formally correct meeting, we settled down to a close, intimate collaboration and went ahead to take charge of all matters relating to the conference, drawing up the final documents and establishing close relations with the Dutch youth.

The coolness that existed in my initial meeting with Held may have been caused by a momentary feeling on his part that this American appeared suddenly to take over conference affairs after he had done so much of the preliminary work. But Held soon realized that this was not so, and he was too friendly a person with too much sense to keep up his initial posture. We not only worked closely but became very warm friends, remaining so up to the time of his tragic and brutal murder by Stalin's secret police.

Held told me of a new antagonism toward us by the Dutch organizers of the conference, and in this attitude they were joined by the representative of the SAP youth, Willy Brandt. The reason for this he could only surmise, but he thought it might be because, having taken the initiative in the call for the new International, they now questioned their own audacity. He had the feeling too, that they feared the delegations of the Trotskyists. My report on the youth conference recorded that:

We found upon our arrival in Amsterdam sharp feeling against us: . . . Comrade Held and I went directly to the buro of the OSP to inquire about the arrival of the delegations. We were told that none had arrived and that all would come to the hotel on the day of the conference. We next inquired for Brandt of the SAP and were told that he was here. When we asked to see him, we were told that he was in Holland but not in Amsterdam.[19]

There was nothing for us to do in these circumstances but to complete all preliminaries for our participation in the conference. The ideas in the documents we prepared were syntheses of those propagated by the Trotskyist movement and came initially from Trotsky.

*   *   *

Nothing worked out the way we planned it. The Dutch organizers were oblivious to the reactionary moods emerging in Western Europe after Hitler's easy victory. No precautions of any kind for the safety of delegates were observed, even of the most elementary kind, even though it was known that a number of delegates were there illegally, without passports or other proper papers. The delegates from Sweden informed the Dutch comrades that they had been turned back at the border. Because the conference was to be held in the town of Laren, at the OSP Camp De-Toorts, on the twenty-fifth of February, all delegates were instructed to meet at the well-known Hotel De Roode Leeuve in central Amsterdam. The comings and goings of the delegates at the hotel were under the eyes of the Dutch police and security personnel, and, as we soon learned, all public telephones were tapped. Thus, the police were as familiar with the preliminaries of the conference as the delegates were. Nay, more so! While individual delegates knew about some of the delegates present, the police had knowledge of all of them.

The conference opened on a Saturday evening. The very first session was taken up with skirmishes between the Dutch, Norwegian, and German delegates on the one side, and the Trotskyists on the other, over a proposal to limit the Trotskyist delegation, the largest in the conference. Ours was not only the largest delegation, but in number and size of the individual youth organizations probably equal to, if not larger than, the non-Trotskyist representation taken together. The proposal they made to the conference was that the national sections of the ICL should have no vote, and, since we were an international organization, we should be limited to one vote. Although it was obvious that we could not control the conference even if all our delegates voted, our adversaries were determined to weaken our influence with a contrived organizational measure. It was bureaucratically motivated.

A second such scheme was a proposal to create a presidium of the conference to control its function in which only the Dutch OSP and the German SAP would be members. No representative from any of the ICL delegations was to be a member. We insisted on one member in the conference presidium of three, and we made a strong fight, because we knew that the proposal was meant to prevent our effective participation. The agenda prepared for the meeting made us all the more determined to work for our membership on the committee to direct its affairs. As presented to us, the agenda guaranteed that politics would be a minor preoccupation of the assembly. As the planners arranged it, a total of nine hours were devoted to meals, two hours for pause, four hours to dance, and a total of four and half hours to political questions, resolutions, and the election of a bureau to direct post-conference activities! My report on the conference records that:

> It became clear that in order to prevent the conference from becoming a huge joke, it was necessary to change the agenda. In this question there was agreement between Brandt and ourselves. I was speaking about the necessity of changing the agenda when the police arrived and changed it for us.[20]

The first organized attempt on a world scale to promote a new Socialist International movement seemed doomed, since the conference as planned by the OSP youth now ended. All the delegates were taken by police bus to the local jail in Laren. We were told by an officer that it was a basic right for the Dutch to meet and speak freely, the Netherlands being a democratic nation, but this right did not apply to foreigners—whereupon the Dutch delegates were released from custody and the foreign delegates underwent rigid passport examinations.

We were divided into two groups. Eight remained in the Laren jail, from where, on the initiative of the local mayor, four German exiles were deported to the New Reich. Eleven delegates were then bused to the Central Investigative Prison in Amsterdam.

In the Amsterdam jail, our papers were reexamined and records were made of the vital statistics of those arrested. We were photographed, fingerprinted, and assigned individual cells. Our personal possessions remained in Camp De Toorts. None of the Dutch delegates were prisoners, subjected to any examination, or fingerprinted.

The delegates confined to the Amsterdam jail were Brandt, Ording, and Moe of Norway; the ISL delegates Craipeau, Fux, Saxe, Brinke, and

Held; and myself and Browner, the Weisbord delegate. After two days the police divided the delegates by national or language groups, as I recall, and proceeded to deport us skillfully in relays to Belgium. We were all taken to Rosendaal near the border, our departure point, and met again in Brussels in two days. Browner and I, carrying American passports, had no travel problems, though we were put on a "milk" train at Rosendaal, which was scheduled to stop at Antwerp, turning a short hour-long trip into a half-day of local stops.

The intervention of the police and the deportations led to a conference in Brussels, which achieved a minor step forward from what seemed impossible in Holland: a minimal organization and propaganda for a new International. It was apparent to me in Laren that given the opening events of the meeting, no agreement of any kind would have been reached there. As it turned out, during the two days of confinement Held and I, after talking it over with our friends, met with Brandt, as spokesman for the Norwegians and the SAP, to propose some means of renewing the conference. We all criticized the Dutch's poor and irresponsible preparations.

The three of us then proceeded to reorganize the conference and draw up a new agenda. Brandt sought support among his political friends for the reorganization plan we three had agreed on. Held and I reported on the final agreement with Brandt to our comrades, who endorsed our action.

All of us knew that the new conference would have to be held in Brussels. In order to mislead the Belgian authorities who, on the announcement by the Dutch that we were deported to Belgium, began a search for us, we stated publicly that we would reconvene in Luxemburg. When the original conference had been halted by the police, the press in Western Europe gave large coverage to the event. The American press, without giving it the same importance as the European, also reported our arrests and deportations. The Brussels press reported that the police were patrolling the borders in a search for delegates; the police of Luxemburg were doing the same in their tiny land.

The new conference opened on February 28 at the Café Maison de Artiste in the central square of Brussels, opposite the central police headquarters. A comrade from the University of Brussels had arranged for the meeting place—for a meeting of his "artist friends" from various European nations who did not wish to be disturbed during their extended discussions of art. That is how the first effort was made for a new International beyond Trotskyist circles. Obviously, our foray was made on a very limited international scale.

The reorganized conference met in haste, for time was short, but with the satisfaction that it had retrieved something that seemed hopelessly lost.

My handwritten notes indicate that there were fourteen delegates present, of which six were from the ICL, two from the SAP (Brandt and Talin), two from Norway's NAP (Labor Party) and Mot Dag (Aake Ording and Fin Moe), one each from the Dutch OSP and RSP, and Browner, who worked closely with the ICL delegation. The Swedish group was represented by proxy.

The conference opened on a note that could have been humorous had it not produced sharp resentment from all the non-Dutch delegates. The youth representative of the OSP announced its participation in the Brussels meeting with a request that all the delegates pay registration fees to the Dutch for the expenditures made for the Laren conference. I remember a figure of thirteen guilders asked of each delegate. This was greeted with gales of laughter from everyone but the Dutch, who did not wish to be reminded that their irresponsibly organized conference had put the rest of us in a financially burdensome situation. The delegates had expended a considerable sum of money to go to Holland; it cost the Dutch delegates nothing. But the OSP was boorishly obstinate in its insistence on payment. However, the Brussels conference was a new one, under new auspices and with a different agenda, as confirmed the previous night at a plenum meeting. And so no one honored the request of the Dutch.

The principal debate in the conference was on the need for a new International and the propaganda for it. Brandt, Ording, and Moe were opposed to the idea as premature and, in the given circumstances, sectarian. Trotsky had predicted they might react this way. Yet, formally, these organizations took the position that the Second and Third Internationals were no longer viable Socialist movements. Hitler's victory made them irrelevant. It was now necessary to create a new International, a new youth section. This was not a radical view; it was stated frequently—in fact, it was this perspective that had impelled the Dutch OSP to call the Laren conference in the first place.

The two Norwegian organizations, while proclaiming the absolute necessity of a new world movement as the logical outcome of the debacle in Germany, were nevertheless opposed to any public declaration that would "tend to split the workers' movement" everywhere, as if this were not already a fact. Brandt supported the Scandanavians in the initial discussion at this opening session. But Jan Molinaar, speaking for the OSP, differed sharply from the position taken by Brandt, calling for a new turn and heightened activity for a new world body. His position was similar to the one I had already stated in behalf of the Trotskyist delegates. As he developed his views in the discussion, however, Molinaar placed his organization squarely between the positions of the SAP, NAP, and Mot Dag on the one hand, and the ICL on the other.

The Brussels meeting reached a momentary impasse because advocates of these positions were adamant. The OSP, acting independently, held views similar to those of the Trotskyists, but they were "opposed to maneuvering," whatever that meant in the given circumstances. Prejudice prevented the OSP from collaborating with us to support the adoption of a formal, public declaration for a new International despite the strong speech for it by Molinaar. I had already stated that the Trotskyist delegates yielded ground in accepting the term "new International" when everyone knew we were for a new, Fourth International. The others understood its ideological nature, that it meant a new movement based on the early years of the Comintern.

The discussion was a very muddy one. The Norwegians supported Brandt, but in order to establish their revolutionary credentials took pains to announce that they were for the "dictatorship of the proletariat," the Soviet system, the struggle for power, a fight against the impending war, and for a non-Stalinist or non-Communist concept of the united front. But, paradoxically, they also made sure that everyone knew they were opposed to *carrying out* these views. It was revealed in our discussions that they had no real belief in them. In accepting the proposal for a new International without defining that it was really a Fourth, we made an amorphous compromise. The alternative to this compromise was a collapse of the conference. We did not want that.

Given the impasse, Brandt, in what he believed was a display of statesmanship, made this proposal: Since the positions in the conference appeared irreconcilable, and in view of the fact that there was agreement on the ultimate goal, we should create *two* post-conference bureaus, one in Stockholm representing the views of the Scandanavians and SAP, and another in Paris to accommodate the views of the ICL. I called an immediate meeting of our delegates to work out a unanimous statement rejecting Brandt's proposal. We made it clear to him and his allies that we understood that his proposal was predicated on a permanent split in the proceedings. Our delegation felt that, even with a compromise, the constant intrigue of Brandt was pushing toward a collapse. While advising Held and me of the difficulties he was having with the Norwegians who resisted any forward step, in his public comments Brandt appeared far more stubborn than they.

We had the choice of forcing that collapse or trying to salvage the meeting and produce a decision that favored the idea of a new International, if not the *Fourth* International. We rejected the idea of two bureaus each functioning in isolation and in competition with each other. Since we were of the unanimous opinion that this was a new conference in the organization of which we played the most important part, we did everything we could to hold it together. In private conversation with Brandt and the Norwegians we pointed out that they would be a laughing stock, after all their public statements and writings attacking the Second and Third Internationals as moribund, proclaiming the need for a new International—to then, after all the difficulties we had already gone through in the Laren and Brussels conferences, conclude with no accomplishment whatever. We pressed them very hard.

A strange thing occurred later in the official discussion. Aake Ording rose to say that he had been adamant in opposing a public declaration for a new International because Fin Moe was present; but now that Moe had departed for Norway, he could speak more freely! Although he still opposed the Trotskyist position, he did not want the conference to end on a bad note. While deploring the "dogmatism and undialectical positions" of the ICL, he would now accept a resolution proclaiming the need for a new world movement for socialism.

With this statement, the conference was ready to vote for a resolution proposed by Brandt, a synthesis of the various positions, with a concluding paragraph advocating a new International and a new youth formation. Before adding the concluding paragraph, the statement had no point. The acceptance of our position in compromised form enabled the conference to achieve one tiny step toward the goal for which it was originally convened.

To give the political decision any meaning, the conference agreed to set up a bureau of representative organizations and a Secretariat of three located in Stockholm. The Secretariat would be made up of representatives of SAP, the Independent Communist Youth of Sweden, and the ICL. The conference adjourned on a warmer note.

Reviewing what happened, Held and I felt that we had achieved a minor goal, despite the inherent limitations of the conference. We had kept the conference from collapsing, and we brought it to a conclusion that we believed, in view of the political situation in those years, to be of some merit. Georges Fux supported us in that opinion, as did most of our other delegates.

I remained in Paris for several weeks after the conference, but I did not see Trotsky again. I learned, however, that Trotsky was sharply critical of the strategy we pursued and the decisions the conference reached. He wrote:

The resolution makes an extremely unsatisfying impression. The entire text rests on half-made points, ambiguities, radical sounding phrases and evasion of consequences. Martov's documents at Zimmerwald and Kienthal were much more radical.[21] In a word, the document is *centrist* through and through.[22]

This was only an introduction to his more elaborate criticism, which began with the title of the adopted resolution, "Conference of Revolutionary Socialist Organizations." "We call ourselves 'Communist,'" he added, "and we should have insisted that the title include that designation." This was obviously an unacceptable gesture, since the organization that initiated the conference and those that came to it were not Trotskyist; they would never have accepted Trotsky's view of the matter. They were fully conscious of the reasons why they called themselves *Socialist* and not *Communist*. Simply put, they were not Leninists in any sense. Furthermore, many organizations of the ICL also used the word *Socialist* in their names, the outstanding example of which was the Socialist Workers' Party in the United States. The designations "Socialist" and "Communist" were used interchangeably all the time by the organizations of the Fourth International. Trotsky went on:

The question of centrism is completely ignored. Only once . . . do we find centrism named between reformism and Stalinism. Thus, the word is used only for a legalistic alibi. . . . I don't find it in the final version of the text concerning the Fourth International. The original version is slippery. . . . It is true that after the departure of Fin Moe, the SAP graciously accepted the new International formulation, but only in connection with transcending [the Second and Third Internationals]. We cannot agree to this under any circumstances. It is not simply a question of a new International; the Two-and-a-half International would be a new International, as would the unification of the Second and Third.[23]

To my astonishment, Trotsky proposed that, in order to overcome this slide into centrism

we can sign this document [agreed to at the conference] (with qualifications, i.e., with a special official statement) only if: 1. the title is changed, 2. "transcending the Second and Third Internationals" is removed and/or replaced by "liberating the workers against all opportunist and centrist currents," and, 3. the goal set is the creation of the Fourth (and not new) International.[24]

As a measure of how seriously he regarded the whole matter, Trotsky concluded:

> These three points must be put forward as an absolute ultimatum and we cannot give an inch. . . . If the three points above are accepted by the SAP we will sign the document. . . . P.S. If our young delegates feel that they are being "repudiated," that is only partially true. The IS is there not just to approve its delegates, but also to repudiate them. With many of our comrades one notices the following: They understand very well how to explain and ridicule the psychology and methods of the centrist bigshots, but not how to combat them on the practical plane.[25]

I was stunned. I knew, as did all the ICL delegates, that had we pursued the course recommended by Trotsky the conference would have broken up immediately. For one, the conference would never have accepted *any* ultimatum from the Trotskyists. It would have ended right then and there. Trotsky must have known this.

We looked upon the Brussels meeting as a beginning step in the political contest for our views. We did everything we could to keep the conference from collapsing and still obtain from it at least an endorsement of a new International. In the isolation in which our whole movement found itself, I believed what we did and achieved was of merit.[26]

None of the points made by Trotsky was mentioned by him in our discussion. They were not part of any preconference discussion with the International Secretariat. On the contrary, I was led to believe that in the discussion with the Secretariat and Trotsky (its appears mistakenly with respect to Trotsky) we would push for our view, but since this was a "united front" conference, we would try to make the most of any opportunities that arose.

The Trotsky movement would shortly abandon its long-held position of regarding itself as an expelled faction of the Communist International. From the very beginning it opposed any idea of building new parties or another International. Those who advocated such a policy could not remain in the Left Opposition. The drastic change came in 1933, and all through that year we used the term "new International." "Fourth International" was employed much later, and the two were used interchangeably.

Trotsky observed, however, that we gave the idea of a new International a specific and different content from others who now spoke of a new world organization. It was the "others" who called the conference, and his appreciation of its problems was unreal if we sought to make something of this bare beginning. His attitude was stiff-backed, formalistic, and ultimatistic. Had his view prevailed, we could have accomplished as much or as little by not attending the meeting at all. While agreeing with Trotsky's criticism, the International Secretariat saw no point in carrying out his proposals and just let the matter slide.

Several years later, under pressure from Trotsky, a reluctant Trotskyist movement proclaimed the existence of the Fourth International. Trotsky's optimism was unfounded, because it never evolved into anything more than an isolated, tiny, uninfluential, and sectarian body.

In the aftermath of the conference, Trotsky continued his sharp criticism, most of it directed at Walter Held, as though he were responsible for everything we did. I thought the reason for that was simply proximity: Held remained in Western Europe. He was at hand, so to speak, as our outstanding youth leader in Europe, our representative on the Stockholm Secretariat of three. He was a leading member of the German Trotskyists, a person of unusual political talents. I always thought that Trotsky felt, because of Held's abilities, he bore a larger responsiblity. Trotsky was often that way with his son Lyova, as well, for whom he was a tough taskmaster.

Trotsky wrote directly to Held on March 29: "The error was that our delegation completely disregarded the instructions they were given."[27] Trotsky's severity with Held, it seemed to me, grew out of the exchange of correspondence they had in which Held defended the tactics we used in Brussels. Because of the special circumstances of my presence in Europe, I knew that the criticisms were also of me, but I did not accept them, as evidenced in my report on the conference. I recalled that, while Trotsky was inflexible in connection with the youth conference, he was much less so when he saw the possibility of a unification of the SAP and the German Trotskyists. He was willing to bend considerably to bring about such a unity, and he was right to do so.

At that particular time, the Communist League in the United States and the centrist American Workers' Party, under the leadership of A. J. Muste, were considering unification. In this case, as I expressed strong skepticism, Trotsky wrote me on April 10, 1934, in a tone entirely different from the one he employed concerning the youth conference. Although the time for both was almost identical, in the case of the possible American unity, flexibility was the watchword:

I read your letter of March 28 to Shachtman with great interest. What you communicate about our experience with the centrists in Europe is completely correct and the American comrades must carefully follow and consider this experience. I would, however, like to call attention to the following point: Regarding the SAP, we (and I personally) insisted on immediate unification.

But the SAP, after a short period of vacillation, opposed this. In the case of the OSP, the course of development proceeded in the opposite direction. The OSP insisted on immediate unification and the RSP opposed this. These two examples show that while completely maintaining our principled relationship to centrism, the practical road toward approaching (and at the same time combating) centrist tendencies can turn out to be very different. If we feel that we are theoretically and practically (also numerically) strong enough, we can accept a centrist organization and then continue the education of its best elements within the unified organization. There is no general formula for these things.[28]

It was easy for me to accept his criticism of my own rather stiff-backed attitude to the prospective unity in the United States. But the views he expressed on organizational unity with centrist organizations could easily have been applied to the youth conference, where no organizational unification was involved.

The International Secretariat did reply to Trotsky's letter of March 19, though I did not know it at the time. A note in the volume of *Trotsky's Writings: Supplement II, 1934-1940* states:

Five days after this letter [March 23, 1934] the IS adopted a resolution expressing political agreement with the points Trotsky had made in his criticism of the youth conference. But the IS did not insist on the changes Trotsky had demanded as a condition for participating in the Stockholm Bureau, concluding only that the youth conference had been just the first step on the road to a revolutionary youth International, and that the ICL members had to remain representatives of Marxist clarity and revolutionary initiative in the new organization.[29]

The IS had a more realistic grasp of the significance of the conference than Trotsky did. Or it may have been that it considered it too late to accept Trotsky's "absolute ultimatum," for to do so meant not even to realize the Committee's view. Even though it expressed agreement with Trotsky's razorlike criticism, it did nothing to carry it out.

In Brussels we had pursued a flexible course, because "there is no general formula for these things," as Trotsky would say. Our judgment was involved in the strategy and tactics we employed. We felt ideologically superior to the other organizations and numerically their equal. More importantly, we believed that if we could create an organizational form in which to function, we would be able to pursue our political aims with a possiblility of success.

Trotsky's criticism of the use of the word *Socialist* rather than *Com-*

munist no longer had any validity in the thirties. Stalinism had identified the latter term with labor camps, frame-up trials, the murder of political opponents, the disruption of the labor movement, and totalitarian dictatorship. Trotsky made much of a point that history has shown to be false. Just because we were unable to push the conference to adopt our resolution and "compromised" by accepting the formula "new International," Trotsky regarded the act a "betrayal and a crime."

By 1937, the schism between the Stockholm Bureau and the Secretariat reached a breaking point. The one achievement of the conference had failed. The pressure of world events—the Spanish Revolution and Civil War, the expansion of fascism, the Moscow Frame-Up Trials and GPU murders of emigrés in Western Europe, followed by the Stalinist betrayal of the Spanish struggle—all of these happenings, instead of bringing greater unity to the non-Stalinist movements of the working class, widened the gulf and increased their tensions.

The two years of the life of the Stockholm committees were marked by constant internal quarrels. The Secretariat, created so it could function in Stockholm, did not do so. The decisions of the Brussels conference were never immediately reproduced and sent to the participating organization, as agreed. Willy Brandt, seeking to create a more difficult situation, now proposed that there be three Secretariats, one each in Oslo (where he was located), Stockholm, and Copenhagen (where Held was temporarily located). The Swedish Forslund would handle matters in Stockholm. Brandt in Oslo would become secretary, and Held would have the task of communicating Stockholm's decisions to the organizations of the Trotskyist movement.

The maneuver was obvious. If accepted, it would concentrate the power of the Bureau and Secretariat in Brandt's hands and prevent the effective participation of Walter Held, who thought Brand intellectually limited and theoretically primitive. In any case, the tiny weak committees could not withstand the internal pressures and intrigue. They collapsed as a result, marking the end of a minor experiment in Socialist politics during an increasingly critical period of history, a demise to which all the participants contributed.

The wind-up of my stay in Paris came as soon as I had finished my responsibilities in connection with the conference and attended all the necessary meetings that had been arranged for me by the IS. Most of my time was spent with Held; we did not know when we would see each other again. Sedov handed me the inscribed photo of Trotsky just before I left; I felt quite proud of my possession as I turned homeward.

Looking back at the experience, it is easy to see that the effort made by the Independent Socialist Party of Holland was doomed to fail. Although their criticisms of the existing two Internationals were often correct, especially when referring to their monumental failures, the epoch did not and does not now support the creation of new international organizations. The Socialist International was reconstituted, and though weak as a world body, it rests upon mass parties in Western Europe. The Communist International was formally dissolved by Stalin—to be replaced by Kremlin intrigue based on its subject parties.

Notes

1. Some of Trotsky's works dealing with these questions are: *My Life, The Stalin School of Falsification, The Revolution Betrayed, The Case of Leon Trotsky,* and *In Defense of Marxism.*

2. Written March 14, 1933, and published in the *Russian Bulletin* No. 34, May 1933, by the Trotskyist press.

3. Robert Conquest, *The Great Terror: Stalin's Purges of the Thirties.* Conquest estimates that twenty million people perished in Stalin's drive to consolidate his personal power as the dictator of the Soviet Union. Estimates by Trotskyist writers and others concerned with the purges were all off the mark, as they underestimated by millions the physical terror carried out by an entirely new party and a secret police twice renewed over the dead bodies of its predecessors. Conquest emphasized a point made before him, that the party Stalin now led was not the party of the Russian Revolution.

4. Heijenoort, *With Trotsky in Exile,* p. 49.

5. Walter Held (Heinz Epe, 1910-1941), a leading member of the German Left Opposition, an émigré from the Nazi regime, was living in Amsterdam at the time of the conference and functioned as secretary to Henricus Sneevliet, a Trotskyist at the time and member of the Dutch parliament. Held, his wife Synnove, and his child, traveling to the United States via the Soviet Union in 1941, all disappeared immediately on crossing the Russian border. They fell into the hands of the secret police and nothing more was ever heard from or about them—as was the custom of the Soviet government.

6. Souzo (Feroci, or Leonetti) was a long-time leader of the Italian Communist Party. He supported the Left Opposition and was a member of the International Secretariat for a number of years. I met with him in 1931 and 1934. After World War II he returned to Italy and was said to have rejoined the Italian Communist Party.

7. Trotsky, a copy of a letter dated November 21, 1933, enclosed with a letter to the author.

8. Colonel De la Rocque was described in the notes to *Trotsky's Diary in Exile–1935* as "a member of Marshall Foch's general staff between 1926 and 1928,

leader of the *Croix de Feu,* [and] one of the principals in the antiparliamentary movement of February 6, 1934. . . . The *Croix de Feu,* the organization he founded, was originally made up of veterans. . . . In the thirties, it became a paramilitary organization with Fascist inclinations," p. 18.

9. Ivan Craipeau (b. 1912) was a leader of the youth in the French Trotskyist organization in the early thirties. He was a member of the executive committee of the French section until 1936, when he resigned because of sharp differences with Trotsky and the ICL on the Russian question: He no longer accepted the theory of the degenerated workers' state. Craipeau was an active participant in the youth conference in Laren, Holland, and joined Held and me in jail to re-plan the conference broken up by the Dutch police. He, too, was deported to Belgium and participated in the reorganized conference there. He was a robust young man and, at the time we met again in 1934, was deeply involved in the struggle against the Fascist encroachments on student life at the University of the Sorbonne.

10. Erwin (or Eugene) Bauer (Prof. Erwin Ackerknecht) was the leader of the German Trotskyists in 1933 and a member of the International Secretariat in Paris in 1933 and 1934. He broke with the ICL and joined the German Socialist Workers' Party (SAP) briefly, before making his way to the United States. In the United States, he no longer involved himself in politics, joining the staff of the Museum of Natural History as a scientist until his retirement.

11. Albert Weisbord (1900–1977), a one-time member of the Socialist Party and secretary of the Young People's Socialist League, graduated from Harvard Law School in 1924. He joined the Communist Party and was a strong supporter of the Ruthenberg–Lovestone faction. He believed in "dual unionism" and felt the Party should organize workers into its own unions. He became a leader of the Passaic textile strike. Weisbord was a strong-minded individual, and thought he was the natural heir to leadership of American communism, in the tradition of Lenin. He was expelled from the CP after Lovestone's ouster.

12. Maslov (Arkady, Isaac Tschereminsky) and Ruth Fischer (Eisler), were husband-and-wife leaders of the German Communist Party up to the mid-twenties, after the first Communist debacle of 1923. They were removed from the leadership by Stalin because they were supporters of Zinoviev and part of his diminishing group in the Communist International, which he headed from its formation until his defeat in the Russian Party. They were adherents of the International Left Opposition for a time. Maslov made his way to Cuba, where he died suddenly in 1941 of what was reported to be a stroke. Ruth Fischer resided in New York during the war years, when she wrote *Stalin and German Communism,* published in 1948. I worked with her on the book, partially as editor. My renewed relations with Fischer in the war years came about through my participation in a committee that brought a number of German Trotskyists to the United States, including Ruth. I lost touch with her after the war, when she returned to Europe.

13. Rudolph Klement was an aide to Trotsky in Barbizon, administrative secretary of the International Secretariat; murdered by the GPU in 1938.

14. Trotsky, letter dictated to author, now in author's personal archives.

15. In subsequent years, there were no relations between Weisbord and the CLA. He became embroiled in an internal struggle within his organization, which led to its dissolution. He then went to work for an AFL union, where he remained until his death in 1977.

16. Fischer served informally on the International Secretariat. It was Trotsky who pushed for her full membership with voting rights. In 1934 he wrote: "As for the Secretariat, I have already communicated my view—my conviction even— to Geneva: Dubois must be formally placed on the Secretariat. The plenum [of the ICL] could agree to the following: 'To strengthen the Secretariat, especially its work in the Anglo–Saxon countries, the plenum decides to include Comrade Dubois [on the Secretariat] with decisive vote.' " This letter led to her full membership on the Committee. Trotsky, *Writings,* Vol. 6, 1934, p. 484.

17. Vereecken broke with Trotsky politically at the time the Belgian Trotskyists entered the Socialist Party of Belgium. He rejoined it later, only to separate himself again on the eve of the proclamation of the Fourth International, forming his own organization. Vereecken died in 1978.

18. Henricus Sneevliet (1883–1942) was an outstanding Dutch Socialist personality, founder of the Communist Parties of Holland and of Indonesia. Sneevliet broke with the Communist Party in 1927, and in 1933 announced his adherence to Trotsky's views. But in 1938 he broke with Trotsky in a dispute over trade-union policy, the Spanish POUM, and Andrés Nin. Sneevliet was shot by the Nazis.

19. Glotzer, "Report on the Youth Conference," in author's personal archives.

20. Glotzer, "Report."

21. Zimmerwald and Kienthal were the meeting places of the newly emerging antiwar and left-wing groupings in the Socialist International during World War I. The single idea that brought these meetings of diverse people together was that the International had collapsed when the leading national sections came to the support of their governments in prosecuting the war, betraying the long-held internationalist doctrine of the movement. These conferences called for a new International and constructed an organizational and propagandistic base for such a new movement as emerged from the Russian Revolution. The new, Third International was established through the initiative of the Russian Bolshevik Party and its sympathetic organizations in other countries. As with the Communist International, Zimmerwald-Kienthal marked a complete break with the ideas and programs of the Socialist International.

22. *Writings,* Supplement, 1934–40, pp. 448–54. By "centrist" Trotsky meant a policy whose political character placed it between revolutionary and reformist policies.

23. *Writings,* Supplement, 1934–40, p. 465.

24. *Writings,* Supplement, 1934–40, p. 466.

25. *Writings,* Supplement, 1934–40, pp. 466–67.

26. One reason this difference with Trotsky was not foreseen by me was that six months before, on August 24, 1933, in a writing entitled *Building a New International and the United Front Policy,* he used the phrase "new International" several times. He was concerned with bringing together the SAP, OSP, RSP, and ILO (Bloc of Four). In August, the words "new International" were perfectly acceptable to Trotsky. Then he did not demand using "Fourth International" nor did he insist that the refusal to accept the latter was a breaking point in creating that Bloc. He did, however, insist on acceptance of the concept that the Soviet Union was a workers' state and that all must join in its defense, as indispensible to the Bloc, or United Front. Whether or not that led to the dissolution of the Bloc, it certainly narrowed its prospects, assuming it had any.

27. *Writings,* Supplement, 1934–40, p. 469.

28. Sidney Hook would have chuckled had he read this, since he was the individual most responsible for the unity, which he thought would strengthen the anti-Stalinist Front.

29. *Writings,* Supplement, 1934–40, p. 896.

"I Am Not a Jew But an Internationalist"

When in 1918 a delegation of Jews came to ask Trotsky to use his influence with his Bolshevik comrades to retain the equal rights they had received for the first time in the democratic February Revolution, Trotsky replied, "I am not a Jew but an Internationalist."[1]

On another occasion, in 1921, at the height of his political power after the consolidation of the Bolshevik Revolution, the chief rabbi of Moscow, Jacob Maze (sometimes spelled Mazeh) came to him on behalf of Jews again deprived of many rights (as they were under Tsarism, when the Russian Orthodox Church wielded an enormous amount of secular, as well as religious, power). Trotsky said: "I am a revolutionist and a Bolshevik, and I am not a Jew."[2] To which Rabbi Maze acutely replied: "The Trotskys make the revolution and the Bronsteins pay the bills."[3]

Prior to these occasions Trotsky is reported to have said to one group of Jews who came to him that Jews did not interest him more than the Bulgars.[4]

In the beginning of his revolutionary career as a Social Democrat, Trotsky had this exchange with the Bundist leader Vladimir Medem:

"When it comes to classifying yourself, you certainly cannot ignore the fact of national allegiance. You consider yourself, I take it, to be either a Russian or a Jew."

"No," cried Trotsky. "You are mistaken! I am a Social Democrat and that's all."[5]

There is a rigid Marxian, assimilationist attitude expressed in these responses. Although Trotsky softened his views in later years, he never changed his basic conceptions.

*   *   *

Trotsky's Jewish origins were repeatedly mentioned by the world press in writing about the Russian Revolution, when his fame became international. The Jewish press, which was most often critical of his Bolshevism, nonetheless expressed a pride and respect for Trotsky because he was a Jew.

Trotsky was born in 1879 to a Jewish family engaged in farming in the south of the Ukraine. Not only was farming an exceptional and unusual occupation for Jews in Tsarist Russia, but by Russian standards the farm was a *kulak* enterprise, since his father owned a large tract of land that increased as he prospered.

The family did not practice Judaism, nor did it speak Yiddish, the language of Russian Jews, or Hebrew. The father tried to induce feelings of Jewishness in his son by sending him to a *cheder,* but the boy's attendance was brief and without significant influence. When he went to Odessa to live with his cousins, the Schprentzas, he first learned something about Jews and Jewish life. Almost all his time, however, was spent in and around the German Lutheran-founded St. Paul School, which he attended.

The absence in his early years of Jewish religious education and celebrations did not conceal from Trotsky how society regarded him. Jews themselves—neutral, friendly, or even hostile—looked at him with varying degrees of pride as one of their own. While he disclaimed his identity as a Jew, he was at an extreme distance from the posture of Marx. As many other leading figures of modern socialism, Trotsky never referred to Marx's writings on the Jewish Question because he, like his fellow political leaders, historians, and ideologists, were embarrassed by them. He could not explain or defend their offensive anti-Semitism.[6]

Marx, the son of a father converted to Christianity who came from a family of rabbis, wrote in his essay "On The Jewish Question" that he detested Jews. If religion was the opium of the people, as he wrote, he obviously meant all religions, and as a European, first and foremost dominant Christianity, the offspring of Judaism. Why then did he express an over-excited hatred of Jews and Judaism in his essay? Egypt expelled the Jews, Marx said, because they were "lepers."[7] Of anti-Semitic Poland, an excessively religious country, Marx wrote that Jews were the "dirtiest of all races." "They multiply like flies," he wrote.

When referring to Ferdinand LaSalle, the founder of the German Socialist movement, as "Itzig" or "Itzel," Marx did so not out of friendship but to call attention to LaSalle's Jewish origins. That LaSalle himself was filled with Jewish self-hatred did not justify Marx's attitude toward him. The fact that Marx, the prodigious intellect of modern socialism, could himself express Jewish self-hatred in such gutter language, remains an anomaly. In private letters, Marx had no compunction about using language like "Levy's Jewish nose," "usurers," "Jew-boy," or "Nigger-Jew."[8]

Eleanor Marx, a Contrast

Eleanor Marx, Marx's youngest daughter, was the only member of the family who acknowledged publicly the Jewish side of her origins; her sisters Laura and Jenny avoided the subject. Eleanor once said to Max Beer, the historian of British socialism:

> I am the only one of my family who felt drawn to the Jewish people, particu-
> larly those who are socialistically inclined. My happiest moments were when
> I was in the East End [of London] amidst Jewish workpeople.[9]

All the daughters of Marx were interested and involved in the labor and Socialist movements, but Eleanor was the one most active in political and union organizational work.[10] In helping to unionize the Jewish workers of East London, she chose the most exploited and poorest, the immigrants. To make of herself a better organizer, more understanding of the problems of these workers, Eleanor learned Yiddish so that she could speak to them in their native tongue. When asked if she could help to get her father to speak to them, she agreed, "the more so that my father is a Jew."[11]

"My linguistic acquisition," she once said, "is Yiddish. I even deliver lectures in Yiddish and easily distort German grammar so that my audience should understand me better." A Russian acquaintance, referring to a discussion they had, wrote:

> Eleanor explained to me that she was active among the Jewish working
> women in Whitechapel, and that in the interests of Socialist propaganda
> it was more sensible for her to learn Yiddish than wait for the ignorant
> masses of immigrants from Eastern Europe to become Anglicised. "Besides,
> the Jewish language is akin to my blood," she said. "In our family it is
> thought that I am like my paternal grandmother, who was the wife of a
> learned Rabbi."[12]

In another expression of her feelings, she wrote to Karl Kautsky, the leading Marxist of the German Social Democracy of the time, on December
28, 1896: "I unfortunately only inherited my father's nose (I used to tell
him I could sue him for damages as his nose had distinctly entailed a
loss upon me) and not his genius."

At a parade in celebration of a congress of the Socialist International
in Zurich in 1893, marching with her union in the long line, Eleanor saw
Morris Vinchevsky (Benzion Novochovits), a world famous Jewish literary
and Socialist figure, standing alone on the side. She pulled him into the
line of march, locked arms with him to show she understood there was
a "Jewish problem," however small, in the International, saying to him,
"We Jews must stick together." These extended references to Eleanor Marx
show not merely her intelligence but her deep sympathies for suffering Jews.
Though Trotsky never spoke of himself in the way Eleanor did, he did
find himself writing in an objective and also often passionate way about
the ever-present anti-Semitism in Europe and Russia. He could never show
the emotions, however, of Marx's youngest daughter.

Russian Social Democracy from its beginnings was touched by the
ideology of anti-Semitism. The founder of Russian Marxism, Georgi V.
Plekhanov, was noted in the movement for his antagonism for Jews. Peter
Pavlov, a leader of the Narodniki, was also a known anti-Semite. Both
refused to protest the pogroms of 1880, 1881, and 1882.[13]

The most indecent attitude, and in sharp contrast to professed Socialist universalism, was toward the Jewish Bund. Plekhanov expressed his
contempt for the Bund quite openly, and his attitude had nothing to do
with the political-organizational differences they had. The Bund was an
integral part of the Russian Social Democratic Labor Party, whose founding congress was due primarily to its initiatives. As early as 1900, at a
meeting of *Iskra,* Plekhanov expressed himself somewhat like Marx. Lenin
revealed Plekhanov's bitterness in a memoir of the meeting:

In the question of our attitude toward the Jewish Bund, G. V. [Georgi
Valentovich Plekhanov] demonstrates phenomenal intolerance, declaring it
plainly not to be a social democratic organization, but in fact an exploitative
organization, exploiting the Russian. He said that our aim is to throw out
this Bund from the Party, that Jews are all chauvinists and nationalists,
that the Russian Party ought to be Russian and not let itself be "imprisoned"
by the "serpent-tribe." . . . All attempts at contradicting this unfair talk was
of no avail, and G. V. stuck to his guns, maintaining that we simply lack
the knowledge about Jewry and the vital experience of having come into
contact with Jews.[14]

At the London Congress of 1903, Trotsky became involved in the Jewish Question by opposing the Bund's demand that it be given special status in the Party, namely, that Socialist activity among Jewish workers be the exclusive operation of the Bund. This position was rejected by the Congress, Mensheviks and Bolsheviks alike. Trotsky engaged himself actively in the debate, so much so that David Riazanov, the Marxist scholar, said Trotsky was "Lenin's big stick" on the issue. Martov played a role equal to Trotsky's in arguing against the Bund's position. The Bund leaders were anything but pleased by Trotsky's vigorous and uncompromising intervention in the dispute, but they did not believe he was motivated by anti-Semitic feelings or was, like Marx, a "Judeophobe." They recognized that their differences were within the boundaries of Socialist ideas.

Several years later, in the fluid relations that existed after the Bund left the Party to function independently, it authorized Trotsky, as well as Paul Axelrod, to act in its behalf at the 1910 Paris Conference, which prepared the next congress of the Socialist International. By that action the organization expressed confidence in the integrity of the two men, one a veteran leader of the movement and the other a new and promising one.

In the turbulent year of 1905, when the movement was young and Trotsky was chairman of the first Soviet in history, he had assisted in the formation of Jewish Defense Groups in Kiev and Petrograd against organized pogroms in these two cities. The act was a forerunner to other interventions by Trotsky in public acts against Jews over the years, up until the time of his assassination.

After 1905

Following the defeat of the 1905 Revolution, the childishly devout and mystical Tsar was personally responsible for 705 pogroms in a score of cities in a single year. The barbarous acts were unleashed by the feeble-minded Romanov Nicholas II against unorganzied, unarmed, and defenseless Jews. The Social Democrats and the Bund were stunned by the brutality of the state-organized gangs, which were assisted by the police and army. Trotsky was distressed by the atrocities of the pogroms and he wrote more than anyone in the Party against the massacres.

In 1911, while Trotsky was in exile in Vienna, the ritual murder trial of the heretofore obscure Mendel Beillis took place. The trial was an epilogue to the pogroms in Kiev, a center of the notorious Ukrainian anti-Semitism. The charges against the helpless Beillis were made by the Ministry of Justice (!), headed by the well-known Russian anti-Semite Schelovitov. So abhorrent was the conduct of the government officials that many countries of the West made public their revulsion to the trial and to the unbridled hatred spread throughout the Russian Empire by the prosection's conduct, in a manner akin to "medieval witch-hunting."

Trotsky wrote about the trial for the famous *Neue Zeit,* in which he said the proceedings left him with a feeling of "physical nausea." He acutely compared the Dreyfus and Beillis trials:

> It cannot be denied that to a certain extent an analogy between the two cases exists, but they are strikingly different from one another as is the French drawing-room Jesuit anti-Semitism from the Russian criminal pogromist Black Hundredism, and as is the cynical and learned Poincare—who professes not to believe in God or the Devil—from Tsar Nicholas—who has no doubt that witches on brooms take off at night through chimneys.[15]

Following the Beillis Trial, Trotsky became the Balkan correpondent for the *Kievskaya Mysl* in the years 1912 to 1913, and he traveled extensively in that part of Europe, particularly Romania. He was struck by the savagery of the monarchy's official anti-Semitism and what he believed to be the indifference of Europe and European Jews to the suffering of Jews in the Balkans, especially the Jews in Romania. Now more familiar with the conditions of Jewish life in that country, he was so appalled by what he observed that he wrote stinging articles about this backward nation, where Jews had no rights, only obligations, including compulsory service in the army. Trotsky was particularly struck by the brutality of the government and the Continental indifference to the barbarism of the country. The Jew was the "perennial scapegoat" for all social ills—a universal view in Western society.

> Anti-Semitism is becoming a state religion, the last psychological cementing factor of a feudal society rotten through and through. . . . The condition of feudal stagnation, legal deprivation, political and bureaucratic corruption, not only degrade the Jewish masses economically but bring about their spiritual disintegration.[16]

Although he regarded himself as a Socialist internationalist and not a Jew—in the tradition of Marxist movements—and was not involved in Jewish affairs in the Russian and European organizations, his public political responses to the persecution of Jews were of interest to many Jewish circles. Historians of socialism who had a special interest in the Jewish Socialist movement wondered about Trotsky's interventions, because they knew that he didn't consider himself a Jew.

Joseph Nedava believed that despite protestations to the contrary, Trotsky did feel more than a formal Socialist reaction to anti-Semitic pogroms and massacres. He wrote:

The humiliating butchery of defenseless Jews in Russia touched him to the core. In this he saw the total degradation of humanity, and this may principally have been his unconscious reaction to the Jewish tragedy.[17]

Nedava then compared him to LaSalle, whom Trotsky greatly admired. A speech by LaSalle before the German court was issued in pamphlet form, for which Trotsky wrote the introduction. The translation of the speech was edited by him, too. Though LaSalle became full of Jewish self-hatred, said Nedava, Trotsky, less conscious of being a Jew, never turned to self-hatred.

Knei-Paz writes that there is no "Jewishness" in Trotsky's works. This is essentially true, although it must be said that a feeling of Jewishness and a special feeling for their sufferings as Jews are not identical. After his reference to Trotsky's writings on Romania, Knei-Paz comes close to amending his view.

Without question, the article constituted one of Trotsky's best comments on the Jewish Question; it was certainly the most openly sympathetic. There was no sense here of a demonstrative detachment; rather one feels that Trotsky was almost identifying with the endurers of injustice whom he described. Moreover, there was in the article no facile economic dismissal of the problem, though the economic position of the Jews entered into his analysis, the Jews were presented as victims of a social system—not to mention of an international diplomatic maneuver, if not conspiracy—rather than its happy beneficiaries. There is of course no reason to believe that Trotsky's empathy for the Jews was any greater for his being a Jew; he could write with no less compassion about the sufferings of non-Jews as well. His identification was with the suffering, not with the identity of the sufferer. But how different was the tone and content of the article, which was, in effect, a definition of the Judenfrage, from Marx's notorious fulminations on same subject.[18]

There is a gray area here in which there is room for legitimate speculation. One has to bear in mind that Trotsky, in writing of the persecution of Jews and the prevalence of active anti-Semitism, even among the most exploited and oppressed non-Jews, showed that despite his strict Internationalist beliefs he understood there was something special and unique in the sufferings of this particular people. He saw it in all countries where they lived, countries in which their small numbers threatened no one. Still,

Trotsky was particularly dismayed and nauseated by the endless pogroms, massacres, and inquisitions of Jews in Russia, the Ukraine, Poland, Romania, and elsewhere.

During the latter half of the thirties, the knot of death was tightened around European Jews, especially in Hitler's Germany. Aside from Jews, there were not many, certainly no world force, concerned with the fate of this ancient people, either in Western Europe or in Stalin's Russia, the self-styled Socialist motherland. Even though he expressed certainty of a Socialist victory emerging from a new war, Trotsky expressed many times his fear for the future of Jews in such a world conflict. Yet he could offer no counsel other than socialism as the future solution to their problem of sheer existence; this solution was made to look ridiculous when the Hitler–Stalin Pact sealed their fate.

In 1938 Trotsky was interviewed by the Argentine newspaperman M. Rubinstein. (The article reappeared in *Die Presse,* a Yiddish paper, on May 22, 1940.) The reporter raised the question of a war declared by Germany and a preventive strike against Hitler to keep down casualties. Trotsky reacted immediately to the idea, exhibiting in his comment that he had thought of the consequences of war on Jews, not as a passing or fleeting consideration, but with fearful concern.

Do not speak lightly of a war. You certainly need not pray for war. Remember, you are Jews and between Warta [a Polish river, the chief right bank effluent of the Oder River] and the Volga there live seven million Jews—in the coming war they will be annihilated.[19]

In a letter to an American friend on December 22, 1938, Trotsky again called attention to the fate of Jews in the world of those years.

The number of countries which expel Jews grows without cease. The number of countries able to accept them decreases. It is possible to imagine without difficulty what awaits the Jews upon the mere outbreak of the future world war. But even without war the next development of world reaction signifies with certainty the physical extermination of the Jews.[20]

The danger for Jews from Hitler's reign grew with the signing of the Hitler–Stalin Pact for two reasons: One, it was a signal that Hitler's annihilation of Jews was of no concern to Stalin. Secondly, the Pact hastened the war, hence increasing the pace of Jewish extermination. Sadly, the movement that bears Trotsky's name exhibited an indifference to the fate of Jews. Although it published historical and theoretical tracts and booklets on the

Jewish Question, these bore no relationship to its political reaction to the Holocaust.

When American troops entered the concentration camps and the American and world press published the photographs of the dead, starving, and skeletonized thousands, the American Trotskyist Socialist Workers' Party and its journal, *The Militant,* cried "fake" and "frame-up," saying with a characteristic overconfidence that this was preparation for the "enslavement" of the defeated German nation. Its sympathy was for Germany, not for the decimated Jews, just as today its views parallel Russian foreign policy in support of the Arab world at all times against the state of Israel, whose dissolution it also favors in its choice of an Arab-Jewish state. Given the many pogroms of Jews in the Arab world before the war, such a state would almost certainly repeat the Jewish experience with Nazi Germany.

Anti-Semitism, the Revolution, and Bolshevism

The anti-Semitism of the Tsar and of Orthodox Christianity pervaded all layers of Russian society, spilling over into the Social Revolutionary and Social Democratic movements. The prejudice was strongest in the Bolshevik wing of Social Democracy, perhaps because it had fewer Jews and because of the early influence of Plekhanov, who gave anti-Semitism a "revolutionary" caché. Lenin, a Great Russian, Internationalist, and "cosmopolitan," was quick to respond to expressions of anti-Semitism in the movement.

To underscore Trotsky's awareness that the October Revolution did not automatically eliminate anti-Semitism, he once wrote what seems obvious, that "legislation alone does not change people." As the foremost authority in the country after Lenin, and as commander of the Red Army in the newly formed state, Trotsky suppressed eruptions of anti-Semitism in the army and in the anarchistic Nestor I. Makhno partisan army. He was supported by Lenin in these acts.[21]

Internationalist though he was and in a revolution that catapulted him to the pinnacle of leadership, Trotsky *was* sensitive to the fact that he was a Jew as it related to his assumption of posts in the new regime. When Lenin proposed that he become the Commissar of the Interior, for example, Trotsky immediately rejected it out of fear of a negative reaction in the Party and the nation at large. One is justified in believing that Trotsky wanted nothing to do with internal police powers, because he did accept the post of Foreign Minister for a brief time—as well as the assignment to create an army and be its commander. He records the incident in *My Life* in the following way:

> Lenin lost his temper. "We are having a great international revolution. Of what importance are such trifles?"
> A good-humored bickering began. "No doubt the revolution is good," I answered, "but there are still a good many fools left."
> "But surely we don't keep step with fools."
> "Probably we don't, but sometimes one has to make some allowance for stupidity. Why create additional complications at the outset? . . . ."
> Was it worthwhile to put into our enemies' hands such an additional weapon as my Jewish origins?[22]

There is no doubt that Trotsky's "sensitivity" heavily influenced his response to proposals for posts in the Bolshevik regime. In later years, he wrote: "If in 1917 and later, I occasionally pointed to my Jewish origins as an argument against some appointment it was simply because of political considerations."[23]

It should be noted that Zinoviev and the half-Jew Kamenev never raised such "political considerations," particularly Zinoviev, who drove hard for leadership.

Up to the death of Lenin and the beginning of the internal struggle in 1924, anti-Semitism was kept in check in the Party and state by the force of Lenin's leadership and a Central Committee vigilant in suppressing manifestations of this retrograde prejudice. With the rise of Stalin, all this changed. National anti-Jewish prejudice, the corrupting influence in the culture of the Russian Empire, was revived to become a force in the political struggle between the rising Stalinist bureaucracy with the Trotskyists, and later with the United Opposition.

In the beginning of Stalin's rise, his path to leadership was made possible by the collusion of Zinoviev and Kamenev. It was they who nominated Stalin for the post of General Secretary, at that time a political-technical post, which Stalin quickly transformed into the major political office in the leadership. Nicolai Bukharin joined in the effort to solidify the new role of Stalin. When Stalin turned on Zinoviev and Kamenev, he still had the strong support of Bukharin and his friends in the Politburo, Rykov and Tomsky. They supported all the measures Stalin employed to reach the sole leadership of the Party and nation, including anti-Semitism.

Trotsky was the first to inform the parties of the Communist International, and then a skeptical world, that Stalin had introduced anti-Semitism into internal political disputes, at first indirectly and then quite open-

ly—until it had become a dominant theme in the new political climate—
indeed, a hallmark of Stalinism. Anti-Semitic occurrences took place in
units of the Party during the first discussions with the Left Opposition,
which had to contend with hooliganism at membership meetings, hooting,
catcalls, whistling, stamping of feet, and shouting of abuses (in addition
to intellectually low-grade debates). The Trotskyists had to bear the burden
of vicious anti-Semitic slanders, too.

At one point, it had come to Trotsky's attention that in a Moscow
factory unit the Left Opposition was denounced because it was led by Jews.
This lie about the ethnic composition of the Trotsky faction leaders was
followed up by anti-Semitic attacks on them. The principal leaders of the
faction next to Trotsky were Rakovsky, Smirnov, Serebriakov, Piatakov,
Preobrazhensky, Krestinsky, Muralov, Belaborodov, and Istchenko—all of
them non-Jews. In Schapiro's history of the party, he records that:

> Among Trotsky's papers there is a record of a meeting held in September
> 1927 in a Party cell to demand the expulsion of Trotsky, which was one
> of the thousands organized by the Secretariat as part of the campaign. The
> principal speech stressed that Trotsky's nationality precluded him from being
> a Communist since "it shows that he must be in favor of speculation" and
> that Trotsky and his supporters had "made a mistake about the Russian
> spirit."[24]

Schapiro comments quite correctly that "such remarks by a Party member at a time when anti-Semitism was a punishable offense are not likely
to have been made without higher authority." Indeed, it is safe to add
that it was very likely written for the speaker by a higher authority.

Despite the new stage in the inner-party life under Stalin, Trotsky did
not believe that the General Secretary was personally anti-Semitic. Trotsky
thought Stalin merely used anti-Semitism in the struggle against him and
the various oppositions. He wrote in "Thermidor and Anti-Semitism" that
"between 1923 and 1926 . . . the play on the stings of anti-Semitism bore
a very cautious and marked character."[25] Historians, writers, and people
close to the Party and its leading staff did not agree with Trotsky about
Stalin; they believed the new leader to be an anti-Semite himself, only
very clever in concealing his deep hatred of Jews. In those years, Trotsky
dealt with the problem on the basis of his evaluation of the situation in
the leadership. We know he was off the mark on Stalin, if only from
the episode with Bukharin in the Politburo cited earlier.

In the middle or late twenties, Trotsky was, despite contrary evidence,
reluctant to accept that part of the struggle against him that was of an anti-

Jewish nature. Trotsky explained in his 1937 essay that one had to remember the October Revolution was only twenty years old, so that it was not surprising that the heritage of anti-Semitism was widespread in the generations that grew up and were educated under Tsarism. But seventy years after that October one finds anti-Semitism just as prevalent in the Soviet Union. The virus is found in all layers of the population, from the highest Party and government officials to the lowest member of a peasant *kolhoz*.[26]

Even while he was writing the biography of Stalin (Trotsky was assassinated before he was finished; it was completed from Trotsky's notes and translated by Charles Malamuth), and when anti-Semitic incidents multiplied and became standard in the struggle against Trotsky and his supporters, he still avoided saying that Stalin was an anti-Semite. Here is how he wrote of the matter in the biography;

> [Stalin] and his henchman even stooped to fish in the muddied waters of anti-Semitism. I recall particularly a cartoon in the *Rabochaya Gazeta (Workers' Gazette)* entitled "Comrades Trotsky and Zinoviev." There were any number of such caricatures and doggerels of an anti-Semitic character in the Party press. They were received with sly snickers. Stalin's attitude toward this growing anti-Semitism was one of friendly neutrality. But matters went so far that he was forced to come out with a published statement which declared: "We are fighting Trotsky, Zinoviev, and Kamenev not because they are Jews, but because they are Oppositionists," and the like. It was absolutely clear to everyone who thought politically that his deliberately equivocal declaration was aimed merely at the "excesses" of anti-Semitism, while at the same time broadcasting throughout the entire Soviet press the very pregnant reminder, "Don't forget that the leaders of the Opposition are Jews." Such a statement gave carte blanche to the anti-Semites.[27]

Suddenly Zinoviev and Kamenev were referred to by their unused patronyms of Radomyslasky and Rosenfeld, and Trotsky by the name he never used in the movement, Bronstein. Stalin's police, on orders from above, in arresting Trotsky's youngest son, Sergei Sedov (he was named after his mother, Natalia Sedov), wrote his name as Bronstein. This was Stalin's "yellow badge" for Party leaders who had used pseudonyms for decades under Tsarism.

In a most sinister way, the Stalinist leadership made "Jewish" Oppositionists part of the issue in the dispute. Trotsky wrote sometime after the internal struggle began, when he had already been deported to Turkey:

> The question of my Jewish origins acquired importance only after I had become a subject for political baiting. Anti-Semitism raised its head with

that of anti-Trotskyism. They both derived from the same source—the petty bourgeois reaction against October.[28]

In the land of October, in the Party that made the Bolshevik Revolution, a Party of intellectual leaders and a large plebian membership? Hardly! Immediately before this reference, he had written the following to show how White Guardist anti-Semitic agitation did not wholly succeed when the Revolution was in the ascendance; whereas under Stalin, it was in the process of degeneration. For proof of a change, he took a quote from a White Guard writer of a Berlin publication, "Archives of the Russian Revolution":

A cossack who came to see us was hurt by someone's taunt that he not only served under but fought under the command of a Jew—Trotsky—and retorted with warm conviction:
"Nothing of the sort. Trotsky is not a Jew. Trotsky is a fighter. He's ours . . . Russian! It is Lenin who is a Communist, a Jew, but Trotsky is ours . . . a fighter . . . a Russian . . . our own!"[29]

Trotsky was as pleased with this reference as he was disturbed by the new reality in the Party. But if Stalin was not personally anti-Semitic, merely using this reactionary ploy as a weapon against the Opposition, Trotsky had to seek an "objective" explanation for its prevalence outside of the Party, which he could not accept as a repository of widespread anti-Semitism. He turned to a historic abstraction, European in character and not always applicable, to explain the phenomenon under Bolshevism. He wrote:

History has never yet seen an example when the reaction following the revolutionary upsurge was not accompanied by the most unbridled chauvinistic passions, anti-Semitism among them.[30]

But in a "Socialistic" workers' state? The problem with this "law" is that Trotsky applied it to the Stalin era, in which nationalized property, Trotsky's *sine qua non* for a workers' state, was solidified. The "reaction" following the revolutionary upsurge came with Stalin's invasion of Finland and the partition of Poland in partnership with Hitler. These two imperialist actions by Soviet armies were followed by the nationalization of property in the areas conquered by the Red Army. This nationalization in Finland and Poland was used by Trotsky to rebuff the minority in the American Trotskyist organization and to demand the "defense of the Soviet Union." Even though he was against Stalin's actions, once accomplished, he argued, their revolutionary significance resided in the extension of a Soviet society. Here we see the consequences of Trotsky's theory of the "degenerated workers' state," based on the nationalization of property.

Was Stalin a Jew-Hater?

Trotsky differed from many in and out of the Party who believed Stalin to be a Jew-hater and Jew-baiter from his days as a seminary student in the early 1890s. They believed him also to be very subtle in concealing his feelings for a long time. Hitherto no one looked for it in him because of the overwhelming dominance of Lenin in the Bolshevik Party and its formal, or official, opposition to the prejudice. There was certainly an absence of it in the Menshevik Party. At this point it is of interest to turn to Bertram D. Wolfe, who cites an episode involving Stalin as early as 1907. There was a London meeting of the Party leadership at which Stalin represented a Caucasian group. On his return from London, Stalin wrote a "Report on the London Congress," which contained the following observation:

> Statistics showed that the majority of the Menshevik faction consists of Jews—and this of course without counting the Bundists—after which came Georgians and then Russians. . . . On the other hand, the overwhelming majority of the Bolshevik faction consists of Russians, after which come Jews—not counting of course the Poles and Letts. . . . For this reason one of the Bolsheviks observed in jest (it seems, Comrade Aleksinsky) that the Mensheviks are a Jewish faction, the Bolsheviks a genuine Russian faction, whence it wouldn't be a bad idea for us Bolsheviks to arrange a pogrom in the Party.[31]

Other references indicate that Aleksinsky did make such a comment. Still, for Stalin to find it of surpassing interest, sufficiently so to include in his report of the Congress, indicates not only his coarseness but his indifference to the prevalence of continuous pogroms and persecution of Jews. Aside from Plekhanov, it is difficult to see any other luminary of Russian Social Democracy enjoying the "jest" enough to incorporate it into an official report of the meeting.

Whatever Trotsky may have thought about Stalin's anti-Semitism, he made no secret of his belief that anti-Jewish feelings were widespread in the Soviet Union, in and out of the Party. We come now to an incident that reveals how successful Stalin was in the People's Front days and just before the Hitler–Stalin Pact in concealing the nationwide presence of anti-Semitism. On January 18, 1937, Trotsky was interviewed by the widely circulated *Jewish Daily Forward.*

> You ask me whether there is a connection between the Moscow Trial and anti-Semitism. That has been shown quite clearly in the press by Franz Pfemfert, a German writer and publisher and a refugee from Nazism. Whoever attentively follows the inner life in the Soviet Union, whoever reads the Soviet press line by line and between the lines, has for a long time clearly seen that the Soviet bureaucrats are playing a double game in the Jewish Question as on other questions. In words, of course, they come out against anti-Semitism; bigoted pogromists are not only brought to court by them but also shot. At the same time, though, they systematically exploit anti-Semitic prejudices in order to compromise every opposition group. In the commentaries on the political trial proceedings, about the artistic taste of the defendants, about the character of their social position, there is always and invariably the hint that the Opposition is an outgrowth of the Jewish intelligentsia . . . .
>
> Take, for example, these trials of the Opposition—there the Jews are constantly pushed to the fore, yet Jews are no worse or better in that respect. That is to say, the Jewish theme had been fully exploited in the struggle with the Opposition, and that has gone on for several years. In 1927 when I established the bloc of the Opposition, there was on the staff of my group not one Jew except myself. The rest, such as Smirnov, Preobrazhensky, Mrachkovsky, et al., included not one Jew. Also the so-called Zinoviev Opposition consisted, except for Zinoviev, of non-Jews, only the best Leningrad revolutionary leaders, like Bakaev, Yevdokimov, Kukla, et al.
>
> And in 1927 Stalin was already writing in official documents—very discreetly but with a clear meaning—that the Opposition consisted in its majority of Jews.
>
> He said there: "We are struggling against Trotsky, Zinoviev, Kamenev, and others, not because they are Jews but because they are Oppositionists." The intention was to clearly indicate that at the head of the Opposition stand Jews.[32]

The interview upset the *Forward's* rival Jewish daily, *The Day,* whose managing editor, B. Z. Goldberg, leaned toward Stalinism. One can see it plainly not only from the words but the juxtaposition of ideas. In two consecutive articles—on January 26 and 27, 1937—attacking Trotsky, Goldberg wrote:

> And here, as regards the Jewish Question, Trotsky did something that is characteristic of every small man in politics—he utilized the Jewish Question for his own political aims. And that is altogether not worthy of Leon Trotsky.

In order to hurt Stalin, Trotsky thinks it is justifiable to proclaim the Soviet Union as anti-Semitic. . . . Is that true, Mr. Trotsky? And if it is not true, is it righteous to say so?

No matter what kind of "reaction" should at this moment exist in Soviet Russia—and I do not want to defend Stalin or the Soviet Union—one thing cannot be said of the present regime and that is that it oppresses national minorities.

Trotsky himself knows very well that not only is every nationality free, but it is greatly encouraged to protect and preserve its own language and culture and the same is true of the Jews.

In the second installment, Goldberg went on:

. . . [Trotsky] also declares that the Bolshevist [sic] leaders are utilizing this anti-Semitic tendency to turn the dissatisfaction of the masses from the bureaucracy toward the Jews. . . .

Even the most orthodox, the most conservative Jew will say: "Stalin may be a confounded cur, but he does not allow anti-Semitism in the Soviet Union."[33]

Goldberg displays a thick-headed naivete; it is more egregious for its defense of Stalin. What a pity not to have a videotape of B. Z. Goldberg on the day of the signing of the Hitler–Stalin Pact!

The managing editor of *The Day* was not alone in his blind acceptance of Soviet and Comintern propaganda, for the notions he expressed in his attack on Trotsky were widespread. This feeling about Soviet defense of Russian Jewry even touched critics of Stalin's Russia. On the same Yiddish daily that Goldberg edited was a well-known popular columnist, Aaron Glanz, who was sympathetic to the struggle of the Left Opposition, had great respect for Trotsky, and was concerned with the plight of his family (which became worse, by the way, with the deportation of the man Lenin once called "the most able man on the Central Committee," with his wife, Natalia).

Shortly after Goldberg's piece, Glanz wrote a letter to Max Shachtman, then in Mexico, in which he expressed regret regarding Trotsky's interview. In telling Shachtman how disturbed he was about it, he described his reaction in language quite different from his managing editor's. He wrote in part:

. . . Trotsky's interview bearing on anti-Semitism in Russia is both bewildering and painful. I must also add on my own behalf that I consider this charge rather unfortunate. Our Jews are very touchy on this matter of anti-

Semitism as I think we should be. In the raging sea of Judeophobia which
the world presents today, the official stand of the USSR, where anti-Semitism is punishable by death, is the one exception, the one habitable island,
so to say. The Jews of all classes and of all countries appreciate this very
much—and I think quite rightly. Now, unless Trotsky can substantiate this
charge of his, he should not have made it. . . .

My profound esteem for the great exile remains, of course, unaltered.
Please convey to him my warmest regards and most fervent hope that the
opportunity may be given to him to present the truth to the world.[34]

*   *   *

In early 1932, after I returned from my visit to Trotsky in Turkey, Glanz
interviewed me, asking questions that revealed his broad knowledge of the
life and ideas of the revolutionary exile. The published interview took almost a whole page of *The Day* and was a faithful reproduction of the
many things we discussed: the danger of Hitler, Trotsky's health and
demeanor in exile, and the Jewish Question.

The story in *The Day* reflected a common worldwide acceptance of
the skillful propaganda of the Stalin machine, which, in this question, ceased
only when pictures appeared everywhere showing Stalin looking on smiling
as his Foreign Minister, Molotov, signed the Pact with his German coun-
terpart, Von Ribbentrop, in Moscow.

Testimony From Russian Sources

Trotsky did not live through the period of "the Great War" and Stalin's
rule. But as we have seen, when he was writing the biography of Stalin
and up to 1940, he maintained his view that Stalin personally was not
anti-Jewish. Trotsky's view was not corroborated by Nikita Khrushchev,
for many years an intimate of the General Secretary, or by and Stalin's
daughter, Svetlana Alliluyeva.

There is no evidence that Khrushchev, no lover of Jews himself, initiated any anti-Semitic acts, as Stalin did. Khrushchev would not concede
that the Jews suffered more from the advance of the German armies and
the SS. Nor did he oppose Stalin's order of deportation of Jews from
the Ukraine to Siberia, and he was silent about the Holocaust and the
massacre at Baba Yar. But he told the truth about the secret murder, ordered by Stalin, of Simon Mikhoels, the famous Russian actor and director, and similarly the shooting of Alan Lozovsky, the long-time head of
the Red International of Trade Unions. These disclosures came after the

Twentieth Congress, for Khrushchev did not mention the two cases in his famous secret speech; neither did he mention the arrest and exile in 1949 of Polina Semiponova, the wife of Stalin's longest associate and devoted collaborator, Molotov, because she was Jewish.[35]

In *Khrushchev Remembers,* he notes that Stalin "took care never to hint of his anti-Semitism in his written works or speeches." But "when he happened to talk about a Jew, Stalin often imitated in a well-known exaggerated accent the way Jews talk." That Stalin should exhibit a strong anti-Jewish bias this way is odd indeed, since he spoke Russian with a marked Georgian accent. His knowledge of the language was said to be poor, and he spoke it without distinction.

At another time, a few years before his death, the State Security reported to Stalin about "trouble" at the Thirtieth Aviation Factory. Stalin's directive, made orally, was that "the good workers of the factory should be given clubs so they can beat the hell out of those Jews at the end of the working day." When Khrushchev left the room, Beria, who followed, asked him ironically: "Well, have you received your orders?"

Khrushchev reported himself as saying: "Yes, I've received them. My father was illiterate but he never took part in a pogrom. It was considered a disgrace. And now this directive is given to me as a Secretary of the Central Committee of the Communist Party of the USSR."

Had Stalin's orders been carried out and it become public, as it certainly would have, Khrushchev said Stalin would have "a Commission appointed and the culprits would be severely punished. Stalin would have stopped at nothing to punish anti-Semitism publicly."[36]

Svetlana, Stalin's daughter, tells the story of her first relationship with a man, Alexei Kagler, a movie-maker and writer, when she was still a young teenager. This was the first such experience of her life and marked her first break from a closely supervised life. Kagler was much older than Svetlana but appeared to be sincerely interested in her. She told Stalin that she was in love with Kagler, and she recorded her father's reaction in this way:

"Love!" screamed my father with a hatred of the very word I can scarcely convey. And for the first time in his life he slapped me across the face, twice. . . .

Apparently the fact that Kagler was a Jew was what bothered him most of all.[37]

The relationship was broken up when Kagler was banished to the frozen north. Svetlana's visits with Kagler and their phone conversations were recorded and made known to Stalin. Svetlana did not see Kagler for eleven years. Meanwhile she continued her schooling and met Grigory Morozov. After a time of courtship they decided to get married. When Stalin was told, he was outraged, especially after he was told Morozov was Jewish:

> "So you want to get married, do you? . . . Yes, it's spring. To Hell with you. Do as you like."
> My father set only one condition on the marriage: that my husband never set foot in his house. We were even glad. There was just one thing he wouldn't give us: his love, warmth, a real family relationship. He never once met my first husband, said quite firmly that he never would.[38]

Some years later, after the marriage had dissolved and Svetlana had given birth to a son of Morozov's, whom she named Joseph (for her father and father-in-law), she records this conversation with Stalin:

> "That first husband of yours was thrown your way by the Zionists."
> "Papa," I tried to object, "the younger ones couldn't care less about Zionism."
> "No, you don't understand," was the sharp answer. "The entire older generation is contaminated with Zionism, and now they're teaching the young people, too."[39]

In his memoirs, Khrushchev closes his chapter on "Stalin's Last Years" with an observation quite opposite to Trotsky's:

> After Stalin came to power, instead of setting an example of how to liquidate anti-Semitism at its roots, he helped to spread it. Anti-Semitism grew like a growth inside of Stalin's own brain. Then, at Stalin's death, we arrested the spread a lot, but only arrested it. Unfortunately, the germs of anti-Semitism remained in our system, and apparently there still isn't the necessary discouragement of it and resistance to it.[40]

We know, too, not only from Khrushchev's speech at the Twentieth Congress, but from many sources since, that just before his death Stalin was preparing a new slaughter in the Party and nation, principally of Jews, to begin with a trial of the Kremlin's doctors, most of whom were Jews. The doctors were charged with poisoning A. A. Zhadanov, Stalin's collaborator. Zhadanov was a "guardian of the faith" and the leader of the campaign against "cosmopolitans" (read "Jews"). Khrushchev described the way Stalin prepared his frame-up of the nation's leading doctors and his personal intervention in the prosecution of the case against them:

Let us recall the "Affair of the Doctor-Plotters." . . . Actually there was no "Affair" outside of the declaration of the woman doctor [Lydia] Tima-shuk, who was probably influenced or ordered by someone (after all, she was an unofficial collaborator of state security) to write Stalin a letter in which she declared that doctors were applying supposedly improper methods of medical treatment.

Such a letter was sufficient for Stalin to reach an immediate conclusion that there were doctor-plotters in the Soviet Union. He issued orders to arrest a group of eminent Soviet medical specialists. He personally issued advice on the conduct of the investigation and the method of interrogation of the arrested persons. He said that the academician Vinograd should be put in chains, another one should be beaten. Present at this Congress as a delegate was the former Minister of State Security, Comrade Ignatiev. Stalin told him curtly, "If you do not obtain confessions from the doctors we will short-en you by a head." . . .

Stalin personally called the investigative judge, gave him instructions, advised him on which investigative methods should be used. These methods were simple—beat, beat, and once again, beat.[41]

*   *   *

As early as the time of the first Five Year Plan in 1928, Stalin began his drive to build up heavy industry at a breakneck speed. The notorious backwardness of the country was expressed at this time in the search for capital. Not only were workers and peasants subjected to unbelievable exploitation, but the state invaded the very living quarters of people to search for capital in personal possessions. Nicolai Tolstoy described this form of state thievery graphically:

Sweeping measures were adopted by the GPU to extort gold and jewelry from hoards, for the most part tiny, held by the population at large. Anyone suspected of concealing a gold watch or a wedding ring was dragged off to the GPU jail and subjected to tortures until he disgorged (assuming he had anything to disgorge). Few were able to resist the horrors of the *parilka* (sweat room) and the "conveyor." Those who did soon succumbed to the next stage in Soviet refinement: watching their own children being tortured before them. Jews in particular were suspected of concealing their wealth, and widespread anti-Semitism amongst GPU agents gave them especial pleasure in inflicting pain and humiliation on the *Zhidovskaya morda* ("Yid snouts"). An aged Jew was forced to drink his own urine before a circle of jeering louts. Others suffered hideous torments as a inducement to make them inform on their fellow religionists.[42]

Tolstoy believed Stalin was anti-Semitic, but he thought this antipathy "was not the all-absorbing obsession it was to Hitler." He backs his opinion with a reference to Ronald Hingley, author of *Joseph Stalin: Man and Legend,* who wrote that "the mature Stalin was not narrowly biased against any specific section of humanity, for his sympathies were broadly and generously anti-human in general."[43]

There is a continuous interplay of anti-Jewish events throughout the years of Stalin's reign. Medvedev spoke of Stalin's "revival of Great Russian chauvinism, the deportation of many peoples of the USSR from their native lands," and his "anti-Semitic policies which led to the physical destruction of the most brilliant representatives of Jewish culture and his plans for the deportation of all Jews to remote regions of the USSR."[44]

By the end of the "Great Patriotic War" in 1945, Stalin's power was secure and beyond challenge, but that did not lessen his hunger for purges, particularly of Jews, and new slaughter. The various Oppositionists were long defeated and dispersed, and their many leaders were physically destroyed. Yet, driven by his anti-Semitic passions, he was preparing his own "final solution" of the Jewish Question.

In this immediate post-war period, a special meeting was convened by Stalin of the Politburo and Central Committee Secretariat, "republic and regional" first Party secretaries, leaders of defense industries, and state security organs to consider the Jewish Question, at which Stalin advocated a "more cautious" attitude to the appointment of Jews to positions in the state and Party institutions. Medvedev reports on this important yet unpublicized meeting in his small volume *All Stalin's Men:*

> A more detailed speech was given on this occasion by G. M. Malenkov, who demonstrated the need for "heightened alertness" in relation to Jewish cadres. A memorandum was circulated to the Party "which listed those jobs that it was thought undesirable to give to Jews. At the same time, certain limitations were imposed on admission to Jews to institutions of higher learning."[45]

Trotsky could not have maintained his evaluation of Stalin's anti-Semitism in the light of all this knowledge.

Contradictions and Changes

In the early years of his political life, Trotsky never hesitated to criticize Zionism, the movement seeking a homeland for Jews following the *diaspora* in Palestine, when it was a Turkish possession, and after World

War I when Great Britain dominated the poorly populated country. He considered Zionism non-Socialist and incapable of achieving anything substantial for Jews. When Theodore Herzl, the founder of Zionism, proposed that Jews seek a homeland in Uganda, having failed to win Palestine from the British rulers, he was chided by Trotsky. Trotsky said that if Jews wanted to realize their right to schools, press, theaters, cultural centers—in short, their own nation—socialism alone would make that possible. These were, he asserted more than once, manifestly unrealizable under world capitalism.

Trotsky called Herzl's proposal on Uganda a "demonstration of impotence," adding, "Herzl promised Palestine—but didn't deliver it." Herzl's was the "reactionary" dream of a "shameless adventurer." He concluded: "It is impossible to keep Zionism alive by this kind of trickery. Zionism has exhausted its miserable contents. Tens of intriguers and hundreds of simpletons may yet continue to support Herzl's adventures, but Zionism as a movement is already doomed to losing all rights to existence in the future. This is as clear as midday."[46]

Trotsky expected that the outbreak of a new world war (World War II) would provoke a Socialist revolution in Europe, if not the whole world. Until that time, Trotsky believed that nothing substantial could be done for Jews; they would continue to suffer as they had for hundreds of years. Their only hope was Socialist revolution—which was certain to come, and soon:

American capitalism has reached its zenith in the capitalist era and is now decaying—the democracy of the capitalist world is doomed. In France, it is giving dying gasps while in Britain it is rapidly decaying.[47]

Trotsky's vision was more than a little cloudy. He was again making a sweeping forecast of abstractions unrelated to the real world. Exactly the opposite took place after the war. Jews around the world were fortunate not to accept Trotsky's perspective. Events in Europe impelled them to help themselves in practical ways through coordinated efforts of large world and national organizations under the very difficult circumstances unique to Jews. There were also uncoordinated efforts by small groups and individuals, who reached for any straw as they watched the massacre of Jews in Hitler's Germany and in Central Europe in the thirties.

One example of these efforts was that of a brilliant Chicago attorney, Harry Ruskin, who wished to enlist Trotsky's aid. Ruskin asked veteran Congressman Joseph Sabath, who represented the city's Jewish West Side for many years, to write to Trotsky. Trotsky sent me a copy of the congressman's letter and asked whether I thought he should meet with Ruskin. I had known Ruskin by reputation as an honest and sincere person. He had preceded me as a student at Crane Technical High School, was an outstanding student and the champion debater in the area. His reputation as a lawyer was impeccable. I wrote Trotsky saying I could see no harm in accepting a visit from Ruskin. He did see him on February 19, 1939, as the danger of war was rapidly intensifying.

Trotsky wrote to me on February fourteenth that Ruskin had tried to enlist his help in behalf of the endangered European Jews, on the assumption that Trotsky's Jewish origins made him a possible participant in any movement for that purpose. But Trotsky told him, "Only the international revolution can save the Jews." It is easy to see why Ruskin would be alarmed by Trotsky's response. In the same letter to me, Trotsky made a forecast about the future of American Jews that was as wide of the mark as his forecast about the democratic West. Here again the opinion reflected the kind of theoretical certainties he often expressed on the large canvas of world events.

> There are 400,000 Jews in Palestine, but Ruskin and his associates hope to place 500,000 more there. (How? When?) I answered him that they were preparing a fine trap for the Jews in Palestine. Before you settle 500,000 people you will have an inner Palestine question with the 2,500,000 United States Jews. With the decline of American capitalism, anti-Semitism will become more and more terrible in the United States—in any case more important than in Germany. If the war comes, and it will come, a good many Jews will fall as the first victims of the war and will be practically exterminated.[48]

Trotsky was utterly out of touch with the real America. His abstractions did not serve him well there. Pockets of anti-Semitism did and do indeed exist in various areas of the country, as it always has, but it has never been an official state dogma, as it was in Germany, the Eastern European monarchies, and the Arab nations, nor has it been sponsored by the government, as in the Soviet Union.

Toward the end of his life, Trotsky was compelled to modify, however slightly, some of his position on Zionism. In an interview with the *Jewish Daily Forward* of January 24, 1937, entitled "Jews Must Have a Land, Trotsky Declares," he startled many:

> During my youth I rather leaned toward the prognosis that the Jews of different countries would be assimilated and that the Jewish Question would

thus disappear in a quasi-automatic fashion. The historical development of the last quarter of a century (this would take us back to 1910, at least) has not confirmed this perspective. Decaying capitalism has everywhere swung over to an exacerbated nationalism, one part of which is anti-Semitism. . . .

Jews of different countries have created their own press and developed a Yiddish language as an instrument adapted to modern culture. . . . Now a nation cannot normally exist without a common territory. Zionism springs from this very idea. . . . Zionism is incapable of resolving the Jewish Question. The conflict between Jews and Arabs in Palestine acquires a more and more tragic and more and more menacing character. I do not believe that the Jewish Question can be resolved within the framework of rotting capitalism and under the control of British imperialism.

And how, you ask me, can socialism solve this question? . . . I can but offer a hypothesis. . . . Human history has witnessed the epoch of great migrations on the basis of barbarism. Socialism will open the possibility of great migrations on the basis of the most developed technique and culture. It goes without saying that what is here involved is not compulsory displacement—that is, the creation of new ghettos for certain nationalities, but displacement freely consented to, or rather demanded by certain nationalities or parts of nationalities. . . . To work for international socialism means also to work for the solution of the Jewish Question.[49]

Trotsky again projects a Socialist utopia as the only solution. Jews only had to wait for it—but for how long, he was far from certain. He had already written about the certainty of the physical extermination of Jews in Europe in the war. Those of us who lived through those years saw the "crystal nights" in Germany, Stalinist Russia's extensive anti-Semitism, the Holocaust, and the refusal of Great Britain and the United States to do much, if anything, to aid Hitler's victims. How pertinently he described the problem of Jewish survival when he wrote:

Today decaying capitalist society (and the decaying Stalinist world) is striving to squeeze the Jewish people from all pores; seventeen million individuals out of two billion populating the globe, that is, less than one percent, can no longer find a place on our planet.[50]

In 1948, eight years after Trotsky's assassination, Zionism, containing a strong Socialist sector, created the nation of Israel, disregarding the ever-present British imperialism that resisted with its armed forces. The Zionists challenged the belief that only a proletarian revolution could establish a "territorial base for Jewry in Palestine or any other country." Given the "final solution" of Nazism, Jews could not follow Trotsky's advice and await their doom. They proceeded to make their own history. Knei-Paz observes:

> In view of the catastrophe which befell Jewish people during the period of the Second World War, in view of the nearly total failure of the Socialist movement to become the international force which Trotsky hoped it would, Zionism proved to be a more realistic response to the Jewish predicament than any other conceivable or conceived solution.[51]

The last chapter of Trotsky's autobiography is entitled "The Planet Without a Visa," and it describes his plight in being forced into exile again— by the nation he did so much to create. Be that as it may, a "planet without a visa" is a vivid description of the life of the Jews of the world until the State of Israel was established. Despite the precariousness of its existence, surrounded by an Arab world bent on destroying it, its borders continually assailed, more than three million people live without fear that the rulers of their country will unleash pogroms upon them.

Notes

1. Nedava, p. 117.
2. Nedava, p. 167.
3. Carmichael, p. 249.
4. Nedava, p. 117. This is quoted from A. Liesin, *Reminiscences and Sketches,* p. 213.
5. The exchange occurred in 1903. See Robert S. Wistrich, *Revolutionary Jews from Marx to Trotsky,* p. 181.
6. The utopian Socialist forerunners of Marx—St. Simon and Fourier, and his contemporary, Proudhon—were also anti-Semites. There was an anti-Semitic thread in the Socialist movement that ran from Marx to Stalin.
7. Marx repeats in this essay a historical falsehood, first propounded by Maneho in 250 B.C.: the legend that Moses was an alienated Egyptian priest who led a revolt of outcasts, Jews, lepers, and Negroes, a myth continued among Mediterranean and European peoples and prolonged over the centuries, which Paul Johnson in his *History of the Jews* observed, "became the fundamental matrix of anti-Semitism" (pp. 26–29).
8. Marx, *The Letters of Karl Marx,* Saul Padover, ed. See especially pp. 306, 308, 338, 435, and 456.
9. Max Beer, *Fifty Years of International Socialism,* p. 72.
10. Yvonne Kapp in her fine two-volume biography of Eleanor Marx details the deep involvement of Marx's youngest daughter in trade-union organization work on London's east side among the poor immigrant Jewish workers. Eleanor Marx was, in modern parlance, a "political activist," the only one of Marx's daughters

to be so totally involved.

11. This quote and the three that follow are from Yvonne Kapp's *Eleanor Marx*, Volume 2, pp. 519–526.

12. There is an error here, for Eleanor Marx's paternal grandmother was the *daughter* of a rabbi, not the wife.

13. The Narodniki—from *Narodnaia Viola*, or "People's Will"—was a terrorist group whose most notable achievement was the assassination of Alexander II in 1881.

14. Quoted in Nedava, p. 10.

15. This was the journal of German Social Democracy, edited by Karl Kautsky for many years during its highest reputation. The quotation is taken from Knei-Paz, p. 346.

16. Knei-Paz, p. 542.

17. Knei-Paz, pp. 544–545.

18. Knei-Paz, pp. 544–545.

19. Nedava, p. 225.

20. Nedava, p. 225.

21. Nedava relates that Bertram D. Wolfe wrote to him stating that Lenin made two phonograph records years before the Revolution, in which he said: "Disgrace and infamy to the damnable Tsarism which tortured and persecuted Jews! Disgrace and infamy to whoever sows enmity against Jews and hatred against nations!"

In the post-Revolution period, a pamphlet *Lenin on the Jewish Question* was put out by the early Communist International and distributed by all Communist Parties. Lenin's political feelings are unmistakable. The pamphlet became for a time an "official" statement of Lenin's rejection of anti-Semitism.

22. *My Life* pp. 340–341, 346.

23. *My Life*, p. 341.

24. Schapiro, p. 304.

25. Trotsky, "Therimidor and Anti-Semitism," in *The Basic Writings of Leon Trotsky*, p. 210.

26. *Basic Writings*, pp. 211–212.

27. *Stalin*, p. 400.

28. *My Life*, p. 361.

29. *My Life*, pp. 360–361.

30. *Basic Writings*, p. 213.

31. Wolfe, *Three Who Made a Revolution*, p. 468. The reference was taken from Stalin's *Collected Works*.

32. Quoted in "Interview with Trotsky," *Jewish Daily Forward*, January 18, 1937.

33. B. Z. Goldberg, "Editorial," in *The Day*, January 26 and 27, 1937, p. 33.

34. Aaron Glanz, letter to Shachtman, dated January 28, 1937.

35. Molotov, Trotsky wrote in *Stalin*, was "just as inclined to rudeness as Stalin," and a cold fish in fear of his leader. He did not even have the courage

to vote against the proposed punishment of his wife in the Politburo; he abstained! On March 9, 1953 (Molotov's birthday), Khrushchev and Malenkov asked him what he would like for his birthday. "Give me back my Polina," he replied coldly. Having feared his leader's wrath, he was now rude to Stalin's successors, who were ready to please him by returning his wife from banishment. See also Roy Medvedev's *All Stalin's Men*, p. 102.

36. *Khrushchev Remembers*, p. 263.

37. Svetlana Alliluyeva, *Twenty Letters to a Friend*, p. 180.

38. Alliluyeva, p. 186–87.

39. Alliluyeva, p. 196.

40. *Khrushchev Remembers*, p. 269.

41. *Khrushchev Remembers*, pp. 600–01.

42. Tolstoy, *Stalin's Secret War*, p. 32.

43. Quoted in *Stalin's Secret War*, p. 27.

44. *All Stalin's Men*, p. 148.

45. *All Stalin's Men*, p. 146.

46. Knei-Paz, 541–43.

47. Knei-Paz, 541–43.

48. *Letters*, p. 827.

49. Quoted in "Jews Must Have a Land, Trotsky Declares," *Jewish Daily Forward*, January 24, 1937.

50. *Writings, 1939–40*, p. 184.

51. Knei-Paz, p. 554.

The Moscow Frame-Up Trials
and the Dewey Commission in Mexico

I next saw Trotsky in Coyoacan, Mexico, in April, 1937. This is how it came about. Natalia and he were now living in the fourth country of their exile since being deported from the Soviet Union in 1929. Stalin had begun his series of Moscow Frame-Up Trials of Party leaders, and these were accompanied by a nationwide mass terror. Trotsky and his son Leon Sedov were the principal unnamed and unindicted defendants in all the trials of the Party leaders.

The American Committee for the Defense of Leon Trotsky came into existence in 1936 to give Trotsky a tribunal from which to defend himself against the charges. Trotsky had prodded his American comrades into creating this body, as he had our European counterparts. The American Committee organized a Commission of Inquiry, composed of outstanding public figures in the United States and Europe. The Commission asked me to go to Mexico in my capacity as a professional verbatim court reporter to record the testimony of Trotsky and his secretary, Jan Frankel, when their depositions were taken. I agreed to do so and prepared to leave for Coyoacan.

The Moscow Frame-Up Trials began with the 1935 trial of Gregory Zinoviev, Leon Kamenev, and several of their comrades. The fact that these two were Old Bolsheviks and long-time collaborators with Lenin indicated the path the Trials would take. By 1938, when Nikolai Bukharin (Lenin's "favorite"), Alexei Rykov, and their associates were tried, Stalin had succeeded in eliminating all of Lenin's staff from the days of the October Revolution. Ironically, the successive trials in Moscow came on the heels

of Hitler's Reichstag fire frame-up trial of Comintern leader Georgi Dimitrov, German Communist Party leader Ernst Torgler, and others—adding force to Trotsky's acute observation that "Stalinism and fascism were
symmetrical phenomena."[1]

The indictments in the Moscow Trials of 1935, 1936, 1937, and 1938
were almost identical in the charges and language. All the defendants in
the four trials, to one degree or another, named Trotsky and Sedov as
responsible for a vast conspiracy against the Soviet government in which
they all participated. They had "treasonable relations with foreign powers,"
were guilty of "undermining the military power of the USSR," and of seeking
to restore capitalism in the Soviet Union. The indictments in the Piatakov-
Radek trial of January 1937, though differing slightly in language, were
in essence an indictment of Zinoviev, Kamenev, Bukharin, Rykov, and
all the rest. Here is how they read:

> The accused Pyatakov [sic], in his turn, relating his conversation with L.
> Trotsky near Oslo in December 1935, testified that L. Trotsky, in demanding
> that the diversive, wrecking, and terrorist activities of the Trotskyite organiza-
> tion in the USSR be intensified, emphasized that as a result of an agreement
> with capitalist states, it was necessary, as he put it, to retreat to capitalism. . . .
>
> Proceeding from this program, L. D. Trotsky and his accomplices in
> the parallel center entered into negotiations with agents of foreign states with
> the object of overthrowing the Soviet government with the aid of foreign
> intervention . . . [gave] permission in the USSR of the development of pri-
> vate capital, the dissolution of collective farms, the liquidation of state farms,
> the leasing of a number of Soviet enterprises as concessions to foreign
> capitalists, and the granting to such foreign states of other economic and
> political advantages, including the surrender of part of Soviet territory.
>
> The preliminary investigation of the present case established that the
> so-called reserve center . . . was actually a parallel Trotskyite center, orga-
> nized and operating under the direct instructions of L. D. Trotsky, now in
> immigration [sic]. . . .
>
> The Trotskyite parallel center developed its criminal activities most
> energetically after the dastardly murder of Sergei Mironovich Kirov. . . .
>
> The main task which the parallel center set itself was the forcible over-
> throw of the Soviet government with the object of changing the social and
> state system existing in the USSR. L. D. Trotsky, and on his instructions
> the parallel center, aimed at seizing power with the aid of foreign states
> with the object of restoring capitalist social relations in the USSR. . . .
>
> The investigation has established that L. D. Trotsky entered into
> negotiation with one of the leaders of the German National Socialist Party
> with a view of waging a joint struggle against the Soviet Union, in which
> Trotsky guaranteed "a favorable attitude towards the German government

and the necessary collaboration with it," "to agree to territorial concessions . . . to permit German industrialists . . . to exploit enterprises in the USSR . . . in time of war to develop . . . extensive diversive activities in war industries and at the front."

These principles of agreement, as Trotsky related, were finally elaborated and adopted during Trotsky's meeting with Hitler's deputy, Hess.[2]

The rest of the indictment continues along similar lines, adding the crimes of sabotage and murder.

All seventeen defendants pleaded guilty!

Looking back to those years, the indictments of the leaders of the Revolution and founders of the Soviet state were nonsensical, which Khrushchev publicly admitted at the Twentieth Congress of the Russian Communist Party. Yet the trials and the bizarre behavior of the State Inquisitor, Andrei Vyshinsky, were endorsed and supported by millions the world over: liberals, radicals, governments in the democratic Western world, as well as the entire Communist International and its intellectual and cultural supporters. The Hitler–Stalin Pact that began World War II disillusioned many, but it did not influence the hardened minds of loyal Communists and intellectual supporters any more than Khrushchev's affirmation that the Moscow Trials were frame-ups. Communist Party resistance to the truth was particularly strong in the United States.

Trotsky's Initial Response to the Charges

As the principal—if unnamed—defendant in all the trials, Trotsky fought the new frame-up of Piatakov and Radek with confidence that he could unmask the new inquisition, even though he was almost alone in a struggle against a great state power and the most powerful police apparatus in the world. When he began to challenge the Kremlin, he was still an exile in Norway—whereupon the Norwegian government, under heavy pressure from the Soviet Union, ordered Trotsky to leave the country immediately. The time was near the end of 1936.

At the moment that Norway made its demand on the Trotskys, they had no place to go. Not a single nation in Europe would accept them as political exiles. The historic right of political asylum was almost impossible for Trotsky to obtain; the pressures of the Kremlin were potent.

Suddenly and quite unexpectedly, however, a new place of exile became available to him and Natalia. The Mexican president, Lazaro Cardenas, a man of deep democratic sensitivity, at the urgings of Diego Rivera, the world-famous muralist, and some of his friends, made Trotsky's exile in

Mexico a reality. Resisting the Stalinist campaign organized by the Latin American headquarters of the GPU in Mexico City, Cardenas held fast in his grant of asylum.

As they had done so many times before, Trotsky and Natalia, with all their belongings, this time on shipboard, were on their way to a new exile, which was to be their last together. They arrived in Mexico on January 9, 1937. Through the kindness of the artist Frida Kahlo, wife of Rivera, they resided in her home in Coyoacan, a suburb of Mexico City and once the summer home of Cortez. From this exile, Trotsky continued his resistance to the Moscow Trials and the savage purges that accompanied them.

Even before he was on his way to Mexico, Trotsky had appealed to the League of Nations for permission to submit his case before its Commission on Political Terrorism. By now totally feeble and incompetent, the League responded in what had become its customary style: It remained totally silent. The government of the Soviet Union was also silent toward Trotsky's request for a public hearing. Trotsky, however, continued to press the matter. He declared (over the telephone) to a public meeting in the city of New York that he was ready to submit to a public and impartial commission of inquiry to examine the charges against him and to accept whatever verdict it came to.

During 1936, as the Trotskyists themselves began to attack and expose the spurious charges of the Kremlin, there appeared very important works by Max Shachtman, Leon Sedov, and Victor Serge, all of them vigorous critiques of the so-called evidence invented by the secret police.[3] The main source material for these trenchant attacks on the Zinoviev–Kamenev trial of 1936 came from Trotsky and the factual material he made public.

The American Committee for the Defense of Leon Trotsky was made up of 120 outstanding figures from academic, literary, cultural, and radical political realms. Among them were Norman Thomas, Edmund Wilson, Sidney Hook, Ernest Sutherland Bates, Meyer Schapiro, Lionel Trilling, Reinhold Niebuhr, John Dos Passos, Horace Kallen, Joseph Wood Krutch, Burton Roscoe, James T. Farrell, B. Charney Vladeck, John Chamberlain, and Edward Alsworth Ross. The Committee issued a tabloid-size journal called *Truth,* which was an important source of information on its work. Most important of all, the American Committee, in collaboration with similar committees in Europe, set up the preliminary Commission of Inquiry into the "Charges Against Leon Trotsky in the Moscow Trials." The purpose of the Commission was to go to Mexico to take Trotsky's depositions. The trip to Mexico was necessary because the government of the United States refused Trotsky permission to enter the country.

*   *   *

The Chairman of the Commission of Inquiry was the venerable Dr. John Dewey, dean of American philosophers and one of the nation's great educators, a humanist and democrat. He was seventy-eight years old at the time he accepted the post, over the sharp objections of his family. Dewey knew it would be an exhaustive inquiry, tiring for him as well as for the other members of the body, which included Otto Ruehle, renowned German Socialist, biographer of Karl Marx, and exile from Nazi Germany; Benjamin Stolberg, a nationally known writer on labor and economic affairs; Suzanne LaFollette, niece of Senator Robert LaFollette, an art critic, journalist, and one-time editor of the *New Freeman;* and Carlton Beals, author of books and articles on Latin America, well-known in liberal circles.

Except for Ruehle, the Socialist, none of the Commission members who went to Mexico for this quasi-legal proceeding were Socialists, let alone Communists. Philosphically and politically, they were all explicitly opposed to Trotsky's political thinking. They were liberals and democrats in the American tradition, some having at one time or another sympathized with the "Russian experiment," but all strong in their beliefs that Trotsky, given the severity of the charges against him, deserved an open, public hearing where he could answer his accusers.

There were, in addition to these five, several European members of the Commission who would figure in its work once the Mexican depositions were taken and they were given copies of the record and exhibits.

Forerunners of the Moscow Frame-Up Trials

To understand the trials of the Old Bolsheviks, it is necessary to note that theirs were not the first frame-up trials to take place in the Leninist state. Jurisprudence in the one-party state moved in that direction in the late twenties, beginning with the Shakhty Trial of "Wreckers" in 1928, continuing with the trials of the "bourgeois remnants," and the GPU-invented "Industrial" and "Peasant" parties, which were charged with being "wreckers." These trials took on the "Union Bureau" of the Menshevik Party. In the Piatakov–Radek Trial of 1937, Inquisitor Vyshinsky referred to Kondratieff's "Toiling Peasant Party" as a *"kulak* organization, the activities of which were examined by the Supreme Court—all of these organizations exposed as organs of wreckers and groups of diversionists who welcomed Trotsky's struggle against our Party, against the Soviet Government."[4]

E. B. Pashukanis, a Soviet authority on law in the new state, denounced "bourgeois jurisprudence" as law of commodity exchange, which he claimed led to the emergence of the "jurisprudence of terror" in Russia in the twenties, but he asserted that this was necessary because Soviet legislation possessed "maximum elasticity"; "revolutionary legality," he said, "is a problem which is 99 percent political." When the state withered away, his idea went, so would the law.[5]

Soviet jurisprudence limited private or individual rights early in the post-revolutionary years. It is important to keep this in mind, because Stalin's revolution from above created vast dissatisfaction in the land, which was dealt with by physical and legal terror against which, under totalitarian conditions, no remedies existed. "In effect," Robert Sharlet wrote, "terror was 'legalized' and the criminal process 'politicized.' "[6] Guilt or innocence did not depend on the facts of the case or of objective proof but only on what suited the interests of the Party. This was true in the very beginning as it is to this day. One must look here for the legal source of the Frame-Up Trials of 1928–1929 and 1931, as well as the later trials of the former Party leaders.

Friedrich Adler, Secretary of the Labor and Socialist International in the years of the Trials, noted in his pamphlet *The Witchcraft Trial in Moscow* (1937) that the charges in the several trials involving the Old Bolshevik leaders, beginning with Zinoviev and Kamenev and the following with proceedings against Piatakov and Radek, *et al.*, were repetitions of the indictments and trials of the Mensheviks. The Mensheviks, too, had been accused of seeking to overthrow the Soviet regime under the direction and leadership of foreign Socialist parties and leaders. All subsequent trials were based on the same charge of involvement either with foreign governments, their military establishments, or, as in the 1936–1938 Trials, with a single diabolical person of unusual powers.

In the Menshevik Trial, Adler pointed out that the defendants were accused of struggling "against the working class." The Menshevik Party (then nonexistent as a party in the Soviet Union) had become a "paid agent of French imperialism and a direct ally of fugitive manufacturers, speculators, *Kulaks,* and White Guardists." They did all this with "the support of the Second International and primarily the German Social Democratic Party." Their aim was the "forcible overthrow of the proletarian revolution and the Soviet Union . . . the occupation of the Soviet, its partition among international brigands; the return of capitalists and landlords, decades of White Terror against the workers in the Soviet Union and torture and murder for the Communists and pioneers of the working class."[7]

THE MOSCOW FRAME-UP TRIALS

These charges, however, were not yet enough for the GPU organizers of the Mensheviks' trial. They had to find leaders who directed the Russian Mensheviks from outside Russia. Since they could not use the bogey of Trotsky, who was long critical of Social Democracy, for this particular trial they turned to Leon Blum in France and Emile Vandervelde in Belgium, both world-renowned leaders and prominent in the affairs of the Socialist International, as the organizers of the anti-Soviet conspiracy. No wonder that Blum, Vandervelde, and the Labor and Socialist International denounced the Menshevik Trial as a crude frame-up.

Even that was not enough. There had to be Russian involvement from abroad. The GPU chose Rafael Abramowitz, noted Socialist and publicist, a Menshevik and a Jew, thus eminently suited to Stalin's purposes. Abramowitz was the individual who directed the day-to-day activities of the Mensheviks in Russia, the regime asserted. But Abramowitz disconcerted the GPU, if only momentarily, because he was able to prove by photographic evidence that the testimony implicating him was incontrovertibly false.[8]

How could Vyshinsky carry out his leading role in these trials? Did he know that he lied? Did he know that the organizations he named never existed? Did he know that the "evidence" he cited in all the trials consisted of pure inventions?

As the chief inquisitor, he could not but know that the indictments in all the trials were more or less identical and that all the defendants were charged with the same offenses. Defendants in 1938 were charged with committing acts that defendants in 1928 and 1929 had already committed. The one difference is that where Blum, Vandervelde, and Albramowitz were organizers and directors of the defendants in the earlier trials, in the later trials it was Trotsky who organized, devised, and directed the ideological programs of the defendants from abroad.

The irony in this situation was that the politically diverse defendants in the four Party trials, who would not accept Trotsky's leadership in the post-Revolution years when they were still more or less equals in the leadership of the Party and state, were now accused of accepting detailed instructions for counterrevolution and murder, no less, from this same longtime political opponent.

Trotsky Misreads the Early Trials

Before the trials of the mid-thirties, Trotsky accepted the validity of the trials against the "wreckers" and the Mensheviks simply because they were charged by the "workers' state." Until charged himself, he could not visualize his new state engaging in a terrorist frame-up. His theory that Russia was a workers' state, albeit degenerated, was an abstraction at odds with the reality of Russian society—and it blinded him. In his mind a workers' state simply could not and would not engage in such malevolent practices. Therefore he accepted all the statements of the police regime as true. The years from 1924 to his deportation from the workers' state were forgotten in a political amnesia.

Medvedev has written:

> He accepted the validity of the Shakhty trial and never doubted the accusations against the so-called "Industrial Party." He even protested against the leniency of the sentence given to the main "leaders" of the nonexistent group. . . .[9]

Trotsky was utterly won over by this farce:

> Trotsky again believed the unsubstantiated accusations of the prosecutor Krylenko rather than the more convincing arguments put forward by the Menshevik Center abroad. He was absolutely convinced of the "guilt" of David Riazanov, who had been dismissed from his job and expelled from the Party, allegedly for keeping archives of the [Menshevik] "Union Bureau" in the depository of the Marx–Engels Institute. And although not one specimen from this "underground" archive was ever produced in court, Trotsky wrote that the guilt of the accused had been "established incontrovertibly."[10]

Trotsky's gullibility here is almost unbelievable, given his own experiences with the regime. Even assuming that the charge against Riazanov was true, how could archives of the Union Bureau, lodged in some dusty corner of the Marx–Engels Institute, threaten the safety of the Soviet Union?

In the *Bulletin of the Russian Opposition* Trotsky wrote of the nonexistent Industrial Party as

> the hired agents of foreign capital and Russian emigré *compradors*. Is it not clear that Krylenko's indictment against the Industrial Party is at the same time an indictment against the Stalinist elite which in its struggle against genuine Bolshevik–Leninists actually became the tool of world capital?[11]

The statement reflected Trotsky's certainty that the regime of Stalin meant a return to capitalism; this, he thought, was the meaning of the Stalinist counter-revolution. This erroneous perception of Stalin's role misled Trotsky in many important ways in subsequent years.

When the trials of the Old Bolsheviks began, Trotsky was compelled to revise his earlier views. At one point he wrote in the *Russian Bulletin* that

The editors of the Bulletin must acknowledge the fact that at the time of the Menshevik trial, they underestimated by far the degree to which the shamefulness had become a feature of Stalinist justice, and for this reason they took the confession of the former Mensheviks too seriously.[12]

After the Zinoviev–Kamenev trial of 1936, he went even further in rationalizing his early views. This is from "Why They Had Confessed Crimes They Had Not Committed" (January 1, 1937):

I remember that my son [Leon Sedov], then living in Berlin, said to me later, in a conversation in France, "The trial of the Mensheviks is a complete falsification."
    "But what are we to think of the statements of Sukhanov and Groman?" I answered. "After all, they aren't venal careerists, not worthless people!"[13]

Trotsky's notion of what an abstract workers' state could do was naive. He tried to explain his error by saying that he lived "outside" political circles, having been expelled from the Party, exiled in Central Asia, and deported to Turkey. He had no confidence in the "degenerate institution," the GPU, but he did have it "in certain of the accused." In further explanation, he wrote,

I underestimated the progress made in the techniques of demoralization and corruption. Later revelations and the trials that followed lifted the veil. . . . [14]

In May, 1936 before the Zinoviev–Kamenev trial, he wrote:

A long series of political trials has shown with what zeal the accused accepted responsibility for crimes they had not committed. . . .[15]

There were the threats against the families of the accused, particularly the children, threats that were often carried out. All of this put a burden on defendants to confess to crimes they could not possibly have committed, in the hope that they and their families would be spared. Neither happened. No one was saved.

    In trying to explain how such trials could take place in the Soviet Union, Trotsky wrote with new clarity:

There is nothing complicated, as can be seen, in this mechanism. It needs only a totalitarian regime, that is, the suppression of all freedom to criticise, the subjection of the accused to the military examining magistrate, a prosecutor and judge in one, a monolithic press whose howlings terrorize the accused and hypnotise public opinion.[16]

It is fitting to point to the anomaly in Trotsky's frequent denigration of democracy as a political form, and Social Democracy as a political movement. However, in this critical personal situation he had nowhere else to turn for help in the struggle against the Stalinist frame-up system, the false charges made against him and his one-time colleagues, the inquisitions, and the unending executions. There was simply no way he could meet this onslaught against innocent people in the Soviet Union except by looking to the democratic West. When he offered to open his archives, to testify freely, to subject himself to public cross examination, no one but movements and people in the West even cared. This irony could not possibly have eluded him. Still, it meant nothing to him, and he never ceased his assaults on democracy. Nor did he ever repudiate the strident views he expressed against democracy in his polemic with the great theorist of Social Democracy, Karl Kautsky, in Trotsky's notorious defense of the Leninist one-party state in his book *Dictatorship Versus Democracy*. With the utmost perversity, he defended a political system that guaranteed his defeat. He was totally helpless in the Soviet Union, and he was able to fight back now only because he resided in the West where, despite the difficulties of living conditions, active resistance to the Stalinist terror *was* possible.

The Kirov Assassination and the Moscow Trials

What triggered the Great Terror? The year 1934 was a turning point in the terrorism that had become constant in Russian society. At this time, a new intensive phase began in Stalin's relentless drive for total individual power, which would not countenance Party or state intervention in his personal rule. In describing this change, Medvedev has written:

Now the axe was to fall on the Party itself, the terror would be directed not only against former oppositionists but against those who in 1920 constituted the basic cadres of the Party apparatus, the government, the Red Army, and all other public organizations.
    It began with the murder of Kirov.[17]

Who was Sergei Kirov and how did his assassination begin Stalin's holocaust? Kirov was largely unknown outside of the Soviet Union. At the
time of his death, however, he was the appointed leader of the Leningrad
organization, the pride of the Bolshevik Party.

From all accounts, Kirov was a new force in the bureaucratic leadership. He was reported to be critical of the widespread terror; he believed
it impeded economic progress and created chaos in the countryside. Some
currents in the bureaucracy thought of him as a replacement for Stalin.
His critical attitude won him support in the Party and state apparatuses.
One thing was certain: Kirov could not be accused of being a Left Oppositionist, Zinovievist, Bukharinite, or Trotskyist. He had always been a
staunch supporter of the Stalin faction and an admirer of its leader. Had
that not been so, he would never have risen in the ranks so rapidly and
reached the summits of the ruling circles.

Kirov had, within a brief period after his rise as a national Party
leader, become an object of Stalin's inner rage. Stalin was always bitterly
envious of any person of talent. Stalin was further angered by Kirov's
criticisms of him, which were tepid when compared to the early quarrels
of the post-Revolution years. He was not yet a fully matured leader, but
in his development he never exhibited the bitterness of his *Vozhd* or many
of his colleagues. Kirov had the reputation of having sympathetic feelings for the terrified Party members. He was said to be alarmed at the
continual terror and to advocate a slower pace of industrial development
for the nation. The Leningrad district membership was reported to be
appreciative and devoted to him, and expressed these feelings in many
public ways. That alone would have been enough to incur Stalin's
pathological hatred.

Given the constant rewriting of Russian Party and state history, one
cannot be certain that any of these things said about Kirov in the early
thirties were true, with the possible exception of the widespread opinion
that he was deeply hated by Stalin.[18] We will never know the whole story
until the secret Kremlin Archives are no longer secret.

Kirov's assassination on December 1, 1934, in the Smolny Institute,
the Party headquarters in Leningrad, by Leonid Nikolaev, a disaffected
young Communist, was a bungled affair for which the GPU, which planned
it all, was totally responsible.[19] Khrushchev revealed some of the circumstances in his famous speech at the Twentieth Party Congress. Kirov,
like all top-rank Party leaders, was under constant protective guard of the
GPU, no matter where he happened to be. The assassin was a worker
in one of the state institutions. But, as Trotsky wrote in one of his several
articles on the Kirov affair, Nikolaev appeared to have free access to the

Smolny, where Kirov's office was and where he was shot in an easily arranged confrontation. Why was Kirov alone at the moment? Where were Kirov's guards? Why didn't the GPU prevent the murder?

The killing of Kirov shocked the Party ranks. Stalin and the internal police apparatus presented the assassination as a counterrevolutionary plot originating inside the Party. The assassination provided Stalin with an excuse to unleash a wave of terror following the earlier Frame-Up Trials and the forced collectivization of private property. Sixty-six Party and non-Party persons, imprisoned long before Nikolaev fired his pistol at Kirov, were immediately executed as though they had something to do with the act or were part of some conspiracy.

Stalin took immediate charge of the "investigation" of the killing by going to Leningrad to direct the inquiry by local officials. One may doubt that he wanted Kirov killed, but the local GPU's apparent bungling gave him the opportunity to lash out against various former opposition groups, now dispersed and ineffectual, on the one hand, and the Leningrad GPU on the other. The play he directed called for new executions of alleged plotters and other Party "malefactors," including the secret police functionaries connected to the Kirov affair. All the new killings came without trials.

The Kirov assassination of 1934 became the catalyst for the unending slaughter during the Great Terror of the next five years.[20] Stalin, now completely dominant in the Party and state, exerted his personal power as he pleased. Was he a modern Ivan the Terrible—or a "Genghis Khan," as Bukharin said to Kamenev in 1929? In an earlier comment on the ostensible GPU-planned assault on Kirov, Trotsky had written that the Stalinist terror "constitutes a phenomemon which is entirely new and directly of Soviet origin."

In his celebrated study of the Russian Party, Schapiro used the phrase "show trial" in referring to the Moscow Trials. He wrote: "The three show trials of 1936–38 have formed the subject of much discussion both at the time and since and they certainly raise important questions for the historian."[21] Elsewhere in this study he wrote: "The three show trials were only the most dramatic aspect of the greater process of Stalin's two-year assault on the Party and on the population at large. . . ."[22]

Robert Tucker, an outstanding historian of Soviet affairs, described the trials in an elaboration of what Schapiro had written years earlier. In the magazine *Dissent* (Spring 1965) he, too, described them as show trials:

> [The] whole proceedings become literally a dramatic performance in which not only the judge and prosecutor but also the defendant or defendants play pre-arranged parts just as actors do on the stage.

Political trials have taken place throughout the history of Soviet Russia from Lenin's time to the present. The show trial, however, is one of the special hallmarks of the Stalin era and Stalinism.[23]

The description of the Stalinist court proceedings as dramas or show trials drew attention to the extraordinary and extra-legal nature of these political trials. Why the unrelenting, fierce, and brutal persecution of powerless political comrades, Party members in general, and the population at large? There was not just one single, overriding reason or purpose, but a coalescence of several in Stalin's determination to take full personal power in the nation, to destroy the old Party physically, and to eliminate any possible rival from the old leadership. In his megolamania and xenophobia he believed this was necessary for a crash program of economic and military growth in the national interest of Great Russia. One completes the picture in noting the murderous personality of Stalin, a factor Trotsky shied away from in those years (until his biography of the General Secretary) but which Tucker described in the following way:

A great lesson to be learned from a study of events at that time is that our theory of totalitarianism has unduly neglected the personal factor. It has not been taken account of, or sufficient account, of the role of the dictator and his personality in determining the conduct of the regimes; the dynamics of totalitarianism itself, in such truly totalitarian situations as Germany under Hitler and Russia in the time of Stalin.[24]

Did Stalin really seek such destruction in the Party and nation? In his article "Eight Ministers," written on March 1, 1938, on the announcement of a pending new trial of Bukharin, Rykov, and others, Trotsky wrote of the role of the Kirov murder in Stalin's scheme as a summary of what Stalin wrought:

Immediately after the murder of Kirov, 104 White Guards, who had presumably come abroad in order to commit terrorist acts, were shot without trial.
    Although the names of the 104 were not published, it is known that among them were Bulgarian, Hungarian, and Polish Oppositionist members of the Communist International. Later the Leningrad "Center" of the Zinoviev group was accused of the murder of Kirov and thirteen men were shot. After this, the "Zinoviev–Trotskyist Center" was accused of the same crime and sixteen people were shot, not counting those shot during the government investigation. In January last year the "Parallel Trotskyist Center" (Radek, Piatakov and others) was accused of the murder of Kirov and thirteen of the accused were shot. Finally, we now learn that the Right Oppo-

sition (Rykov, Bukharin) was likewise occupied with plotting the murder of Kirov. [Eighteen were shot.] Thus all the leaders of the Bolshevik Party . . . plotted the murder of one and the same Kirov. . . .

The victim of this infernal conspiratorial activity beginning with 1918 proves to be no more than the same Kirov who was killed in turn by the White Guards, Leningrad Zinovieivists, the United Center, the Trotskyists, and finally the Bukharinists.[25]

Furthermore, when the White Guardists were accused and executed for the murder of Kirov, nothing was said about the involvement of Trotsky, Zinoviev, or Kamenev. The secret police, which could have invented anything Stalin demanded, did not indict the Left Opposition at the time of the assassination simply because they weren't *asked* to. In the Zinoviev–Kamenev trial of 1936, no mention was made of a "parallel center" of Piatakov-Radek. Yet in the Piatakov–Radek trial, the prosecutor obtained the confession that they were the Parallel Center, ready to act in case something happened to Zinoviev and Kamenev. But in the same Piatakov–Radek trial no mention was made about Bukharin or Rykov in connection with the Kirov affair. The subject was introduced for the first time only in their indictment.

Was Stalin really responsible? At the time of the Trials, Trotsky believed that Stalin personally was the instigator of the charges and the trials in order to have a legal cover for the murder of his comrades. This idea permeated his testimony in Mexico, and was received with considerable skepticism around the world. But years after the trials, Tucker stated that

A critically important point that emerges from the post-Stalin Soviet revelations about the Great Purge is that Stalin personally conceived and directed the whole process, including the planning, preparation, and actual conduct of the purge trials.[26]

What Stalin sought and achieved was the complete atomization of Russian society. Schapiro wrote that this was Stalin's goal, that "atomization" was "the most characteristic feature of totalitarian rule [and] was completed in the years of the terror."[27] Inside Russia, the terror engulfed all, no matter what one's social and political roles or positions were. All public information on the Trials and terror was composed either by Stalin personally or by the secret police at his direction. The Russian Empire had become a nation of fear.

Ilya Ehrenburg, the noted Russian journalist and a long-time writer and propagandist for the regime, described these hectic years in his post-Stalin *Memoirs 1921–41:*

We thought (perhaps we wanted to think) that Stalin knew nothing about the senseless violence committed against the Communists, against the Soviet intelligentsia. Mayerhold said: "They conceal it from Stalin." . . . One night I met Boris Pasternak in Lavrushensky Lane, he waved his arms about as he stood between the snowdrifts, "If only someone would tell Stalin about it. . . ."

Yes, not only I, but many other people, thought the evil came from the small man [Yezhov] they called Stalin's People's Commissar.[28]

In my opinion, Babel was more intelligent than I, and cleverer than most. He had known Yezhov's wife before her marriage. He sometimes went to see her, aware that this was unwise, but wanting, as he told me, "to find the key to the puzzle." One day he said, shaking his head, "It is not a matter of Yezhov. Of course, Yezhov plays his part, but he's not at the bottom of it."[29]

Is this a post-Stalin rationalization, or is Ehrenburg telling the truth? He was a propagandist for Stalin's Russia for so long that it is difficult to tell, for he had an unusual relationship with the Kremlin. Uncritical opinion always regarded him highly. Ehrenburg was an anti-Bolshevik who left Russia in 1921 because he felt stifled there, unable to carry on as a journalist. Nevertheless, he maintained his ties to the Soviet Union, which became close during the Stalin era. He was *Izvestia's* correspondent in Spain, where his journalistic reporting supported and praised the activities of the Russian Party's representatives and the secret police. In repayment for his services to the state, his chest bore two rows of decorations honoring his loyalty to the Stalinist leadership. There is no more apt description of Ehrenburg than his own:

Life is like a vaudeville show, with innumerable changes of costume, but I'm no one in particular. I try simply to obey.

I believe in absolutely nothing. It isn't my fault.

That's how I'm made. My spine is so supple that nothing can straighten it out.

I've changed my shirt again. Now, I'm a despicable swindler, doubling as an indecent fellow with dreamy and idealistic eyes.[30]

By 1939, so great was Stalin's power that when the Party leadership met, Schapiro noted, "It was a cowed and servile assembly. . . . There was no debate, no criticism, no discussion."[31]

*   *   *

Stalin received some world support for his terror regime and the great purge. Such support came, for example, from the noted British historian of Russia, Sir Bernard Pares, who regarded the charges of wrecking activities against the defendants, among the most ludicrous of the charges, as "proved up to the hilt." Walter Duranty, Moscow correspondent for the *New York Times,* lied shamelessly about events during the Trials, knew that he did, and laughed about it to his newspaper colleagues. He was the most cynical of reporters, and he relished the high standing he had in Moscow as the result of his sympathetic reporting of the leadership's conduct. The *New York Times,* zealous in its reputation of truth and accuracy, published all of Duranty's fictional reports from Moscow under its rubric "All the news that's fit to print."

Louis Fischer, Russian correspondent for *The Nation,* wrote a weekly propaganda column in support of the Kremlin. Among literary people, Lion Feuchtwanger, an outspoken supporter of Stalin's regime, was a very active propagandist in behalf of the Trials and purges. Perhaps the most dangerous person speaking up for the Trials was Joseph Davies, the American ambassador to the Soviet Union in the years of the great terror. Totally ignorant of the history and politics of Stalinist Russia, he lived for the handouts from the GPU. His vanity led him to produce a scurrilous book called *Mission to Moscow,* later made into a low-grade Hollywood movie justifying the purges and terror to American and world audiences.

Davies informed the Secretary of State that there was proof "beyond reasonable doubt to justify the verdict of guilty of treason." Robert Conquest described how, "during wartime lectures, Davies used to get a laugh, which he greatly appreciated, to his answer to the questions about fifth-columnists in Russia: 'There aren't any, they shot them all.' "[32]

The Trials of 1936 and 1937

In August 1936 Zinoviev, Kamenev, and fourteen Old Bolsheviks were put on trial. These were men who had high posts in the revolutionary state they helped create from the very beginning of its existence. But they were "capitulators" in the struggle against Stalin, men who in 1927 accepted defeat, acknowledging the triumph and leadership of Stalin and his faction. They were broken men, incapable of threatening anyone since then. Yet they were charged with unbelievable crimes against the state. None of these men had the moral or physical courage, above all the desire, to carry out any of the charges of counterrevolutionary activities, spying for imperialist powers, sabotaging industry, killing workers, murdering Kirov, or threatening the leadership of Stalin, the Torquemada of the Soviet Union.

Notwithstanding all of this, they were tried, found guilty, and executed immediately upon pronouncement of the verdict. So ended, in the summer of 1936, the lives of Zinoviev, Kamenev—the two leaders, long-time coworkers, and companions of Lenin—and their codefendants.

Almost immediately after the Zinoviev–Kamenev trial, a lesser known trial took place in Novosibirsk, Siberia, as a seeming rehearsal for the trials of Piatakov, Radek, Sokolnikov, *et al.,* in January 1937. The trial was a "minor" one and unpublicized, but the defendants were lesser-known alleged Trotskyists in exile. They, too, were charged with plotting together with a Hitler spy (a German engineer) to overthrow the Soviet government. Imagine, a plot to overthrow the powerful police regime from the distant recesses of Siberia—with the aid of a single German engineer, no less! Six of these defendants were executed immediately upon the close of the trial. The defendants in the January 1937 trial, Piatakov, Radek, Sokolnikov, and others, were charged with exactly the same plots as the now-dead Siberian exiles.

The trial of Piatakov and his comrades involved Trotsky directly as the intellectual, political, and moral influence on the defendants. A long catalog of charges were presented in this new trial. They included the usual charges made in all trials—counter-revolutionary plotting against the state, the planned assassination of Soviet leaders in league with foreign imperialism—but now the defendants were acting in behalf of Hitler, and/or Emperor Hirohito, and, not to leave anyone out, British and/or French imperialism. They were also charged with the murder of Kirov.

The indictment stated that Leon Trotsky was behind all of these activities. He gave the orders, just as he did in the murder of Kirov and the assassination of other leaders. How he was able to accomplish these miracles, in face of the most rigidly controlled totalitarian police regime the world has ever seen, went unexplained. The use of GPU agents, poorly prepared but eager to provide the "proofs," turned out to be a clumsy and ludicrous performance.

The eagerness of the GPU to act swiftly in this trial only compounded their bungling and made for obvious doubts about the trial among those not committed to the cult of the Soviet Union and Stalin. This explains in part why the organizers of this bizarre trial moved swiftly. The court hearings, examinations, pretended cross-examinations, verdicts, and execution all occurred within a single week. Such haste prevented any appeals of the verdict, protests from the outside world, or demands for stays of execution.

Hotel Bristol and Oslo

In linking Trotsky to the defendants, the secret police needed "events" to prove that the trumped-up confessions were true. Trotsky's son, Leon Sedov, was charged with acting as Trotsky's intermediary in transmitting instructions to the defendants through one E. S. Goltsman (Holzman). They met, the indictment said, in November 1932, in the vestibule of the Hotel Bristol in Copenhagen. But the Hotel Bristol had burned down in 1917! At one time Trotsky had jestingly suggested that the GPU had used an old Baedeker. D. N. Pritt, British barrister and propagandist on behalf of the Frame-Ups (Trotsky called him a GPU lawyer), explained away the name "Bristol" as a slip of the stenographer's pen. As a former verbatim court reporter, I can assure you that such a slip is virtually impossible. How did the honorable barrister arrive at such a nonsensical explanation? Was it supplied to him by his good friend Vyshinsky, the policeman-prosecutor in all the trials?

It turned out that the organizers of the Trials didn't mean the Hotel Bristol but a confectionary shop call the Bristol. What now becomes of Mr. Pritt's "slip of the stenographer's pen"? A confectionary store is not a hotel, obviously. Well, there was a store next to the hotel, but the hotel was called Grand Hotel Copenhagen. In pointing to this clumsiness, Trotsky wrote:

> To this must be added that, as it appears even in the sketches published in the Comintern press, the entrance to the shop and to the hotel are in different streets. Now, where did the meeting really take place? In the vestibule without the "Bristol" or in the "Bristol" without the vestibule?[33]

If Goltsman was confused about where the Hotel Bristol was located, or even whether that was its name, it would seem that the zealous ex-Menshevik Vyshinsky should have rehearsed his witness beforehand. Sheer arrogance of his complete control of the trial dictated his failure to prepare Goltsman in his earlier disposition. To top off the series of GPU bunglings, it was easily shown that Leon Sedov was in Berlin at the time of the alleged meeting and had never been in Copenhagen in his life. For example, he was unable to obtain the necessary papers and permission to make the trip to meet his parents when Trotsky spoke to university students in Copenhagen in 1932.

We come now to the charge involving Trotsky's personal meeting with Vladimir Romm, a defendant, in July 1933, in the Bois de Boulogne, Paris. Before the trial began, *Isvestia* had been instructed to say that the meeting took place in a Parisian alley. As the documents in the Dewey

Commission hearings revealed, Trotsky was in Turkey during most of July or on shipboard on his way to France. He did not arrive in Marseilles with his party until July 24, and then he was met by the French police and directed to Royan on the Atlantic coast near the Gironde River. He remained there for two months because he was ill.

Vyshinsky pressed on in trying to establish a personal link between the defendants and Trotsky. For the purpose of strengthening the frame-up, it was alleged that Piatakov, a principal defendant in the January 1937 trial, flew to Oslo from Berlin, where he was a member of a Soviet mission, in December 1935, to receive instructions from Trotsky in how to carry out his counter-revolutionary work. Moreover, he made this flight in a Nazi plane, thus nicely establishing a link to German fascism as well.

Why, it might be asked, would a man whom Lenin said was one of the two most able younger leaders of the Party need to receive instructions on how to put glass in the food of workers or how to destroy trains? And why should he so foolishly use a Nazi plane for a flight to Norway, where everyone knew Trotsky was living in exile? Had he really done so, it would have made Lenin's estimate of Piatakov's ability entirely mistaken.

Alas, for its case, the GPU neglected to prepare well. It was confident of its unchallenged power inside the Soviet Union. In the sporting world, it would be called overconfidence. Airfield records in Oslo showed that no airplane of any kind landed at the Oslo airfield in December 1935—it was ice-bound and not open to traffic. Norwegian government officials confirmed this fact. Piatakov simply could not have met Trotsky in Norway.

*   *   *

From the very beginning of the American Committee and its Dewey Commission, the American Stalinist movement—orchestrated by the Kremlin, the Party, its institutions and "transmission belts," fellow-traveling writers, and cultural representatives—began a massive and costly campaign to destroy them both. The campaign was an international one, but because the hearings would take place on this side of the Atlantic, the attacks were most strongly organized and most hysterical in the United States.

For weeks and months members of the Committee and its Commission were hounded, threatened, and cajoled to resign from these bodies. In the case of writers, the threat was that their books and articles would not be published. Stalinists and their sympathizers had penetrated some areas of the publishing industries and were quite capable of carrying out these threats. So that on top of the many indignities members of the Committee and Commission had to undergo, they were now threatened with economic reprisals.

The main pressure was put on Dewey personally. The Communists urged Dewey to make a second visit to the Soviet Union (he had been there in the twenties). Had he gone, he would have been fêted as no one else. But Dewey was too honorable to bend under such pressures. He also knew a crude bribe when he saw one. Thereafter he was continually and alternately praised and abused. Eventually, when the Stalinist dullards saw that Dewey was immovable, they denounced him as senile. The political line they used on Dewey and other Commission members was that giving Trotsky the opportunity to answer the charges of the Moscow Trials threatened the safety of the USSR and heightened the danger of war!

The leaders and main participants in the furious effort to prevent the hearings in Mexico were: Heywood Broun, a noted American journalist who was particularly vicious in his attacks on the Commission; Malcolm Cowley, literary critic and long-time Stalinist, an active member of the pack who, fifty years later, finally acknowledged how mistaken he had been; Theodore Dreiser, who had joined the Communist Party near the end of his life. Lillian Hellman, the playwright, was a very militant supporter of the Soviet Union and the activities of the Communist Party. Robert Morse Lovett served on countless Communist committees nationally and in Chicago, using his liberal reputation to champion the "cause." There was Carey McWilliams, one-time editor of *The Nation,* and Dorothy Parker, Henry Roth, Paul Sweezy, Lillian Wald, and hard-bitten Stalinist Nathaniel West.

These were the most active. Most of them believed in Stalinism politically and philosophically. And they had important assistance from the very wealthy Corliss Lamont (the noted humanist philosopher), Mauritz Hallgren, Vincent Sheehan, John Howard Lawson (a prominent Party member in Hollywood), Erskine Caldwell, and the ever-willing Frederick Schuman.

Few of them ever apologized for the part they played in attempting to destroy the Dewey Commission with their public abuse of its members and their nightly telephone calls to pressure and denounce the Committee. They supported the mass purges and the Moscow Frame-up Trials militantly, clamoring for the blood of the victims. Just as the Hitler–Stalin Pact did not shake them, so too were they unmoved by Khrushchev's denunciation of Stalin's endless murders of innocent Party leaders. They publicly hailed Stalin's murderous drive for total personal power over the Party and nation as the essence of freedom and socialism.

On the Eve of the Hearings

The Dewey Commission was getting ready to leave New York for Mexico to take Trotsky's depositions in April 1937. On March 30 I received the following telegram from Felix Morrow, author of *The Civil War in Spain,* acting for the American Committee: "Important you go to Mexico to take court proceedings Commission of Inquiry. Expenses paid. Write answer immediately."

In a letter of the same day, Morrow advised me that:

> The hearings will probably open on the 7th [of April]. We should like you to leave for Mexico Thursday at the latest and you need not have any hesitation so far as money is concerned. We can fully finance your expedition. . . . Naturally, we hope that you will be able to go for nothing more than full expenses both ways in Mexico.[34]

I replied immediately that I would leave for Mexico within a few days. Though I had doubts that the Committee would finance my "expedition" fully, I knew that my professional and political qualifications made it necessary that I make the record for the Commission. In any case, the political and historical importance of the hearings would have determined my willingness to go. In addition, I would see Trotsky and Natalia once more. As it turned out, the financial pressures were constant during my stay in Mexico—as they were back in Chicago, when I was transcribing my notes into written text. The Committee was unable to ease the pressures significantly.

I took the long train ride to Mexico City at a time when the railroad was the most convenient way to one's destination. In St. Louis I changed trains and boarded the Missouri Pacific for Mexico City. I awakened in the early morning hours to the changing mountain scenes and a variety of cacti silhouetted against a light dawn sky. I had been interested in Mexico for many years, an interest kindled by an old comrade in the Communist Party who lived there and was involved in Latin American affairs.

The sunshine, mountains, deserts, cacti, and people were what I always imagined them to be from reading, and arriving from a just-ending dull, grey, and bleak Chicago winter made a deeper impression on me of this land. This feeling about Mexico, even after many other visits, has never been dulled.

On my arrival in Mexico City, I was met by George Novak, Secretary of the American Committee, and Pearl Kluger, Secretary to the Commission. They, too, had arrived on the Missouri Pacific "Sunshine Special," along with Dewey, Stolberg, Suzanne LaFollette, and James T. Farrell. We went directly to Coyoacan, to the temporary residence of Trotsky and Natalia on Avenida Londres. It was also the residence of the secretaries and staff working on preparations for the hearings, which were to be held in the same building. This was the very attractive house made available to us by Frida Kahlo Rivera.

I then had a friendly reunion with the "Old Man" and Natalia. It was three years since I had seen and talked with Trotsky and six since I had been in Turkey, when I saw Natalia daily for many weeks. We talked briefly in our first personal meeting. Trotsky told me how excited and busy everyone was with the preparations for the event, but he hoped it would be possible to sneak in some conversation, particularly about affairs of the American organization. Natalia, with her usual concern for one's welfare, ushered me into lunch with a large group of old and new friends.

Trotsky appeared unchanged physically from when I saw him in Paris. He had regrown his goatee and resumed his characteristic appearance. Natalia, in contrast, now seemed tired and worn. I also met my old comrade and friend from Turkey, Jan Frankel, whom I had not seen since, except for a brief encounter in France. Although we enjoyed seeing each other again, he, too, was absorbed in hearing matters, for he would be the only other witness. An acquaintance from France, Jean van Heijenoort, was also in Coyoacan to help in the preparations. (He had been secretary to Trotsky in Turkey, France, and now Mexico.)

Everyone was busy sorting documents, letters, and other materials for the sessions, which would begin in a matter of days. Ruth Ageloff, a Trotskyist from New York, was giving technical help. Bernard Wolfe, the novelist, then a Trotskyist living in New York, had been sent to Mexico to assist in the prehearing work. Together with Frankel and Van Heijenoort, they made up the "secretariat" in the house.

There was another technical staff, which had arrived earlier, headed by Herbert Solow, a brilliant intellectual and journalist, former member of the Trotskyist organization in New York. Solow was assisted by John McDonald, who worked with him at *Time* and *Fortune* magazines. Dorothy Eisner, McDonald's wife, was also a member of the staff. An artist, she was painting Trotsky's portrait amidst the turmoil and din of the intense activities surrounding her.

Charles Rumford Walker, author of *American City,* and his wife, Adelaide, were in Mexico to assist in public relations. Charles was in charge of press matters. Adelaide's mother, Mrs. Robert Latham George, had a residence in Mexico City on Avenida Amberes, around the corner from the famous Hotel Geneva. The Walkers resided with her. My first night in the city was spent in Mrs. George's house. Solow, who put me there, thought the house was getting too crowded and assured me I would have a permanent place to stay soon. And so it was that on the following day I moved into a large modern penthouse on Avenida Londres in Mexico City, together with George Novack, Pearl Kluger, and James T. Farrell. We became a very close group, going to and from the daily hearings and eating together often.

Farrell and I became personal friends at that time. I had read *Studs Lonigan* soon after it appeared and admired it, and I was therefore most pleased to meet its author. He had become, in the course of his struggles in the Stalinist cultural movement, a sympathizer of the American Trotskyists. Our Chicago origins no doubt also helped to create some kind of bond, but it was more our political interests and our passionate devotion to baseball, its lore, history and "science." Once during our stay, Farrell became ill with severe chills and a rough shaking of his body. I administered to him, piling blankets and coats over him and forcing him to take hot drinks that I had made. After hours of such attention, the chill was broken, so that before too long Farrell was back in good shape, meeting and talking with visitors in Coyoacan and the press.

The last-minute gathering of materials for the hearings made it a busy time for the staff. Everyone understood, whether or not all the materials would be used, they needed to be available immediately once the examination of Trotsky began. So the staff in the household and the friends who wandered in were busy gathering, typing, and organizing a great mass of documents. Much of this material became exhibits that the Commission would use in reaching its verdict. The testimony Trotsky gave reflected this careful preparation. *The Case of Leon Trotsky,* my verbatim record, reproduces it all.

I talked to Trotsky several days before the opening session about the situation of the American Trotskyists, who had liquidated their organization, the "Workers' Party of 1934" (a fusion of the Communist League of America and the American Workers' Party led by A. J. Muste), to enter the Socialist Party. Even though he devoted almost all of his time to preparation for his testimony, he made sure he communicated his feelings about the work of the Americans in the Socialist Party.

Before he arrived in Mexico, he was familiar with the internal crisis in the Workers' Party over the proposal made by James P. Cannon and Max Shachtman, the two main leaders of the majority faction, to dissolve the new Party and enter the Socialist Party. The reasoning behind their proposal was to provide a wider political arena for Trotskyist activity. They believed the political times ripe for such a tactical maneuver. Trotsky supported their position, but it soon became clear that they did not really share political perspectives.

I was talking to Trotsky in his study about the presentation of his testimony when I said I wanted to take up with him the situation in the States, indicating my critical observations. I had opposed the entry into the Socialist Party and voted against the motion to do so, but I felt that once we had done so, we had an obligation to carry it out seriously. Our work in the Socialist Party was very uneven. While our faction was completely integrated into the Socialist Party in Chicago, and fairly well in California and New York, there were areas where our people were hesitant and uncertain about their presence in the party. These sections did not do well in their work. They seemed to be uncomfortable outside the cozy sectarian relations in their old organization with their long-time comrades and friends.

Trotsky told me, "I am very dissatisfied with the way the American comrades are working in the Socialist Party. It is opportunist."

I interjected to say, "I am dissatisfied, too, and I want to discuss the entry and the future with you."

"The comrades should be looking to a conclusion to the experiment. They seem to think we have a long time to spend in this reformist movement," he said. Then he mentioned the events in Spain and elsewhere coming to a head, which required us to be free to carry out a revolutionary policy. We would be unable to do this if we remained in the Socialist Party, he told me. I was taken aback by the perspective he sketched so briefly. This was too abrupt a turn so soon after our entry and completely opposite to what I believed our policy should be. It was a repetition of the policy in France that ended so poorly for the Trotskyists there.

Our conversation was coming to an end, since he was impatient to get back to the preparations for his testimony. He merely added that he thought we had already won considerable support in the party and a majority of the young Socialists. It was now necessary to draw the curtain on this American version of the French experience, he advised. The French experience was a disaster and I was certain, given Trotsky's views, the American would follow a similar course. I knew, standing there in his study, that our life in the Socialist Party would be short.

The Hearings Begin

The hearings began on April 10, 1937. It was a festive occasion. The press, mainly American and Mexican, understood the political importance of the event, and their reporters were present throughout the proceedings of the next eight days.

The hearing room, the one best suited to be a "courtroom," ran along the south side of the house on Avenida Londres. The windows leading into the long hearing chamber were filled with adobe brick to prevent a possible attack by Stalinist hooligans and *pistoleros*. Police assigned to guard duty were alerted to prepare for any kind of disruption. There had to be a selection of visitors because of limitations of space, and there was an area marked off for these visitors. Many were turned away, but each day brought new attendants.

The rest of the chamber was occupied by the five members of the Commission and its counsel, John Finerty, a respected veteran labor attorney, once closely associated with the IWW but reputed to be a philosophical anarchist. Trotsky, with Natalia at his side, sat to the right of the Commission. Alongside them was Jan Frankel. Van Heijenoort was also in that area and assisted in the identification of documents and other references. Albert Goldman, Trotsky's attorney, sat opposite this group and to the left of the Commission, examining Trotsky from that position. I sat in between Goldman and Finerty.

Trotsky, modestly dressed in a suit, shirt, and tie—his usual neat and formal attire—was enspirited by the occasion. The gathering was a culmination of his long struggle. He had been endlessly abused and lied about by the Kremlin. His family was brutally destroyed, one by one, to satisfy the blood lust of the vengeful Stalin. And he had watched helplessly the murder of countless numbers of his friends and followers, in a terror so generalized and continuous as to seem almost monotonous to the average person viewing the Soviet Union.

The hearings for Trotsky were an opportunity to speak out, to challenge the vast machinery of the Stalinist bureaucracy and prove that the charges in the several Moscow Trials were frame-ups consisting of invented evidence and extorted confessions. He fought back, many acknowledged, with intensity, vigor, skill, and intelligence. It was done, as we were soon to see, with a thorough command of the accumulated material, historical and current, and a first-hand knowledge of the functioning of the Stalin regime's police apparatus.

While Attorney Goldman asked the necessary preliminary questions to lead Trotsky into a recital of his personal history, the evolution of the political struggle against Tsarism and absolutist Russia, and the October Revolution, the guiding hand was Trotsky's. He was closely cross-examined by the Commission Chairman and its members, themselves intellectually accomplished, and, again, with the exception of Otto Ruehle, not sympathetic to Trotsky in philosophical and political terms.

*   *   *

The first two sessions dealt with Trotsky's relations with the numerous defendants in the 1936 and 1937 Trials. These were followed by three sessions on the charges and evidence of the two trials in which Trotsky stated his rebuttals to the indictments and the so-called proofs of the trials' officials, prosecutor, and confessing defendants. After these depositions, he was examined on his theoretical and political views as they bore on the indictments: the nature of and his attitude toward the nationalized Russian economy, the defense of USSR terrorism, his thinking regarding fascism, the meaning and role of the movement for a Fourth International, in addition to other subjects.

Jan Frankel, the only other witness, was cross-examined in the middle of Trotsky's testimony as to numerous events and documents according to his own independent memory of them and in corroboration of parts of Trotsky's statements. A fine linguist, Frankel had quickly acquired a fluency in English so that he was able to testify in the language.

The direct examination by Goldman elicited from Trotsky a recital of biographical-political material: when he joined the Socialist movement, his political and organizational life, his exiles and escapes, the events of the Russian Revolution, the much disputed Kronstadt sailors' rebellion, his literary activities, and, finally, the events that led to his deposition in Coyoacan, made possible through the fortunate right of asylum given him by President Cardenas and Mexico.

If for Trotsky the hearings' *raison d'etre* was to absolve him of accusations made against him in the Frame-Up Trials, the bulk of his testimony described his views on the Stalinist state and the future of communism. Trotsky's testimony embodied his brilliant insights into the corruption of the Soviet regime as well as his tragic dogmatism regarding the inevitability of communism's victory over capitalism and fascism. The principal focus was on the growth of the bureaucracy. Trotsky's lawyer, Albert Goldman, asked if this growth began during Lenin's rule:

> TROTSKY: During Lenin's time? . . . I believe we did what we could to avoid the degeneration. During the Civil War the militarization of the Soviets and the Party was almost inevitable. But even during the Civil War I myself tried in the army—even in the army on the field—to give a full possibility to the Communists to discuss all the military measures. I discussed

these measures even with the soldiers and, as I explained in my autobiography, even with the deserters. After the Civil War was finished, we hoped that the possibility for democracy would be greater. But two factors, two different but connected factors, hindered the development of Soviet democracy. The first general factor was the backwardness and misery of the country. From that basis emanated the bureaucracy, and the bureaucracy did not wish to be abolished, to be annihilated. The bureaucracy became an independent factor. Then the fight became to a certain degree a struggle of classes. That was the beginning of the Opposition. For a certain time the question was an internal question in the Central Committee. We discussed by what means we should begin the fight on the degeneration and the bureaucratization of the state. Then it became not a question of discussions in the Central Committee, but a question of the fight, the struggle between the Opposition and the bureaucracy.

The Commission rigorously questioned Trotsky concerning the relationship between the "dictatorship of the proletariat" and the now-ingrained bureaucracy. Trotsky was asked by John Finerty to define the "dictatorship of the proletariat."

TROTSKY: The dictatorship of the proletariat signifies that all the exploiters are eliminated from the right of determining the fate of the country, and all the elements who support them are automatically eliminated. Only the revolutionary of the proletariat and all the exploited masses which support the proletariat have the right to determine the fate of the country.

FINERTY: What I want to know is, if within that definition is included the meaning of a dictatorial government?

TROTSKY: Yes; of a dictatorial government. It is a government which represents the dictatorship of the proletariat. The class cannot be the government. The class—

FINERTY: What I really want to ask you, is, if the more correct designation would be the dictatorship for the proletariat, rather than the dictatorship of the proletariat?

TROTSKY: The question is of the relationship between the Party and the class and between the Central Committee and the Party. If the Party has the full confidence of the workers and the elections are free, then these two formulae coincide, because it is impossible for a class directly to form the government. The whole class cannot do it. There is the trade union with secretaries and directing bodies. If the secretaries are selected freely—if a GPU does not have the means of oppression—it is a democratic means of election in the trade unions.

FINERTY: It is a democratic method of selecting the dictatorship?

TROTSKY: We named that the dictatorship of the proletariat as the first experience of genuine proletarian democracy.

FINERTY: But the government in essence is a dictatorial government?

TROTSKY: Dictatorial government? You must make it precise. The question is, if its dictatorial power is directed against the people—if the GPU, if the function of the GPU—is to oppress the masses, or if the GPU and the newly acquired rights of the masses are against the exploiters. It is a simple definition.

FINERTY: Well, the dictatorship, whether for better or worse, is a dictatorship?

TROTSKY: Formally, yes. But my opinion is, that in Norway, where the government is Socialist, we have a genuine dictatorship of the shipowners. The state is governed exclusively by the shipowners. The Socialist government is a decorative ornament in this instance.

FINERTY: Now, I understand that your belief is that even such a democratic organization of the Communist Party and of the Soviet government as was possible within the limits of the theory of dictatorship has been set aside by Stalin through the means of the bureaucracy.

TROTSKY: Transformed into its contrary; not only changed, but transformed into its contrary.

FINERTY: Into its contrary?

TROTSKY: Yes.

FINERTY: In other words, it has become a purely bureaucratic government?

TROTSKY: Defending the privileges of the new caste, not the interests of the masses. Because, for me the most important criterion is the material and moral interests of the masses, and not only constitutional amendments. It is important, but it is subordinated in my conceptions to the real material and moral interests of the masses.

DEWEY: Might I ask one question? Just on what you said, did I understand that you hold that these privileges have reached a point where there are class divisions in the Soviet Union?

TROTSKY: It is difficult to get a strict social formula for this stage of development, because we have it for the first time in history, such a social structure. We must develop our own terminology, new social terms. But I am inclined to affirm that it is not a genuine class division.

DEWEY: Yet it is a real class. That is the reason why I asked the question.

INTERPRETER: A caste.

TROTSKY: I said a caste.

DEWEY: I beg your pardon.

FINERTY: In the Socialist state, Mr. Trotsky, the state controls the forms of production, does it not?

TROTSKY: Yes.

FINERTY: The sources of production and the methods of production.

TROTSKY: Yes.

FINERTY: And in order to have an effective control, the state itself must employ technicians. Isn't it then inevitable in a Socialist state that the bureaucracy will grow up automatically?

TROTSKY: What do you name a Socialist state? The Socialist state is a transitory form which is necessary to prepare to build up the future Socialist society. The Socialist society will not have any state.

FINERTY: I understand that. But in the intermediate form of the Socialist state, you have an inevitable bureaucracy.

TROTSKY: It depends on two factors which are connected with one another: the productive forces and the power of the country. It is the function of the new régime to satisfy the material and moral needs of the popuation. Secondly, and what is connected with it, the cultural level of the population. The more the population is educated, the easier it is that everyone can realize the simple functions of an intermediary regulation of distribution. The bureaucrat in a cultivated, civilized country has not the possibility of becoming a half-god.

FINERTY: Demi-god.

TROTSKY: Demi-god, yes.

FINERTY: What I mean is this: It is obviously impossible in a Socialist state, as an intermediary organization, to have a democratic control of industry. I mean, a truly democratic control. It must be a bureaucratic control.

TROTSKY: I repeat, the relationship between the bureaucracy and the democracy depends—the elements of bureaucracy are inevitable at the beginning, especially because we inherited all the past, the oppression and misery of the people, and so on. We cannot transform it in twenty-four hours, this relationship. Here the quantity is transformed into quality. The relationship between them depends upon the material prosperity and the cultural level of the population.

FINERTY: I understand, but we cannot now discuss what the relationship should be between the democracy and bureaucracy. But it is the inevitable result of a Socialist state?

TROTSKY: Not only a Socialist state. Bureaucracy—

FINERTY: Just confine it, if you will, to the Socialist state. Whatever may be good in the Socialist state, the bureaucracy is inevitable from the start?

TROTSKY: I cannot accept that formula, as a Marxist. The first period of the Socialist state is the victory over the bourgeois state. That is the formula of the Marxist—until the time we have reached a state to satisfy freely, as with a *table d'hôte*. The rich people have a *table d'hôte*, wines and jewels. It is not necessary to have a dictatorship when you have a *table d'hôte*. On the contrary, everybody gets the same things, especially the ladies. When the table is very poor, everybody forgets whether it is a lady or a man. He will take all he can. Then it is necessary to have a dictatorship. The reason for the existence of *gendarmes* is the misery of the people. In other words, the economic condition has a basic influence on this question.

FINERTY: Limit it this way: When the revolutionary Socialist state takes the place of the former capitalist state, the bureaucracy is inevitable at the start.

TROTSKY: It is an inheritance, just as misery is an inheritance.

FINERTY: Inherited or not, it is inevitable?

DEWEY: May I, before we adjourn for recess, ask one question along the same line? On page forty-four of the English translation of [Trotsky's] *The Revolution Betrayed,* I find this statement:

> If the state does not die away, but grows more and more despotic, if the plenipotentiaries of the working class become bureaucratized, and the bureaucracy rises above the new society, this is not for some secondary reasons like the psychological relics of the past, etc., but it is a result of the iron necessity to give birth to and support a privileged minority, so long as it is impossible to guarantee genuine equality.

. . . Isn't that a statement that this dictatorship in the early stage is a matter of iron necessity?

TROTSKY: In a poor, backward, and isolated workers' state, yes. To a certain degree, not an absolute measure, but to a certain degree it is an historical necessity.

*   *   *

The questions then turned to Stalin:

FINERTY: . . . What has Stalin done to perpetuate the bureaucracy instead of shortening it, and what would you have done to shorten it?

TROTSKY: He declared in 1927, openly, "You cannot remove these cadres except by civil war." That is, the bureaucracy cannot be removed, except by civil war. He proclaimed officially that the bureaucracy is independent of the people, of the Party and non-Party people. . . .

FINERTY: Can you briefly state how you would have shortened its dominion, or controlled the power of the bureaucracy?

TROTSKY: First, the Left Opposition was not expelled accidentally. It was the defeat of the German proletariat, the defeat in China, and the defeat in Austria. We were also defeated with the world proletariat. It explains why we are not in office. Secondly, in our platform we gave measures which were not a panacea, but which we considered necessary measures to attenuate the oppression of the bureaucracy. It was the secret vote in the Party, in the Soviets, in the trade unions, and the different enterprises.

FINERTY: You advocated the secret vote beginning with, I believe, 1926–1927?

TROTSKY: Then, freedom of speech, discussion and criticism against the bureaucracy. Then, the abolition of the civil paragraph in the penal code, by which the bureaucracy tries to stifle the workers, the more critical workers. That is the gradation of measures which we proposed in our platform.

FINERTY: The recent Constitution does purport to accord the secret vote. Now, do you think that will not operate to control the bureaucracy?

TROTSKY: It will have the same consequence as the secret vote in Germany. Hitler did not touch the Weimar Constitution, the democratic Constitution. It was an astonishment for everybody. Everybody believed that Hitler would change the Constitution, but the Constitution remains. But he broke the backbone of the Constitution. That is all he did, and even the secret vote gave him the majority.

FINERTY: In other words, you don't believe the new Constitution affords any means of controlling the bureaucracy? The only possibility is a revolution against the bureaucracy?

TROTSKY: Yes.

*   *   *

From my seated position as the reporter, I could observe Trotsky giving his testimony and the fluency with which he gave it. I have already written of his interest in the English language. When I saw him in Paris in 1934, I noted that his English was much improved since 1931. There were several opportunities for him to use it in the intervening time in Turkey and Norway, and I know he read English frequently, given the increased amount of material issued by the American and British Trotskyists. Even so, the language was not his "natural" one. Still, he sat as a witness for many hours during the eight days, examined by the attorneys and cross-examined by the Commissioners—all of which he answered in English for a total of 554 printed pages in thirteen sessions.

Although his English was excellent, Trotsky's accent was pronounced. There were moments of laughter arising from his occasional confusion of languages, which caused difficulties for me as the reporter. A single example might suffice. Questioned about his early revolutionary activity, the following exchange took place:

TROTSKY: I have patience. Three revolutions have made me patient. It is absolutely necessary for a revolutionist to be patient. It is a false idea that a revolutionary must be impatient. Adventurers are impatient. [Trotsky here pronounced the word "patient" as "passion" and "patience" as "passions."]

INTERPRETER: You mean "impatience."

TROTSKY: Yes, a revolutionary must know English, and with the help of patience, I will learn English. (*Laughter*)

It was an astonishing performance by Trotsky in the use of a language essentially foreign to him. One loses sight of this aspect of the hearings when reading its results, assuming the testimony in English to have been an ordinary or usual thing for the witness.

As a professional court reporter with some prior experience of Trotsky's English and accent, I was prepared for the technical difficulties of transcription. It required unusual concentration to catch the strange and ambiguous uses of English he sometimes made. What helped me was not so much knowledge of Trotsky's English as my own political experience. Political knowledge and experience made it possible for me to extricate myself from several difficult passages in my notes—as, for example, Trotsky's use of a French word for assassinate or kill, which I wrote in shorthand. In transcribing it, I could not make out the shorthand note because I kept seeking an English word until it suddenly occurred to me that he had spoken in French at the moment. Such recall is not unusual to professional court reporters.

Commissioner Carleton Beals
and the Long Arm of the GPU

What Stalin and his secret police were unable to achieve from the outside to prevent the hearings they tried to accomplish from the inside. Two incidents disrupted the Commission's task: the attempt by Carleton Beals, a member of the Commission, to create embarrassment and difficulty for Trotsky in Mexico by asking several pointed questions about Trotsky's alleged revolutionary activity in the country; and the misleading, antagonistic and pro-Stalinist reports to the *New York Times* by its reporter Frank L. Kluckhohn.

The Beals matter was the more important, dangerous, and significant. It represented the penetration by the GPU in Mexico into the work of the Commission in order to disrupt the examinations from within. Very suddenly, and without any relationship to the examination of Trotsky at the moment, Beals asked Trotsky whether or not it was true that he sent a Russian agent to Mexico at the time he was a Soviet Commissar to foment trouble in the country. Trotsky called the charge a lie and asked Beals where he got the information. Beals replied: "Then General Borodin is a liar." The implication that he got the information from Borodin was followed by Beals's antagonistic behavior towards the proceedings and the work of the Commission. Ben Stolberg, anguished by Beals's behavior, was certain that there was something wrong in the incident, but at the moment it happened was not quite sure what produced it.

Stolberg and Beals were personal friends for many years, a fact known to members of the Commission. They turned to Stolberg to see if he had any inkling as to why Beals asked such an inflammatory question. Was this his purpose in agreeing to serve as a member of the Commission? Stolberg believed that Beals's intervention was out of character. He then recounted to listeners how he and his party on the "Sunshine Special" met Beals at the United States-Mexican border on their way down to the capital. They had a very warm reunion there, he said, not only with him but with Dewey and LaFollette as well.

Beals and his wife had driven to the border meeting place from the West Coast, where he told Stolberg about his difficult financial situation. He was given some money to tide him over until he reached Mexico City.

Beals did not participate in the prehearing meetings of the Commission. Nor was he present at the first session. Where had he been? Why did he not inform the Commission, its Chairman, or his friend Stolberg, that he had arrived in the city? His conduct was certainly suspicious. The Commission members were convinced that he had been with a person or persons who hoped to disrupt and damage the taking of Trotsky's deposition. This was compatible with GPU strategy. If his intervention fell flat, it was in part because of his ignorance of the history involved in the questions he asked. He was merely repeating what his mentors told him. Furthermore, Beals simply lacked the skill for the disruptive role he tried to play. All in all, his performance was sad and embarrassing for him.

Years later, in a letter of April 1977, James T. Farrell wrote to me:

Kluckhohn of the *New York Times* told me that the man who played the big role in swinging Carlton Beals was Harry Block. Block was editor-in-chief at Covici-Fried. In about 1935, he quit and went to Mexico. . . . He did marry Toledano's daughter. He worked for a Mexican general.

He was a Stalinist. I believe, but I am not certain, that Herbert Solow tagged him as an agent.[35]

I met Harry Block in the Communist Party and was not overly surprised by Farrell's comments. I told him so. Farrell wrote to me again on April 18, 1977, as follows:

We are both writing to one another of the one and the same Harry Block. And as I believe I told you, Kluckhohn told me that he was the person who got to Carlton Beals.[36]

When Beals resigned from the Commission and left the hearings—thinking it would be a fatal blow to its deliberations—the action had not the slightest effect. The Commissioners were not in any way uneasy because of Beals's action; it did not prevent them from completing their work. As an act calculated to cause public concern or reflect on the integrity of the Commission, it misfired badly.

For a brief time after he left the Commission and the sessions, Beals continued his efforts to discredit both. He wrote an article for the Mexican magazine *Futuro,* repeating the GPU invention that Trotsky sent Borodin to Mexico to foment a revolution. In this article, he confused the GPU theft of Trotsky's archives in Paris, which did in fact happen, with an alleged stealing of archives in Norway by native Fascists, which did not happen. As evidence that his tutors were sloppy, Beals wrote in this article that Trotsky's sister had committed suicide in Paris, when, in fact, it was his daughter, Zinaida, who took her life, and not in Paris but in Berlin.

In his *Futuro* article Beals described his own role on the Commission as that of a valiant, courageous searcher for truth. This was at best an unjustified boast. From the language used in the article, one could assume that it was written by his Stalinist mentors or that he was assisted by them. On the other hand, the style could not be entirely alien to him, since he was at one time a correspondent for Tass, the Russian news agency abroad, which was populated by agents of the secret police.

Beals, for example, wrote that he challenged the authenticity of Trotsky's documents. In fact, he did not do so in the hearings; he merely claimed to be concerned about the originals and their whereabouts. (This was the concern of the GPU, too.) He went on to write:

> I could not find out how the Commissions in Europe were created nor who were their members. I suppose that they will be members of the Trotskyist groups.

Everything in this statement is false. The suggestion that the European Commissions of Inquiry were made up of Trotskyists was the propaganda of the police agents who were now using Beals. Undaunted, he claimed:

> I questioned [Trotsky] on the secret activities of Borodin in Mexico in 1919–20. The result was a violent explosion. Trotsky branded my informers as liars and lost his composure. My informer, among others [Beals mentioned no others], I told Trotsky, was Borodin himself.[37]

Here again, everything is untrue. There was no explosion and no loss of composure, as any person attending the hearings could verify. A question that arises here is why Borodin, in Mexico on a secret mission, would tell Carlton Beals, of all people, his purpose for being in Mexico, when even members of the Communist Party were not privy to the information. Be that as it may, Trotsky commented on Beals's statement:

> When I said that Mr. Beals's informer is a liar, it was only a polite expression of the idea that Mr. Beals himself departs from the truth. Or will he agree to confirm his testimony before the Commission?[38]

Trotsky pointed out that in 1919–1920 he could no more send Borodin to Mexico than anywhere else, because such activities were the concern of the Comintern, and Zinoviev, head of the International, would never tolerate such interference. On the other hand, neither could Zinoviev appoint Red Army commanders over the head of, or unbeknownst, to Trotsky, the Commander-in-Chief.

*   *   *

The affair of reporter Kluckhohn was less damaging to the hearings from within, but capable of greater mischief in the world of public opinion. Kluckhohn's news stories for the *New York Times* were meanly antagonistic. They distorted the atmosphere of the Coyoacan event, and they were openly biased in favor of the Kremlin and its Trials. The apparently single object of his reporting was to cast doubt on the validity of the Commission and its inquiry. The reporting was so outrageous that Chairman Dewey wired a protest to Edwin L. James, foreign editor of the paper. Dewey informed the Commission in open session that he had received a reply from James advising that he had instructed Kluckhohn to quit editorializing his new reports or face removal from his assignment.

Kluckhohn's background was actually rather unusual for an "impartial" newspaper reporter. His conduct, which was in fact publicly hostile, brought to mind the journalism of Walter Duranty, with this difference: While Duranty was simply an unprincipled person who cared nothing about the truth, Kluckhohn's interest had ties, through his friendship with Frank Jellinek, with the Communist movement. Jellinek was known in radical circles of the United States and England as the author of *The Paris Commune* (published by Left Books, part of the Victor Gollancz publishing venture in England). In England, Jellinek was known as a militant Stalinist. As several events strongly suggested, Jellinek's presence in

Mexico appeared to be an assignment from the GPU. He came to Mexico City in the fall of 1937, some months after the Dewey Commission hearings. Kluckhohn brought him to a Trotsky press conference, where Jellinek's conduct was so disruptive that Trotsky called him to order. In bringing Jellinek to this press conference, Kluckhohn continued his own kind of disruption begun at the April hearings, showing once more where his political sympathies lay.

In the trial of the Communist Party leaders involved in the May 1940 attempt to assassinate Trotsky, sometimes known as the "Siqueiros attack," Jellinek sat at the defendants' table in the courtroom advising Pavon Flores, a member of the Political Committee of the Party and a defendant. The role of Jellinek at the trial could only have been an assignment by those in charge of his political activity, the GPU. The whole apparatus of the GPU in North America, located in Mexico City, had one goal: the assassination of Trotsky. Jellinek was part of that apparatus, as was Ramon Mercader, Trotsky's murderer, a Spanish member of the Western European Stalinist secret police.

Trotsky was suspicious of Jellinek's political and organizational affiliation and of his reasons for being in Mexico, which is why he refused to see him in 1937 when Jellinek arrived from England. The fact that Kluckhohn was a personal friend of Jellinek might ordinarily have no significance, but the events in Mexico disclosed an obvious political bias in favor of the Stalinist murder machine.

*   *   *

One day, during a recess, Trotsky spoke to me about his fears for the security of my shorthand notes: The GPU network was obviously surrounding us. He spoke of his personal knowledge of the technical resources and experience of the secret police, and he was certain they would do anything to prevent the publication of the minutes of the hearings. It might even act, he suggested, on the train on my return to Chicago, or after I returned to my home.

Whether the danger was real or not, it would have been foolish to deny the possibility mentioned by Trotsky, in view of the long murderous history of GPU. After giving it some thought, I suggested that I make an announcement at the next session, since we were nearing the close of the hearings, that most of my notes had already been transcribed, that there remained only the last day or so, and these I would do before I left Mexico. The Commissioners agreed that I should make this statement before the entire assembly. On page 544 of the published record the following white lie is recorded:

> DEWEY: I wish now to refer to quite another matter. A considerable and quite legitimate interest has been expressed in the question of the official transcript of the testimony. I am going to ask the official stenographer if there is a statement to make on that.
>
> GLOTZER: I have most of the record finished, and I am going to stay several days to complete the record of the last day and a half.

*   *   *

After days of detailed refutation of one charge after another with the use of documents or verifiable references, we came near the end of the examinations to Trotsky's summary of his case against the Moscow Trials. That session began at 4:00 P.M., ended at 8:45, and consisted almost entirely of Trotsky's analysis of the Trials and their purpose.

And when he finished, the audience, a singularly diverse one, burst out into applause, which was, believe me, most spontaneous. This moment I shall never forget.

*   *   *

There was yet another final "session," a social gathering at the home of Mrs. George on the evening of the day the hearings ended. The Commissioners, members of their staff, the technical corps at Coyoacan, the attorneys, Trotsky and Natalia, as well as his secretaries, specially invited people, and I, all came together as a farewell to the event and to each other.

During the convivial interchanges between the people that crowded the main rooms in the house, a great laughter broke out in one corner of the large room where Dewey and Trotsky were conversing. They were surrounded by several people listening to their conversations. I asked Frankel what happened in the corner. He smiled, "Dewey said to Trotsky, 'If all Communists were like you, I would be a Communist.' And Trotsky replied, 'If all liberals were like you, I would be a liberal.' " This banter expressed the respect that the two principal people at the hearings had for each other.

Farrell wrote that Dewey left the house upon declaring the hearings closed.

> Moved deeply, John Dewey immediately left. Most of those present thought that he had been so touched by Trotsky's speech. But they were mistaken.

He had been watching Mrs. Trotsky, not only during Trotsky's final summation but on and off, during the entire hearing. A faded, tired-looking, brave woman, dressed in simple but distinctive, almost chic, manner, she sat near Trotsky, looking, listening intently. She did not understand English. . . .[39]

I left for Chicago almost immediately. George Novack asked me to accompany Dewey and share his suite to St. Louis, where he was to be met by his son. Novack did not want Dewey to travel alone, given his age and the physically taxing sessions. Novack was mistaken about Dewey's condition, and it proved embarrassing to me, for when we went to board the train in Mexico's Central Station, I tried to help Dewey into the car. He jerked his powerful arm from me and went swiftly up the steps alone. Despite my gaffe, we had a very pleasant journey as the train made its way slowly northward. We talked for almost two days of riding, much of it spent with me answering questions he asked about the American Communist Party and how it functioned. My notebooks never left my person during the entire trip.

The transcription of my shorthand notes took a number of weeks. It was a laborious task made doubly difficult by the sudden introduction of foreign words as Trotsky searched for proper English expressions. The grammatical constructions he used often slowed the transcription in my search for clarity; and I was not a grammatical expert in any sense. However, the day arrived when the work was completed. I had been sending copies of the sessions as they were done to Dewey, LaFollette, the Commission of Inquiry, and Trotsky. At one point, Dewey wrote me:

Dear Albert:

Thanks for copy of the report which I found on my return Thursday P.M. I'm sure you're doing a good job. We have our meeting Sunday evening. Got good advance notices in *Times* and *Herald Tribune* this A.M.

From Trotsky I received acknowledgement on June 3, 1937:

We have now received the complete record and everybody admires your work, especially in view of my terrible English. You functioned not only as a stenographer but also as an English teacher and editor. . . . Without your work (and the help of comrade Reva) we would never have such a record and the hearings in Mexico would lose half their value. I thank you wholeheartedly.[40]

The *National Reporter* of June 1937, the official journal of the National Shorthand Reporters Association, published a facsimile of a page of my shorthand notes of the opening of the hearings.

The echoes of the hearings resounded for a long time and did much to counteract the hideous propaganda of the Kremlin in support of its "judicial" murders. *The Case of Leon Trotsky* was followed by *Not Guilty,* the book-form verdict of the Commission. The integrity of the Commission and the respect in which it was held lent great force to its findings that Trotsky was not guilty of any of the charges made in the spurious Moscow Trials. Almost twenty years later, Khrushchev said the same thing. Here is how the Commission concluded its findings:

> We are convinced that the alleged letters in which Trotsky conveyed alleged conspiratorial instructions to the various defendants in the Moscow Trials never existed; and that the testimony concerning them is sheer fabrication.
>
> We find that Trotsky throughout his whole career has always been a consistent opponent of individual terror. The Commission further finds that Trotsky never instructed any of the defendants or witnesses in the Moscow Trials to assassinate any political opponent.
>
> We find that Trotsky never instructed the defendants or witnesses in the Moscow Trials to engage in sabotage, wrecking, and diversion. On the contrary, he has always been a consistent advocate of the building up of Socialist industry and agriculture in the Soviet Union and has criticized the present régime on the basis that its activities were harmful to the building up of Socialist economy in Russia. He is not in favor of sabotage as a method of opposition to any political régime.
>
> We find that Trotsky never instructed any of the accused or witnesses in the Moscow Trials to enter into agreements with foreign powers against the Soviet Union. On the contrary, he has always uncompromisingly advocated the defense of the USSR. He has also been a most forthright ideological opponent of the fascism represented by the foreign powers with which he is accused of having conspired.
>
> On the basis of all the evidence we find that Trotsky never recommended, plotted, or attempted the restoration of capitalism in the USSR. On the contrary, he has always uncompromisingly opposed the restoration of capitalism in the Soviet Union and its existence anywhere else.
>
> We find that the Prosecutor fantastically falsified Trotsky's role before, during, and after the October Revolution.
>
> We therefore find the Moscow Trials to be frame-ups.
>
> We therefore find Trotsky and Sedov not guilty.
>
> JOHN DEWEY, Chairman
> JOHN R. CHAMBERLAIN

ALFRED ROSMER
E. A. ROSS
OTTO RUEHLE
BENJAMIN STOLBERG
WENDELIN THOMAS
CARLO TRESCA
F. ZAMORA
SUZANNE LA FOLLETTE, Secretary
JOHN F. FINERTY, Counsel, Concurring.

New York, September 21, 1937.[41]

* * *

After the hearings, I was able to reflect on its proceedings, how fortunate it was that John Dewey agreed to act as chairman of the Commission, and how important were the efforts made by Sidney Hook to convince this giant of American philosophers to assume that responsibility. He was indeed an outstanding chairman. He kept the sessions in proper order and ensured its democratic procedure. Farrell wrote about Dewey from Coyoacan several days after the event:

> He also did everything for himself and would let no one help him. He is a very shrewd man, and a very wise one, and he gets to the gist of things in a quite unobtrusive way. He does not get fooled by speeches and tricks. . . .

Sometime after the Mexican experience Farrell, who was close to everything that happened there, wrote that Dewey's "thinking was much sharper and clearer than the thinking of anyone else in the group."[42]

This historic gathering in Mexico was the last time I saw Trotsky.

Postscript on Diego and Frida Kahlo Rivera

Diego and Frida Kahlo Rivera were adherents of the Trotskyist movement during the years of the Moscow Trials. Rivera was involved in the successful efforts to obtain asylum for Trotsky and Natalia in Mexico. The Riveras not only provided a residence for their exiled comrades, they became personal friends. However, the relations between the famous revolutionary leader and the famous artist were not easy. There were tensions arising from Rivera's organizational relations with the Mexican Trotskyist group. For the most part, politics was a minor cause for the difficulties and the impending rupture. But politics inevitably became part of the eventual political and personal break between Trotsky and Rivera. The break was rooted in the difficult "artistic" temperment of Diego Rivera.

In his *Life in Two Centuries,* Bertram D. Wolfe describes Rivera as a teller of "tall stories," "fantasies," and "inventions." Wolfe wrote that if he did "enjoy a friendship with Diego for over three decades and [had] become his biographer it was not because I did not take truth seriously, but because I took Rivera seriously as a creative artist."[43] For this reason Wolfe successfully urged Rivera in 1924 to resign from the Communist Party, in which he was a noted personality.

Wolfe wrote that "it had become increasingly clear to me that the best service he could give was with his brush." Wolfe said to him: "Look, Diego, you are one of the greatest revolutionary painters in the world. It is a shame for you to waste a day or an hour of such exceptional talent as yours"—which membership in the Party and routine organizational life would undoubtedly do.[44] Rivera was finally convinced and resigned from the Party. But in 1926, sometime after Wolfe left Mexico, the Party Central Committee arranged for him to rejoin the Party. In 1929, however, he was expelled as the personification of the "Right Wing Danger" in the organization, which was how, like all parties in the Comintern, the Mexican responded automatically to Stalin's new "left turn" in preparation for the "Third Period" of revolutionary upheavals.

Trotsky, too, had a high regard for Rivera's great talent and considered him "a revolutionary artist" who ought not to get enmeshed in the meaner details of organizational life in the movement, but be free to paint without diminishing his role as a revolutionary. When I arrived at the Avenida Londres house on my daily visits, Rivera was often present, talking to Trotsky, assisting in the physical preparations of the house for the hearings. The photos I took during the hearings show Rivera in a relaxed mood throughout.

Rivera was a large presence during the sessions themselves, bringing with him many personal friends and various political associates, including artist friends and his ex-wife, the well-known Guadalupe.

At one point before the sessions began, Trotsky said he agreed that Rivera's presence was important to the hearing, but he added that there was a very difficult problem brewing in the Mexican League between Rivera and most of the other members, a problem that threatened to explode without warning. It existed, he said, because of Rivera's objection to his "exalted" place in the organization. Rivera was demanding a more direct organizational role, where he would be regarded more seriously as a "Party man." In short, he wanted to be the National Secretary of the League. But the members of the Mexican Trotskyist League did not want

Rivera in the post of National Secretary. They thought him too irresponsible for its organizational requirements. In any case, they felt that his position as a world-famous revolutionary artist meant much more to the movement than to have him waste his talents in an area for which he was tempermentally, and by training and experience, quite unsuited. This dispute was already sharp in early 1937, when Trotsky and Natalia were newly arrived.

For two more years this conflict went on, expanding to include a variety of vague political questions raised by Rivera, in the course of which he became more and more estranged from Trotsky, who tried to help Rivera through his difficulties with his Mexican comrades. He thought Rivera ought not to function in the League but join the Trotskyist Pan-American Commission, which had broader perspectives and involved the Spanish organization as well. Initially, Rivera agreed that might be best. But, reversing himself shortly thereafter, he accused Trotsky of conspiring against him; subsequently, he dropped this charge. He then agreed to continue as an editor together with Trotsky, Charles Curtiss, and others of the theoretical journal *Clave,* which had no formal organizational affiliations. But then he attacked Trotsky for his "methods" and withdrew.

Relations with Rivera became more complicated with the arrival in Mexico in 1938 of André Breton, a leader of the French Surrealist movement. Breton was sympathetic to Trotsky and a pronounced anti-Stalinist. In his conversations with Breton, Trotsky suggested the possibility of creating a world organization of revolutionary writers and artists as an answer to the Stalinist intellectual and cultural movements. They talked about a manifesto for such an organization, and Breton agreed to write one. At this very time, Breton and his wife, Jaquelin, close friends of Diego and Frida, were staying at their home.

There were increasing difficulties over the manifesto between Trotsky, Breton, and Rivera, who was "drafted" into the scheme. The differences over the manifesto affected relations among the three, but mainly between Trotsky and an increasingly hostile Rivera.[45] This conflict and the tensions it produced led to an eventual break between Trotsky and Rivera. Trotsky and Natalia faced an embarrassing situation: the impossibility of continuing as the guests of the Riveras in Frida's house, given the breach in their relations. The political-organizational differences quickly evolved into personal ones.

Rivera charged that Trotsky had intrigued against him, a charge Trotsky described as "more false and fantastic than all the others, but since Rivera claimed that he was hindered in his functions in the League, the matter should be taken before a commission appointed by the Pan-American Committee or by the International Secretariat."

Meanwhile, in the *Casa del Pueblo,* which Rivera organized as an arena for his personal political activity, he made a speech in which he described Trotsky as a "bourgeois, exhibiting his flirtations with anarchism." He was now an open antagonist of Trotsky. In his autobiography, Wolfe, aware of this break between the two, wrote of his old friend Rivera:

> When Leon Trotsky was his honored guest, he drove him to distraction by outrageous inventions of fact and doctrines in Mexican politics, until the argument ended by Leon Trotsky's packing his bags and leaving his and his wife's goods on the sidewalk while he looked for another habitation.[46]

I have already indicated that the relationship was far more complicated to end in the impulsive manner described by Wolfe. In fact, it didn't happen that way at all. By February 14, 1939, when Trotsky and Natalia felt they could no longer accept their position as guests of the Riveras, Trotsky wrote to Curtiss, a long-time Trotskyist:

> You know, as do all the other comrades, of the generosity with which Diego Rivera and his family helped us during our installation and ultimate sojourn in Mexico. I accepted this help, especially the housing, because it came from a person whom I considered not only a devoted militant of the Fourth International, but also a personal friend. Now, as you know, the situation has undergone a radical change. I did everything I could to settle the crisis provoked by Diego Rivera's attempts to perform political miracles. . . . I did not succeed. . . .
>
> We are now looking for another house. . . . [It] is very difficult, if not impossible, to find a house which is more or less convenient from the point of view of security. In any case, we are compelled to live in this house until we find another. . . . I proposed to pay a monthly rental to Diego Rivera, but he refused categorically. . . .
>
> I am enclosing two hundred pesos (a modest monthly rental) and I ask you to visit Diego Rivera and explain to him again . . . that under the given conditions he cannot refuse to accept the payment. If in spite of all this he refuses, please transmit this payment to the treasury of "Clave," noting it as the rent which Diego Rivera has not accepted. In this case, I shall consider Rivera's attitude as moral pressure to force me to move immediately, regardless of whether we have or have not found another.[47]

Wolfe's description of the Trotsky's departure is literary license. In response to Trotsky's letter, Curtiss made the proffer of rent money to Rivera, who refused it, making the Trotskys stay in Frida's house even more difficult and embarrassing. Meanwhile, the search for new quarters continued for a long time; there was so much to move that it was much more than a matter of packing some bags. There was by this time a large library, an accumulation of archives, a "central political buro" and its appurtenaces.

The relationship had almost totally deteriorated. Rivera felt that Trotsky considered him to be a liar and an "anti-Trotskyist traitor." He resigned from the Trotskyist movement in early 1939. Even so, after he moved, Trotsky visited Rivera in an effort to placate him, and to convince him that he did not hold the views Rivera attributed to him. The peace did not last. Rivera continued to say that Trosky had made unjustified accusations against him. In explanation, Trotsky wrote on March 22, 1939:

> I simply insisted on my opinion that by his character, his occupation, and his life, he was not suited to be a Party functionary. But that does not indicate a lack of appreciation. Not every member of the organization, nor even of the staff, is obliged to be a secretary.

Trotsky added that Rivera had "a tremendous impulsivity, a lack of self-control, an inflammable imagination and an extreme capriciousness—such are the features of Rivera's character."[48]

*   *   *

On April 12, 1939, *Excelsiro,* a leading Mexico City newspaper, carried a headline: *Trotsky Breaks His Relations With the Painter Diego Rivera.* In a letter of the same date to Jan Frankel, Trotsky commented on the newspaper's report:

> The note is very vicious and contains various slanders as is very natural in such cases. One thing is clear from the note: The whole thing came from Rivera himself, from his babbling to different painters, artists and so on. The whole question of the house is largely and falsely presented. . . .[49]

After their complete break with Trotsky, Rivera and Frida rejoined the Communist Party and, as Wolfe informs us, the Catholic Church, thus making of their reaffiliations political low comedy.

Trotsky and Natalia found new living quarters on Avenida Viena, in close proximity to the Kahlo house. It was here that in May 1940 the artist-gunman, David Siqueiros, led an armed attack, orchestrated by Stalin's secret police, on the new household.[50] The Riveras were totally silent about this event, as they were when the GPU killer, Ramon Mercader, assassinated Trotsky in August. No one knew better than Diego Rivera and Frida who ordered the murder of Trotsky, yet so personally bitter had they become that they accepted the brutal murder without the slightest remorse. During the period of the Hitler–Stalin Pact they had fully accepted Stalinism, which now determined their political views. So they no longer considered GPU murders and slanders as outrageous; to them they were perfectably acceptable political policy.

Wolfe noted in his biography of Rivera that while the artist was a "professional" in painting, "in politics, he was an amateur and a passionate dilletante."[51] When Rivera resided in Europe in his early years, he was an anarchist. There was also a strong element of buffoonery in his political life, no better illustrated than in his repeated applications for readmission into the Communist Party. One day, in 1946, he demanded that Frida give him Trotsky's pen, decorated in silver with his facsimile signature (a gift from Frida that Trotsky left in her house when Natalia and he left), so that he could write and sign his application to the Stalinist Party with it. Why she refused to give it to him, in view of her embrace of the Communist Party, is difficult to understand. She may have felt too much sentiment over the immediate past to grant Diego's politically crude, vulgar, and childishly revengeful demand.

Frida Kahlo Rivera died in 1954; Diego in 1957. Their one-time political and personal friendship with the Trotskys was a matter of history without any other significance. They had been loyal Stalinists for fifteen years or more. Frida's home on Avenida Londres, where the ghosts of the Dewey Commission hearings reside, is now a museum of pre-Columbian art that had been collected by the Riveras. It is now known as the Frida Kahlo Museum. But it is not only a museum, but a political statement, for the house maintains intact the rooms in which Frida lived, with all the memorabilia of her family and of her Stalinism. On top of the bureau in her bedroom is a bust of Stalin, so placed as to peer down upon her bed. Thus, it would seem, she fell asleep each night secure in the knowledge that her newly found god (more murderous than any Aztec chief) watched over her, protecting her from the many goblins of the night. In an adjacent room hangs her portrait of Stalin, lovingly painted as a bright, warm sun, with a beatific smile, safeguarding all mankind from its many enemies. In still another room in the museum are Mao posters and other political juvenilia.

It became obvious to me as I walked through the museum that politics to the Riveras was much too difficult a discipline for such subjective, impressionistic, and explosive people.

Notes

1. *The Revolution Betrayed,* p. 278.

2. Indictments in the Piatakov–Radek trial, January 1937, pp. 5, 6, and 7.

3. Max Shachtman, *Behind the Moscow Trial;* Leon Sedov, *The Red Book on the Moscow Trials;* Victor Serge, *Sixteen Executed in Moscow;* also Francis Heisler, *The First Two Moscow Trials—Why?,* published by the National Office of the Socialist Party of the USA, 1937.

4. *Not Guilty,* Report of the Dewey Commission of Inquiry, p. 387.

5. Robert Sharlet, "Stalinism and Soviet Legal Culture," in *Stalinism,* edited by Robert Tucker, p. 161.

6. Sharlet, "Soviet Legal Culture," p. 164.

7. Friedrich Adler, "The Witchcraft Trial in Moscow."

8. *Not Guilty,* Report of the Dewey Commission, pp. 387–388.

9. Medvedev, *Stalin and Stalinism,* p. 20–91. Medvedev's reference to Trotsky's statement is taken from the *Bulletin of the Russian Opposition,* nos. 17–18, 1931, p. 21.

10. *Stalin and Stalinism,* p. 91.

11. Trotsky, *What Does the Trial of the Wreckers Teach Us?,* p. 21.

12. Trotsky, *Russian Bulletin* (No. 51) 1936.

13. *Writings,* Supplement, 1936–37, p. 56.

14. *Writings,* Supplement, 1936–37, p. 56.

15. *Writings,* Supplement, 1936–37, p. 57.

16. *Writings,* Supplement, 1936–37, p. 57.

17. *Stalin and Stalinists,* p. 97. About Kirov, see *Not Guilty,* Report of the Commission of Inquiry and "Judicial Investigation in the USSR As I Saw It," by Anton Ciliga, in *Le Revolution Proletarienne,* January, 1937.

18. For further discussion of Kirov and his story see *Stalinism,* edited by Robert C. Tucker, particularly the following essays: "Stalinism as Revolution from Above," by R. C. Tucker; "The Social Background of Stalinism," by Moshe Lewin; "Stalinism and Soviet Legal Culture," by Robert Sharlet. See also Robert Conquest, *The Great Terror;* Roy Medvedev, *Let History Judge;* Robert C. Tucker, *The Soviet Political Mind;* Leon Trotsky, *The Stalin School of Falsification;* and Schapiro.

19. Under the Tsar, Smolny Institute was a school and convent for "gentle-women," with gardens adjacent to the Neva River. It became the seat of the Central Executive Committee of the Petrograd Soviet. When the capital moved to Moscow, it was the headquarters of the Leningrad Party.

20. Conquest, *The Great Terror,* p. 423.

21. Schapiro, p. 423.

22. Schapiro, p. 428.

23. Robert Tucker, "Show Trials?," *Dissent,* Spring 1965 issue.

24. Tucker, *Dissent,* Spring 1965. Medvedev wrote that "the overwhelming passion of his life was power. . . ." in *Stalin and Stalinism,* p. 34.

25. Trotsky, "Eight Ministers," in *Writings, 1937–1938*, p. 124.

26. Tucker in *Dissent*.

27. Schapiro, *Communist Party*, p. 431.

28. Yezhov was Stalin's hand-picked chief of the GPU at the moment.

29. Ilya Ehrenburg, *Memoirs, 1921–1941*, p. 426–427.

30. *Memoirs*, p. 427.

31. Schapiro, p. 432.

32. Conquest, *The Great Terror*, p. 505.

33. *Writings*, Vol. 9, p. 147.

34. Personal correspondence from Felix Morrow to the author.

35. Personal correspondence from Farrell to the author.

36. Personal correspondence from Farrell to the author.

37. Carleton Beals, *Futuro*, 1937.

38. Trotsky, *Writings*, Vol. 9, p. 68.

39. *John Dewey, Philosopher of Science and Freedom*, p. 369.

40. Personal correspondence from Trotsky to the author.

41. *Not Guilty*, Report of the Dewey Commission, pp. 14–15.

42. Personal correspondence between Farrell and unidentified associate.

43. Wolfe, *A Life in Two Centuries*, p. 645.

44. Wolfe, *A Life in Two Centuries*, p. 645.

45. The manifesto eventually appeared and was called "Toward a Free Revolutionary Art." In *LaCles des Champs*, Breton wrote that it was a product of discussions among Trotsky, Rivera, and he, but that Trotsky contributed most of it.

46. Wolfe, *A Life in Two Centuries*, p. 645.

47. Trotsky, *Writings*, Vol. 10, p. 287.

48. Trotsky archives, Houghton Library, Harvard University, Cambridge.

49. Letter to Frankel, April 12, 1939.

50. Siqueiros fled Mexico in the midst of his trial for the attack on Trotsky's household. He was aided in his escape by Pablo Neruda, noted Chilean poet and militant Stalinist who worked in the Chilean Embassy in Mexico for the Allende government.

51. Wolfe, *The Fabulous Life of Diego Rivera*, p. 383.

The Russian Question and the Split in American Trotskyism

In the year before the actual opening of hostilities in World War II, the political crises in the world had reached their most intense and threatening stage. Hitler completed the rearmament of Germany and was fully prepared for war in a way the Allies were not. England and France began an energetic wooing of the Soviet Union and quibbled with Stalin over the price of a tenuous alliance against Nazi Germany. And in the the United States there was a reenactment of the struggle with the forces of isolationism, whose powerful forces hindered any move of the Roosevelt government to assist its Western Allies.

In the midst of Stalin's negotiations with England and France, on August 23, 1939, Stalin and Hitler made their joint surprise announcement in Berlin and Moscow: *They* had established a political and military alliance. The West knew that war was only days away, for through this macabre alliance Hitler secured his Eastern front. A week later, on September 1, the German armies invaded Poland, while the Russians occupied the Eastern half of the country. (The Russian press of 1989, fifty years after the Pact, acknowledges that there was a secret agreement between Nazi Germany and Stalinist Russia to divide Poland between them, create separate spheres of influence, and give Russia domination of the Baltic states and Finland. For fifty years, the various regimes in the post-Stalin period denied or remained silent about the secret agreement. In the era of Gorbachev's reform, the regime admits that the agreement was a fact and that the Baltic states were incorporated into the Soviet Union under the Pact. While Gorbachev acknowledges this, he denies these states the right to right to withdraw and reestablish their national independence.)

The war vindicated Stalin's critics, none more than Trotsky, who warned that the Stalinist sabotage of a unified anti-Nazi struggle against German fascism would be followed by a wave of reaction in Europe, leading to a new world war. The signing of the Hitler–Stalin Pact determined the immediate course of history in a reactionary way, the consequences of which continue to plague the world. The Pact was shattering to the American Communist Party, the Kremlin's most abjectedly loyal supporter. The American Party had made progress with the political tactic of the People's Front Against Fascism, and the thirties saw it reach a membership of almost a hundred thousand, an unprecedented number for the United States.

For different reasons the Pact and the war were destined to tear apart the American Trotskyist movement. The traditional positions of Trotskyism on the so-called Russian Question and "the Defense of the Soviet Union" were to be seriously challenged by a large section of its membership.

Early factional conflict in the Trotskyist American Communist League was never too deep; fundamental ideological questions never divided it. Now there arose a new internal conflict in response to European events, which concerned programmatic principles related to the Soviet Union. The defense of the Soviet Union had become a religiouslike dogma of all Trotskyists. If you challenged them, you could be, and usually were, excluded from the Trotskyist world organization and any of its sections.

Trotsky not only established the principle but the political mood of any discussion that questioned the doctrine. As early as 1934, he warned about deviations in the matter:

> We have been informed by various sources that there is a tendency among our friends in Paris to deny the proletarian nature of the USSR, to demand that there be complete democracy in the USSR, including the legalization of the Mensheviks, etc. Please convey our position on this matter to the Central Committee officially: We regard this tendency as *treason* which must be fought implacably. One does not change one's attitude toward a question of such dimensions lightly: We have resolutions which state clearly that denying the proletarian character of the USSR is incompatible with membership in the Bolshevik–Leninists. . . .
>
> The Mensheviks are the representatives of bourgeois restoration and we are for the defense of the workers' state by every means possible. . . .
>
> I repeat: no compromise on this question! Lay all the cards on the table! It is necessary to eradicate the bohemian influence which is poisoning certain elements in our organization and which drives them to change their position

on fundamental questions as the spirit moves them. No, no compromise and no equivocation on this question![1]

No event in the later thirties—the Pact, the outbreak of war, the joint Hitler and Stalin occupation of Poland, the seizure of the Baltic states of Estonia, Latvia, and Lithuania, or the war on Finland by the Red Army —softened Trotsky's position in any way. Those who rose to challenge the views he described and which he repeated in many different ways over the years had reason to be prepared for a bitter quarrel.

*   *   *

The first indication that all was not serene on the Russian Question came in a 1938 resolution presented to the convention of the Socialist Workers' Party (SWP) by Joseph Carter[2] and James Burnham,[3] both members of the National and Political Committees. The resolution pointedly denied that the Soviet Union was any longer a "workers' state." Oddly enough, it still called for the defense of the USSR as long as it maintained nationalized property!

There were concerns about the nature of Stalinist Russia in the early thirties in the American Trotskyist movement, but these were tentative probings rather than sharply defined views that could prove to be internally explosive. The decade was itself so filled with sharp political events as to cause concern with the nature of the Soviet Union to be constant, though the intensity of the concerns varied with the pressures of the continually changing political scene. For the American Trotskyists, the Moscow Trials and the Commission of Inquiry hearings in Mexico, the entry of the Workers' Party into the Socialist Party, the tragedy of the Spanish Civil War and its repercussions in the internal life of the Socialist Party, and the eventual expulsion of the Trotskyists—all postponed for a time a breaking out of the dissatisfactions with the long-held position of Trotskyism on the Russian issue.

By 1939, the dissatisfactions could no longer be contained. Events of that year shattered the internal peace of the newly formed Socialist Workers' Party. A factional fight broke out in earnest even before the Pact and the invasion of Poland, which became sharper as the discussion ensued. The critical group that emerged was large. It challenged the movement's dogma concerning the Russian Question. Supported by a majority of the youth organization, the Minority in the Party made up almost half of organized Trotskyism in the United States. Having already questioned the principles of the Workers' State and the defense of the Soviet Union, the two cornerstones of Trotskyist ideology on the USSR, it is easy to see why the Hitler–Stalin Pact, the Soviet invasion of Finland, and the subsequent partition of Poland by the New Reich and Stalinist Russia deepened the disaffection of the Minority with traditional modes of thinking about the "workers' motherland." Merely questioning the validity of Trotsky's "no compromise and no equivocation" on the Russian Question caused the most intense and far-reaching internal dispute ever experienced by the world Trotskyist movement.

Trotsky was deeply anguished by the fact that some of the most able, experienced, and influential leaders in the most cohesive of Trotskyist organizations created this most dangerous rift. He knew that if the differences were not reconciled by compromise, the consequences would be irreversible. He regarded the situation as so critical that he was drawn to intervene and participate in it as he had never done in any factional dispute in a national section of the Fourth International. So continuous was Trotsky's involvement in the American dispute that a whole volume of his writings regarding the debates with the Minority and various individuals was published with the exegetic title *In Defense of Marxism.*

Trotsky's intervention only made the conflict more intense. He sided completely with the ineffectual Majority. Despite Trotsky's efforts, the cohesiveness of the Minority developed swiftly. The first skirmish in the Party went badly for the Majority. Cannon, supported by veteran leaders Arne Swabeck, Vincent Ray Dunne, Karl Skoglund, Albert Goldman, and younger men like Bert Cochrane and George Clarke, fought back unsuccessfully. They were unable to overcome the theoretical and political questions of the opposition: How could a workers' state possibly be allied with a Fascist one? Was the Soviet Union a true Communist state or a totalitarian, bureaucratic one? Cannon felt the weakness of his faction's ability to debate the views of the Minority and appealed to Trotsky to come to its aid. He didn't have to beg very hard. One of the reasons Cannon was quick to intervene was that he knew personally that the leadership and membership of the opposition were not bohemian elements "who change their position on fundamental questions as the spirit moves them."[4] He knew all too well from personal experience, too, that among the Minority were founders and leaders of the American Trotskyist movement; dissent from them warranted serious personal engagement on the part of Trotsky.

As the dispute on the fundamental Russian positions became more intense, it also became more bitter. Trotsky's introduction of the "defense of the dialectic" into the dispute (in order to defend it, he said, against the "revisionists" led by Burnham), was calculated to affect the *mood* of the discussion. Trotsky was certain that it was Burnham's theoretical deviations that led the Minority to doubt the nature of the Soviet Union. Trotsky argued that Burnham was using the Hitler–Stalin Pact and the Finnish invasions merely as vehicles for developing what he regarded as untenable theoretical views. Such speculation was, however, ludicrous on Trotsky's part. It is quite likely that Cannon and his faction misled Trotsky as to Burnham's role in the leadership, or that he misled himself. In any case, his attack on Burnham's good faith poisoned the minds of leaders and members alike on the dialectic; it played no role whatever in the inner discussions of the Minority faction on the Russian Question.

Despite the evident bitterness Trotsky expressed in the discussion and *In Defense of Marxism,* he did not regard the presence of the Minority as incompatible with membership in the Party at this stage of the dispute. He was doing his utmost to maintain the unity of the Party in the heat of the factional struggle, and yet at the same time made that impossible by the manner of his intervention, by introducing the non-issue of the dialectic and then designating the Minority as the "petty bourgeois opposition."

The Minority believed that Trotsky had become theoretically immobilized by his adherence to a ritualized position on the Soviet Union. It believed that he was therefore unable to address the critics of his position except in a fierce, unyielding polemic. Yet some of us had a feeling that he was himself disturbed over this issue and that he, too, was concerned more fundamentally with the social direction of the Soviet Union than ever before. By this time he had already published his strangely critical and instructive study *The Revolution Betrayed.* While it affirmed his position that the Soviet Union was a workers' state, he subjected the Stalinist society to the most withering criticism, saying several times that the Stalinist state would be totalitarian and its leaders Fascist—if it were not for nationalized property.

Trotsky's intervention in the American discussion was not one of his finer moments. His strong attacks on the Minority because of its social composition—not very different from that of the Majority—did not seriously affect the opposition because it was patently unwarranted.[5] A few people caved in under his attack; they did not wish to remain in a faction led in part and briefly, to be sure, by Burnham, the enemy of the dialectic. They felt the pressure of Trotsky's enormous intellectual and theoretical authority to accept the dictum that having a wrong position on the dialectic made one's position on the nature of Soviet society automatically false.

Aside from a few oppositionists who succumbed to Trotsky's pressure, the Minority remained united and intransigent in the long and intense discussion. Trotsky's attack on it as "an enemy of the dialectic" was unavailing; there were many in the Minority who accepted the validity of the Marxian dialectic and considered themselves more educated and informed in Marxism than most of the leaders of the Majority. Having sharpened the dispute as I have described, Trotsky had reason to be concerned about a split, if only for the reason that he was familiar with the long history of the American Trotskyists and was aware of Cannon's penchant for resolving theoretical and political disputes of great magnitude by organizational means. Despite his own heavy responsibility for sharpening the debate, he warned Cannon against taking an organizational approach to a resolution of the differences. Trotsky wanted to maintain the unity of the Party as long as possible in face of an impending world war. Thus, while he deplored devoting so much of his time to the factional situation and a defense of his ideas, he wanted to settle ideological accounts because he saw great revolutionary events on the immediate political horizon.

*   *   *

As early as 1937 Trotsky had forecast a Hitler–Stalin alliance. In an interview with the Sydney, Australia, *Sunday Sun,* he said:

> Hitler seeks the "friendship" of England. Stalin seeks a military alliance with France and through France a rapprochement with England. If these plans do not succeed, a union of Hitler and Stalin will become not only possible but inevitable . . . but only if Hitler and Stalin are still in power at the time. . . . *I don't guarantee it. . . .*[6]

Unrealistically, he looked for the Fourth International to triumph over these appalling events. These great expectations may have led Trotsky to seek a conclusion to the internal differences without splitting the largest Trotskyist organization in the world. In *With Trotsky in Exile,* the late Jean van Heijenoort refers to the question of Cannon and the factional struggle in the American Party and the dilemma Trotsky faced at the time when Van Heijenoort was leaving for the United States to be active in the American movement. He recalled the eve of his departure in November 1939, when he had his last conversation with Trotsky:

> Trotsky feared that Cannon, with whom he was politically allied, would tend to replace the discussion of political differences with organizational measures, thereby precipitating the expulsion of the Minority. Cannon has

to be held back on the organizational plane and pushed forward on the ideological plane.[7]

The internal dispute, given the issues, did unavoidably sharpen. How could it be otherwise? In the nature of things, compromise was truly impossible. The Minority gathered in its own national conference in Cleveland in February 1940, where it made an assessment of the situation and considered political and organizational perspectives for the next period. The conference observed that a split during the next stage was likely. At one point in the discussion, in the Party and before the Cleveland conference Cannon actually proposed a "cold split" to Shachtman. Since reconciliation was impossible, he said, why go through the agony of further dispute and discussion? Why not agree just to sever relations, go our separate ways, and save a lot of time and heartache? Afterward, taxed with this, Cannon insisted he was not serious; he had only been joking. Those who had been associated with Cannon for more than fifteen years and were familiar with his style knew, however, that his humor did not run in this direction and that he was in earnest when he made his proposal to Shachtman. He had wearied of the discussion and the intellectual and physical energy it demanded. This was not the first time he evidenced a malaise in a difficult and prolonged political debate. Now certain of the irreconcilability of the differences, he wanted to end the fight. As it turned out, there was political logic to his joke.

The discussion within the Party went on for a year until the special convention in New York in April 1940, when the split formally occurred. The Minority organized its own workers' party, issued a weekly paper, *Labor Action,* and retained the magazine *The New International,* supported mainly by the Minority members and often ridiculed by the self-styled proletarians of the Majority. (Under the pseudonym "Albert Gates," I was at various times editor of both journals.)

By this point in the dispute James Burnham was nowhere to be seen. Actually, he had not been involved in the final preparations for the convention of the new organization, and questions about him were being asked by members of the Minority. The concern was reasonable, because Burnham was to make the report on the organization question and the new Party. On the very eve of the Minority convention, the directing committee of the faction received a letter from Burnham stating that he had been rethinking his theoretical and political positions and had determined that he was not a Marxist or Socialist of any kind, that he was severing all relations with the new party and would no longer participate in any of its affairs. This was, without a doubt, a blow of sorts to the Minority, though it was no surprise to some people in the leadership, especially Shachtman. Burnham had indicated signs of leaving for some time. After their initial disappointment at this development, the delegates went on with their convention affairs. Burnham attended none of the sessions of the convention he was partly responsible for organizing, and the report on the formation of the Workers' Party and its organizational principles he was to have made was assigned to me at the very last moment.[8] Forty years ago, I still presented the "traditional Leninist" view of a democratic centralist party, though given our experiences and internal history, I emphasized the democratic side of organizational life.

In expressing obeisance to the Leninist principle, at least in a formal sense, the new party acted in an automatic way, merely repeating what it had affirmed for many years as second nature, so to speak. The criticisms the Cannonite Socialist Workers' Party made of the Minority's Bolshevism had more than a kernel of truth in them, since our new party was never, in fact, a Leninist organization. The centralist aspect of a Leninist party was always, in the Workers' Party, subordinated to its democratic character. Discipline was never of a "barracks" type, so to a Leninist the new party was a loose affair. The theoretical precepts of the traditional Leninist organization, while honored in speech intermittently and ceremoniously, had no practical place in the internal life of the Workers' Party.

In real life the Workers' Party was highly democratic and featured continuous discussions of theoretical and political questions. This aspect stood out when the Workers' Party took the name "Independent Socialist League," a more suitable cognomen considering its propagandistic and political nature. It lived out its remaining years as an internally free organization, to the surprise of many who were aware of the Communist, Trotskyist, and Left Socialist antecedents of a considerable number of its leading members, national and local. It did make small gains during the years of its existence, especially when thousands of copies of its weekly journal, *Labor Action,* were circulated at selected industries and unions. The paper enjoyed a limited success in those circles because of its intense and skillful anti-Stalinism and its exposure of the inanities of the American Communist Party. However, neither the Workers' Party nor its successor, the Independent Socialist League, made significant progress in the form of important growth. The standing of the organization and its press was respected in the circles of left anti-Stalinist organizations and in academic circles to a significant degree. This was nowhere better reflected than at the time of the successful suit of the Workers' Party and Independent Socialist League against the government over its placement on the Attorney General's

List of Subversive Organizations alongside the Communist Party and its many fellow-traveling organizations. The government was unable, despite its long efforts, to obtain any witness against us from the colleges and universities—except a Russian expert, Gerald T. Robinson of Columbia University, who spent two days reading from volumes of Lenin, and James Burnham, who was mercilessly cross-examined by Attorney Joseph Rauh. The government was unable to prove its case, and the organizations were then removed from the list.

The Debate on the Russian Question

Once finished with the factional struggle in the SWP, the new organization began a long and intensive review of the Russian Question, drawing a balance sheet for the severe discussion it had just had with Trotsky. The discussion was free of the fetters of worn-out and outlived conceptions of official policy and lasted for many months in debates, internal bulletins, and the public press. After long study and dispute, the party arrived at the view that the Soviet Union represented a new type of economic exploitation and social oppression in which the immense bureaucracy had become transformed into a new ruling class, that it was a new kind of society. We termed it "Bureaucratic Collectivism."

Although this bureaucratic class did not possess productive property as its own private estate, by its monopoly of the state power it "owned" all of the nationalized property, i.e., the production and distribution of all goods. Unable to own privately and juridically the productive property in a capitalist sense, the bureaucracy nevertheless controlled all the production and corollary riches of the society through its political monopoly. So acute an observer as Andrei Sakharov saw that the economic gulf between the bureaucracy and the working class, or the mass of ordinary people, was infinitely greater than between the capitalist class and the working class in the United States. As the development of the Soviet Union has revealed, this bureaucratic class renews itself in the sense that, having become all-powerful internally in a police state, and, above all, exclusive, its replacement comes not from the population at large, but literally from its own progeny.[9]

The "free" capitalist market as known in the West and elsewhere did not then and never did exist in the Soviet Union to influence the production of goods. There, a "planned economy" exists, poorly functioning as it is, initiated entirely from above. The Party governs all social, economic, as well as political decisions. The situation of the Soviet Union is historically unique, because it is a society in which the state is subordinated to a single party, the only one permitted by law to exist. The state acts as the national coordinating means to carry out the decisions of the Party. It does not have the power to veto or ratify, to discuss or debate matters, only to execute.

Lacking democracy of any kind and at any level, no institutions exist to challenge, contest, criticize, amend, propose alternatives, debate policies, or oppose decisions made from on high. The name aside, there are no soviets (workers' councils) in the Soviet Union. There are no independent free-trade unions or any other independent free social organizations or institutions. The statification of the total economy in the Soviet Union is accompanied by the atomization of the classes (the peasantry and what was once a proletariat in the capitalist sense). There are no means for the classes to be involved in political activities and thus intervene in the social processes. They have no *legal* right to do so. As a police state in which all the forces of control and coercion are in the hands of the ruling party, the Soviet Union is an ideal totalitarian society next to which fascism is a relatively anemic likeness. In this land, the "blind laws of economics" are only a historical relic, replaced by the conscious political power, the Party, as the determining factor in economic policy. Finally, there is no private property in the means of production and, therefore, no capitalist class.

In adopting its position that the Soviet Union was not a workers' state of any kind, "degenerated" or otherwise, the Socialist Workers' Party deepened its differences with official Trotskyism, precluding any reconciliation with it. The new organization declared that nationalization of the means of production was *not* the determining characteristic of a workers' state. Nationalized property was not such a measure when the new state was founded and it was not Trotsky's view in the early years of the Revolution. Trotsky came to that formula only after some years of the deepening struggle against Stalinism and seemingly as an afterthought. In the very beginning, in the first years of the revolutionary power, it was the position of the Left that the new Russia was a workers' state *because the political state and its control was in the hands of the working class* (the great myth of the Revolution). This view reflected Lenin's theory that the Party represented the essential social interest of the working class, which could, as we learned, never "rise in consciousness" above the trade-union level. The Party and the Party alone would reach the highest level of social consciousness, according to this theory, and so would speak and act in the name of the proletariat.

Not everyone accepted this view. After the Revolution, the still-existing though powerless Social Revolutionaries and Mensheviks, as well as some Party members, believed the proletariat had already lost political power by 1920. That was the contention of the Democratic Centralist Faction led by Sapronov and Vladimir M. Smirnov. They argued then that the bureaucracy had triumphed and that a new revolution was necessary to restore power to the working class. The activity of the Democratic Centralist Faction, with its telling criticism, is one of the reasons for Lenin's determination to end all factions in the Party through the famous resolution of the Tenth Party Congress. Such criticism, however sporadic and unorganized, did continue during the twenties, however. Toward the end of that decade, the view that the workers' state no longer existed was expressed by young Trotskyists in Siberian exile.

In an earlier chapter, I have referred to Trotsky showing me their letters (received from exile, written in tiny handscript, in "disappearing ink") which were very brilliant analyses, Trotsky said, of Russian society under Stalin. They no longer considered the Soviet Union a workers' state. Trotsky said their analyses, while wrong, were nonetheless very learned. He attributed their "incorrect" views, in part, to their severe isolation.

Nineteen twenty-seven was the year Trotsky wrote his important *Letter to Borodai,* which gave a different answer to the question from the one he developed in a variety of ways during the next decade.[10] Borodai was a militant member of the Democratic Centralist Faction, which held that the "Thermidorean reaction"—i.e., the counter-revolution—had already occurred. Borodai himself formally concluded that a new revolution was necessary to reestablish the political power of the working class. Trotsky denied that a counter-revolution had occurred. What made the country a workers' state, he wrote, was the *political power of the working class.* If that power no longer existed, the Soviet Union would cease to be a workers' state. And although he believed that nationalized property was the economic form in such a state, it was not the determining criterion. At the time of writing this letter, he considered the Bolshevik Party still to be a revolutionary Socialist party representing the best interests of the working class—badly to be sure, but still speaking and acting for the Russian proletariat. His view of the revolutionary character of the Party did not change until Hitler took power in Germany; only then did he castigate the Bolshevik Party as a counter-revolutionary force inside Russia and in the International.

The historical reality, however, was that the working class *never* had political power in Russia. The Party had all the power, total power. Before the Stalinist degeneration, the assertion that the Party represented, spoke for, and *was* the working class was widely accepted. It was the cardinal doctrine of Leninism. And it was never true.

*   *   *

One month after the split in American Trotskyism, the GPU made its first attempt to assassinate Trotsky, in May, 1940. It was led by artist-turned-gunman David Siqueiros, a well-known leading Mexican Stalinist. He was able to penetrate the guard system at the fortified house where Trotsky, Natalia, and the guards resided, through admittance by one of the guards, Sheldon Harte.[11] The circumstances will probably never be completely known, as Harte was later found murdered. The Siqueiros gang proceeded to shoot up the house and garden areas in the hope that the sweep of bullets would reach Trotsky. Trotsky and Natalia escaped the heavy fire by lying prone on the floor of their room. The only one hit in this bizarre attempt was their grandson, Sieva Volkow.

In August of that year Stalin and his GPU succeeded in assassinating Trotsky with the aid of a trained agent of the secret police, Spanish Communist Ramon Mercader, who penetrated the household through a ruse and struck the fatal blow with an alpenstock into Trotsky's head during a private and unguarded meeting in the leader's workroom.[12]

Trotsky always believed that Stalin could murder him whenever Stalin wanted to. Still, Trotsky's followers tried to make it difficult for Stalin. For that reason, the residence in Coyoacan, Mexico, was made into a fortress, with guards always present as a system of defense. One of the difficulties in the guard system, however, was that Trotsky violated its rules. He objected to having a guard in his room when he met with visitors and to having a guard outside the door of his room when such visitors were present. When Trotsky was struck and screamed, the guards had to come running from another part of the "fortress."

Mercader was a well-trained, tough agent to whom carrying out the assignment of the GPU was as "God given." He did his job with cunning and managed, despite the warning of Sylvia Ageloff (his companion and a member of the WP) that he not be invited into the house. But he was able to do so by pretending he was politically interested in the conflict with the Minority over the Russian Question. Ironically, Trotsky was reading a peurile document Mercader wrote *in support* of Trotsky when he was struck. When the guard Harold Robins rushed into the room and proceeded to beat Mercader, Trotsky still had the presence of mind and the strength to yell out not to kill the assassin, but let him live to be questioned. But Mercader was a true Stalinist who remained silent. He understood his role.

The Russian Question in Retrospect

I am no longer a Trotskyist and have not been for many years. The Russian Question destroyed my political and personal relations with Trotsky, as it did for many of my former associates.

Still the question persists: What might have happened had Trotsky lived through the Second World War, Hitler's invasion of Russia, and observed the triumph of the Stalinist state, its solidification and expansion? We can only guess, since at one point he stated that if the proletariat did not take power in the war, it would force the question: Is it incapable of doing so, or was the Socialist perspective an unrealizable dream? We do know from other things he had written that had he witnessed the thrust of German arms across the Russian borders, he would have called for universal support of the Soviet Union, and offered his services to the Stalin regime in any capacity and without any conditions to help its war effort. It would not be a wild guess, to be sure, that the offer would have been rejected by Stalin, accompanied with vicious attacks on Trotsky for trying to insinuate his counter-revolutionary aspirations. No doubt he would have been charged once again with being Hitler's agent.

All through the thirties, we saw an uncertainty about the nature of Russian society reflected in Trotsky's often contradictory analyses.[13] What was the nature of the regime of Stalin? Early in the decade we were told that the Stalinist bureaucracy represented a "Thermidorean" degeneration; later it was defined as "Bonapartism," and then as Centrism and "national Bolshevism." In one place he wrote that the bureaucracy "protects the workers' state with its own peculiar methods," but also that the "Stalinist bureaucracy is nothing else than the first stage of bourgeois restoration." His most persistent theme was that Stalin was preparing to bring capitalism back to Russia.

Trotsky published *The Revolution Betrayed* in 1936. Despite his reaffirmation that Russia was a workers' state, the work contained the most compelling descriptions of the basic characteristics of the society. At one point, referring to the new Stalin constitution and its equation of " 'state property' as the possessions of the whole people," Trotsky wrote, "this identification is the fundamental sophism of the official doctrine."[14] In a sharply sketched analysis he went on to say:

> In order to become social, private property must as inevitably pass through the state stage as the caterpillar in order to become a butterfly must pass through the pupa stage. But the pupa is not a butterfly. Myriads of pupae perish without ever becoming butterflies. State property becomes the property

of "the whole people" only to the degree that social privilege and differentiation disappear, and there with the necessity of the state. In other words: State property is converted into Socialist property in proportion as it ceases to be state property. And the contrary is true: The higher the Soviet state rises above the people, and the more fiercely it opposes itself as the guardian of property to the people as its squanderer, the more obviously does it testify against the Socialist character of this state property.[15]

Trotsky was relentless in his critical descriptions of the Stalinist state, which lend no support to his own theory of the workers' state even on the grounds he postulates. For a time, we were all hypnotized by the "nationalized property" formula. It became a religiouslike faith in the Trotskyist movement. And this was so even though we were taught in Trotsky's book that "Stalinism and fascism, in spite of a deep differentiation in social foundation, are symmetrical phenomena. In many of their features they show a deadly similarity."[16]

Trotsky, in further description of the new state, wrote:

The regime had become "totalitarian" in character several years before this word arrived from Germany. "By means of demoralizing methods, which convert thinking Communists into machines, destroying will, character, and human dignity," wrote Rakovsky in 1928. "The ruling circles have succeeded in consolidating themselves into an unremovable and inviolate oligarchy, which replaced the class and the party."[17] Since these indignant lines were written, the degeneration of the regime has gone immeasurably farther. The GPU has become the decisive factor in the inner life of the Party. . . . The old Bolshevik Party is dead, and no force will resurrect it.[18]

By 1928 Rakovsky had already described the regime as an "unremovable and inviolate oligarchy, which replaced the class and the party." Trotsky agreed with that view and added that the "old Bolshevik Party is dead, and no force will resurrect it."[19] Even as late as 1939, in one of his lesser writings (the very factional and dreary *In Defense of Marxism*), Trotsky repeats that totalitarianism had become a characteristic condition of Soviet society: "The USSR minus the social structure of the October Revolution would be a Fascist state."[20] The main direction of the state had gone further and further away from a loosening of the regime's stranglehold on the economy, the political and social life of the country. In all important respects, the state had become even more omnipotent, assuming there was any room left for such further development. Social differentiation and privilege of the bureaucracy have become greater in the seventy years following the Revolution.

Trotsky wrote that "free labor is incompatible with the existence of a bureaucratic state."[21] True, but as is evident from the history of the Russian Revolution and the course of the post-World War II world, especially in the newly arisen nations and the Third World, *free labor is compatible only under conditions of democracy.* So far as the Soviet Union goes, labor has never been free, but has always been a regimented class functioning under conditions of police terror.

Despite his belief in the "Socialist" character of the state and a reaffirmation of his theory of Russian society, objectivity compelled Trotsky to write, in the closing pages of *The Revolution Betrayed,* an observation that anticipated the views of the Minority and the Workers' Party:

> The Soviet bureaucracy has risen above a class which is hardly emerging from destitution and darkness, and has no tradition of dominion or command. Whereas the Fascists, when they find themselves in power, are united with the big bourgeoisie by bonds of common interest, friendship, marriage, etc., the Soviet bureaucracy takes on bourgeois customs without having beside it a national bourgeoisie. In this sense we cannot deny that it is something more than a bureaucracy. It is in the full sense of the word the sole privileged and commanding stratum in the Soviet society.
>
> Another difference is no less important. The Soviet bureaucracy has expropriated the proletariat politically in order by methods of its own to defend [its] social conquests. But the very act of its appropriation of political power in a country where the principle means of production are in the hands of the state, creates a new and hitherto unknown relation between the bureaucracy and the riches of the nation. The means of production belong to the state. But the state, so to speak, "belongs" to the bureaucracy. If these as yet wholly new relations should solidify, become the norm, and be legalized, whether with or without resistance from the workers, they would, in the long run, lead to a complete liquidation of the social conquests of the proletarian revolution. But to speak of that now is at least premature.[22]

And what of today? As far back as 1936, "the mass Soviets have entirely disappeared from the scene, having turned over the function of compulsion to Stalin, Yagoda, and Company." And now, for more than fifty years we have had a Soviet Union without soviets! Given a nation without a "bill of rights," no democratic institutions of any kind, and without the possibility of any class, group, or institution's intervention, challenge, criticize, or offer alternatives, disenfranchisement of the people has become the nation's hallmark.

Have the "new relations" solidified? Have they become the norm? The Minority and the Workers' Party believed they had. And *The Revolution*

Betrayed, on page after page, described the society in many details that forced the question: What is left of the October Revolution? Trotsky said that it was premature to answer. It may have been premature in 1936, but it has not been so for many decades. The Old Bolshevik Party is long gone, having been replaced by an entirely new party of the bureaucracy.[23] The "soviets" and "trade unions" are state organizations that exist to enforce government policy in the workplace. The conditions Trotsky wrote about have indeed solidified long ago.

To further complicate things for himself and his loyal followers, Trotsky, the classical and objective Marxist, wrote:

> Theory is not a note which you can present at any moment to reality for payment. If a theory proves mistaken we must revise it or fill out its gaps. . . . We must not wander in the dark, repeating ritual phrases, useful for the prestige of the leaders, but nevertheless slap reality in the face.[24]

Which is exactly what reality did to Trotsky's theory. He was unable to adhere to his own idea, though he came close to it. His view of the Russian state was an abstraction shattered by the ways in which Stalinism functioned with relation to the economy and classes in Russian society. With great literary sweep he could write, "The laws of history are stronger than the bureaucracy." What laws? Why did they not operate? Evidently the bureaucracy proved stronger than the "laws of history," whatever they may be.

Trotsky's acute intellect and searching mind led him in many directions in dealing with the Russian phenomena, so that even allowing for the possibility of a new social development in the nation, he rejected the prospect in 1936 because it was "premature." But he also rejected the possibility in 1939 because he was unwarrantedly optimistic about the impending doom of the Stalinist regime. In answer to the Minority, he wrote:

> Might we not place ourselves in a ludicrous position if we affixed to the Bonapartist oligarchy the nomenclature of a new ruling class just a few years or a few months prior to its downfall?[25]

Whence sprang this optimism? How in the face of the evolution of Stalinism, of which he had been the premier historian, could Trotsky write such arrant nonsense? A downfall through a coup in the Kremlin? A military *putsch?* The spontaneous uprising of the unorganized masses, the cowed working class, and the oppressed, dispersed peasants, each totally leaderless? Had Trotsky reverted to his pre-Bolshevik faith in the masses and

a form of spontaneous rebellion in contradiction to the essence of Leninism on the role of the Party? The answer is difficult to find if one searches
for it in political theory. His own analyses of Stalinism gave no support
to the expectation of an early fall of Stalin. Since he could not accept
the inherent implications of *The Revolution Betrayed* or the view of the
Minority in American Trotskyism, he still spoke of the possibility of impending revolutionary social change in Soviet society in 1936, and repeated
it on the eve of the war. In his essay "The USSR in War," Trotsky set
down the following theoretical possibility:

> The historic alternative, carried to the end, is as follows: Either the Stalin
> regime is an abhorrent relapse in the process of transforming bourgeois so-
> ciety into a Socialist society, or the Stalin regime is the first stage of a new
> exploiting society. If the second prognosis proves correct, then of course
> the bureaucracy will become a new exploiting class. However onerous the
> second perspective may be, if the world proletariat should actually prove
> incapable of fulfilling the mission placed upon it by the course of develop-
> ment, nothing else would remain except openly to recognize that the So-
> cialist program, based on the internal contradictions of capitalist society, end-
> ed as a utopia. It is self-evident that a new "minimum" program would be
> required for the defense of the interests of the slaves of the totalitarian
> bureaucracy.
>
> But are there such incontrovertible or even impressive objective data
> as would compel us today to renounce the prospect of the Socialist revo-
> lution? That is the whole question.[26]

But that was really *not* the whole question. In 1939, no one involved in
the dispute with Trotsky thought, spoke, or wrote about *giving up* the
Socialist perspective. I would add that even in this rapidly changing world
of varying perspectives, a general Socialist perspective suited to our epoch
has viability to one degree or another. But because Trotsky posed the question in the way quoted above, Max Shachtman replied to him for the
Minority, saying: "The essence of the question, however, relates *not* to
perspective, but to the theoretical characterization of the Soviet state and
its bureaucracy."[27] Had Trotsky recalled the statement in his *Letter to Borodai* in 1928 that "the character of the economy as a whole thus depends
upon the character of the state power,"[28] he would have been able to see
more clearly the evolution of Stalinist society as it neared the war.

The Russian bourgeoisie was no factor in the new society after 1917,
because it disappeared almost immediately. No matter; the bourgeoisie was
not any kind of factor during the development of the statified economy.
The fruits of the "primitive accumulation of capital" after the Revolution

was based on an unprecedented exploitation of the nation's resources, most particularly of its working class and peasantry; it accrued to the bureaucracy, enriching it economically, providing it with social privileges granted to no one else, and strengthening its despotic rule. Shachtman's view of Trotsky's great error—believing that "Stalin is creating conditions for a bourgeois counter-revolution and reestablishment of capitalism was fundamentally wrong"—remains uncontradicted. What happened during this period of "primitive accumulation of capital"? In the rapid industrialization of the country and the forced complete collectivization of agriculture and its murderous subordination to industry, Shachtman went on to say:

> . . . a new coagulation that was to perform—one way or another—the social task awaiting it. In so doing it was to consolidate itself as a new, reactionary ruling class, which established and continues to maintain its domination over society by means of the most ruthless, most unashamed, most intensely organized, centralized, and consciously directed terror against the people it exploited that has ever been known to history—without exception.[29]

Had Trotsky lived out his full natural life and observed Russian developments in the next decade or more after his death (and those of Eastern Europe and later China), what would he have said in the light of his last pronouncements about this inhuman, reactionary, and culturally conservative and backward society, which, armed to the teeth, stifles its people, the national minorities, particularly the Jews, and where terror is a never ending state policy against dissidents? Would he have repeated that this was a "degenerated workers' state" because "property is nationalized," or would he have finally recognized that the "Stalin regime is the first stage of a new exploiting society"?

*   *   *

Nearly fifty years after Trotsky's death, his followers remain intellectually and politically in the social period of 1940, the year of his assassination. No, even worse: Their policies reflect the undue influence of Isaac Deutscher, Trotsky's biographer, more than they do of Trotsky. Accepting Trotsky's conception of a workers' state, Deutscher developed a view of Stalinism that Trotsky would never have tolerated, as I have stated. It was Deutscher's idea that Stalin was building a Socialist society, though his policies were indeed dreadful. In his way, Stalin was really carrying out Trotsky's program! Deutscher observed that revolutions were made by utopians, but the "practicals" take over because the revolutionary founders of the new society cannot achieve their aims, the masses tire, the revolutionary ebb occurs, and the practicals, in one way or another, assume the responsibility of state power.

Even though Deutscher acknowledged the backwardness of the USSR, he made light of Trotsky's struggle against the theory of "socialism in one country." He knew that it violated a long Socialist tradition of internationalism. But to Deutscher, the very backwardness of Russia supported Stalin's historic role, because Stalin retained nationalized property while bullying his way to socialism. In his *Ironies of History* he described Stalinism as

> an amalgamation of Marxism with semi-barbarous and quite barbarous traditions and primitive magic of an essentially pre-industrial, i.e., not merely pre-Socialist but pre-bourgeois, society.[30]

This explained to Deutscher why Stalin took such a cruel course on his way to triumph. Deutscher is also certain that the inexorable laws of the dialectic would in the end govern the conduct of Stalin and the Kremlin and would, in the end, lead to socialism. Thus in *The Prophet Outcast,* Stalin's victory over Trotsky "concealed a heavy element of defeat where Trotsky's defeat was pregnant with victory." In such a development, Deutscher, with a religiouslike certainty, knew that socialism would come to Russia but without the intervention or assistance of the Fourth International or any other such movement. He was certain, too, that after Stalin's death Malenkov and Khrushchev would continue the historic march to socialism begun by Stalin, forced to do so by objective circumstances. In that way, they would be caused "to act up to a point as the executors of Trotsky's political testament." How shameful! How false! This is not political science but mumbo jumbo.

Again: "What Malenkov's government is carrying out now specifically is the 'limited revolution' envisaged by Trotsky." This is an allusion to Trotsky's view that the revolution against the bureaucracy would be a political and not a social one, because nationalized property was already in existence. As to the general conception of Deutscher in this area, Shachtman observed in his penetrating criticisms of Deutscher's biographies of Trotsky and Stalin that

> the alloy in Trotsky's argument was already a base one [nationalized property equals a workers' state]; in Deutscher it is far worse because he mixes into it what was so absent to Trotsky—a wholesale capitulation to Stalinism historically, theoretically, and politically.[31]

Many decades have passed since Trotsky wrote his ideas about the Soviet Union, and almost three since Deutscher completed his biographies. Recent developments in Russia have made their views untenable, assuming they ever had any validity. Toward the end, Deutscher was said to have wondered about it all. His young supporter, Marcel Liebman, was resigned to the long existence of the present regime "in an atmosphere of contentment and apathy." We know of the apathy; we are not so sure about the contentment.

In his searching essay "Trotskyist Interpretations of Stalinism," Robert H. McNeal observes with particular reference to Deutscher's role and Liebman's reflections that

> it leads toward the intellectual option that Trotsky resisted so desperately in his last year (against the Shachtman faction and the newly formed Workers' Party) and which Deutscher, too, resisted: that the October Revolution led to a new form of exploitation by a ruling class.[32]

Fifteen years after the "Shachtman faction and the newly formed Workers' Party" made known its position on the nature of Stalinist society as a new class society, Milovan Djilas wrote his book *The New Class*. In no way did it approach the depth of analysis characteristic of the Workers' Party on bureaucratic collectivism, but because he was, next to Tito, perhaps the most important or best-known leader of the dissident Yugoslav Communist state, his book received wide notoriety.

More recently, Paul M. Sweezy, for many years an ardent supporter of Stalin's Russia, made a complete break with his old view in his article "Is There a Ruling Class in the USSR?" "I shall argue in favor of the thesis that there is a ruling class in the USSR and that it is of a new type," he wrote.[33] He proceeded to examine some of Trotsky's and Deutscher's writings preliminary to a polemic with Ernst Mandel, the theoretician of the Fourth International. Most curious in Sweezy's statement, however, is that twenty-five years after the Workers' Party made public its theory of bureaucratic collectivism, i.e., that "there is a ruling class in the USSR and that it is of a new type," Sweezy, who could not possibly have missed Trotsky's long polemics with "the Shachtman faction," makes no reference whatever to the Workers' Party position. Was he protecting his "originality"?

Sweezy's article devotes a good deal of space to Deutscher, because Trotsky's biographer pronounced the certainty of the Socialist progress of the Soviet Union as late as 1956. Among the many wrong observations Deutscher had written on the subject, perhaps the most crass appeared in *Ironies:*

With the traditions of a Socialist revolution alive in the minds of its people, the Soviet Union breaks with Stalin in order to assume its advance towards equality and Socialist democracy. . . . No matter how much one may dislike Stalin's epigones, one must acknowledge that they have proved themselves capable of a much more sensitive response to the need for reform than was generally expected of them. . . . Once they have matured they are certain to transform profoundly the whole moral and political climate of communism and transform it in a spirit of Socialist democracy.[34]

A pure and simple fairy tale. How could this knowledgeable historian write such nonsense? Even more than Trotsky, Deutscher believed that nationalized property made Russia a workers' state traveling the high road to socialism. And so Deutscher is of the opinion that though Trotsky may have done it better than Stalin, more efficiently, relatively more democratically, and without the murderous intent of Stalin, still, for all his evils, the Georgian carried out the historic task that is now continued by his successors—who "have proved themselves capable of a much more sensitive response to the need for reform than was generally expected of them. . . . " Brezhnev? Andropov? Chernenko? Wishful thinking is presented as history.

*   *   *

Deutscher creates serious problems in evaluating Trotsky's works. The fact that he wrote a very significant biography of Trotsky, some of it brilliant, all of it sympathetic and informative, can be misleading unless it is understood that he was a critical supporter of the Stalinist state and the society it molded. McNeal called attention to an important aspect of Deutscher's style when he wrote, "One of Deutscher's great assets, his allusive and metaphorical style in a language he learned as a mature man, is an obstacle to the analysis of his ideological position."[35]

An obstacle, to be sure, but not insurmountable, as can be seen in the criticisms of Deutscher's biographies, and illustrated sharply in Shachtman's reviews. Deutscher contributed much to the disorientation of many young radicals, including many in the Trotskyist movement. The latter-day Trotskyists did not need his help. McNeal was on target when he wrote:

Having called attention to the conception of Stalinism as something more deeply rooted in society and the political institutions of this century, the Trotskyists could not, however, follow up this insight as uninhibited Marxists without threatening their eschatalogical faith, which was (and is) more fundamental than their commitment to a science of society.[36]

The dogma of the degenerated workers' state made it possible for Stalinism and the Soviet Union to "exercise a magnetic attraction upon the Trotskyist movement," wrote Shachtman, "forcing it into reluctant alignment in most of the fundamentally important political developments and leaving it essentially only with the criticism not so much of what Stalinism does as the 'methods' by which it does it."[37] Nothing has changed for the Fourth International since Trotsky died. Their slavish adherence to a static conception of the Soviet state, which has degenerated for fifty years without "quantity changing into quality," with the odd philosophical view that *their* dialectic has application to the capitalist world only.

One noted European Trotskyist, observing the world scene and reaffirming that the Soviet Union is a degenerated workers' state, settles the matter forever, for himself at least, when he writes: "Where you have capitalism, it isn't state capitalism, and where you have stratified planned economy, you don't have capitalism."[38]

But do you have a workers' state, even a degenerated one? Do you have a "Socialist" state? Is any other alternative possible? Something new, perhaps? Something not foreseen? Evidently nothing has changed in the USSR in the past fifty years. Changes of dramatic proportions have taken place in Western capitalism. There has been a dissolution of the old colonial empires (except the Russian) and the rise of Third World nations. Everywhere there is change of great depth; but to the Trotskyists nothing changes in Stalinist Russia or, since Stalin is no longer the revered figure, from the time of Khrushchev on. Although even Trotsky projected the possibility of a social change in the Soviet Union, his followers remain stonily indifferent to such a possibility and deeply rooted in a historically untenable theory.

Without direction from Trotsky, the Fourth International went into ecstasy over Tito, and even gave way to a one-sided and unreciprocated love for the Stalinist demon of Latin America, Castro. The abject adulation of Fidel by the Socialist Workers' Party was similar to the "frenzy" of enthusiasm for Tito, only it went a little further in the coupling of Castro with Marx, Lenin, and Trotsky; he became the fourth member in this new pantheon of leaders created by the philosopher of the SWP, George Novack. The party's paper, *The Militant,* regularly prints the speeches of Castro with evident enthusiasm. Castro, the true Stalinist type, who supplies the Soviet Union with its "foreign legion" in Africa and the Middle East in repayment for Russia's economic aid to his bankrupt economy, is unresponsive to this courtship, refusing to admit the party's representatives to any "international" gatherings held in Havana. Finally, the Socialist Workers' Party in the United States has ceased to be a Trotskyist organization. It has expelled all the old-time Trotskyists, with or without trial, and announced its intention to work for a "new mass Leninist International," signifying that the Fourth International is superfluous and ought to be dissolved.

A Note on Natalia Sedova Trotsky

In one of her several trips to the United States from Mexico, Natalia Sedova Trotsky told Shachtman and me that Trotsky was reconsidering the Russian Question, which was troubling him more than ever just before he was assassinated. Natalia did not believe that the USSR was a degenerated workers' state, nor did she accept the theory of bureaucratic collectivism, holding that it was a state capitalist society. Important to her, however, was that we agreed politically. She made public her break with the Fourth International when she resigned from it in 1951. She felt it had misinterpreted Trotsky's views and carried out policies she could not abide.

Part of her statement of resignation from the Fourth International appears below:

> I find I must tell you that I see no other way than to say openly that our disagreements make it impossible for me to remain any longer in your ranks. . . .
> Obsessed by old and outlived formulas, you continue to regard the Stalinist state as a workers' state. I cannot and will not follow you in this. . . .
> I find it impossible to follow you in the question of the Tito regime in Jugoslavia [sic]. . . . Your entire press is now devoted to an inexcusable idealization of the Titoist bureaucracy for which no ground exists in the traditions and principles of our movement.[39]

Had she lived on she could have added Castro to this commentary, but she would not have been listened to in that case either.

Notes

1. *Writings,* Vol. 6, pp. 538–539.

2. Joseph Carter (Friedman) (1910–19??) though expelled from the Young Communist League, was a founding member of the Trotskyist organization in New York in 1928. He was a member of the Young Peoples' Socialist League as early as 1924. He initiated the idea that Russia was a bureaucratic collectivist society. He won Burnham to his view and obtained Burnham's agreement to present the resolution jointly. Although Bruno R. (Rizzi) first used the term in France when he was connected with the French Trotskyist League, his concept of bureaucratic collectivism was unknown in the SWP, as was his use of the term itself. More important, his concept was different from Carter's and certainly from the Workers' Party resolution on the Russian state (1942), drafted by Max Shachtman and developed by him in his book *The Bureaucratic Revolution.* To emphasize this difference, Rizzi's views were corroded by anti-Semitism. Even as late as 1942, with the war on in Europe, Rizzi's views were unknown to Americans except for a reference to them by Trotsky in his polemic with the Minority.

Carter was the original driving force behind the idea in its earlier form and contributed substantially to the final position of the Workers' Party. Rizzi's book, entitled *La Bureaucratisation du Monde,* was discussed in *The New International* (September 1948) by James M. Fenwick, in "The Mysterious Bruno R." The subject was also discussed in an exchange between Max Shachtman and Ted Grant, a leading British Trotskyist, which also appeared in *The New International,* in 1947.

3. James Burnham (1905–1987). A leader of the American Workers' Party and National Committee of the Workers' Party after unification with the Communist League of America in 1934, he was also a leading member of the SWP, on its National and Political Committees, and was active in the Minority until just before the split in the SWP, when he left the movement entirely, advising the convention that formed the Workers' Party of 1940 that he was no longer a Socialist and would not join the new organization. Afterward he became a voice of conservatism and a pundit for the *National Review,* issued and edited by William F. Buckley, Jr. Burnham quickly lost interest in the theory of bureaucratic collectivism; his *Managerial Revolution* makes no reference to the idea or the descriptive phrase itself.

4. In the fall of 1939, aboard a train to New York with Albert Goldman to attend a meeting of the National Committee, I found myself involved in a long discussion with him on the meaning of the events during the year and how they affected our Russian position. Although he was supporting the Majority, his was a very shaky support, and he was beset with grave doubts about the position of the official leadership. I pressed Goldman very hard in an effort to win his support to the Minority. He had been shocked by the Moscow Trials, and only his almost total involvement in the Mexican hearings kept him from dealing with the question at any great depth. Finland's invasion and the partition of Poland

saw him more affected than any member of the Majority, but he succumbed to the pressure of Trotsky and the National Committee. He remained in the SWP for several years, at which time he and a new group of supporters left the SWP and joined the Workers' Party.

Goldman was a veteran of the Socialist and Communist movements, a labor attorney of considerable reputation, with long political experience. After the Commission of Inquiry hearing he was Trotsky's American counsel.

5. The original National Committee of the Communist League had nine members, some of whom formed its Political Committee. Of the nine, four were leading members of the Minority: Max Shachtman, Martin Abern, Maurice Spector, and myself. Joe Carter, an important person in the discussion, was a founding member, as were many leading figures throughout the country. The youth leadership consisted of many who were among the earliest Trotskyists in the United States: Emanuel Geltman, Reva Craine, Nathan Gould, Paul Bernick, Henry Malter; out of the YPSL movement were Ernest Erber and Hal Draper. The "petit bourgeois opposition" was peopled by many workers, but the faction was the younger section of the party, most of them part of the unemployed "army." Trotsky's designation could have been applied to the Majority with equal justification (or lack of it).

6. Trotsky, *Writings, 1936–37*, pp. 404–06.

7. *With Trotsky in Exile,* p. 145–46.

8. Confusion over Burnham's relations with the Workers' Party arose because he was one of the speakers at the first public meeting of the new organization. Why did he speak for an organization he rejected? We must speculate. Was it because, having contributed so much to the political group, he did not want to let it down and so paid his last respects to its struggle? To explain it further we must enter the field of psychology. No doubt it was automatically assumed on the outside that he was still associated with his faction, now independently organized. The leadership of the Workers' Party did not see Burnham again—until he appeared as a government witness in the successful suit of the Workers' Party and Independent Socialist League against the Attorney General of the United States to remove them, and its affiliated youth organization, from its "List of Subversive Organizations."

With the departure of Burnham, only the late Ernest Rice McKinney, at one time on the staff of the American Workers' Party, remained in the Trotskyist or quasi-Trotskyist movement. He became an important leader of the Workers' Party.

9. This is how the Workers' Party resolution on Russia defined its theory:

> The reaction and the counterrevolution in Russia took fundamentally different forms, however, from those which had been forseen by the Marxists. . . . They envisaged the collapse of the workers' state as the culmination of a process in which the capitalist elements would grow and finally triumph by a counterrevolution which would restore the rule of capitalism in Russia. In this, their predictions have not been confirmed. The workers' state was crushed by the Stalinist counter-revolution, but it was not replaced by a capitalist state. . . .

The bureaucracy, contrary to prediction, did not proceed to denationalize the land or the industries, and the banks and transportation system; it did not wipe out the monopoly of foreign trade; it did not facilitate the "gradual" development of small capitalist production and exchange into a full-fledged capitalist system. On the contrary, it directed an assault against the capitalist elements in the country that was no less ruthless than any before known in the Soviet Republic; it enormously increased the importance and specific gravity of the state property and state production sector of Society economy. . . . The workers' state gave way to the bureaucratic collectivist state. . . . For the bureaucratic-collectivist development of the productive forces in the Soviet Union, a new ruling class was necessary, that is, a particularly brutal gendarme converting "inequality into a whip for the spurring on of the majority," and steadily accentuating the inequality in favor of the ruling class. . . .

The Workers' Party rejects the theory that the Soviet Union is a degenerated workers' state which must be unconditionally defended against any capitalist society regardless of conditions and circumstances. This theory covers up the class nature of the Stalinist bureaucracy and the reactionary character of the regime. By the same token, it tends to underestimate the full, reactionary significance of the bureaucracy. . . .

10. Max Shachtman's *The Bureaucratic Revolution* contains Trotsky's letter and Shachtman's important explanatory introduction (p. 88). The letter also appeared in *The New International*, April 1943.

11. Sheldon Harte, a new recruit to the SWP, was sent to Mexico as a new guard, reputedly after only six months of membership. His actions on the night of the attack were strange. In violation of guard rules, he opened the door to Siqueiros and his gang and was himself taken with them when they left. Harte's body was later discovered by the police. Suspicion remains over Harte's role. His father, upon receiving the news of his son's involvement, was reported to have said that he was surprised to learn that Sheldon was a Trotskyist because he knew there was a picture of Stalin in his room and assumed that Sheldon was a supporter of the Kremlin. Trotsky defended Harte against the suspicions raised, but it is doubtful that the real answer will be found unless and until the archives of the Russian secret police are opened. What is certain is that it was most unusual for the SWP to send a guard to Mexico, especially someone who was in the organization for so short a time.

12. In the custody of the Mexican police, Mercader pretended he was a Trotskyist who had had a falling out with his leader. He said he was so outraged that he had no recourse but to murder him. Various representatives of the press toyed with the notion, obviously suggested by the GPU and Mercader, that an affair of the heart was involved, in which Trotsky betrayed this Spanish Russian police agent. Any doubts about Mercader's role were resolved when, having served his twenty-five year sentence, he flew to Cuba and then to Czechoslovakia, from where he made his way to the Soviet Union. In Russia, he was awarded the honor

"Hero of the Soviet Union" for his murderous service to the Stalin regime. Not too many years later he was reported to have died of cancer while residing in the "Socialist Motherland."

13. See bibliography for complete list.
14. *The Revolution Betrayed*, p. 236.
15. *Betrayed*, p. 237.
16. *Betrayed*, p. 278.
17. Christian Rakovsky (1873–1941) was a Bulgarian Socialist Internationalist who joined the Russian Social Democratic organization in 1890 at the time of Plekhanov, Axelrod, and Zasulich. A renowned Socialist leader in the Balkans, he went to Russia in 1899 and was arrested many times by the Tsarist police and in the Balkan countries. He was one of the initiators of the Left Zimmerwald Conference during World War I. At the time of the Russian Revolution he was residing in Stockholm but made his way to Russia, where he was assigned by the new regime to work in the Ukraine and Romania. He was a leading member of the Left Opposition and a long-time personal friend of Trotsky, until he gave up the struggle during Siberian exile under Stalin. He was a learned and thoughtful leader of the Russian Opposition.
18. *Betrayed*, p. 100.
19. *Betrayed*, p. 100.
20. *In Defense of Marxism*, p. 53.
21. *Betrayed*, p. 242.
22. *Betrayed*, pp. 248–249.
23. Conquest, *The Great Terror*, p. 236.
24. *Betrayed*, Chapter 5.
25. Trotsky, *The New International*, November 1939.
26. "The USSR in War," in *The New International*, November 1939.
27. Quoted in *Bureaucratic Revolution*, p. 225.
28. "Letter to Borodai," *The New International*, April 1943.
29. *Bureaucratic Revolution*, p. 286.
30. See Robert H. McNeal's "Trotskyist Interpretations of Stalinism," in *Stalinism*, edited by Robert C. Tucker, p. 30.
31. Max Shachtman's articles in *The New International* were incorporated into his *Bureaucratic Revolution*, p. 225. This reference is on p. 272.
32. Quoted in Tucker's *Stalinism*, p. 30.
33. Sweezy, *Modern Monthly*, October 1956, p. 1.
34. See *Stalinism*, above.
35. McNeal, "Trotskyist Interpretations," in Tucker's *Stalinism*, p. 48.
36. McNeal, "Trotskyist Interpretations," p. 52.
37. *Bureaucratic Revolution*, "Introduction."
38. See Ernst Mandel's odd analysis in his book *Studies in Comparative Commuinism*.
39. N. Sedova, Resignation from the Fourth International.

Trotsky's Legacy

In the summer of 1938, when it was absolutely certain that another world war was about to break out, Trotsky again announced the demise of the Second and Third Internationals and called for the immediate organization of a new, Fourth International to replace them. His active memory recalled that the antiwar, left-wing Socialists in the First World War had then, too, pronounced the Second International dead and laid the foundations for a new International. In the several years before 1938, he and his movement had propagandized for a repeat of this early experience—but with little or no response from other movements that had defected from the mass Socialist and Communist world bodies.

Who was to constitute the Fourth International? It was obvious at the time the call was made, and even more so at the conference itself, that no matter the claims made for it, the Fourth International was only another name for the world Trotskyist movement: It had no support from any labor movement, political faction, or mass party of political significance anywhere in the world. Moveover, the Trotskyist organizations were themselves skeptical of the step Trotsky was insisting on. Some were more than skeptical and were opposed to the calling of the conference at all. Nevertheless, Trotsky persisted, overcoming the opposition; he pressed on with historical references to the small band of antiwar Socialists at Zimmerwald in 1915, a number of whom not only made a revolution in Russia, but created the Third International. Size was no barrier to a determined movement that carried on the struggle despite the odds against it.

Didn't Trotsky know that his movement was small, isolated, and separated from the great organizations of Social Democracy and communism? Indeed he did. But he saw the coming world war as the catalyst for political turmoil in Europe. He foresaw the revolutionary overthrow of Hitler and Stalin by the militant working classes of those countries. In seeing the forthcoming unfolding of revolutionary upheavals through the mirror of the First World War, he was applying the policies of that era to qualitatively different world situations. Trotsky's may have been the most striking example of political self-hypnosis ever observed in the broad Socialist movement.

The conference in Paris in the summer of 1938 brought together a happy reunion of comrades from many countries who had not seen each other for a long time, but it was nonetheless most unpromising. Aside from the Trotskyist organizations—not one of them a true party in membership or influence—no one responded to the conference call. The membership of the various organizations could be counted in the tens, perhaps hundreds. I doubt that the total combined world membership ever surpassed a thousand. In any case, the affair was an act of true political sectarianism, matched only by the perspectives adopted in the document. Not one resolution, from the Transitional Program to the statement on the impending war and the struggle for power, had any relation to the social reality of the period. Even the language of the resolutions and programs had an old-world, archaic quality.

The Transitional Program, while it contained many provocative proposals for social reform, was meaningless to a movement without influence or measurable support. A transitional program conceived of as the instrument to guide the masses into power as a Socialist state, in the circumstances where the working class political parties and other similar organized forces were nonexistent, or so tiny as to be invisible, was doomed. Most important, however, was that the labor movements of Western Europe were largely led by Social Democracy and, to a lesser extent, by Stalinism. This factor acted as an unbreachable wall against any 1917-type revolutionary upheaval. The world was not going in that direction either. The denouement of the Leninist–Stalinist state is revealed in the emergence of Gorbachevism, in its Russian and Chinese forms, and in the upheavals in Poland, Hungary, and the national-minority movements held captive in the Soviet Union.

*   *   *

Many people in the Trotskyist movement were conscious that a mistake was being made, but they did not articulate their feelings that to launch the Fourth International on grounds too feeble to secure it was a hopeless task. Trotsky's vision was of a vast revolutionary upheaval, at least in Europe, and this inevitable spontaneous rebellion would change everything overnight. This is a quotation from the program of the Fourth International:

During the next ten years, the program of the Fourth International will be the guide of millions, and these revolutionary millions will know how to storm heaven and earth.[1]

Why will this happen? Because, said the Transitional Program, "democratic as well as Fascist regimes stagger on from one bankruptcy to another . . . [and there is] no new exit from the economic blind alley."[1] Trotsky then forecast the worst economic crisis in the history of the United States and the rise of the mass revolutionary movement there. And for that reason, he wrote, "the best theoreticians of Marxism will appear on American soil."

Trotsky was wrong on all counts, for there was more than one "new exit from the economic blind alley." The "worst crisis in the United States" was a period of vast expansion, and the "best theoreticians of Marxism" never made their appearance.

Trotsky wrote to James P. Cannon in 1939 that "the perspective of the Socialist revolution becomes an imminent reality."[2] But the world at large ignored the "imminent reality" Trotsky envisioned, as did the Fourth International and its members. Their own day-to-day lives told them to discount what Trotsky wrote when he said: "Social Democracy and Stalinocracy even today represent stupendous fictions. But the Fourth International is an impregnable reality."[3] Who knew better than they that it was not a reality at all, let alone an "impregnable" one?

The Fourth International, oddly enough, still exists at the end of the 1980s. It's no larger than it was at the founding conference in 1939. In almost fifty years, through a devastating world war, the end of the prewar imperialist empires, the rise of the Third World, continuous upheavals, and the spread of world Stalinism, it has advanced nowhere. Internal crises and splits have wracked almost every national section. In France, England, and the United States, there are multiple Trotskyist groups at war with each other. In the United States, where the largest movement was once located, there are not only several groups, but the heart of the movement, the Socialist Workers' Party, has begun to prepare its migration toward Stalinism in the form of "Castroism," beginning with its literary campaign to prove that Trotsky, in every major theoretical and political difference he had with Lenin and the Bolshevik Party, was wrong. The new leaders of the Party announce that they are Leninists, not Trotskyists, and call for a new Leninist International, making clear they have really left the Fourth.

In the International Center in France, the leadership has conflicting perspectives. There was a political current led by the late Pablo, a well-known figure in the world movement, which believed that the Trotskyists should dissolve and join the mass Stalinist parties, clandestinely of course, and work in that arena. In sum, the Fourth International lost what little strength it had when Trotsky died. Without him to guide its politics and activities, the Fourth foundered.

How the Errors Escalated

Trotsky regarded the Axis and Allied powers as equally culpable for World War II. Moreover, as he looked at the conflict merely as a reenactment of the First World War; he believed that no important new elements needed to be taken into account.

Trotsky was not the only one to hold this view. In the United States there were many pacifists, liberals, and old-line isolationists who opposed the war. Norman Thomas, the spokesman for American socialism, and the conservative Liberty League made up other antiwar voices in the country. The Workers' Party, except for its view on the Soviet Union (which did not change during the war), rejected support for the war in favor of a Third Camp, recognizing the difference between the two world wars in the participation of Nazi Germany and Fascist Italy. This absurd view called for military and material aid to this nonexistent Third Camp. Trotsky justified his view by writing in his statement:

> It inevitably must become an international war, since each camp contains
> . . . Fascist, semi-Fascist, Bonapartist, and "democratic" states. . . .[4]

One can explain such inaccurate analysis by the need to reaffirm views that had no validity. The Western Alliance did not contain Fascist, semi-Fascist states—with the exception of Stalinist Russia. Putting the word *democratic* in quotes implies that there were no differences between the West and the Axis. If one thinks he could justify this view at the beginning of the war, there was no way it could be done with logic *after* the war. Yet in the United States today there are Fourth Internationalists who continue this kind of thinking. The Cold War is explained as Western aggression, absolving Soviet expansion under Stalin and its imperialism in Eastern Europe of any responsibility for European instability. This view makes hollow their defense of the Czech and Hungarian "masses" or the Solidarity movement in Poland. The contradictions of this position arise from the programmatic necessity to defend the Soviet Union.

Looking at Trotsky's statement regarding "democracy," it is easy to see how the movement that bears his name became blind to history. In *The Imperialist War and the Proletarian Revolution,* Trotsky wrote:

> In these circumstances is not the working class obliged to support democracy in its struggle with German fascism? . . . It is with indignation that we reject such a policy. Differences undoubtedly exist among the political regimes of bourgeois society, just as there are degrees of comfort in different class railway carriages. But when the whole train is heading for the precipice, the contrast in comfort between the different carriages loses all significance. Capitalist civilization is sliding toward the precipice. Differences between decaying democracy and barbarian fascism disappear in the face of the collapse of the entire capitalist system.
>
> As victors, imperialist Britain and France would be no less fearful for the fate of mankind than Hitler and Mussolini. Bourgeois democracy is not to be saved. Lending aid to its own bourgeoisie against the foreign fascism, the workers would only hasten the victory of fascism in their own country. The task set by history is not to support one part of the imperialist system against another but to cast the entire system over the precipice.[5]

Would it really have made no difference to the working class anywhere if Hitler and Mussolini had won the war? To pose the question is to show how dreadfully wrong Trotsky was in repeating archaic ideas in a swiftly changing world. Bourgeois democracy saved itself. It also made possible the defense and the saving of the Soviet Union, so that it was the West, not the Fourth International, that carried out that part of the Trotskyist program. The colonial empires of the West disappeared with the victory over the Axis and the imperialist empires were not extended—except the Soviet's.

*   *   *

Few challenge the view that the Hitler–Stalin Pact began the Second World War. Nor is there any doubt that it led to the partition of Poland by Hitler and Stalin. The Russian invasion of Finland had already occurred. These events were trumpeted by world Stalinism as measures taken to secure the borders of Mother Russia and thus strengthen the defense of the nation, and they exacerbated the internal crises in the Fourth International. While criticizing the war on Finland and the invasion of Poland, Trotsky defended these reactionary acts of the Soviet Union on the grounds that it had nationalized property in Poland, which was, of course, a progressive achievement.

Hitler's invasion of the Soviet Union once more posed the question of the Soviet Union's defense, not to mention the problem of the Kremlin's alliance with the "imperialist Allies." Trotsky had left guideposts for his followers. In June 1941 the Fourth International adopted a resolution called *For the Defense of the USSR:*

> The Fourth International has declared time and time again what the Soviet working class instinctively understands: The Soviet Union must be defended unconditionally. We defend the USSR irrespective of the betrayal of the bureaucracy and despite its betrayal. Our support is absolute and not dependent on any concessions on the part of the Stalinist bureaucracy. But we will defend the USSR with our own methods. We represent the revolutionary interests of the proletariat and our weapon is the struggle of the revolutionary class. The imperialist Allies of the Kremlin are not our allies. We will carry on the revolutionary struggle everywhere, and that includes the "democratic camp" as well. If we were to support the imperialist bosses of England and the United States, it would mean assisting Hitler in his domination of the German workers. We place our stake on revolution, and the best way to serve the revolutionary future of the German workers is to extend the revolutionary struggle in the camp of the enemy. . . .[6]

The view expressed here is almost a word-for-word repetition of what Trotsky had written; and it was just as wrong. There is considerable bombast in it, but in attacking Russia's allies the Fourth supported the Russian side in the war. It would appear from the results of the war that the Allies contributed more, much more than anything the world Trotskyists could possibly have achieved in the defense of the Russian empire. Allied arms and American Lend-Lease aid sustained the Soviet Union, making possible its resistance to Hitler's invasion with a revival of Russian arms and the war effort. Unfortunately, the Allied victory brought with it a solidification of Stalin's rule and the expansion of the Great Russian empire. The expansion of Leninist society to Eastern Europe under Stalin's leadership showed Trotsky's predictions before 1940 to have been mistaken.

In 1937, in predicting the Hitler–Stalin Pact, he also predicted an early demise for both regimes. As the war neared, his optimism was unchanged; he was certain that they would fall through revolutionary overthrow by the working classes of both countries. Optimism was all he really had:

> Stalin's clique, as the Moscow Trials demonstrated, has entered the last stages of its death agony. The Soviet Union will live and develop as the new social basis created by the October Revolution; it will produce a regime of true democracy and will become the greatest factor for peace and for the social emancipation of humanity.[7]

In November 1939 he continued this mode of thinking:

> The military crash of Hitler will inevitably provoke a revolution in Germany and the consequences will be the overthrow of Stalin's oligarchy in the USSR. Already at this early date these two occurrences loom as the most likely to materialize from the bloody chaos.[8]

Trotsky's repetitious forecast of the certain overthrow of Hitler and Stalin by revolutionary working classes of Germany and Russia violated his own teachings, which were that such a social upheaval—where the working class was disorganized and lacked leadership—was not possible, even if the nation's ruling elite fell apart.

Despite this strong optimism in his writings, he nevertheless appeared to be concerned whether he was in fact correct in his optimistic predictions. In contradiction to his certainty that the end of Hitler and Stalin was an immediate prospect, he expressed another possible perspective, a pessimistic one, in his *USSR in War,* also written in 1939. It startled even his own supporters:

> The historical alternative, carried to the end, is as follows: Either the Stalin regime is an abhorrent relapse in the process of transforming bourgeois society into a Socialist society, or the Stalin regime is the first stage of a new exploiting society. If the second prognosis proves to be correct, then, of course, the bureaucracy will become a new exploiting class. However onerous the second perspective may be, if the world proletariat should actually prove incapable of fulfilling the mission placed upon it by the course of development, nothing else would remain except to recognize that the Socialist program, based on the internal contradictions of capitalist society, ends as a utopia. It is absolutely self-evident that a new "minimum" program would be required for the defense of the interests of the slaves of the totalitarian bureaucratic society. . . . Have we entered the epoch of social revolution and Socialist society, or, on the contrary, the epoch of the declining society of totalitarian bureaucracy? . . . It is absolutely self-evident that if the international proletariat, as a result of the experience of our entire epoch and the current new war, proves incapable of becoming the master of society, this would signify the foundering of all hope for a Socialist revolution, for it is impossible to expect any other more favorable conditions for it.[9]

There is no doubt that despite his sharp polemics with the Minority in the factional struggle, he was deeply concerned that his optimism might have been unwarranted as far as Russia was concerned. As he wrote in his *Defense of Marxism:*

Either the Stalin state is a transitory formation, a deformation of a worker state in a backward and isolated country, or "bureaucratic collectivism" . . . is a new social formation which is replacing capitalism throughout the world. Who chooses the second alternative admits, openly or silently, that all revolutionary potentialities of the world proletariat are exhausted, that the Socialist movement is bankrupt, and that the old capitalism is transforming itself into "bureaucratic collectivism" with a new exploiting class.[10]

Of especial interest here is that Trotsky, in acknowledging the possibility of a new social formation, does so for the first time in the dispute. What if there is no proletarian victory as a result of the war?

There remains another alternative: the further decay of monopoly capitalism, its further fusion with the state and the replacement of democracy wherever it still remained by a totalitarian regime. . . . An analogous result might occur in the event that the proletariat of advanced capitalist countries, having conquered power, should prove incapable of holding it and surrender it, as in the USSR, to a privileged bureaucracy. Then we would be compelled to acknowledge that the reason for the bureaucratic relapse is rooted not in the backwardness of the country and not in the imperialist environment but in the congenital incapacity of the proletariat to become a ruling class. Then it would be necessary in retrospect to establish that in its fundamental traits the present USSR was the precursor of a new exploiting regime on an international scale.[11]

Trotsky was saying, in contrast to almost all of his writings from *The Revolution Betrayed* on, that a third alternative to capitalism and socialism was possible. He also raised the possibility that Marx's prophecy about the evolution of capitalism might well be in error. When these lines were written by him, they came as a total surprise to his supporters.

Trotsky never developed these "pessimistic" views any further, as he continued to struggle against the Minority and the Workers' Party as though no alternatives to "the degenerated workers' state" were real. Aside from Natalia Sedova's personal statement to me that at the time of his assassination Trotsky was reconsidering the Russian Question, nothing of such a nature was ever communicated publicly or privately to anyone.

*   *   *

The post-war world has seen some very unexpected changes. Most unexpected of all, not only to Socialists but to the leaders of Western capitalism, was the liquidation of the imperialist empires in the colonial world and the creation of new countries in Asia, Africa, and other parts of the world. Despite the forecast of a severe post-war economic crisis throughout the capitalist world, it expanded and prospered, with the rise of Japan and West Germany as the most outstanding expressions of that development.

Along with this development in the West, however, there was an expansion of the Stalinist states in Eastern Europe, Central America, and Africa. Moreover, China was refashioned as a Maoist–Stalinist nation. Characteristic of these states, aside from the poor economic conditions in all of them, is that they are all to one degree or another *one-party states,* totalitarian in character. They have not fulfilled Marx's expectation of a socialism based on advanced capitalist industrial society. Indeed, many of the new states have been formed in economically backward peasant countries, some with one-crop agricultures.

In Western Europe there was a post-war revival of Social Democracy. Unless he changed his contemptuous views of this movement, a position he adopted with his late conversion to Bolshevism, Trotsky would have had difficulty tolerating this unexpected development. The surge of the working masses in Europe and the United States was in a *democratic* direction. They were a powerful force for social progress, reacting sharply to the dictatorships of the thirties and forties that brought nothing but chaos and destruction to the world.

The only prediction that Trotsky made that came true was the tragic extermination of millions of European Jews by German fascism and its war allies. Since he did not believe an independent nation of Jews was possible except under socialism, he did not and could not foresee the post-war creation of the state of Israel by Zionist forces. Israel was born of a mass migration of Jews Trotsky thought impossible.

The Tragedy of Trotsky

Trotsky was undoubtedly one of the most tragic political figures of our century. Yet more than fifty years after his assassination, he remains a "living" historical figure in many parts of the world. Joel Carmichael writes in "The Marxist Hall of Mirrors" that

> the interest in him is undeniable; it even seems to grow. His name *stands* for something—a little vague no doubt. . . . Trotsky is certainly a central hero of history to many—the only Marxist popular with non-Marxists during the thirties. . . .[12]

To many he is a romantic hero: the man of the Revolution, the creator of the Red Army he led with confidence, skill, and distinction—and the victim of a brutal dictatorship that expunged his name from the histories of the country he did so much to create. Robert Wistrich, too, believed that Trotsky's enormous contributions to his party and country served him little. In *Trotsky, Fate of a Revolutionary,* he wrote:

> As a revolutionary politician, his undeniable merits were long buried by a mountain of slander which sought to efface entirely his decisive role in the creation of Soviet Russia.
>
>   The ghost of the murdered Trotsky would appear to be very much alive in the minds of a leadership that after sixty years of absolute power still fears to rehabilitate one of its founding-fathers.[13]

There is no doubt that, as Wistrich writes, "the mystique of Trotskyism derives in large part from the charisma of its founding figure." Trotsky, however, was unable to build a movement after his expulsion from the Soviet Union, just as he had been unable to do so in the years between 1903 and 1917. He was a man of the pen and the sword; the patient, grinding, prosaic requirements in building a party were unsuitable to his temperament and skills. Carmichael writes that

> in overestimating ideas, in rationalizing his refusal to "stoop," "deign," and "demean" himself, [Trotsky] was evading the unmistakable fact that he was simply incapable of navigating in the protean relationships of a large organization. While capable of expressing with mystical conviction the generalizations of Marxism, he was blind to the real-life interests of his opponents, who exploited such generalizations, in order to make them dovetail with their private ambitions.
>
>   Trotsky despised intrigue to the point of incomprehension. . . . His seeming obtuseness was no doubt another rationalization of his ineptitude in personal relationships.[14]

Two things should be emphasized again regarding this last stage of Trotsky's life:

One, apart from the few years he spent in the Bolshevik Party, half of those in factional conflict, he never belonged to a mass party with authentic social power. His role in Social Democracy after 1905, after Russia's first democratic revolution, were years spent in exile and in European parties, with spokesmen and other leaders of the International. In those years he functioned alone as a writer and speaker.

Two, as a leader, before and after the October Revolution, he never surrounded himself with a large circle of political friends whose devotion to him would withstand the harsh blows from his enemies. He had very few personal friends, despite his more than forty years in the Russian and world Socialist movements. Only Christian Rakovsky and Adolphe Joffe could claim personal friendship of an intimate kind with Trotsky. There was always a measure of stiffness in Trotsky's relations with people. Even with close and loyal followers, he never went beyond a given point set by him.

After the Revolution and the Civil War, for example, there was a period of relaxation in the new state. The Party cadre settled into an active social life, accompanied by a great deal of drinking. Trotsky described his relation to this socialization:

> If I took no part in the amusements that were becoming more and more common in the lives of the new governing stratum, it was not for moral reasons, but because I hated to inflict such boredom on myself. The visiting at each other's homes, the assiduous attendance at the ballet, the drinking parties at which people who were absent were pulled to pieces, had no attraction for me. The new ruling group felt that I did not fit in with this way of living, and they did not even try to win me over. . . .
>
> I am here limiting myself to the psychological aspect of the matter and disregarding its social base, the changes in the anatomy of the revolutionary society. . . .
>
> The out-and-out philistine, ignorant, and simply stupid baiting of the theory of permanent revolution grew from just these psychological sources. Gossiping over a bottle of wine or returning from the ballet, one smug official would say to another: "He can think of nothing but permanent revolution." The accusations of unsociability, of individualism, of aristocratism, were closely connected with this particular mood. . . .[15]

Over the years, when time permitted, and in a very limited way, he wrote about other aspects of life; he had, after all, a deep interest in literature and the arts. He loved to hunt and fish; in his Mexican exile he liked to gather cacti; and he cared for his pets with great tenderness. He was always most aware and concerned with the physical welfare of his family, his political friends, and followers. Political disputes and differences, however, even of the most temporary nature, often resulted in an end to any relationship he may have had with a disputant. He broke with the noted French Socialist Alfred Rosmer, a founder and leader of the early French Trotskyist movement with whom he was extremely close, both politically and personally, in a temporary dispute over a volatile and adventuristic French Trotskyist, Raymond Molinier, a man of limited ability. A political dispute with Andrés Nin, a popular leader of Spanish Trotskyism and an important figure in the Communist International, a close political friend for years, led to a termination of their relations. In almost every case, political differences, major or minor, would end Trotsky's relations with erstwhile comrades.

*   *   *

Not many leaders could have survived the political and personal persecution Trotsky underwent. After his deportation from Russia in 1929, his exile was a continuous trek from country to country. His family in Russia was destroyed, as were many of his political followers. His closest coworker in Europe, his son Leon Sedov, was murdered by Stalin's agents. Neither he nor Natalia lived to know they had a granddaughter, Yulia, born to their son Sergei, with whom they lost all contact when he was sent to the gulag; Stalin murdered him. Personal secretaries were assassinated one by one; few doubted that Stalin's secret police were roaming freely around the world and were guilty of these crimes. But Trotsky's revolutionary zeal gave him strength. He did not feel alone, for even though his movement was small, his confidence in an ultimate victory over Stalinism was overriding.

Trotsky was an uncommon Bolshevik. He stood out over almost all of the Bolshevik leadership, who, for that very reason, felt envy and antagonism toward him. His wide-ranging interests, which included a concern for literature and the arts under the new regime, were noted by many historians and political writers. Knei-Paz, for example, observes that

> Trotsky, it needs hardly reminding, was a political animal *par excellence* and his writings, like his life, were devoted to politics. Yet he was amongst the least narrow-minded of the Russian revolutionaries: His intellectual curiosity was boundless, his interest wide and varied, and his attitude to politics never so crude as to see in it the complete essence of human life and endeavor.[16]

This open-mindedness, while in contrast with the rigidity of the Marxism he espoused, expressed itself in his love, respect, and deep appreciation of literature and the arts. As Knei-Paz wrote of *Literature and Revolution,* "whatever one thought of its literary opinions," the book is "one of Trotsky's most fascinating works."[17]

One can understand Trotsky's revulsion to the Stalin regime's treatment of writers and artists, of literature and the arts. In the May–July 1939 issue of the *Russian Bulletin,* Trotsky savaged Soviet culture:

It is impossible to read Soviet verse and prose without physical disgust, mixed with horror, or to look at reproductions of paintings and sculptures in which functionaries armed with pens, brushes, and scissors, under the supervision of functionaries with Mausers, glorify the "great" and "brilliant" leaders, who are actually devoid of the least spark of genius or greatness. The art of the Stalinist period will go down as the most concrete expression of the profound decline of the proletarian revolution.[18]

*   *   *

Trotsky did not become a Socialist because of his own class position in society. He was not an industrial worker driven to rebellion by exploitation and oppression. Trotsky became a Socialist and a Marxist by intellectual conviction and reason. In *Three Who Made a Revolution,* Bertram D. Wolfe quotes from a writing by Trotsky in Prinkipo in 1929 on his political evolution:

The feeling of the supremacy of the general over the particular became an integral part of my literary and political work. The dull empiricism, the unashamed, cringing worship of the fact, which is so often only imaginary and falsely interpreted at that, were odious to me. Beyond the facts I looked for laws. Naturally, this led me more than once into hasty and incorrect generalizations, especially in my younger years when my knowledge—book-acquired, and my experience in life—were still inadequate. But in every sphere, barring none, I felt that I could move and act only when I held in my hand the thread of the general. The social-revolutionary radicalism which has become the permanent pivot for my whole inner life grew out of this intellectual enmity toward the striving for petty ends, toward out-and-out pragmatism, and toward all that is ideologically without form and theoretically ungeneralized.[19]

Wolfe points out that this approach was different from Lenin's, who repeatedly stressed that "the truth is always and everywhere concrete." Wolfe adds that for Trotsky socialism was the "effort to rationalize life, that is, transform it according to the dictates of reason. . . . It is only socialism that has set itself the task of embracing reason and subjecting all the activities of man to it." The strong element of faith is present here, too.

To be sure, faith was a driving element in Trotsky's life. Just as in his youth he considered himself an optimist who did not believe that "human horrors, murder, starvation, and racial hatred" would be permanent features of human life, so to the very end, when the Bolshevik world destroyed him, he continued to believe in his dream of humankind's redemption and its glorious future. In his "Testament," written in February, 1940 he said of himself:

> I shall die a proletarian revolutionist, a Marxist, a dialectical materialist, and, consequently, an irreconcilable atheist. My faith in the Communist future of mankind is no less ardent, indeed it is firmer today than it was in the days of my youth. . . .
> Life is beautiful. Let the future generations cleanse it of all evil, oppression and violence, and enjoy it to the full. . . . Whatever may be the circumstances of my death, I shall die with unshaken faith in the Communist future.[20]

Long before he wrote this, in *Literature and Revolution* he wrote of the future with a lyricism a whole generation of young Socialists found inspiring. A utopian thread runs through this vision of future man, but there is no doubt he believed in it strongly. As he wrote in the final paragraph of the book:

> It is difficult to predict the extent of self-government which the man of the future may reach or the heights to which he may carry his technique. Social construction and psycho-physical self-education will become two aspects of one and the same process. All the arts—literature, drama, painting, music, and architecture will lend this process beautiful form. More correctly, the skill in which the cultural and self-education of Communist man will be enclosed, will develop all the vital elements of contemporary art to the highest point. Man will become immeasurably stronger, wiser, and subtler; his body will become more harmonized, his movements more rhythmic, his voice more musical. The forms of life will become dynamically dramatic. The average human type will rise to the heights of an Aristotle, a Goethe, or a Marx. And above this ridge new peaks wlll rise.[21]

The idealization of man in the utopian terms employed by Trotsky reflected the great faith he had in the future. How, then, could this man of faith have written "no one can be right against the Party" or "the Party is always right"?

A man of Trotsky's innate feelings of social justice and a utopian overview of mankind and its future could have thrived best only in democratic society. Once, Trotsky knew this. He had simply forgotten it in the fire of the revolution to which his temper was attuned. N. N. Sukhanov, the great historian of the Russian Revolution, said that Trotsky could not do without Lenin, but also that Lenin could not do without Trotsky. Unfortunately, this was true. They were "monumental partners." The Soviet

Union is the creation of this monumental partnership, and Trotsky must share responsibility with Lenin for the rise of Stalin and Stalinism.

Notes

1. *The Founding Conference of the Fourth International,* p. 15.
2. *Writings,* 1939–1940.
3. *Writings,* 1939–1940.
4. *Writings,* 1939–1940.
5. "Imperialist War," in *Writings,* 1939–1940, p. 183.
6. Fourth International, *For the Defense of the USSR,* p. 231.
7. *Writings,* Supplement II, p. 847.
8. *Writings,* Supplement II, p. 847.
9. *The New International,* November 1939, p. 327.
10. *Defense of Marxism,* p. 1.
11. *Defense of Marxism,* p. 9.
12. Carmichael, "Marxist Hall of Mirrors."
13. Wistrich, pp. 210–211.
14. Carmichael, *Trotsky,* p. 307.
15. *My Life,* pp. 504–505.
16. Knei-Paz, pp. 445, 447.
17. Knei-Paz, p. 469.
18. Quoted in *The Bulletin of the Opposition,* Russian edition, May–July 1939, p. 8.
19. Wolfe, *Three Who Made a Revolution,* p. 193.
20. *Trotsky's Diary in Exile,* 1935, p. 165.
21. Trotsky, *Literature and Revolution,* p. 256.

Bibliography

Abramovitch, Rafael. *The Soviet Revolution*. New York: International Universities Press, Inc., 1962.

Alexander, Robert. *The Right Opposition: The Lovestoneites and the International Communist Opposition of the 1930s*. Westport, Conn.: Greenwood, 1981.

Alliluyeva, Svetlana. *Twenty Letters to a Friend*. Priscilla J. McMillan, trans. New York: Harper and Row, 1967.

Antonov-Ovseyenko, A. V. *The Time of Stalin: Portrait of a Tyranny*. New York: Harper and Row, 1981.

Arendt, Hannah. *The Origins of Totalitarianism*. 1958. Reprint. New York: Harcourt Brace Jovanovich, 1973.

Balabanoff, Angelina. *My Life as a Rebel*. 1938. Reprint. Westport, Conn.: Greenwood, 1968.

Barron, John. *The KGB Today: The Hidden Land*. New York: Readers Digest Press, 1983.

Beer, Max. *A History of International Socialism*. New York: Macmillan Co., 1935.

Bell, Daniel. *The End of Ideology*. New York: The Free Press, 1962.

———. "The Strange Tale of Bruno R.," in *The New Leader,* September 28, 1959.

Berlin, Isaiah. *Karl Marx: His Life and Environment*. New York: Oxford University Press, 1959.

Bernstein, Eduard. *Evolutionary Socialism: A Criticism and Affirmation*. London: Schocken, 1899.

Borkenau, Franz. *The Communist International*. London: Faber, 1938.

Braunthal, Julius. *History of the International: World Socialism Nineteen Forty-Three to Nineteen Sixty-Eight*. 2 volumes. New York: Westview Press, 1967.

Burnham, James. *The Managerial Revolution*. Bloomington, Ind.: Indiana University Press, 1962.

Carmichael, Joel. *Leon Trotsky: An Appreciation of His Life.* London: n.p., 1975.

Carr, Edward H. *The Bolshevik Revolution, Nineteen Seventeen to Nineteen Twenty-One.* Harmondsworth, England: Penguin Books, Ltd., 1966.

————. *Socialism in One Country.* Volumes 5–7 of *A History of Soviet Russia.* New York: Macmillan, 1972.

————. *The Twilight of the Comintern.* New York: Pantheon Books, 1982.

Chamberlin, William. *The Russian Revolution, Nineteen Seventeen to Nineteen Twenty-One.* New York, n.p., 1965.

Ciliga, Anton. *The Russian Enigma.* Ferdnand G. Renier and Anne Cliff, trans. 1940. Reprint. Westport, Conn.: Hyperion, 1973.

Cohen, Stephen F. *Bukharin and the Bolshevik Revolution: A Political Biography, 1888–1938.* New York: Oxford University Press, 1973.

Conquest, Robert. *The Great Terror: Stalin's Purges of the Thirties.* London: Macmillan, 1971.

————. *Harvest of Sorrow: Soviet Collectivization and the Terror-Famine.* New York: Oxford University Press, 1986.

————. *V. I. Lenin.* New York: Viking Press, 1972.

Crossman, Richard, ed. *The God That Failed.* Salem, N.H.: Arno, 1949.

Dan, Theodore. *Origin of Bolshevism.* London: n.p., 1964.

Day, Richard. *Leon Trotsky and the Politics of Economic Isolation.* Cambridge, Mass.: Cambridge University Press, 1973.

Dewey, John. *The Later Works of John Dewey.* Carbondale, Ill.: Southern Illinois University Press, 1987.

Deutscher, Isaac. *The Prophet Armed: Trotsky, 1879–1921.* New York: Oxford University Press, 1954.

————. *The Prophet Unarmed: Trotsky, 1921–1929.* New York: Oxford University Press, 1959.

————. *The Prophet Outcast: Trotsky, 1929–1940.* New York: Oxford University Press, 1963.

————. *Stalin: A Political Biography.* New York: Oxford University Press, 1967.

————. *Ironies of History.* New York, 1966.

Djilas, Milovan. *The New Class: An Analysis of the Communist System.* 1957. Reprint. New York: Harcourt Brace Jovanovich, 1982.

Draper, Theodore. *American Communism and Soviet Russia.* New York: Octagon, 1960.

————. *The Roots of American Communism.* New York: Octagon, 1957.

Eastman, Max. *Since Lenin Died.* 1925. Reprint. Westport, Conn.: Hyperion, 1973.

————. *Heroes I Have Known.*

Ehrenburg, Ilya. *Memoirs: 1921–41.* Cleveland and New York: The World Publishing Co., 1963.

Fenwick, J. "The Mysterious Bruno R.," in *The New International,* September 1948.

Fischer, Ruth. *Stalin and German Communism: A Study in the Origins of the State Party.* Cambridge, Mass.: Cambridge University Press, 1948.

Frolich, Paul. *Rosa Luxemburg.* 1940. Reprint. New York: Gordon Press, 1987.

Ganken, Olga H., and Harold H. Fischer. *The Bolsheviks and the World War: The Origins of the Third International.* Stanford, Calif.: Stanford University Press, 1940.

Gay, Peter. *The Dilemma of Democratic Socialism: Edward Bernstein's Challenge to Marx.* 1952. Reprint. New York: Octagon, 1970.

Glotzer, Albert. *The Case of Leon Trotsky: Verbatim Report.* London: Martin Secker and Warburg, Ltd., 1937.

Hayward, Max, and Leopold Labedz, eds. *Literature and Revolution in Soviet Russia.* 1963. Reprint. Westport, Conn.: Greenwood, 1976.

Hook, Sydney. *From Hegel to Marx: Studies in the Intellectual Development of Karl Marx.* Ann Arbor, Mich.: University of Michigan Press, 1960.

———. *The Hero in History: A Study in Limitation and Possibility.* New York: Beacon Press, 1955.

———, ed. *John Dewey: Philosopher of Science and Freedom.* 1950. Reprint. Westport, Conn.: Greenwood, 1976.

———. *Out of Step: An Unquiet Life in the Twentieth Century.* New York: Harper and Row, 1987.

———. *Revolution Reform and Social Justice: Studies in the Theory and Practice of Marxism.* New York: New York University Press, 1975.

———. *Toward an Understanding of Karl Marx.* New York: The John Day Company, 1933.

Howe, Irving. *Leon Trotsky.* New York: Viking, 1979.

Johnpoll, Bernard K., and Harvey Klehr, eds. *Biographical Dictionary of the American Left.* Westport, Conn.: Greenwood, 1986.

Johnson, Paul. *A History of the Jews.* New York: Harper and Row, 1987.

Kapp, Yvonne. *Eleanor Marx: Family Life (1855–1883)* vol. I and *The Crowded Years, 1884–1898,* vol. II. Woodstock, N.Y.: Beekman Publishers, 1972, 1976.

Kautsky, Karl. *The Dictatorship of the Proletariat.* Ann Arbor, Mich.: University of Michigan Press, 1964.

———. *Terrorism and Communism.* 1920. Reprint. Wesptort, Conn.: Hyperion, 1973.

Khrushchev, Nikita S. *Khrushchev Remembers.* Strobe Talbot, ed. and trans. Boston: Little, Brown, 1970.

Klehr, Harvey. *The Heyday of American Communism: The Depression Decade.* New York: Basic Books, 1984.

Knei-Paz, Baruch. *The Social and Political Thought of Leon Trotsky.* New York: Oxford University Press, 1978.

Koestler, Arthur. *Darkness at Noon.* New York: Macmillan, 1941.

Kolakowski, Leszek. *Main Currents of Marxism: The Founders, The Golden Age, The Breakdown.* Three volumes. New York: Oxford University Press, 1978.

Labedz, Leopold. *Revisionism: Essays on the History of Marxist Ideas.* 1962. Reprint. Salem, N.H.: Arno, 1987.

Lenin, V. I. *Collected Works.* Moscow: Progress Publishers, 1947.

――――. *Lenin on the Jewish Question.* (Pamphlet) 1934. Reprint. Hyman Lumer, ed. New York: International Publishing Co., 1974.

――――. *Selected Works.* Moscow: Progress Publishers, 1947.

Levine, Isaac Don. *The Mind of an Assassin.* New York: Signet, 1954.

Lichtheim, George. *Marxism in Modern France.* New York: Columbia University Press, 1961.

――――. *Collected Essays.* New York: Viking Press, 1973.

Lunacharsky, A. V. *Revolutionary Silhouettes.* Moscow: Progress Publishers, n.d.

Luxemburg, Rosa. *The Future of the Soviet System.*

――――. *The Russian Revolution and Leninism and Marxism?* Ann Arbor, Mich.: University of Michigan Press, 1961.

Maksudov, L. *Ideological Struggle Today.* New York: State Mutual Books, 1982.

Martov, J. *The State and the Socialist Revolution.* New York: n.p., 1938.

Marx, Karl, and Frederich Engels. *The Communist Manifesto.* Riazanov edition. 1930. Reprint. New York: Russell, 1963.

――――. *Selected Correspondence.* New York: n.p., 1942.

――――. *Selected Works.* Two volumes. New York: International Publishing Co., 1933.

Medvedev, Roy. *All Stalin's Men.* New York: Doubleday, 1984.

――――. *Let History Judge: The Origins and Consequences of Stalinism.* David Joravsky and Georges Haupt, eds. New York: Knopf, 1971.

――――. *Nicolai Bukharin: The Last Years.* A. D. Briggs, trans. New York: W. W. Norton, 1980.

――――. *Stalin and Stalinism.* London: Oxford University Press, 1979.

Nedava, Joseph. *Trotsky and the Jews.* Philadelphia: n.p., 1972.

Nettl, J. P. *Rosa Luxemburg.* Two volumes. London: n.p., 1966.

Nicolaevsky, Boris. *Power and the Soviet Elite: "The Letter of An Old Bolshevik" and Other Essays.* Janet P. Zagoria, ed. 1965. Reprint. Ann Arbor, Mich.: University of Michigan Press, 1975.

Nove, Alex. *Was Stalin Necessary?* London: n.p., 1964.

Padover, Saul, ed. *The Letters of Karl Marx.* Englewood Cliffs, N.J.: Prentice Hall, 1979.

Rizzi, Bruno. *The Bureaucratization of the World.* Adam Westoby, trans. New York: The Free Press, 1985.

Samuel, Maurice. *Blood Accusation.* New York: Alfred A. Knopf, 1966.

Schapiro, Leonard. *The Communist Party of the Soviet Union.* New York: Random House, 1959.

Serge, Victor. *Memoirs of a Revolutionary, 1901-1949.* Peter Sedgwick, trans. New York: Writers and Readers Publishers, Inc., 1963.

――――. *Russia Twenty Years Later.* 1937. Reprint. Westport, Conn.: Hyperion, 1973.

Serge, Victor, and Natalia Sedova Trotsky. *The Life and Death of Leon Trotsky.* New York: Basic Books, 1975.

Shachtman, Max. *The Struggle for the New Course.* Bound with *The New Course* by Leon Trotsky. Ann Arbor, Mich.: University of Michigan Press, 1963.

———. *The Bureaucratic Revolution.* New York: The Donald Press, 1962.

———. *Behind the Moscow Frame-up Trials.*

Shipler, David. *Russia: Broken Idols, Solemn Dreams.* New York: Times Books, 1983.

Shub, David. *Lenin.* Garden City, N.Y.: n.p., 1948.

Solzhenitsyn, Alexander. *The Gulag Archipelago, One, Parts I and II.* Thomas P. Whitney, trans. New York: Harper and Row, 1974.

Souvarine, Boris. *Stalin: A Critical Survey of Bolshevism.* 1939. Reprint. Salem, N.H.: Arno, 1972.

Stalin, Joseph. *Problems of Leninism.* New York: International Publishers, 1934.

Sukhanov, N. N. *The Russian Revolution, 1917.* Joel Carmichael, ed. New York: Oxford University Press, 1955.

Tolstoy, Nicolai. *Stalin's Secret War.*

Trotsky, Leon. *History of the Russian Revolution.* New York: Anchor Foundation, 1980.

———. *In Defense of Marxism.* New York: Pathfinder Press, 1973.

———. *Leon Trotsky on the Jewish Question.* New York: Pathfinder Press, 1987.

———. *Literature and Revolution.* New York: Russell and Russell, 1957.

———. *My Life: Authorized Translation and Edition.* Magnolia, Mass.: Peter Smith Publishing, 1977.

———. *Portraits, Political and Personal.* George Breitman and George Saunders, eds. New York: Pathfinder Press, 1977.

———. *The Real Situation in Russia.* New York: Harcourt, Brace, and Co., 1928.

———. *The Revolution Betrayed: What is the Soviet Union and Where is it Going?* New revised edition. Max Eastman, trans. New York: Pathfinder Press, 1973.

———. *Stalin: An Appraisal of the Man and His Influences.* Harper and Row, 1941.

———. *The Stalin School of Falsification.* George Saunders, trans. New York: Pathfinder Press, 1980.

———. *Terrorism and Communism: A Reply to Karl Kautsky.* 1961. Reprint. Westport, Conn.: Greenwood, 1986.

———. *Trotsky's Diary in Exile, 1935.* New York: Atheneum, 1964.

———. *What Next? Vital Questions for the German Proletariat.* New York: Pioneer Publishers, 1932.

———. *Writings of Leon Trotsky, 1929–1940.* Twelve Volumes. George Breitman and Sarah Lovell, eds. Various trans. New York: Pathfinder Press, 1947–1978.

Tucker, Robert, ed. *Stalinism: Essays in Historical Interpretation.* New York: W. W. Norton, 1977.

Tucker, Robert. *Stalin as Revolutionary, 1879–1929: A Study in History and Personality.* New York: W. W. Norton, 1973.

———. *The Soviet Political Mind.* New York: W. W. Norton, 1972.

Ulam, Adam. *The Bolsheviks.* New York: Macmillan, 1965.
———. *Stalin: The Man and His Era.* New York: Beacon Press, 1972.

Valentinov, Nicolay (Volski). *Encounter with Lenin.* New York: Liberal Social Science, 1968.
———. *The Early Youth of Lenin.* Ann Arbor, Mich.: University of Michigan Press, 1969.
Van Heijenoort, Jean. *With Trotsky in Exile from Prinkipo to Coyoacan.* Cambridge, Mass.: Harvard University Press, 1978.

Weeks, Albert L. *The First Bolshevik: A Political Biography of Peter Tkachev.* New York: New York University Press, 1968.
Wilson, Edmund. *To the Finland Station: A Study in the Writing and Acting of History.* 1940. Reprint. New York: Doubleday, 1953.
Wistrich, Robert. *Trotsky: Fate of a Revolutionary.* New Haven, Conn.: Yale University Press, 1957.
———. *Revolutionary Jews from Marx to Trotsky.* New York: Barnes and Noble Books, 1976.
Wittfogel, Karl A. *Oriental Despotism.* New Haven, Conn.: Yale University Press, 1957.
Wolfe, Bertram D. *The Fabulous Life of Diego Rivera.* New York: Stein and Day, 1969.
———. *A Life in Two Centuries.* New York: Stein and Day, 1981.
———. *Revolution and Reality: Essays on the Origin of the Soviet System.* Chapel Hill, N.C.: University of North Carolina Press, 1981.
———. *Three Who Made a Revolution.* 1948. Reprint. New York: Dell, 1964.
Wood, Neal. *Communism and British Intellectuals.* New York: Columbia University University Press, 1959.

Index

Abern, Martin, 21, 23, 24, 26n, 28, 69, 306n
Abramowitz, Rafael, 241
Adler, Alfred, 78
Adler, Friedrich, 239
Adler, Raisa, 78
AFL-CIO, 25n, 60
Ageloff, Ruth, 256
Ageloff, Sylvia, 293
Akselrod, Yulia (Sergei Sedov's daughter), 320
Alexander II, 10
Alliluyeva, Svetlana (Khrushchev's daughter), 224, 225, 226
All Stalin's Men, 228
Amalgamated Clothing Workers, 12
American Committee for the Defense of Leon Trotsky (the Committee), 235, 238, 253, 255
American Communist Party (American Workers' Party, 1921–1925), 9, 15, 16, 17, 18, 19, 23, 25n, 26n, 27n, 67, 69, 154, 160, 174n, 179, 180, 188, 201, 237, 255, 257, 267, 272, 283, 306n
American Trotskyism, Trotskyists, 20, 24, 27n, 80
anti-Semitism, 208–232; and Karl Marx, 209–210; and Plekhanov, 211, 216, 221; and the Soviet Union, 141, 219–224, 227, 228; and Stalin, 167, 217–218, 219, 220, 221–228
Antonov-Ovsyenko, Anton, 166, 170, 171, 173
April Theses, 145
Armand, Inessa, 118
Axelrod, Paul, 87, 90, 94, 96, 100, 105, 125, 212, 308n

Balabanoff, Angelica, 166
Balham Group, 54–55
baseball, 11
Bates, Ernest Sutherland, 238
Bauer, Erwin (Ackerknecht), 182, 186, 191, 205n
Beals, Carleton, 239, 266–270; disrupts Dewey Commission, 266–270; resigns, 268
Beech, Richard, 55, 81
Beilis trial, 212–213
Benson, Allan, 14

Bernick, Paul, 305n
Bloc of Four (Declaration of Four), 179, 180, 207n
Block, Henry, 267
Blum, Leon, 241
Bolshevik, Bolshevism, 9, 14, 15, 18, 20, 21, 24, 25n, 34, 39, 57, 58, 70, 74, 80, 92, 93–94, 95, 97, 99, 100–111, 113, 115, 117, 118, 121, 122, 124, 126, 129, 130–131, 132, 135–138, 143n, 146, 148, 150, 157, 158, 162, 163, 164, 165, 166, 169, 173, 179, 208, 209, 212, 216, 217, 223, 235, 239, 240, 243, 245, 250, 283, 292, 311, 317, 320, 322
Bolshevik Party, 19, 28, 74, 79, 99, 117, 119–120, 121, 123, 125, 133, 134, 145, 159, 170, 178, 206n, 221, 248, 295, 297
Bolshevik Revolution, 121–122, 222. See also October Revolution, Russian Revolution
Borodin, General M., 266, 268, 270
Brandt, Willy, 192–198, 203
Brecht, Bertolt, 186
Breitscheid, Rudoph, 62, 63, 177
Breton, André, 276, 281n
British Communist Party, 30, 43, 81, 82
Bronstein. See Trotsky
Broun, Heywood, 254
Browder, Earl, 19, 24, 174n
Browner, Fred (Raphael), 189, 195
Bruno R. See Rizzi, Bruno
Buckley, William, F., 305n
Bukharin, Nicholai, 20, 21, 24, 25n, 70, 120, 124, 133, 149, 156, 162, 164, 166, 167, 169, 217, 218, 235, 236, 245, 246, 247, 248; weeps, 36; death, 169
Bulletin of the Russian Opposition.

See Russian Bulletin
Bund, the (General Jewish Workers' Union-Jewish Labor Bund) 13, 87, 92, 94, 96, 114, 116, 118, 119, 141n, 208, 211, 212, 221
Bureaucratic Revolution, The, 305n, 307n
Burnham, James, 284, 287, 305n, 306n; resigns from Minority, 288, 305n

Cahn, Abraham, 14
Caldwell, Erskine, 254
Cannon, James P., 17, 18, 21, 22, 24, 25n, 26n, 27n, 69, 70, 84n, 257, 285, 287–288, 311
Cardenas, Lazaro, 237–238, 260
Carmichael, Joel, 56, 65–66, 86n, 166, 172–173, 317, 318
Carr, Edward H., 67, 146; and Trotsky on Nazi Germany, 67
Carter, Joseph (Friedman), 284, 305n, 306n
Case of Leon Trotsky, The, 257, 273
Castle Garden, N.Y., 9
Central Committee, 20, 22, 23, 25n, 26n, 94, 96, 97, 104, 108, 111–118, 146–149, 151, 153, 155, 158–160, 163, 167n, 217, 223, 225, 228, 261, 276, 283
Chamberlain, John, 238, 274
Cherneshevsky, Nicholas 6., 97–98; and his What Is to Be Done, 97, 98
Chicago, 9–11, 14, 17, 23, 24, 85n, 271
Childs, Jack, 26n
Childs, Morris, 26n
Civil War, 16, 123, 125, 146, 147, 172, 260, 261, 319
Cohen, Stephen F., 134, 140, 168–169; and his Bukharin, 168–169
Commission of Inquiry. See Dewey

Commission

Commune Herald, 16

Communist International (Comintern), 17–21, 23, 25n, 26n, 27n, 29, 31, 34, 46, 58, 61–70, 73, 83n, 147–148, 150, 154, 160, 168, 177, 180, 185–187, 189, 191, 197, 200, 204, 205n, 206n, 217, 223, 237, 247, 269, 275, 292, 319, 320

Communist League of America (CLA), 24, 25n, 26n, 27n, 28, 30, 31, 38, 54, 58, 68–69, 82, 180–181, 185, 188–190, 201, 206n, 257, 283, 305n

Communist League of Struggle (CLS), 26n, 184, 188, 189, 194

Communist Manifesto, 95

Communist Party (CP). *See* Russian Communist Party

Connally, Margaret, 55

Conquest, Robert, 101, 127, 136, 170, 250; on Lenin's Marxism, 126–127; on Stalin's Terror, 170, 204n

Constitutional Democratic Party, 119–120

Cowley, Malcolm, 254

Craine, Reva, 305n

Craipeau, Ivan, 182, 194, 205n

Cunea, William, 14

Curtiss, Charles, 277–278

Dan, Theodore, 99, 125, 126

Davies, Joseph, 250

Day, The, 222–223, 224

Debs, Eugene V., 14, 36

Declaration of Four. *See* Bloc of Four

De la Rocque, Casimir (Colonel), 181, 204n

"defense of the Soviet Union," 283

Democratic Centralists, 292

Deutscher, Isaac, 65, 101, 143n, 299–302; believes Stalin completed Trotsky's program, 102, 299; on the Sobolevicius brothers, 79, 80

Dewey Commission (Commission of Inquiry), 46, 74, 84n, 110, 137, 239, 252–254, 255, 257, 258–270, 272, 274, 279, 284, 305n; Stalinist opposition to, 253; summary of findings, 273

Dewey, John, 137, 254, 256, 267, 272; as chairman of Commission, 239, 259, 262, 264, 269, 272, 273–274; Communist attacks on, 254

dictatorship of the proletariat, 58, 127, 197, 261–264

Dimitrov, Georgi, 236

Djilas, Milovan, 301

Dos Passos, John, 238

Draper, Hal, 305n

Dreiser, Theodore, 254

Dreyfus affair, 213. *See also* Beilis trial

Duclos, Jacques, 19

Durant, Will and Ariel, 42

Duranty, Walter, 250, 269

Dzerzhinsky, Felix E., 89, 150, 151, 167n

Eastman, Max, 46, 85n, 160–161, 162–163; translator of Trotsky's *History,* 38, 72

Eisler, Gerhardt and Hans, 186

Eisner, Dorothy (McDonald), 256

Eleanor Marx, 232n

Engels, Friedrich, 32, 42, 56, 91, 92, 95, 98, 99, 100, 123, 126–127, 128, 139, 142n; and emancipation of the working class, 107, 108; on Erfurt program, 107

Erber, Emest, 305n

Erhenburg, Ilya, 248–249

Fabulous Life of Diego Rivera, The, 279
Farrell, James T., 238, 256, 267, 271, 274
February Revolution, 119, 208
Fenwick, James M., 305n
Feuchtwanger, Lion, 186, 250
Fifteenth Party Congress (1927), 163, 164; expulsion of United Opposition from, 164
Fifth Party Congress (1907), 113, 114–116, 160
Finerty, John, 259, 261–265, 274
First International (1893), 95
First Party Congress (1898), 87, 91, 160
First World War. *See* World War I
Fischer, Louis, 250
Fischer, Ruth (Dubois), 184, 186–187, 190, 205n, 206n
Foster-Cannon Faction (Fosterites), 17, 22, 23, 174n
Foster, William Z., 17–19, 24
Fotieva, Lydia, 148, 149
Fourier, Charles, 232n
Fourteenth Party Congress (1926), 159–160, 162
Fourth International, 83n, 179, 191, 197, 199–201, 206n, 260, 278, 286, 288, 300–303, 309, 310–311, 312, 313; defends Soviet Union in World War II, 314; Natalia Sedova resigns from, 304
Fourth Party Congress (1922), 25n, 27n, 46, 111–112, 113, 114
Franck, Jakob, 78
Frank, Pierre, 29, 30, 83n, 182
Frankel, Jan, 34–36, 39, 43, 44, 46–53, 54, 58, 71, 74, 83n, 84n, 172,

271, 279; testifies before Commission, 235, 256, 259, 260
French Communist League, 29, 32, 40, 68, 83n, 181–182, 205n, 305n
French Communist Party, 19, 32, 181
Futuro, 268
Fux, Georges, 192, 194, 198

Geltman, Emanuel, 305n
Gary Steel Strike (1919), 12
George, Mrs. Robert Latham, 256–257, 271
German Communist League, 186
German Communist Party, 59, 64–66, 76, 85n, 177, 184, 186, 205n, 236
German Social Democrats, Democracy, 95, 105–108, 115, 212, 233n, 240
German Socialist Workers' Party (SAP), 178, 179, 185, 192–202, 205n, 207n
Gitlow, Benjamin, 25n
Glanz, Aaron, 223–224
Glotzer, Albert, 9, 10, 11, 13, 15–17, 23, 24, 26n, 28, 34, 35, 41–43, 48–51, 52–54, 56, 58–60, 80–82, 83n, 84n, 85n, 108, 150, 154, 160, 172, 173, 201, 224, 289, 292, 294 304, 306n; first ballot, 14; in Paris, 30–33, 182, 183, 186, 187, 203; meets Trotsky, 36–40; fishing, 44, 45; hunting expedition, 52, and halvah, 46–47; political discussion in Kadikoy 68–78; meets Maria Reese, 184–185; and Weisbord, 188–190; and Youth Conference, 181, 184, 191, 192–198, 199, 200, 202; with Trotsky in Mexico, 256, 259,

271; as Commission court reporter, 235, 255, 257, 259, 266, 271, 271, 272, 275, 276; discussion with Goldman, 306n
Glotzer, Fred, 11, 13, 14
Glotzer, Nate, 12, 13, 15
Glotzer, Sholem, 10
Goldberg, B. Z., 222–223
Goldman, Albert, 259, 260, 264, 283, 306n
Goltsman, E. S., 252
Gorbachev, Mikhail, 136–137, 138, 139, 140, 163–164, 282
Gorky, Maxim, 10, 132
Gould, Nathan, 305n
GPU (early Soviet secret police), 44, 47, 48, 52, 67, 68, 78, 80, 83n, 85n, 86n, 151, 179, 186, 203, 205n, 227, 238, 239, 241, 243, 245, 246, 250, 252, 253, 261–262, 264, 266, 267, 268, 270, 279, 280, 281n, 292, 293, 295, 307n
Great Terror, The, 136, 170, 204n
Green, P. *See* Gusev, Sergei
Groves, Reg, 54, 80, 81
Grylewicz, Anton, 75
Guesde, Jules, 32
Gusev, Sergei, 18

Hallgren, Mauritz, 254
Hart, Schaffner, and Marx, 12
Harte, Sheldon, 292, 293, 307n
Hathaway Clarence, 23–24; and Lenin school, 22
Held, Walter (Heinz Epe), 181, 191, 192–193, 195, 197, 198, 201, 203, 204n
Hellman, Lillian, 254
Helphand, Alexander (Parvus), 91, 110
Heroes I Have Known, 161, 162

Hilferding, Rudolph, 112
Hingley, Ronald, 228
History of the Jews, 232n
History of the Russian Revolution, The, (History), 38, 39, 50, 51, 53, 57, 68, 72, 124
Hitler, Adolf, 51, 57, 58, 59, 62–68, 82, 85n, 86n, 138, 170, 176, 177, 179, 182, 183, 191, 193 196, 215, 220, 224, 229, 231, 236, 237, 251, 265, 282, 286, 292, 294, 310, 313, 314, 315
Hitler–Stalin Pact, 64, 67, 179, 215, 221, 223, 224, 237, 254, 279, 282, 283, 285, 286, 313, 314
Homestead strike, 12
Hook, Sidney, 207n, 238, 274
Hotel Bristol, 252

In Defense of Marxism, 285, 295, 316
Independent Communist Youth, 196
Independent Labor Party, 178–179
Independent Socialist Party (OSP), 178, 179, 190–191, 193, 194, 196, 197, 202, 204, 207n
Industrial Party, 239–240, 242
International Communist League (ICL), 179, 180, 182, 184, 192, 196, 197, 199, 200, 202, 205n, 206n
International Secretariat (IS), 30, 31, 54, 55, 83n, 84n, 181, 182, 190, 191, 192, 200, 201, 202, 203, 204n, 205n, 206n, 218, 277
International Socialist Congress (1893). *See* First International
International Socialist League, 194
International Workers of the World (IWW), 12, 26n, 27n, 259
International Youth Conference, 179, 180–181, 184, 190, 196–198;

opens, 193; police raid, 194; foreigners deported, 195; reconvenes in Brussels, 195
Ironies of History, 300, 301
Iskra (The Spark), 87–88, 90, 91, 94, 96, 99, 104, 105, 122, 125, 212
Isserman, Morris, 19

Jacobins, 105
James, Edwin L., 269
Jellinek, Frank, 269, 270
Jewish Daily Forward, 14, 230, 231
Jewish Group (French League), 30, 39, 40
Jewish Question, 209, 212, 214–215, 222, 224, 228, 230–231
Johnson, Paul, 232n
Joseph Stalin: Man and Legend, 228

Kahlo, Frida (Rivera), 238, 256, 274, 276, 279
Kamenev, Lev (Rosenfeld), 20, 74, 116, 123, 145, 147, 149, 152, 153, 155, 156, 157, 158, 160, 162, 163, 164, 167, 172, 246, 248; and anti-Semitism, 217, 219; trial, 235–236, 238, 240, 243, 248, 250–251
Kamo (Semyon Ter-Petrosyan), 113–114
Kapp, Yvonne, 232n
Kautsky, Karl, 105–106, 112, 124, 127, 131–132, 211, 233n, 244; and his *Terrorism and Communism,* 131
Kerensky, Alexander, 146
Key, The (Germany: The Key to the International Situation), 61, 64, 85n, 86n
KGB, 137
Khrushchev, Nikita, 135, 138, 224–225, 226, 233n, 237, 245, 254,
273, 300, 303
Khrushchev Remembers, 225
Kirov, Sergei, 171, 236, 244–248, 250–251, 280n
Klement, Rudolph, 80, 187, 205n
Kluckhohn, Frank, 266, 267, 269, 270
Kluger, Pearl, 255–256, 257
Knei-Paz, Baruch, 102–103, 121–122, 124, 142n, 166, 214, 232, 320
Kohn, Joseph, 75
Kolakowski, Leszek, 57, 65
Kremlin, 17, 18, 19, 21, 24, 33, 52, 74, 124, 139, 152, 154, 179, 204, 226, 237, 238, 245, 249, 250, 253, 259, 269, 273, 283, 297, 299, 307n, 314
Krizhanovsky, Anton, 90
Kronstadt Rebellion (sailors' rebellion), 131, 155, 260
Krupskaya, Nadezhda, 90, 125, 151, 161, 162; delivers Lenin's Testament, 156
Krutch, Joseph Wood, 238

Lafarge, Paul and Laura (Marx), 32–33
LaFollette, Suzanne, 239, 256, 267, 272, 274
Lamont, Corliss, 254
LaSalle, Ferdinand, 209–210, 214
Lawrence textile strike, 12
Lawson, John Howard, 254
Left Opposition, 21, 30, 31, 51, 54, 72–74, 78, 80–82, 110, 152, 159–162, 166, 167, 172, 177, 200, 205n, 218, 223, 228, 245, 248, 261, 264, 308n; of Germany, 75, 204n
Lenin school, 22, 23, 24
Lenin, Vladimir, 9, 15, 18, 25n, 31,

34, 56, 75, 76, 80, 88, 108–111, 114–118, 126, 133–135, 141, 142n, 147, 148, 154–159, 162, 163, 164, 165, 169, 170, 172, 177, 223, 235, 247, 253, 260, 289, 291, 303, 311, 320, 323; and *Iskra,* 87, 91; meets Trotsky, 90; and second Congress, 92–94; and illegal Third Congress, 96–97; and Cherneshevsky, 97–99; and Tiflis affair, 113–115; and Malinovsky, 79–80, 118; and Bolshevik Revolution, 120–137; and suppression of Mensheviks, Social Revolutionaries, 131–132; and April Theses, 145; and Georgian affair, 148–153; and "bomb" for Stalin, 148–149, 150; and Testament, 73, 151, 156, 160, 161, 162, 163, 173; and anti-Semitism, 211, 216, 217, 220, 221; *On Jewish Question,* 233n; death, 125, 134, 173

Letter to Borodai, 292, 298

Liebknecht House, 75

Life in Two Centuries, A, 161, 275–276, 278

Lovestone Faction (Lovestoneites), 17, 18, 22, 23, 24, 161, 162, 174n, 175n, 205n

Lovestone, Jay, 17, 20, 24, 25n

Lovett, Robert Morse, 254

Ludlow massacre, 12

Lunacharsky, A. V., 94n–95n, 110–111

Luxemburg, Rose, 108, 115, 117, 133, 142n

MacAlpin, Ned, 55, 81

Majority, The, 285, 288, 305n

Makhno, Nestor I., 216

Maksudov, 171

Malamuth, Charles, 219

Malenkov, G. M., 228, 233n, 300

Malinovsky, Roman, 79–80, 118

Malter, Henry, 305n

Mandel, Ernest, 301, 303

Maneho, 232n

Mann, Heinrich, 186

Manutsky, Dimitry, 62

Mark Twain Society, 41

Martov, Julius 87, 92–94, 99, 105–106, 111, 125, 143n, 199, 212

Marx, Eleanor, 210–211

Marx-Engels Institute, 242

Marx, Karl, 32, 42, 56, 89, 91, 92, 95, 99, 100, 107–108, 112, 123, 126–127, 139, 142n, 171, 239, 303, 316, 317, 322; on Jewishness, 210–211, 214, 232n

Marxian League (Riddley-Ram), 30, 31, 54, 55, 56, 58, 81

Maslov, Arkadi (Isaac Tschereminsky), 184, 186–187, 190, 205n

Masses, The, 46

Maze, Jacob, 208

McDonald, John, 256

McKinney, Ernest Rice, 306n

McNeal, Robert H., 301, 302

McWilliams, Carey, 254

Medem, Vladimir, 208

Medved, Filipp, 171

Medvedev, Roy, 134–135, 152–153, 166, 167–168, 169, 171, 228, 242, 244, 280n–281n

Mencken, H. L., 40, 41

Mensheviks, Menshevism, 79, 80, 93–94, 95, 99, 100–102, 105, 109–126, 129–132, 143n, 148, 159, 160, 165, 166, 212, 221, 239, 283, 291; expulsion from Communist Party, 131–132

Menshevik Trial, 240–243
Mercader, Ramon, 9, 270, 279, 292, 307n
Mexican Trotskyist League, 276, 277
Militant, The, 26n, 28, 39, 59, 69, 71, 216, 303
Mill, M. (Pavel Okun), 30, 83n
Minority, The, 84n, 284–288, 293, 295–298, 305n, 316
Minsk Congress. *See* First Party Congress
Mission to Moscow, 250
Moe, Fin, 194, 196, 198, 199
Molinaar, Jan, 196, 197
Molinier, Raymond, 29, 33, 83n, 85n, 182, 320
Molotov Viacheslav, 65, 158, 177, 224, 225, 233n–234n
Montague, Ivan, 82
Morrow, Felix, 255
Moscow Frame-Up Trials (Show Trials), 110, 127, 169, 179, 203, 235–281, 284, 305n, 315
Munzenburg, Willi, 65
Mussolini, Benito, 41, 59, 170, 313
Muste, A. J., 201, 257
My Life, 117–118, 122, 124–126, 143n–144n, 149, 153, 217
Myrtos (Oscar Rosenweig), 30, 31, 32, 68, 83n

Narodniki, 211, 233n
Nation, The, 250, 254
National Reporter, The, 273
National Review, The, 305n
Naville, Pierre, 29, 30, 32, 80, 83n
Nazi, Nazism (German National Socialists), 57, 58, 60–64, 75, 76, 86n, 138, 176, 177, 183, 204n, 206n, 216, 222, 231, 236–237, 239, 253, 282, 312

Nedava, Joseph, 57, 67, 167, 214, 233n
Neue Zeit, Die, 106, 213
New Class, The, 301
"New Course, The," 154, 157, 166
New York Times, 161, 250, 266, 267, 269
Nicholas II, 28, 114, 119, 212, 213, 216
Niebuhr, Reinhold, 238
Nin, Andre, 206n, 320
Nogin, V. P., 116, 117
Norwegian Labor Party (NAP), 196–198
Novack, George, 255–256, 257, 272, 303

October Revolution, 34, 129, 130, 133, 146, 147, 158, 216, 219, 220, 235, 259, 274, 295, 296, 300, 314, 319
Opposition Bloc. *See* United Opposition Bloc
Ording, Aake, 194, 196–198
Ordzhonikidze, Serge, 149, 150, 167n
Origins of Bolshevism, The, 99–100
OSP. *See* Independent Socialist Party

Pan-American Commission, 276–277
Pares, Sir Bernard, 250
Parker, Dorothy, 254
Pasha, Kemal, 84n
Pashukanis, E. B., 240
Pavlov, Peter, 211
Pere Lachaise cemetery, 31–32, 39
permanent revolution, 91, 112, 121, 319; theory of, 92
Pero (the Pen), 90. *See also* Trotsky
Petrograd (Petersburg) Soviet, 103,

109, 121, 145, 158
Pfemfert, Franz, 76–77, 222
Piatakov, Grigori L., 127, 156, 218, 236, 237, 239, 240, 247, 248, 251, 253
Plekhanov, Georgi V., 87, 91, 94, 96–99, 111, 114–116, 117, 118, 124, 308n; and anti-Semitism, 211, 216, 221; and Party split, 118
Politburo, 20, 137, 147, 149, 151, 152, 161, 166, 167, 172, 173, 217, 218, 228, 233n
Potresov, Alexander N., 87, 88, 94
Powers, Charles T., 139
Pravda, 89, 116–118, 154, 155; name stolen by Lenin, 118
Preobrazhensky, Eugene A., 72, 156, 163, 218, 222
Presse, Die, 215
Pritt, D. N., 252
Prophet Armed, The, 143n
Prophet Outcast, The, 300
provisional government, 121, 145, 146, 158
Proudhon, Pierre, 232n

Radek, Karl, 156, 236, 237, 239, 240, 247, 250, 251
Rakovsky, Christian, 161, 162, 218, 295, 308n, 319
Ram, Chandu (Aggrawala), 30, 54, 55, 56, 81
Ramm, Alexandra, 76
Ramzin. *See* Industrial Party
Rappaport, Charles, 126
Red Army, 34, 41, 60, 102, 146, 157, 173, 216, 220, 244, 269, 284, 318
Red Referendum, 62, 75, 177
Reese, Maria, 184–185, 190
Reiss, Ignace, 80
Remmele, Herman, 65, 86n

Revolution Betrayed, The, 130, 132, 163, 264, 286, 294, 296–297, 298, 316
Revolution of 1905, 9, 91, 108–110
Revolutionary Silhouettes, 84n–85n
Revolutionary Socialist Party (RSP), 178, 196, 202, 207n
Riazanov, David, 212, 242
Ridley, F. A., 55, 56, 81
Rivera, Diego, 237–238, 274–279, 281n
Rivera, Frida Kahlo. *See* Kahlo, Frida (Rivera)
Rizzi, Bruno (Bruno R.), 305n
Rodriguez, William, 14
Romm, Vladimir, 252
Roscoe, Burton, 238
Rosmer, Alfred, 274, 320
Ross, Edward Alsworth, 238, 274
Roth, Henry, 254
Rubenstein, M., 215
Ruehle, Otto, 239, 260, 264, 274
Ruskin, Harry, 229, 230
Russia: Broken Idols, Solemn Dreams, 138
Russian Bulletin (Bulletin of the Russian Opposition), 44, 51, 77, 80, 183, 321; and Industrial Party, 242; and Moscow Trials, 243
Russian Communist Party (CP, the Party), 9, 17, 18, 21, 23, 36, 71, 74, 77, 101, 116, 118, 119 122–125, 127, 130, 132, 133, 135, 137, 138, 140, 145–147, 154, 157–161, 163, 165, 168, 169, 171, 179, 212, 216–221, 225, 226, 228, 237, 240, 242, 246, 249, 253, 254, 260, 261, 264, 269, 270, 285, 291–292, 298
Russian Question, 66, 84n, 205n, 283, 284–285, 289, 291–292, 293, 295–

304, 316

Russian Revolution (Revolution of 1917), 9, 13–14, 15, 24, 25n, 26n, 53, 54, 71–72, 90, 104, 119–123, 127, 139, 143n, 157, 158, 160, 163, 164, 167, 168, 171, 173–174, 206n, 209, 212, 237, 260, 291, 298, 308n, 318, 323

Russian Social Democratic (Labor) Party, 13, 87, 90, 93, 94, 96, 99–101, 103, 108, 111–113, 115, 117, 118, 119, 120, 125, 141n, 165, 211, 221

Ruthenburg, Charles E., 17, 25n

Ruthenburg-Lovestone Faction. See Lovestone Faction

Rykov, Alexei, 124, 156, 166, 169, 217, 235, 236, 247, 248

Sabath, Joseph, 229

Saint Simon, Claude H., 232n

Sakharov, Andrei, 290

Sapranov, Timothei, 291

SAP. See German Socialist Workers' Party

Saxe, Nora and Camille, 192, 194

Schapiro, Leonard, 93–94, 96–97, 108, 111, 113, 115, 132, 149, 157, 218, 246, 249

Schapiro, Meyer, 238

Schuman, Frederick, 254

Second International, 114, 191, 196, 198, 199, 240, 309

Second Party Congress (1903), 87, 88, 91–96, 100–102, 104, 105, 107, 108, 111, 119, 124, 141n, 212

Second World War. See World War II

Sedov, Leon (Lyova), 36, 44, 72, 75, 77, 78, 80, 85n, 86n, 235; with Glotzer in Paris, 182–184, 186, 187, 191, 192, 201, 203; and Moscow Frame-Up Trials, 236, 237, 243, 252, 273; murdered, 320

Sedov, Sergei, 219, 320; and daughter Yulia, 320

Sedova, Natalia, 28, 35, 39, 44, 48, 50, 68, 72, 74, 78, 83n, 84n, 85n, 86n, 112, 180, 187, 219, 223, 304, 316, 320; meets Glotzer, 36; Mexican exile, 235, 237–238, 255–256, 259, 271, 274, 276, 277, 279, 293; resigns from Fourth International, 304

Seipold, Oskar, 76

Serge, Victor, 238

Shachtman, Max, 22, 23, 26n, 28, 44, 45, 53, 54, 56, 58, 69, 74, 78, 81–82, 168, 173, 180, 188, 201, 223, 238, 257, 288–289, 301, 304, 305n, 306n, 307n; expelled from Communist Party, 24; on Trotsky's error, 299; on Deutscher, 300, 302

Shachty trial of "Wreckers," 239–240, 241

Sharlet, Robert, 240

Shaw, George Bernard, 37, 42

Sheehan, Vincent, 254

Shipler, David, 138

Sieva (Vsievolod Volkow) 35, 36, 49–50, 77–78, 85n, 182, 293

Since Lenin Died, 85n, 160, 162

Sinclair, Upton, 42

Siqueiros, David, 85n, 270, 278, 281n, 293, 307n

Sixth Party Congress (1928), 19–20, 24, 25n, 27n

Skoglund, Karl, 24, 26n, 285

Sminnov, I. N., 218, 222, 292

Smolny Institute, 245–246, 280n

Sneevliet, Henricus, 192, 204n, 206n

Soblevicius, Abraham (Senin, A.

Soblem), 76, 78–79, 80, 186
Soblevicius, Ruvin (Roman Well, Dr. Soblen), 76, 79–80, 186
Social and Political Thought of Leon Trotsky, 102, 103, 142n
Social Democracy, Democrats, 13, 15, 16, 57, 58, 59, 61, 62, 63, 65, 75, 85n, 88, 90, 91, 99, 100, 103, 108–109, 110, 115, 122, 123, 131, 142n, 156, 169, 176, 177, 208, 216, 241, 244, 310, 311, 317, 319; cannot be Jacobins, 105
Social Revolutionaries, 119, 120, 129, 130, 148, 216, 291; suppressed by Lenin, 131–133
Socialist International, 119, 179, 191, 204, 206n, 211, 212, 241, 307n
Socialist Party, 13–16, 19, 25n, 26n, 27n, 55, 58, 192, 205n, 257, 258
Socialist Workers' Party, 66; American, 26n, 27n, 199, 216, 284, 289, 291, 303, 306n, 307n
Sokolnikov, G. Y., 163, 251
Solow, Herbert, 256, 267
Solzhenitzyn, Alexander, 171
Souvarine, Boris, 129; and his *Stalin,* 129
Souzo (Ercoll), 30, 181, 182, 191
Soviet Union, 17, 19, 21, 22, 24, 34, 39, 40, 52, 53, 57, 66, 68, 77, 82, 129, 130, 133, 134, 138–141, 160, 163, 169, 204n, 207n, 235–238, 240, 243–247, 249–251, 254, 259, 260, 264, 265, 274, 282, 283, 285, 286, 291–292, 294, 300, 303, 304, 307n, 310, 313, 314, 318, 323; and anti-Semitism, 219–224, 227, 228
Spartacus League, 69–70, 181
Spaulding baseball guides, 11
Spector, Maurice, 21, 22, 24, 26n, 69, 306n

Stalin, Joseph, 9, 19–21, 24, 28, 36, 37, 51, 52, 64, 65, 70, 72–74, 78–80, 84n, 86n, 102, 126–127, 134–136, 138, 141, 145, 146–147, 154, 156, 159, 162–166, 168–170, 172, 187, 204, 205n, 214, 242, 264, 276, 280, 283, 292, 294, 298, 299, 302, 303, 307n, 308n, 310, 312, 314, 315–316, 323; and Tiflis affair, 113–115; and Georgian affair, 148–153, 167n; rule of Soviet Union, 133–140; and Triumvirate, 124, 147, 155, 156, 158, 160, 162, 166; and Terror, 35, 128, 130, 132, 136, 171, 178, 192, 240, 244, 245, 249–250, 259, 279, 281n, 320; and anti-Semitism, 167, 217–218, 219, 220, 221–228, 232n, 233n; and Hitler, 61–63, 67, 177, 282, 287; and Moscow Frame-Up Trials, 235, 241, 266; and Kirov, 245–248; death, 300. *See also* Hitler–Stalin Pact
Stalin and German Communism, 205n
Stalinism, 280n
Steadman, Seymour, 25n
Stolberg, Benjamin, 239, 266, 267, 274
Sukharov, N., 143n, 323
Swabeck, Arne, 23, 24, 185, 190, 286
Sweezy, Paul, 254, 301

Tanner, Jack, 55, 81
Tenth Party Congress (1920), 131, 147–148, 154, 155, 291
Thaelman, Ernst, 61, 62, 63, 85n–86n, 177
Third Party Congress (1905, "illegal" Congress), 96–97, 111

Third International, 178, 191, 196, 198, 199, 309

Third World, 296, 303, 311

Thirteenth Party Congress (1924), 155–157

Thomas, Norman, 238, 312

Three Who Made a Revolution, 321

Tiflis affair, 113–115

Time of Stalin, 166, 170

Tkachev, Peter, 97, 98

Toiler, The, 25n

Toiling Peasant Party, 239. *See also* Industrial Party, Shacty trial

Tolstoy, Nicolai, 227

Tomsky, M. 124, 156, 166, 169, 217

Torgler, Ernst, 184, 185, 236

Trachtenberg, Alexander, 26n

Transitional Program, 310, 311

Trient, Albert, 29, 83n

Trilling, Lionel, 238

Trotsky: An Appreciation of His Life, 65–66, 86n

Trotsky: Fate of a Revolutionary, 66, 143n, 318

Trotsky, Leon (Lev Davidovich), 9, 15, 18, 20, 22, 24, 63, 68–74, 77–82, 83n–86n, 90–91, 93, 97, 98, 104–112, 126, 129–131, 134, 137, 140, 142n, 143n, 146, 147, 154–157, 165, 169, 173, 177, 198, 206n, 299, 302, 305n, 311–313, 316–317; Siberian exiles, 21, 36, 88–90, 112; meets Lenin, 90; first break with Lenin, 100–107, 123; and Russian Revolution, 103, 121, 158–159, 168, 291; and Petrograd soviet, 102, 145; and *Pravda*, 116–117; joins Bolsheviks, 103, 120–125, 127; and Dan, 124–125; and Kautsky, 131–132; and Georgian affair, 148–153,
167n; and Lenin's Testament, 161, 162; expulsion from Communist Party, 164, 166, 167; deported to Kadikoy, 28–56, 164, 223, 252–253; meets Glotzer, 36–40; and fishing, 44, 45; and hunting, 51–53; and Nazi Germany, 57, 61, 64–67, 76, 176, 183, 287, 315; and anti-Semitism, 167, 208, 210–232, 233n; French exile, 180, 185, 186, 189–190, 253; and Youth Conference, 181, 183–184, 187, 191, 192, 193, 196, 199, 202; and Fourth International, 179, 180, 191, 196, 200, 201, 203, 206n–207n, 309, 314–315; on Stalin, 172, 178, 191, 236, 242, 247, 280n, 283, 299, 293, 294, 296, 298, 310, 315–316, 321; and Kirov, 247–248; and Moscow Frame-Up Trials, 242–243, 243–244, 251, 252; and Russian Question, 205n, 284–287, 291–292, 295–299, 303, 307n; Mexican exile, 235, 237–238, 258, 274–279, 281n; and Commission of Inquiry, 255–256, 259–272, 273; assassination, 292–293; Testament, 322

Trotsky and the Jews, 67, 167

Trotsky's Diary in Exile, 158

Tsarism, Tsarist, 9, 13, 15, 51, 79, 87, 90, 94, 107, 110, 113, 119, 120, 126, 127, 136, 138, 148, 165, 209, 219, 233n, 259, 308n

Tucker, Robert, 246–247, 280n

Twelfth Party Congress (1923), 148–149, 152–153

Twentieth Party Congress (1956), 137, 225, 226, 237, 245

Twilight of the Comintern, The, 67

Ulam, Adam, 98, 126
United Opposition Bloc, 29, 161–164, 172, 217, 219, 220, 222, 228

Vandervelde, Emile, 241
Van Heijenoort, Jean, 49, 80, 85n, 180, 256, 259, 287
Van Nam, Nguen (Anthony), 182
Vereecken, Georges, 192, 206n
V. I. Lenin, 126–127
Vladeck, B. Charney, 238
Volkow, Vsievolod. *See* Sieva
Volkow, Zinaida, 35–36, 49, 77–78, 85n, 86n, 182, 268
Vyshinsky, Andre, 169, 237, 239, 241, 252, 253

Wald, Lillian, 254
Walker, Adelaide and Charles Rumford, 256
Weber, Sara, 180
Weil, Simone, 187
Weisbord, Albert, 188, 189–190, 205n, 206n
Weisbord organization. *See* Communist League of Struggle
Wells, H. G., 42–43
West, Nathaniel, 254
What Is to Be Done? (Lenin's), 88, 94, 155
Wilson, Edmund, 124, 238
Wistrich, Robert, 57, 66, 90, 108–109, 143n, 172, 173, 318
Witchcraft Trial in Moscow, The, 240
With Trotsky in Exile, 49, 80, 85n, 180, 287
Wolfe, Bernard, 256
Wolfe, Bertram D., 25n, 93, 161, 162, 211, 233n, 275–276, 278, 279, 280, 321

Wood, Neal, 82
Workers' Opposition, 155, 157
Workers' Party, 1921–1925. *See* American Communist Party
Workers' Party, 1934–1939, 289, 296, 301, 316
Workers' Party, 1940–1958 (Independent Socialist League), 26n, 84n, 304n, 305n, 306n–307n, 312. *See also* Socialist Workers' Party, American
Workmen's Circle, 14
World War I (the Great War), 13, 63, 119–120, 175n, 177, 204n, 206n, 228
World War II, 224, 229, 232, 237, 282, 283, 294, 296, 307n, 309, 312, 313

Yezhov, Nikolai, 249
Yeltsin, Boris, 137
Young Communists' League (YCL), 16, 305n
Young People's Socialist League (YPSL), 26n, 205n, 305n
Young Workers' League, 26n

Zakovsky, Leonid, 171
Zasulich, Vera, 87, 90, 94, 307n
Zborowski, Mark, 80
Zimmerwald-Kienthal Conference, 121, 143n, 199, 206n, 308n, 310
Zinoviev, Gregory, 20, 29, 70, 85n, 115, 152, 153, 157–159, 163, 166, 169, 186, 187, 189, 205n, 245, 247, 248, 269; and Stalin, 124, 147–148, 155, 160, 172; and anti-Semitism, 217, 219, 222; trial, 235, 236, 238, 240, 243, 248, 250–251; expulsion from Communist Party, 164, 167